Social History of the
United States

Titles in ABC-CLIO's
Social History of the United States

Social History of the United States
The 1950s

John C. Stoner
Alice L. George

Series Editors
Daniel J. Walkowitz and Daniel E. Bender

A B C ⬥ C L I O

Santa Barbara, California   Denver, Colorado   Oxford, England

Library of Congress Cataloging-in-Publication Data

Stoner, John Charles.
    Social history of the United States. The 1950s / John C. Stoner, Alice L. George.
        p.   cm.
    Includes bibliographical references and index.
    ISBN 978-1-85109-897-2 (alk. paper) — ISBN 978-1-59884-127-5 (set)
    EISBN 978-1-85109-898-9 (ebook)
    1. United States—Social conditions—1945– 2. United States—Politics and government—1945–1953.   3. United States—Politics and government—1953–1961.
I. George, Alice L., 1952–   II. Title.   III. Title: 1950s.
    HN58.S76   2009
    306.0973'09045—dc22   2008021591

12 11 10 09   1 2 3 4 5

Production Editor: Vicki Moran
Production Manager: Don Schmidt
Media Editor: Julie Dunbar
Media Resources Manager: Caroline Price
File Management Coordinator: Paula Gerard

This book is also available on the World Wide Web as an eBook.
Visit www.abc-clio.com for details.

ABC-CLIO, Inc.
130 Cremona Drive, P.O. Box 1911
Santa Barbara, California 93116–1911

This book is printed on acid-free paper ∞
Manufactured in the United States of America

Contents

Contents

Series Introduction

Ordinary people make history. They do so in ways that are different from the ways presidents, generals, business moguls, or celebrities make history; nevertheless, the history of ordinary people is just as profound, just as enduring. Immigration in the early decades of the 20th century was more than numbers and government policy; it was a collective experience of millions of men, women, and children whose political beliefs, vernacular cultural expression, discontent, and dreams transformed the United States. Likewise, during the Great Depression of the 1930s, President Franklin Delano Roosevelt advanced a broad spectrum of new social policies, but as historians have argued, ordinary Americans "made" the New Deal at the workplace, at the ballot box, on the picket lines, and on the city streets. They engaged in new types of consumer behavior, shifted political allegiances, and joined new, more aggressive trade unions. World War II and the Cold War were more than diplomatic maneuvering and military strategy; social upheavals changed the employment patterns, family relations, and daily life of ordinary people. More recently, the rise of the Christian Right in the last few decades is the expression of changing demographics and emerging social movements, not merely the efforts of a few distinct leaders.

These examples, which are drawn directly from the volumes in this series, highlight some of the essential themes of social history. Social history shifts the historical focus away from the famous and the political or economic elite to issues of everyday life. It explores the experiences ordinary Americans—native-born and immigrant, poor and rich, employed and unemployed, men and women, white and black—at home, at work, and at play. In the process, it focuses new attention on the significance of social movements, the behavior and meanings of consumerism, and the changing expression of popular culture.

In many ways, social history is not new. American historians early in the 20th century appreciated the importance of labor, immigration, religion, and urbanization in the study of society. However, early studies shared with political history the emphasis on leaders and major institutions and described a history that was mostly white and male—in other words, a history of those who held power. Several cultural shifts combined to transform how social history was understood and written in the last half of the 20th century: the democratization of higher education after World War II with the GI Bill and the expansion of public and land grant universities; the entry of women, children of immigrants, and racial minorities into the universities and the ranks of historians; and the social movements of the 1960s. Historians created new subjects for social history, casting it as "from the bottom." They realized that much was missing from familiar narratives that stressed the significance of "great men"—presidents, industrialists, and other usually white, usually male notables. Instead, women, working people, and ethnic and racial minorities have become integral parts of the American story along with work, leisure, and social movements.

The result has not simply been additive: ordinary people made history. The story of historical change is located in their lives and their struggles with and against others in power. Historians began to transform the central narrative of American history. They realized that—in the words of a popular 1930s folk cantata, "Ballad for Americans"—the "'etceteras' and the 'and so forths' that do the work" have a role in shaping their own lives, in transforming politics, and in recreating economics. Older themes of study, from industrialization to imperial expansion, from party politics to urbanization, were revisited through the inclusion of new actors, agents, and voices. These took their place alongside such new topics as social movements, popular culture, consumption, and community. But social history remains socially engaged scholarship; contemporary social issues continue to shape social historians' research and thinking. Historians in the 1970s and 1980s who focused on the experiences of working people, for instance, were challenged by the reality of deindustrialization. Likewise, historians in the 1990s who focused on popular culture and consumer behavior were influenced by the explosion of consumerism and new forms of cultural expression. Today's historians explore the antecedents to contemporary globalization as well as the roots of conservatism.

The transformation of the questions and agendas of each new era has made it apparent to historians that the boundaries of historical inquiry are not discrete. Social history, therefore, engages with other kinds of history. Social history reinterprets older narratives of politics and political economy and overlaps both areas. Social historians argue that politics is not restricted to ballot boxes or legislatures; politics is broad popular engagement with ideas about material wealth, social justice, moral values, and civil and human rights. Social historians, naturally,

remain interested in changing political affiliations. They have, for example, examined the changing political allegiances of African Americans during the 1930s
and the civil rights movement of the 1960s. So too have they examined the
relationship of socialist and communist parties to working-class and immigrant
communities. At the same time, social historians measure change by looking at
such issues as family structure, popular culture, and consumer behavior.

For the social historian, the economy extends far beyond statistical data about
production, gross domestic product, or employment. Rather, the economy is a
lived experience. Wealthy or poor, Americans have negotiated the changing reality of economic life. Social historians ask questions about how different groups
of Americans experienced and resisted major economic transformations and how
they have grappled with economic uncertainty. The Great Depression of the
1930s, for example, left both urban workers and rural farmers perilously close
to starvation. During the 1970s and 1980s, factories in the Rust Belt of the Midwest and Northeast shuttered or moved, and many Americans began laboring
in new parts of the country and working new kinds of jobs, especially in the service sector. Americans have also grappled with the unequal distribution of wealth;
some people advanced new ideas and engaged with emerging ideologies that
challenged economic injustice, but others jealously guarded their privilege.

As social history has broadened its purview, it has transformed our sense of
how historical change occurs. Social history changes our conception of chronology; change does not correspond to presidential election cycles. Social history
also changes how we understand sources of power; power is constituted in and
challenged by diverse peoples with different resources. Social historians, then,
look at the long history of the 20th century in the United States and examine
how the terrain has shifted under our feet, sometimes slowly and sometimes
dramatically and abruptly. Social historians measure change in complex ways,
including but also transcending demographic and geographic expansion and
political transformation. How, for example, did the institution of the family change
in the face of successive waves of immigration that often left spouses and children separated by national borders and oceans? Or during years of war with
rising rates of women's wage and salary employment? Or following moralist
reaction that celebrated imagined traditional values, and social movements that
focused on issues of sexuality, birth control, homosexuality, and liberation? Historical change can also be measured by engagement with popular culture as
Americans shifted their attention from vaudeville and pulp novels to radio, silent
films, talkies, television, and finally the Internet and video games. The volumes
in this series, divided by decades, trace all these changes.

To make sense of this complex and broadened field of inquiry, social historians often talk about how the categories by which we understand the past
have been "invented," "contested," and "constructed." The nation has generally
been divided along lines of race, class, gender, sexuality, and ethnicity. However,
historians have also realized that analysts—whether in public or professional

discourse—define these "categories of analysis" in different ways at different moments. Waves of immigration have reconfigured understandings of race and ethnicity, and more recent social movements have challenged the meanings of gender. Similarly, to be working class at the dawn of the age of industry in the 1900s meant something very different from being working class in the post-industrial landscape of the 1990s. How women or African Americans—to cite only two groups—understand their own identity can mean something different than how white men categorize them. Social historians, therefore, trace how Americans have always been divided about the direction of their lives and their nation, how they have consistently challenged and rethought social and cultural values and sought to renegotiate relationships of power, whether in the family, the workplace, the university, or the military. Actors do this armed with differing forms of power to authorize their view.

To examine these contestations, social historians have explored the way Americans articulated and defended numerous identities—as immigrants, citizens, workers, Christians, or feminists, for example. A post–World War II male chemical worker may have thought of himself as a worker and trade unionist at the factory, a veteran and a Democrat in his civic community, a husband and father at home, and as a white, middle-class homeowner. A female civil rights worker in the South in the 1960s may have seen herself as an African American when in the midst of a protest march or when refused service in a restaurant, as working class during a day job as a domestic worker or nurse, and as a woman when struggling to claim a leadership role in an activist organization.

Social historians have revisited older sources and mined rich new veins of information on the daily lives of ordinary people. Social historians engage with a host of materials—from government documents to census reports, from literature to oral histories, and from autobiographies to immigrant and foreign-language newspapers—to illuminate the lives, ideas, and activities of those who have been hidden from history. Social historians have also brought a broad "toolbox" of new methodologies to shed light on these sources. These methodologies are well represented in this series and illustrate the innovations of history from the bottom up. These volumes offer many tables and charts, which demonstrate the ways historians have made creative use of statistical analysis. Furthermore, the volumes are rich in illustrations as examples of the new ways that social historians "read" such images as cartoons or photographs.

The volumes in this series reflect the new subject matter, debates, and methodologies that have composed the writing of the United States' 20th-century social history. The volumes have unique features that make them particularly valuable for students and teachers; they are hybrids that combine the narrative advantages of the monograph with the specific focus of the encyclopedia. Each volume has been authored or co-authored by established social historians. Where the work has been collaborative, the authors have shared the writing and worked to sustain a narrative voice and conceptual flow in the volume. Authors have written the social history for the decade of their expertise and most have also taught its history. Each volume begins with a volume introduction by the author or authors that lays out the major themes of the decade and the big picture—how the social changes of the era transformed the lives of Americans. The author then synthesizes the best and most path-breaking new works in social history. In the case of the last three volumes, which cover the post-1970 era, scholarship remains in its relative infancy. In particular, these three volumes are major original efforts to both define the field and draw upon the considerable body of original research that has already been completed.

The ten volumes in the series divide the century by its decades. This is an avowedly neutral principle of organization that does not privilege economic, political, or cultural transformations; this allows readers to develop their own sense of a moment and their own sense of change. While it remains to be seen how the most recent decades will be taught and studied, in cases such as the 1920s, the 1930s, and the 1960s, this decadal organization replicates how historians frequently study and teach history. The Progressive Era (ca. 1890–1920) and postwar America (ca. 1945–1960) have less often been divided by decades. This highlights the neutrality of this division. In truth, all divisions are imposed: we speak of long decades or short centuries, and so forth. When historians teach the 1960s, they often reach back into the 1950s and ahead into the 1970s. The authors and editors of these volumes recognize that social processes, movements, ideas, and leaders do not rise and fall with the turn of the calendar; therefore, they have worked to knit the volumes together as a unit.

Readers can examine these texts individually or collectively. The texts can be used to provide information on significant events or individuals. They can provide an overview of a pivotal decade. At the same time, these texts are designed to allow readers to follow changing themes over time and to develop their own sense of chronology. The authors regularly spoke with one another and with the series editors to establish the major themes and subthemes in the social history of the century and to sustain story lines across the volumes. Each volume divides the material into six or seven chapters that discuss major themes such as labor or work; urban, suburban, and rural life; private life; politics; economy; culture; and social movements. Each chapter begins with an overview essay and then explores four to six major topics. The discrete essays at the heart of each volume give readers focus on a social movement, a social idea, a case study, a social institution, and so forth. Unlike traditional encyclopedias, however, the narrative coherence of the single-authored text permits authors to break the decade bubble with discussions on the background or effects of a social event.

There are several other features that distinguish this series.

- Many chapters include capsules on major debates in the social history of the era. Even as social historians strive to build on the best scholarship available, social history remains incomplete and contested; readers can benefit from studying this tension.

- The arguments in these volumes are supported by many tables and graphics. Social history has mobilized demographic evidence and—like its sister field, cultural history—has increasingly turned to visual evidence, both for the social history of media and culture and as evidence of social conditions. These materials are not presented simply as illustrations but as social evidence to be studied.

- Timelines at the head of every chapter highlight for readers all the major events and moments in the social history that follows.

- A series of biographical sketches at the end of every chapter highlights the lives of major figures more often overlooked in histories of the era. Readers can find ample biographical material on more prominent figures in other sources; here the authors have targeted lesser known but no less interesting and important subjects.

- Bibliographies include references to electronic sources and guide readers to material for further study.

- Three indices—one for each volume, one for the entire series, and one for all the people and events in the series—are provided in each volume. Readers can easily follow any of the major themes across the volumes.

Finally, we end with thanks for the supportive assistance of Ron Boehm and Kristin Gibson at ABC-CLIO, and especially to Dr. Alex Mikaberidze and Dr. Kim Kennedy White, who helped edit the manuscripts for the press. But of course, these volumes are the product of the extraordinary group of historians to whom we are particularly indebted:

The 1900s: Brian Greenberg and Linda S. Watts
The 1910s: Gordon Reavley
The 1920s: Linda S. Watts, Alice L. George, and Scott Beekman
The 1930s: Cecelia Bucki
The 1940s: Mark Ciabattari
The 1950s: John C. Stoner and Alice L. George
The 1960s: Troy D. Paino
The 1970s: Laurie Mercier
The 1980s: Peter C. Holloran and Andrew Hunt
The 1990s: Nancy Cohen

Daniel J. Walkowitz, Series Editor
Daniel E. Bender, Series Associate Editor

Volume Introduction

Given the somewhat arbitrary limits of decades, historians have begun talking about "long" decades in order to reflect the difficulty in accurately assessing the past in 10-year increments; social history is no exception. In this volume, for instance, that limit is 1950–1959, yet it is impossible to talk about demographic change, suburbanization, civil rights activism, unionization, or anticommunism without looking at a "long" 1950s. This approach looks back to preceding decades and looks forward to the effect of social movements and social change on subsequent ones. Fortunately, other authors in this series are addressing many of those connections, just as we attempt to in this one.

There are, however, a number of things that characterize the social history of the decade as a whole. One of the principal narratives of the 1950s is a story of demographic change. The central decade of the so-called baby boom, the 1950s was a time of population growth and population shifts. After a much smaller increase from 1940 to 1950, the population of the 50 states rose almost 19 percent between 1950 and 1960, from 151 million people to 179 million people. Given the relatively low rates of immigration of the period from the mid-1920s to the mid-1960s, much of this was a result of natural increase—the births of the baby boomers. Population shifts were another hallmark of the decade. On a local level, white middle-class Americans sought new suburban homes far removed from the close-knit urban neighborhoods that had fostered many of them. Farther afield, the core industrial cities of the Midwest and Northeast experienced either little population growth or actually lost inhabitants while the booming cities of the South and West gained large numbers.

In the more recent popular imagination, the 1950s is seen as a time of cultural stagnation and homogeneity, although this was not the case. For years, the image seemed to be one of Americans seeking a return to normalcy in the wake of World War II; they were intent on ensuring economic and military security for themselves and their families while denying opportunities to those who threatened to disrupt an "American" way of life and an increasingly suburban ideal. Popular culture reflected those impulses. The grittier urban cityscapes of *The Honeymooners* and *The Goldbergs* thus gave way to the manicured neighborhoods of *Leave It to Beaver* and *The Adventures of Ozzie and Harriet*. Similarly, another popular image of the 1950s is one of relative political and social quiescence, especially compared to the dramatic victories over fascism and the Great Depression in the 1940s and the chaotic protests of the 1960s. Yet, the origins of 1960s' social activism in the civil rights, peace, and youth movements lay in the 1950s, when supporters of those movements began to clash at various points both with the government and with other Americans who preferred the status quo.

Overseeing much of the decade's change (and in some ways having sponsored it) was the government, both in terms of development at home and in its aggressive foreign policy. Equally concerned with economic and military security, government officials sought to ensure American supremacy internationally against what was perceived as an aggressive competitor in the Soviet Union. The government thus fought communism at home and abroad. The Korean War (1950–1953), while remembered today as the "Forgotten War," was increasingly unpopular with Americans for whom World War II was all too recent a memory. At least in part, Dwight D. Eisenhower owed his election to the presidency in 1952 to the fact that he promised to "go to Korea" and negotiate an end to that conflict.

The government was equally, if not more, vigilant about the perceived threat of communism at home. The convictions of Julius and Ethel Rosenberg and Alger Hiss early in the decade seemed to confirm that there was a credible threat of espionage among employees at all levels of the government. The apocalyptic warnings of Sen. Joseph McCarthy about Communists in many government departments only seemed to fan the flames of anticommunism. Some of America's most prominent icons, from Secretary of State Gen. George Marshall to television sweetheart Lucille Ball, came under the scrutiny of the anticommunist microscope; while both escaped any significant career damage, that they could be accused at all reveals the power of the sentiment in the early 1950s.

Setting the stage for a public backlash against McCarthy and his ilk, many Americans grew increasingly leery of the anticommunist fervor that swept the nation in the first half of the 1950s. In the wake of blacklists in education, entertainment, and the government, many Americans understood all too well the coercive and undemocratic nature of some of the public and private groups (including McCarthy's famous "one-man committee") investigating alleged subversion. Eventually, politicians, editors, television producers, and the public more broadly began to encourage moderating the excesses of McCarthy's crusade. While thousands of Americans lost their livelihoods as a result of the investigations, much of that fervor had subsided by 1954.

As is often the case, the images of a bucolic 1950s America obscured many more complicated dynamics in American society. For those who remained on the sidelines of economic growth that characterized the late 1940s and early 1950s, the suburban ideal was literally unattainable because of race or economic insecurity. Many workers looked to trade unions to achieve the gains they hoped would allow them to realize that dream. What they often found, however, were less rosy outcomes. Imbued with the same anticommunism that swept the nation after World War II, liberal and conservative leaders of the American labor movement took steps to oust radical union leaders (and in some cases entire unions like the United Electrical Workers) who were alleged to have suspect political beliefs and refused to sign loyalty oaths required by the 1950 McCarran Act. Sadly, many of the unions affected had been leaders in organizing service workers, workers of color, and those in lower-wage positions. Other unions continued to discriminate against women and African American workers, reflecting the limits of the "liberal" attitudes of the day. While the merger of the American Federation of Labor and the Congress of Industrial Organizations should have heralded a new era of labor activism and cooperation, the resulting organization was unable to take any bold new steps. Already hampered by employer antipathy, new laws that limited the ability of unions to consolidate their control in the workplace, and a relatively conservative leadership, the AFL-CIO was perhaps at its most influential just as it was founded.

Nonetheless, the organized labor movement did secure historic gains for its members during the decade. Through negotiation and strikes, many industrial workers enjoyed increasing incomes, better benefits, and some protection against the arbitrary effects of inflation. Some of the largest mass strikes in American history—in the steel and electrical industries—took place during the 1950s and helped to pressure employers into concessions on wages, seniority, and other benefits. In many cases, however, those gains either failed to appear or disappeared in the face of hostile employers and worsening economic conditions by the end of the decade. Some, like women and African American workers, enjoyed significant increases in income during the 1950s but continued to lag as far behind their better-paid male white peers as they had in previous decades. That did not stop many of them from pushing for change, however. In service sectors like health care and elsewhere, new efforts were made to organize the growing number of workers, many of them racial minorities and women, who had less access to the industrial unions that had formed the backbone of the union movement for several decades. Local 1199 in New York City is a prime example of these efforts.

American workers, through increased income and, in some cases, white-collar respectability, dreamed of greener pastures. The suburbs seemed to allow

Americans of diverse economic backgrounds to join the amorphously defined "middle class." Working-class suburbs, while very different from more established and wealthier ones, could at least claim some of the same benefits that differentiated life in the city from the new suburban wonderland. Whether mass-produced Cape Cod homes in one of the Levittown developments or the increasingly ubiquitous "ranch," suburban homes provided more privacy, more space, and at least some green space for urbanites seeking to escape aging central cities. Stocked with the latest modern conveniences, American suburban homes became barometers of middle-class success. They also became important symbols of American dominance in Cold War cultural contests: the famous 1959 "kitchen debate" between Vice President Richard Nixon and Soviet Premier Nikita Khrushchev hinged on the alleged superiority of modern American consumer goods and the benefits they purportedly gave American housewives.

Perhaps no other consumer innovation defined the decade or contributed to the creation of a national consumer culture more than the television. While driven by advertising, product placement, and corporate sponsors, television also brought a variety of programming into most American households by the end of the decade. By the early 1960s, Americans owned more TVs than refrigerators. As with the introduction of some previous technologies, like movies or automobiles, some decried the potential influence of television on society, especially younger Americans. Critics feared (perhaps presciently) that too much television would result in a more sedentary, less intellectually engaged populace. They worried particularly about the impact of TV on America's children. Yet Americans tuned in by the millions to watch popular shows like *I Love Lucy* and *Gunsmoke*. They also had access to more socially relevant programming as well. From televised government hearings on corruption to the spectacular self-destruction of Sen. Joseph McCarthy, television became an important medium for children's programming, news, and other shows.

Suburbanization and its attendant consumerism, however, was not a process open to all Americans regardless of race or creed. The process of leaving central cities for suburbs became known as "white flight" for a reason: suburbs remained more than 95 percent white in the largest metropolitan areas. Population increases in cities tended to come from those leaving even less desirable situations elsewhere; migrants from the rural South, Puerto Ricans, and Hispanic migrants are three such examples. Like their immigrant predecessors, they sought better lives for themselves, but for the most part were not permitted the ultimate escape to greener pastures in suburban communities.

In many ways, cities bore the brunt both of the population growth that strained finite resources as well as the consequences of a declining tax base and real estate values in the North and East where suburbanization took its toll on central cities. Congestion, decaying infrastructures, crime, and other issues forced city governments to address an increasing number of commuters who needed roads, parking, and services but took their incomes to the suburbs to spend. By

1960, almost as many people were living in suburbs as in the central cities they surrounded. Some cities (especially in the South and West) incorporated the surrounding communities, thus shoring up some of the financial losses associated with suburbanization. This was not an option in older cities, thus imposing the need for more innovative reform upon city leaders.

Officials at the local, state, and federal levels all sought answers for urban problems while simultaneously struggling to avoid spending the money required to address many of them. "Slum" clearance got some support, but those who faced displacement had few options for adequate new housing to replace the demolished housing stock. Environmental crises caused by heavy manufacturing and higher population densities also generated little reaction; people and governments recognized the problems, but there was little interest in (and relatively little money for) addressing them in a substantive way, especially if the solutions threatened to derail economic growth. As the number of automobiles in the United States grew more than 50 percent during the decade, there was little room in cityscapes for expanding existing roads or building new ones. At the same time, there was little funding for improving public transportation; rail travel dropped as more and more Americans opted for their own cars or for the airlines that offered jet service by the end of the decade.

Cities, however, continued to serve as cultural and intellectual hubs; they also provided social spaces for those Americans whose identities did not fit into the suburban ideal. For example, while a far cry from the public rallies of the early 1970s, the activities of the Mattachine Society provided support and networking for gay men. Lesbians created a similar organization in 1955. For social critics who denounced the ever-more-influential suburban consumer culture, cities were a last bulwark against a vanilla, conformist society. In some ways the inspiration of some of the critiques by the New Left and the counterculture of the 1960s, the beatniks (or "Beats") warned of the consequences of these changes. Usually young, and very disenchanted with mainstream culture, Beats like Jack Kerouac and Allen Ginsberg used fiction and poetry to express their ennui.

At the same time, those young people who found themselves less disaffected than their beatnik peers were fast becoming an important demographic group. Postwar prosperity, coupled with larger numbers of boomer children, helped to increase the prominence of American youths. Kids adopted the clothes and haircuts of prominent stars; rock 'n' roll music became increasingly sexualized and the suggestive gyrations of Elvis and other singers characterized the popular music of the decade. By the end of the 1950s, teenage consumers were seen as crucial in maintaining economic prosperity at the same time as aspects of youth culture generated fears of juvenile delinquency.

Even in the more prosperous suburbs, Americans faced many pressures to conform to social norms. This burden fell particularly heavily on women. Cut loose from traditional social networks in urban neighborhoods, suburban women were often tasked with domestic responsibilities, child care, and, in many cases, jobs of their own. Despite shifts in popular psychological thinking about sexual equality and the arrival of child psychology gurus like Benjamin Spock, women worked at least as hard as in previous eras. Commuting husbands spent more time driving to and from work, making it harder to get the quality time with their children that psychological advice now suggested. New appliances and other innovations saved time, but also validated higher standards of cleanliness and order that required just as much, if not more, time than before.

Especially in the West, both urban and suburban development were possible only because of huge infrastructural investments by the government. In his 1955 State of the Union address, President Eisenhower cited as "essential" a highway system to satisfy the nation's "growing population, our expanding economy, and our national security." The formal establishment of the Federal Interstate Highway system the next year represented a massive outlay for road building, the effects of which were long reaching. Reinforcing America's love affair with the automobile, the spending on highways precluded, at least to a degree, the creation of efficient local and national public transportation options.

While intended for specific purposes, like building up the West Coast ports during the war, many of the government-sponsored improvements of previous decades opened up the American West for even greater development. Dams, highways, and new industries related to fighting the Cold War all encouraged population growth in the West. The shifting of prominent national sports teams like the Brooklyn Dodgers and the New York Giants to Los Angeles and San Francisco, respectively, reflected the new prominence of the West Coast in national culture. Further, the opening of Disneyland in the summer of 1955 symbolized many of the consumerist values that had become so prominent in the postwar period. Celebrating the automobile, highways, and future development, this theme park hosted 18 million Americans before the end of the decade.

Those changes in the West did not come without a price, however. Both public and private developers sought to acquire land for highways, stadiums, and housing projects. Many of those projects would never benefit the residents then living there, making conflict inevitable. Groups of residents and homeowners often fought development, knowing all too well the likely outcome of future construction. Racial tension also continued as both Hispanic and African American residents felt themselves to be largely excluded from the booming economy. The environmental consequences of encouraging water-intensive development in arid parts of the country continue to be thorny issues today. In Nevada, Las Vegas came to represent what damming and irrigation could permit in a desert. "Sin City" began its casino boom during the 1950s, when many of the first generation of the major casinos (the Sahara, Sands, Dunes, and Tropicana) all opened. A less-innocent version of Disneyland, Las Vegas also celebrated various kinds of consumer excess.

In addition to the cult of consumption, Cold War pressures also shaped the suburban household. On the one hand, parents were encouraged to be less strict with their children than in years past. On the other, mothers were encouraged not to treat their sons too sensitively lest they become "sissies"; the fear of "Momism," an allegedly unhealthy attachment to mothers, threatened the developing masculinity of suburban boys who would be expected to continue the struggle against communism. Fear of a nuclear apocalypse further haunted many Americans in the 1950s. With the creation of the People's Republic of China in 1949 and the detonation of the first Soviet atomic bomb in that same year, Americans had new reason to fear the atomic age. That fear intensified with the explosion of the first hydrogen or H-bomb in 1952. With a destructive yield almost 100 times as powerful as the bomb dropped on Hiroshima, the H-bomb did little to lessen that concern.

The possibility (and at times seeming probability) of being attacked with nuclear weapons presented a number of thorny practical and philosophical questions. Given that the government was unwilling to allocate enough money for a widespread bomb and fallout shelter program, Civil Defense efforts concentrated on encouraging people to protect themselves. Most immediately, they encouraged young people to "duck and cover" in what has since become a classic Civil Defense film. Glossing over the fact that being in close proximity to a nuclear explosion would render useless any such efforts, these directives encouraged Americans to believe they could survive a nuclear attack. Similar prescriptions to build home fallout shelters would follow, although relatively few Americans ever did so. From a philosophical and political perspective, some critics of shelters worried that they sent a negative message, that Americans were afraid and wanted to hide should conflict come. Some argued against evacuation of cities, contending that in case of an attack, manufacturing and other essential economic activity had to continue if the United States hoped to successfully weather a Soviet onslaught. Others worried that the limited availability of shelters might lead to conflicts between Americans who had them and those who did not.

The fact that the United States was the only nation to have used nuclear weapons on other people caused great consternation among moral and religious leaders in the United States. Priests and ministers struggled to reconcile their anticommunist, hawkish messages with the destructive capacities of weapons that could vaporize millions in an instant.

Some were not willing to be so passive about the prospect of war, nuclear or otherwise. In addition to religious sects like the Quakers, which had historically opposed war more broadly, some Americans began to advocate for an end not just to nuclear weapons, but also nuclear testing. Citing moral and environmental imperatives, they organized in a variety of organizations that came to be known collectively as the peace movement. Although suppressed in the more virulent anticommunism of the first half of the decade, pacifists and antinuclear activists had reorganized by the later 1950s. One of the most prominent organizations, the National Committee for a Sane Nuclear Policy (SANE), formed in 1957.

Many Americans approved, however, of the government's course both in foreign policy and in its anticommunist domestic program. Funded by Cold War defense spending, the growth of suburbs in California and elsewhere helped to spawn the eventual conservative backlash against liberal activism that defined the political culture of the 1970s and 1980s.

Increasingly, historians connect the grassroots activism of the 1960s' Black Freedom Struggle to the efforts of the previous decade. From the educational efforts of the Citizenship Education Project in Georgia and elsewhere to the overwhelming support of African Americans for a year-long bus boycott in Montgomery, Alabama, African Americans were asserting their rights as never before. The Reverend Dr. Martin Luther King Jr. came to the fore of a re-energized civil rights movement. With landmark legal victories like that of *Brown v. Board of Education* in 1954, African American activists who had been struggling for decades against the negative effects of Jim Crow racism in the South finally got at least tepid government support for eliminating segregation in the United States.

Regardless, in addition to ongoing job discrimination and political disenfranchisement, those seeking to change race relations continued to confront stubborn attitudes, especially in the South. Bombings, shootings, and other violence were not new to the region; some of the more infamous cases like the brutal 1955 murder of Emmett Till, however, began to impress upon Americans inside and outside of the South the need for legal and political change. From all-white juries to the inaccessibility of adequate legal counsel, African Americans faced a stacked deck all too often in their efforts to secure justice. While organizations like the National Association for the Advancement of Colored People (NAACP), and even the Communist Party, had been steadfast advocates of more equitable race relations, their efforts were not sufficient to change several centuries of institutionalized racism. When the Eisenhower administration refused to implement the *Brown* decision in any aggressive fashion, it became even clearer that a more broad-based, grassroots movement was necessary.

African Americans from all walks of life acted both as individuals and collectively to challenge the segregationism that was the norm, especially in the South. In education, efforts to integrate public secondary and higher education institutions began; unfortunately, Autherine Lucy's effort to attend graduate school at the University of Alabama was ultimately unsuccessful. An even higher profile case occurred in Little Rock, Arkansas, where nine courageous African American students successfully weathered white public antagonism and a state governor committed to preventing them from attending Little Rock's Central High School. They eventually made it into school, although only under the watchful eye of soldiers ordered there by the White House. Despite their efforts, and showing the tenacious nature of racist thinking in the South, it would be another 15 years before Little Rock's schools integrated fully.

Groups committed to civil rights activism also began to make themselves heard. One such organization that many would see as key for the civil rights movement in the 1960s had its roots in the 1950s: the Southern Christian Leadership Conference (SCLC). Under the leadership of Martin Luther King Jr., SCLC would serve as one of the highest-profile civil rights organizations in American history. After the success of the Montgomery bus boycott, King became an increasingly recognized figure, both nationally and internationally; his efforts would eventually earn him the Nobel Peace Prize. Stressing Gandhian nonviolent protest and New Testament Christianity, King appeared less threatening than more aggressive activists (like Malcolm X) to many Americans who were beginning to embrace the need for change.

Despite popular notions of the 1950s as a decade of quiescence sandwiched in between the war-torn 1940s and the protest-driven 1960s, this 10-year period is better understood as part of the much-longer continuum of the social history of the 20th century. Social movements, even those officially begun in the 1950s, could not be disconnected from the decade past any more than the activism of the 1960s could be divorced from its antecedents in the 1950s and before. As Americans struggled to come to terms with integrating the egalitarian ideals that had motivated so many to fight fascism in World War II, they began pushing for the changes that would transform New Deal liberalism into a broader and more inclusive conception of America.

References and Further Readings

Branch, Taylor. 1989. *Parting the Waters: America in the King Years, 1954–63.* New York: Simon and Schuster.

Breines, Wini. 1992. *Young, White, and Miserable: Growing Up Female in the Fifties.* Boston: Beacon Press.

D'Emilio, John. 1983. *Sexual Politics, Sexual Communities: The Making of a Homosexual Minority in the United States, 1940–1970.* Chicago: University of Chicago Press.

Doherty, Thomas. 2003. *Cold War, Cool Medium: Television, McCarthyism, and American Culture.* New York: Columbia University Press.

Jackson, Kenneth T. 1985. *Crabgrass Frontier: The Suburbanization of the United States.* New York: Oxford University Press.

May, Elaine Tyler. 1988. *Homeward Bound: American Families in the Cold War Era.* New York: Basic Books.

Sitkoff, Harvard. 1993. *The Struggle for Black Equality, 1954–1992.* Rev. ed. New York: Hill and Wang.

Issues of the
20th Century

Communism and American Society

OVERVIEW

McCarthyism (the term applied to the efforts by both the public and private sector to root out suspected Communists in the United States) was a phenomenon of the late 1940s and early 1950s. At the same time, however, the United States has a long-standing and zealous antiradical tradition. From blaming anarchists for the Haymarket Riot in the late 19th century to persecuting the Wobblies and other radical groups during the Red Scare of the immediate post–World War I period, the government has sought to use legal and extralegal means to contain radical dissent, particularly at moments of societal stress. The American relationship to communism was not always so clear-cut. Antiradical diatribes of the late 19th and early 20th centuries often lumped together anarchists, socialists, Wobblies, and Communists as equally dangerous prophets of revolution (albeit not the same one). American participation in two world wars did little to lessen that antipathy. Socialist pacifism during World War I further alienated the American public and its lawmakers, who fought back with the Espionage and Sedition acts. The Palmer Raids gathered up thousands in their nondiscriminating nets, some of whom were deported before the government's excesses could be reined in.

In the wake of the Bolshevik Revolution and the institution in Russia of the Marxist-Leninist Union of Soviet Socialist Republics, the United States kept the new government at arm's length, withholding recognition until 1933. For American Communists, however, the 1930s were a time of opportunity. The New Deal

1

dovetailed nicely with the Communist International's (Comintern) Popular Front, which permitted Communists to assist labor unions in organizing workers and seek reform (and eventual revolution) from within the capitalist system rather than attempting to destroy it.

The foreign policy of the Soviet Union further complicated matters. Solidly antifascist during much of the 1930s, Soviet policy changed drastically in 1939 with the announcement of the Soviet-German nonaggression pact. The abrupt reversal gave many American Communists whiplash and began the process of alienating many from the Communist Party of the United States (CPUSA). That policy reversed again, with the Soviet Union embracing antifascism once Hitler reneged on his pact with Stalin. These policy shifts wrought havoc on the CPUSA and drove many out of the party. Political alliances between nations did little to make more Americans comfortable with the idea of domestic Communists. That unease increased with the exposure of alleged Soviet espionage in the United States in the late 1940s. The cases of Alger Hiss and Julius and Ethel Rosenberg in particular suggested nefarious Soviet schemes to undermine American foreign policy and level the atomic playing field. Coming on the heels of the first successful Soviet nuclear test in 1949, and the "loss" of China to Mao Zedong's Communists, American Communists seemed all the more suspect.

TIMELINE

1950   Alger Hiss convicted of perjury.

Special Senate committee chaired by Millard Tydings begins hearings on McCarthy's charges of Communists in the State Department.

President Truman denounces McCarthy during a press conference.

FBI arrests Julius and Ethel Rosenberg.

Angry debate in Senate over Tydings Committee report; Senate accepts report on strict party lines.

The Hollywood Ten exhaust their legal appeals, report to various prisons.

1951   Julius and Ethel Rosenberg convicted and sentenced to death.

Alger Hiss begins five-year prison sentence.

Senate Internal Security Subcommittee begins hearings on Institute of Pacific Relations.

Sen. William Benton calls for expulsion of McCarthy.

HUAC issues subpoenas for second round of Hollywood hearings.

1952   Lillian Hellman appears before HUAC.

Moses Finley called before Senate Internal Security Subcommittee.

Simon Heimlich called before Senate Internal Security Subcommittee.

Rutgers Board of Trustees fire Finley and Heimlich.

1953   Dalton Trumbo wins Academy Award for writing *Roman Holiday* using a friend (Ian Hunter) as a front.

Zechariah Chafee and Arthur Sutherland release statement on Fifth Amendment.

Ohio State's Byron Darling goes before HUAC; he is later fired.

Association of American Universities (AAU) releases "Rights and Responsibilities of Universities and their Faculties."

After a brief Supreme Court stay, Ethel and Julius Rosenberg executed in Sing Sing Prison in Ossining, New York.

CBS airs two *See It Now* episodes—"The Case of Milo Radulovich" and "An Argument in Indianapolis"—that criticize McCarthyism.

1954   Two more *See It Now* episodes—"A Report on Senator Joseph R. McCarthy" and "Annie Lee Moss before the McCarthy Committee"—appear on CBS.

Senator McCarthy responds on *See It Now*.

Army-McCarthy hearings are held.

Salt of the Earth released to limited audiences.

Alger Hiss is released from prison.

Senate votes 67–22 to "condemn" McCarthy's actions.

Wayne University (now Wayne State University) in Detroit, Michigan, suspends Gerald Harrison and Irving Stein; neither is reinstated.

1956   American Association of University Professors (AAUP) condemns assaults on academic freedom of professors.

Dalton Trumbo wins Academy Award for *The Brave One*, which he wrote under a pseudonym.

1957   Joseph McCarthy dies.

1996   Alger Hiss dies, never having admitted guilt.

BACKGROUND: EARLIER ANTICOMMUNIST INITIATIVES

As many historians of McCarthyism note quite correctly, the 1950s efforts of the House Committee on Un-American Activities (HUAC), the Senate Internal Security Subcommittee, and Republican senator Joseph McCarthy's (R-WI) famous "one-man committee" represented at most an intensification of the ongoing efforts of various governmental agencies (and nongovernmental organizations) to stamp out subversive organizations and punish their supporters. One of the most notable examples came in the first incarnation of HUAC.

Authorized by Congress for the first time in 1938, the House Committee on Un-American Activities (referred to in the prewar period as the Dies Committee after its chairman, Martin Dies (D-TX), and later referred to simply as HUAC) began its investigations into various types of subversion in American society. Its initial mandate was significantly broader than that of investigating Communist subversion, but that is where the committee focused many of its efforts. Dies (and many of the members of the committee) saw the hearings as a way to further discredit the New Deal, which had come increasingly under siege from Republicans and southern Democrats (Navasky 2003, 20–21).

As the first chairman of the House Committee on Un-American Activities (HUAC) from 1938 to 1945, Martin Dies endeavored to discredit New Deal programs and labor unions by exposing alleged Communist infiltration. (Library of Congress)

Anticommunist crusaders got a new weapon in their arsenal with passage in 1940 of the Alien Registration Act, more popularly known as the Smith Act after its principal sponsor, Rep. Howard Smith of Virginia. According to the Smith Act, it was illegal to "knowingly or willfully advocate, abet, advise, or teach the duty, necessity, desirability, or propriety of overthrowing or destroying any government in the United States by force or violence." The Smith Act became a useful tool in curbing radical influence in labor unions and later efforts against the Communist Party.

In 1945, HUAC became a permanent standing committee, this time under the chairmanship of John Rankin, another southern Democrat. HUAC continued to put pressure on labor unions, government, and other American institutions to root out supposed subversion. It was responsible for several high-profile rounds of hearings, including the hearings involving the so-called Hollywood Ten (see below) and a second round in Hollywood during the early 1950s. While Joseph McCarthy's efforts often took center stage, HUAC conducted a broader and more systematic attack on alleged subversion; its efforts resulted in many prosecutions for contempt of Congress and the blacklisting of numerous Americans in a variety of fields.

The other prominent cases of subversion in the United States appeared in the late 1940s in the prosecutions of Alger Hiss and Julius and Ethel Rosenberg. In both cases, the accused were thought to have been involved in espionage against the United States, which tapped into public fears, particularly in the wake of the detonation of the first Russian atomic bomb in 1949. That the cases played out in the anticommunist hysteria of the early 1950s reflects how Cold War anxieties gripped many Americans.

RADICALISM AND COMMUNISM IN THE 1950S

American Communists in the 1950s

The American Communist Party of the 1950s was a pale shadow of its former self. In the late 1930s, party membership approached 100,000, itself a small fraction of the broader electoral support that Socialist candidate Eugene Debs had gotten earlier in the century. Many of its supporters lived in urban areas, especially in New York City. In the 1930s, the Nazi-Soviet pact weakened the party's ability to claim doctrinal consistency. As Ellen Schrecker notes, it also pitted the rest of the liberal-labor coalition against the party. Even with this adversity, however, tens of thousands of Americans still belonged to the party; membership was as high as 75,000 in 1947 although it began to fall precipitously before the anticommunist onslaught (Schrecker 1994, 4–8).

In addition to the domestic offensive against communism, which eventually included the Smith Act and other legislative measures to weaken dissent without technically abridging First Amendment rights, American Communists also faced more ideological challenges coming from Moscow. By 1956, when Nikita Khrushchev denounced Joseph Stalin and his leadership of the Soviet Union, they had even less keeping them in the party. Only two years later, the Communist Party in the United States had only 3,000 active members. While some may have been driven underground by the public offensive against them, the vastly reduced numbers reflected the final disillusionment of many on the American Left with the Soviet Union and its leadership of international communism.

The Families Committee of Smith Act Victims

The initial prosecutions of 11 leaders of the Communist Party took place in 1948 under the terms of the 1940 Smith Act (which provided for prosecution of those seeking the "overthrow" of the government of the United States). In the early 1950s, a second and larger round of prosecutions followed; more than 120 faced indictment. Those families targeted by the government had to scramble to maintain some semblance of normalcy in the face of the inevitable turmoil.

In the fall of 1951, several prominent women Communists formed the Families Committee of the Smith Act Victims. While on the one hand a political advocacy organization, the group sought more immediately to respond to the needs of the families affected by the indictments. Those indicted were not the only victims of this process; ongoing government surveillance and harassment further complicated the lives of spouses and children (Gerson 1994, 157–158). The Families Committee in many ways capitalized on the Cold War rhetoric that placed the family at the center of American social structure, thus using tropes common in anticommunist rhetoric to justify the need to support the families of suspected subversives.

The Families Committee raised monies for publicity, visits to the prisoners, and summer camp tuition (Gerson 1994, 161). Despite its relatively limited political activities, the organization was added to the attorney general's list of subversive organizations in 1953. The Families Committee disbanded in 1959. Deborah Gerson, a scholar whose own family was one of those affected, argues that, despite traditionalist aspects of the committee's rhetoric, the committee furthered the efforts of committed and politicized women engaged in breaking down gender barriers.

Hiss/Chambers Case

Few espionage cases captured more national attention than that of Alger Hiss. Ironically, however, by the time the allegations of Hiss's actions came to light, it was no longer possible to prosecute him for espionage. Instead, the federal government had to settle for a perjury conviction, which resulted in a five-year sentence for Hiss.

Coming from a modest middle-class background, Alger Hiss became a law student at Harvard University, a secretary for legendary Supreme Court justice Oliver Wendell Holmes, and an official in the New Deal's Agricultural Adjustment Administration (AAA). Probably while working at the AAA, Hiss became involved in a Communist discussion group; one of his more recent biographers alleges that it was at this point, sometime around 1934, that his espionage began (White 2004, 28–29).

The principal courier for the intelligence that Hiss was able to get first from the AAA and later from the State Department was Whittaker Chambers, who had been involved with a variety of Communist organizations for several years. By the mid-1930s, he had been recruited by Soviet military intelligence to contact Hiss and others like him to gather the material they had collected. By the late 1930s, however, Chambers had decided he had had enough. He secreted copies of some of the documents he had transported as an insurance policy and started to let some of his friends and contacts know that he intended to stop working for the Soviet Union. Chambers warned them, including Hiss, that he might have to disclose their actions in the future.

Unlike others who switched sides during this period, Chambers made no immediate moves. His first effort to contact the government came a year and a half later. Even then, the government downplayed the information. Government officials did not acquire corroborating evidence that suggested Hiss was a security risk until the mid-1940s.

After anticommunist informant Elizabeth Bentley and others provided details of a supposed espionage network that may have included Hiss, the Federal Bureau of Investigation (FBI) took a harder look at the State Department employee. By early 1946, it was clear that Hiss would have to answer much harder questions about his past affiliations. His career stalled and he subsequently left the State Department in late 1946 to become the president of the Carnegie Endowment for International Peace at the urging of associates, including Dean Acheson and John Foster Dulles, who told him his career at the State Department was over (White 2004, 49–51).

Leaving the government did not solve Hiss's problems. When HUAC called Whittaker Chambers to appear in 1948, Chambers provided the names of the former study group members, including Alger Hiss. Hiss immediately offered to testify before HUAC and denied knowing Whittaker Chambers, thus setting up the eventual charge that landed him in prison.

When Hiss appeared two days later, he maintained that story at first, although he later admitted that he might have known Chambers under a different name (which was not uncommon for Communists seeking to avoid public scrutiny). His equivocation prompted the committee to take a closer look and Richard Nixon, then a young congressman from California, suggested that he head a special subcommittee to get to the truth of the matter. Nixon's role in the Hiss case certainly helped to catapult him into greater national prominence and the 1952 Republican nomination for vice president.

Investigators from both HUAC and the FBI increased their examination of Hiss's past and his increasingly strained denials of a shared past with Whittaker

Whittaker Chambers (right), senior editor for Time *magazine, takes the stand before the House Committee on Un-American Activities (HUAC) on August 25, 1948. In his testimony, Chambers identified Alger Hiss, a State Department official, as a member of the American Communist Party assigned to infiltrate the U.S. government and pass government secrets to the Soviet Union. (Library of Congress)*

Chambers. The revelations of the so-called Pumpkin Papers (several rolls of microfilm that Chambers had produced from a pumpkin) seemed to bolster his claims of espionage and guaranteed that HUAC would act against Hiss.

When a grand jury asked Hiss once again whether or not he had known Whittaker Chambers and/or given government documents to him, Hiss continued his steadfast denials, which earned him an indictment for perjury. When the case went to trial, little evidence existed to bolster the government's claim other than the testimony of Chambers, an admitted former Communist and courier for the Communist Party. The government refused to release other evidence it had implicating Hiss for fear that it would expose sources who still had value. One of the more visual elements of the trial came from the search for and production by the defense of the typewriter upon which Hiss had copied documents to give to Chambers (White 2004, 68–71).

Even though the copies Chambers had saved suggested Hiss was lying, the jury in his first perjury trial failed to reach consensus. The government retried Hiss and was able to secure a conviction in 1950 using evidence very similar to

Historians' Debate: Alger Hiss

Historians continue to debate the role of Alger Hiss both in terms of his likely participation in espionage and the ways in which his case became a cause celebre for those who charged the government with having persecuted an innocent man for decades following his conviction. While more recent evidence from former Soviet archives does nothing to clear Hiss of involvement, the true nature of Hiss's role remains opaque and is an ongoing source of controversy among diplomatic historians and historians of American communism.

For the two decades following the Hiss case, most writers who addressed the topic came to their studies already convinced of the guilt or innocence of Alger Hiss; this included Hiss and Whittaker Chambers, both of whom wrote books on the subject. Hiss also coauthored a book with his son Tony in the 1970s. By that time, however, at least one historian sought to treat the case more on its merits than on the passions it produced. Allen Weinstein's *Perjury: The Hiss-Chambers Case* concluded that Hiss had at the very least misled investigators and his own defense team. In addition, Weinstein could find no evidence of a government conspiracy against Hiss. Almost immediately, however, Weinstein's book became part of the still-bitter debate over the Hiss case and what it represented. Hiss continued to deny any wrongdoing and challenged Weinstein's methods and motives.

By 2000, many in the academic community who had previously maintained the innocence of Alger Hiss began to admit that the preponderance of the evidence pointed more convincingly toward his guilt. Ellen Schrecker, who in 1998 had maintained that the Hiss case "remains problematic in many ways," admitted just two years later that it was no longer possible (at least in some cases) to protest the innocence of Hiss, Rosenberg, and others (Schrecker 1998, 175; Schrecker 2000).

Despite these often-grudging admissions, the Hiss case continues to remain less clear-cut than, for example, that of Julius and Ethel Rosenberg. Historians and other scholars debate (at times seemingly endlessly) the significance of the one decoded message from the Venona decryptions that referenced an agent with the code name of "Ales"; someone in the government added a handwritten note that Alger Hiss was the likely culprit. These ongoing debates raise some issues that appear more political than historical while others, such as differences over translations in the Russian decryptions, do have real implications for a better, more nuanced understanding of the role of American Communists in Soviet espionage.

that presented before. Jurors were skeptical of the defense claims that not only had someone else stolen State Department government documents to which Alger Hiss had access but that they had also copied those documents on a typewriter owned by Hiss and his wife. After two failed appeals, Hiss went to prison in March 1951. He remained at the federal penitentiary in Lewisburg, Pennsylvania, for more than three years. After his release, Hiss struggled to find work and maintain family relationships in the wake of his ordeal (White 2004, 81–115).

What made Alger Hiss unique was his refusal to admit having been involved with espionage in his testimony before HUAC, during his trial, while he was in prison, and indeed for the rest of his life. He never admitted to having been a member of the Communist Party or having been associated with the party in any way. After the furor over McCarthyism had quieted, Hiss's persistent denials convinced many during the 1960s and 1970s of his innocence. He became a frequent public speaker and to a great degree was able to rehabilitate his damaged reputation. He died in 1996.

The Rosenberg Case

The prosecution of Julius and Ethel Rosenberg for espionage was one of the highest-profile legal cases in American history. This was not only because of the espionage itself, which resulted in the passage of some atomic research materials to the Soviets, but also because the likely result was the Soviets speeding up their quest for their own nuclear weapons. It was also notorious because of the fact that the government executed the Rosenbergs for their crimes and that the couple's experience took on, at least for many on the Left, an air of martyrdom, some of which remains to the present day.

While the evidence linking Alger Hiss to espionage remained sketchy and obscured, there was ample evidence (including the testimony of Ethel Rosenberg's brother David Greenglass) showing that Julius Rosenberg was (depending on the account) either on the periphery or in the center of a spy ring that sought to transmit atomic secrets to the Soviet Union.

Julius and Ethel Rosenberg married in 1939, shortly after Julius graduated with an engineering degree from City College of New York. In 1940, Julius took a civilian job with the U.S. Army Signal Corps. Five years later, he lost that position for alleged prior membership in the Communist Party, membership that Rosenberg denied. For several years, little happened; Rosenberg opened a machine shop that struggled financially (Radosh and Milton 1997, 52–56).

By the late 1940s, the U.S. government had begun to uncover some evidence of Soviet espionage during the war. Using information in particular from German physicist Klaus Fuchs, who had worked on the Manhattan Project, American authorities sought the man who acted as a courier between Fuchs and other Soviet agents. Referred to by Fuchs as "Raymond," the courier quickly became the most sought-after character in the increasingly public drama. Raymond proved to be Harry Gold, a chemist who had started passing industrial information to the Soviets in the mid-1930s. Shortly after being confronted by FBI agents, Gold confessed that he had received information from Fuchs and others. He implicated Greenglass, an American soldier working at Los Alamos. Upon being questioned, Greenglass admitted stealing sensitive material and giving it to Gold (Radosh and Milton 1997, 20–47, 81–82).

After leaving the army, Greenglass joined Julius and several others in a machine shop venture that never prospered. As the shop's fortunes soured, so too did the relationship between the Rosenberg and Greenglass families. Despite a warning from Julius Rosenberg that Greenglass should take his family and leave the country, Greenglass demurred and was thus easy for the FBI to find. Greenglass implicated both his wife, Ruth, and Julius Rosenberg, although he insisted that Ruth be protected from prosecution. On June 16, 1950, agents showed up at the Rosenberg apartment for the first time. Only a month later, the government filed charges against Julius. Several weeks after his arrest, the government indicted Ethel Rosenberg; it did so almost certainly in the hopes that Ethel's indictment would pressure Julius to cooperate. While the evidence produced during and since the trial suggests that Ethel was certainly aware of her husband's activities, little directly implicated her in the espionage itself (Radosh and Milton 1997, 98–103).

Despite the government's best efforts, Julius showed no signs of caving under the increasing pressure. The government then raised the stakes once more by deciding to seek the death penalty against Julius, an unusually harsh penalty given that Julius had been charged with conspiracy to commit espionage, not the more serious, and much harder to prove, crime of treason.

A combination of prosecutorial zeal and popular anticommunism made defending the Rosenbergs very difficult at the beginning of the decade. Their attorney, Emanuel Bloch, was not up to the task. In the face of a vindictive judge and a prosecutor who wanted the public (and jury) very much to believe that the Rosenbergs were traitors, Bloch failed to mount an effective defense. Both David and Ruth Greenglass testified against the couple, further damaging any likelihood of a reprieve. When Julius himself took the stand, he admitted certain facts of the case while either denying more incriminating allegations or taking refuge in the Fifth Amendment.

In the end, the only dilemma facing the jury was about the guilt of Ethel Rosenberg; one juror in particular remained unconvinced. They had few if any doubts about Julius, however. The statement made by the judge during sentencing removes any doubts about what

Ethel and Julius Rosenberg ride to separate prisons following their espionage convictions on March 29, 1951. The Rosenbergs' trial for conspiracy to commit espionage took place in New York City during the height of the Red Scare. (Library of Congress)

The Rosenberg Case

For many years, activists, scholars, and others felt passionately that the Rosenbergs had been denied justice on a number of different levels. Given the backlash against McCarthyism that occurred from the mid-1950s onwards, and particularly after the rise of New Left scholarship in the late 1960s and 1970s, many even questioned whether or not the Rosenbergs had been involved in espionage at all.

As was the case with Alger Hiss, some who defended the Rosenbergs did so because of personal or family connections. This was particularly true of Michael and Robert Meeropol, the two sons of Ethel and Julius. In a 2002 PBS television episode of *Nova,* Michael essentially conceded that his father had engaged in espionage but labeled him a "small fry spy" and went on to say that the government had "murdered" Ethel Rosenberg "in cold blood" when Julius refused to break (*Nova* 2002).

Others decried the conduct of the prosecution for other reasons. One of the more critical attacks on the proceedings was *Invitation to an Inquest,* a 1965 book by Walter and Miriam Schneir. After laboriously going through the details of the alleged spying and pointing out what they saw as the liberties taken by the government with the truth, the Schneirs ended by saying, "The Rosenbergs . . . pressured by a vast state apparatus to tell a story they knew to be untrue, stood firm" (Schneir and Schneir 1965, 426). Their account, influenced at least in part by a more sensitive appreciation for the misconduct that did occur during the trial, is one of the most sympathetic toward the Rosenbergs.

In 1983, Ronald Radosh and Joyce Milton published the first edition of *The Rosenberg File,* which used newly available evidence (with the exception of the Venona transcripts that have since revealed much more about Soviet espionage in the United States) to show links between Julius Rosenberg and various others implicated in espionage. They repudiated much of what the Schneirs had suggested, especially the contention that Harry Gold had simply lied about Julius Rosenberg's involvement.

With books titled *The Murder of the Rosenbergs* and *Fatal Error* published since then, it is clear that the debate over the guilt of the couple and the harsh punishment meted out to them continued into the 1990s. Increasingly, however, more and more people (including the Schneirs) accepted that Julius had in all likelihood been significantly involved. Much of the criticism then shifted focus to the government's conduct during the trial and the cynical and ultimately deadly way in which it used Ethel's prosecution to try to force Julius into confessing.

As with much of the ongoing debate of the Cold War, political agendas seem to dominate the discussion. Those sympathetic to the Rosenbergs (or to the Left more broadly) emphasize the abuse of power by the government and note that much of the information was already known to scientists on both sides. Those engaged in what some have termed Cold War "triumphalism" remind readers (and listeners) that spies like the Rosenbergs knowingly engaged in illegal acts with the intention of helping the Soviet Union at the expense of the United States.

he (and perhaps more broadly the public) perceived as the high stakes involved. "I consider your crime worse than murder," he said. He blamed the Rosenbergs for the Soviets getting the atomic bomb earlier than they would have otherwise, blamed their acts for the Korean War, and opined that their actions might lead to millions of deaths in the future. Judge Irving Kaufman emphasized that Ethel was equally culpable. Both were convicted and sentenced to death (Radosh and Milton 1994, 276–285).

Those who supported the Rosenbergs and who rightly suspected a vindictive agenda behind the harsh penalty mounted a spirited campaign. It gained momentum in late 1952 when many Europeans joined the cause. Citing American hypocrisy, anti-Semitism, and the harsh sentences imposed, the French in particular saw the case as an opportunity to vent displeasure with Cold War pressures. The unwillingness of the government to consider "new" evidence discovered by supporters of the couple only seemed to confirm the mean-spirited nature of the prosecution.

Despite legal appeals, an international campaign for clemency, and appeals to Presidents Truman and Eisenhower, there would be no reprieve for either Rosenberg. Despite questions about evidence, judicial misconduct, and the government's obvious desire to make an example of the Rosenbergs, they received little sympathy from the public; what they did get was reserved mostly for Ethel as the mother of two soon-to-be-orphaned children.

On June 19, 1953, prison authorities at Sing Sing prison in upstate New York executed Ethel and Julius Rosenberg. Their deaths marked the end of one of the highest-profile prosecutions in modern American history. The flaws in the case, and the aggressive tactics used by the government, ensured that their deaths would spark a continuing debate.

THE RISE OF JOSEPH MCCARTHY

McCarthyism's Namesake

More has been written about Joseph McCarthy than most other political figures in American history, especially among those who never achieved the White House. Few people had lukewarm feelings about the senator from Wisconsin and the literature on his life and career reflect the fact. Yet the man who became eponymous with antiradicalism in the post–World War II period became a political force not only in his home state but around the nation. He voiced, however crudely and cynically, the fears of many Americans about hidden Communists in their midst. His downfall similarly seems to represent a moment when those fears began to relax. While still locked in the Cold War struggle with the Soviet Union, Americans no longer saw Communists behind every bush; some of those who had been tarred with McCarthy's brush or that of HUAC or the

Senate Subcommitee on Internal Security (known during this period by the sur-
name of its chairman, Senator McCarran of Nevada, as the McCarran Committee) were able to emerge once more, although rarely unscathed.

McCarthy's performance in the Senate provided indications of his later
tactics once the Republicans were in the majority. He engaged in grandstand-
ing, bent the truth when it suited his purposes, and managed to alienate a not-
insignificant number of his colleagues early in his career. Even before he had
the bully pulpit of his own committee, Joseph McCarthy had latched onto concerns about subversion in the U.S. government as his ticket to stardom. It was
in that environment that he first made public startling charges of disloyalty in
the State Department. The speech in Wheeling, West Virginia, during which he
claimed that there were hundreds of Communists working in the State Department, marked it as McCarthy's first, but hardly last, target.

In the wake of McCarthy's accusations at Wheeling and those that followed
shortly thereafter (which were an explicit challenge to a Democratic Senate and
a Democratic president), Democrats in the Senate decided to take the initiative.
They called for the convening of a special subcommittee to examine McCarthy's
"evidence." Chaired by Maryland senator Millard Tydings, the committee put
McCarthy uncomfortably on the spot. This was particularly the case when Mc-
Carthy tried to use the case of Owen Lattimore in order to save face before his
peers. There is little question that the Democratic senators hoped to put McCarthy
in his place and keep him out of the limelight in the future. While McCarthy's
performance before the committee did little to further endear him to his peers,
it certainly raised his public profile (Schrecker 1998, 243–249).

McCarthy's charges could only have succeeded in a Cold War climate that
sensitized Americans to the possibility of fifth columnists, or subversives, in their
midst. In the process of accusing revered Army general and postwar secretary
of state George Marshall of effectively colluding with worldwide communism
and its effort to conquer the United States, the senator warned of "conspiracy
so immense and an infamy so black as to dwarf any previous venture in the
history of man" (Oshinsky 1983, 197). This apocalyptic vision not only criticized
an American hero, but also suggested something truly sinister happening in the
highest levels of government. McCarthy was not alone in his criticism of Marshall and the State Department, but, as was often the case, his pronouncements
won him at least as many enemies as converts.

After his censure at the end of 1954, the senator lost most of his political influence and was ostracized both by his peers in the Senate and a fellow Republican in the White House. Most of his biographers agree that McCarthy's health
and his drinking took a turn for the worse after 1954. By 1956, he was seriously
ill and he died in May 1957.

Joseph McCarthy took too many risks; he gambled, he drank, and he ma-
nipulated the facts to serve his own ends. His actions had very negative consequences for those who came under the scrutiny of his "one-man committee."

Sen. Joseph McCarthy, 1954. (Library of Congress)

Yet, McCarthy was, however extreme, a bellwether of popular concerns about communism in the United States. He tapped into those concerns (some of them justified) and used them in his quest for political influence. Writers continue to argue about McCarthy's character and his actions, yet most agree that the senator was fundamentally insecure and desperate for affirmation.

McCarthy Comes to the Fore

While Joseph McCarthy's election to the Senate in 1946 made him a national presence, it was only after the 1952 elections that McCarthy, basking in the new Republican majority in both the U.S. House of Representatives and the U.S. Senate, had enough power to unleash his crusade. At least temporarily a darling of the Republican leadership in the Senate, McCarthy saw his stock rise rapidly with the Republican ascendancy.

For all members of Congress, committee appointments are key to the influence wielded by individual members. In the wake of the election, McCarthy did not receive the appointment he perhaps hoped for—that of the chairman of the

Internal Security Subcommittee. Instead, he assumed the chair of the Committee on Government Operations.

At least initially, this seemed to stymie McCarthy's ambitions; what few realized, however, is that McCarthy would make his committee do what he wanted it to do. He appointed himself chair of its Permanent Subcommittee on Investigations, which had wide discretionary powers to investigate the working of the government. This became McCarthy's famous "one-man committee." The Senate did give McCarthy some leeway by appropriating additional funding for the committee's operation. This allowed him to start building his staff and planning strategy. One of the key appointments was that of Roy Cohn as chief counsel; another interesting appointment was that of future attorney general (and brother of future president John F. Kennedy) Robert F. Kennedy as an assistant counsel.

Dozens or Hundreds of Communists?
Joseph McCarthy and His Wheeling Speech

Contrary to some accounts, Sen. Joseph McCarthy's speech to the Ohio County Women's Republican Club in Wheeling, West Virginia, on February 9, 1950, received relatively little press attention right away. But McCarthy's words resonated with those who recognized in the Wisconsin senator's warning a new campaign against supposed subversion in the government. Of greatest concern to those in attendance, and the various media outlets that picked up on the story, was the number of supposed Communists who Joseph McCarthy *claimed* were working in the State Department. Initial accounts put that number at 205; by the next day, however, McCarthy had revised it downward to 57. While analysts of the event continue to debate the exact numbers (which seemed to change regularly), doing so obscures the fundamental power of what McCarthy unleashed that day.

By quoting numbers without naming names, Joseph McCarthy established himself in one fell swoop as an authority on Communists in the executive branch while continuing his outspoken opposition to the Democratic administration of President Harry Truman and its policies. Because McCarthy only ever mentioned a few names in connection with this supposed list, the specter of unnamed individuals inside the department was alarming to many, particularly following the alleged shortcomings of the State Department in the "loss" of China to Mao Zedong's Communists the previous year; Mao had been fighting the Chinese Nationalists for control of the country for more than two decades. What was even more troubling was the assertion, both implicit and explicit, that the Truman administration had failed to act in removing these potential menaces to democracy. This gave McCarthy, at least for a time, the moral and political high ground to further his anticommunist quest.

Professional Anticommunists

In addition to the growing federal investigative efforts, particularly by the FBI, anticommunist efforts often relied upon testimony by people who claimed prior experience with those under investigation. One estimate puts the number of informants paid by the Justice Department at more than 80. Some of these informers became regular witnesses, testifying in most cases as to whether or not they had evidence of Communist affiliations. One witness testified in more than 60 cases. Several others appeared several dozen times each. In some cases, they simply lied. While few of the professional informers had the impact of Elizabeth Bentley, who unmasked the existence of Soviet spy rings in the United States in the late 1940s, they still had a powerful effect on the lives of those against whom they testified (Schrecker 1998, 227–231; Lichtman and Cohen 2004, 2–5).

By the 1950s, the professional anticommunists had become minor celebrities; book deals were not uncommon and Matthew Cvetic's account *I Was a Communist for the FBI* became a feature film and short-lived radio series. In some cases, the more-popular informants reaped significant financial rewards both from the government directly and from the cottage industry it spawned in ex-communist biographies.

One of the more prominent informers in the early 1950s was Harvey Matusow, a young New Yorker who found a home in the Communist Party at some point in 1947. For the next three years, Matusow worked in a variety of posts. By 1950, however, he had become disillusioned. He offered his services to the Bureau shortly thereafter and remained in regular contact with agents for the next months. The Communist Party expelled him in early 1951. His only opportunity to remain in the limelight and guarantee further income was as a paid confidential informant and a witness "naming names" before HUAC.

What makes Matusow's case especially notable is the fact that in 1954, just as Joseph McCarthy's house of cards began to crumble, Matusow publicly recanted some of his earlier testimony. This led to media coverage and government scrutiny about whether or not Matusow could be prosecuted for lying on the stand. After his trial for perjury in September 1956, Matusow served more than three years in prison. His change of heart discredited the government's paid informant program and led, at least in part, to a Supreme Court decision that mandated that the government had to disclose reports that supposedly provided evidence of culpability (Lichtman and Cohen 2004, 112–154).

McCarthyism and Hollywood

Background

While McCarthyism as a process arguably began years prior to the Wisconsin senator's election, other similar campaigns reflected the anticommunist imperatives of the period. The most wide-ranging investigation that did, in fact, occur came at the behest of President Harry Truman in 1947. At that time, Executive Order 9835 mandated an investigation of all civilian employees of the federal government. His concern was that "the presence within the Government service of any disloyal or subversive person constitutes a threat to our democratic processes." Thus, membership in any organizations that were "totalitarian, fascist, communist, or subversive" constituted grounds for removal (reproduced in Schrecker 1994, 151–154).

Truman's loyalty oath did permit those charged with disloyalty to present a defense at a hearing with an attorney present. Unfortunately, however, the order permitted the likely sources of much of the evidence to be kept confidential. The accused did not have the right to cross-examine or question directly the informants who provided the damning evidence, making it nearly impossible to refute anonymous charges.

Truman's loyalty oath had both immediate and long-term effects. During the rest of Truman's administration, more than 500 people lost their jobs as a result of investigations and more than 2,600 chose to resign. Others may have voluntarily resigned even prior to the executive order. In the longer term, loyalty investigations could rightly be seen as a way for the federal government to circumvent civil service rules that gave employees some redress when accused of misconduct. President Eisenhower expanded the program to focus on security rather than loyalty alone, widening the potential number of people affected.

In the same year that Truman imposed his loyalty oath on government employees, the House Committee on Un-American Activities turned its attention to the motion-picture industry. In 1947, HUAC came to Hollywood. In the fall, it issued subpoenas to more than 40 people. Not all of those called were thought to be Communists or fellow travelers (those sympathetic to Communists but not members of the party). Indeed, HUAC expected that more than half of those subpoenaed would testify on their own struggles against Communist influence in the industry. Witnesses included then-president of the Screen Actor's Guild (SAG) and future president of the United States Ronald Reagan, who testified that a small minority of SAG members (a group thought to be dominated by Communists) had been attempting to gain control over the organization. Other witnesses included Walt Disney and film star Gary Cooper (Schrecker 1998, 318–321; Navasky 2003, 78–96).

Of the 19 witnesses expected to be "unfriendly," only 11 actually testified before HUAC; Bertolt Brecht (who would flee to East Germany) answered the committee's questions—ten refused to do so. In the face of growing animosity within the studios and the possible legal ramifications from the government, these men, who would become known as the "Hollywood Ten," faced unenviable choices. Admitting Communist Party membership (most of the 10 had been or were members) could result in further ostracism and even more pressure from HUAC to "name names." Refusing to answer questions citing the Fifth Amendment was not yet a recognized strategy and could have resulted in a charge of contempt of Congress. As a result, each witness sought to read a statement before answering questions; the committee denied the witnesses' request to make statements and had each witness removed from the room when he denounced the committee's efforts. Most subsequently received prison terms of one year for contempt of Congress. Even more important, studio executives met shortly after the debacle of the HUAC hearings. They promised that not only would the Hollywood Ten be fired but that none of the major studios would employ Communists in the future (Schrecker 1998, 321–327).

Hollywood screenwriter Ring Lardner Jr. being led away in handcuffs to serve a one-year jail sentence for refusing to answer questions before the House Committee on Un-American Activities (HUAC). Lester Cole and Herbert Biberman are in the background, 1950. (Library of Congress)

The Hollywood Blacklist

Movie studio executives gathered in New York City in 1947 at the Waldorf-Astoria Hotel to decide upon a standardized policy for how the industry would treat potential Communists or subversives. In its statement (which came to be known as the Waldorf Statement), the executives claimed to recognize the danger of hurting the reputations and careers of innocent men and women; at the same time, however, they pledged not to "knowingly employ a Communist" or those who sought to "overthrow" the U.S. government (Schrecker 1994, 216).

Unfortunately for those caught in its web, the Hollywood blacklist became the model for the smear tactics used in other parts of the industry. Upon release of *Red Channels* in 1950, an anticommunist publication that purported to list the names of more than 150 with suspect ties, the studios and media companies had immediate fodder. *Red Channels,* like many anticommunist accusations, presumed guilt, not innocence, and it became incumbent on those accused to prove their loyalty if they hoped to work again. This was contrary to usual expectations that suspects would be considered innocent until proven guilty.

Thus began the Hollywood blacklist, a campaign that eventually spread to radio and television as well. For some of the Hollywood Ten, the blacklist meant permanent exile; others worked in obscurity for years, writing under pseudonyms in order to maintain some income. While studio executives eventually relaxed their use of the blacklist after the hysteria of the McCarthy period had cooled, it was often small comfort to those who found their lives forever altered.

As the blacklist expanded to other forms of media, it worked more subtly toward the same end as the highly publicized dismissals of the Hollywood Ten. Studios and broadcasting companies employed consultants to vet employees for any possible hints of disloyalty. Thus, instead of losing an existing job because of concerns, job opportunities simply disappeared. This also made it much more difficult to establish the existence of the blacklist; companies could simply say they were making editorial decisions.

The Hollywood Ten

Alvah Bessie, writer, 1904–1985
Herbert Biberman, director, 1900–1971
Lester Cole, writer, 1904–1985
Edward Dmytryk, director, 1908–1999
Ring Lardner Jr., writer, 1915–2000
John Howard Lawson, writer, 1894–1977
Albert Maltz, author and screenwriter, 1908–1985
Samuel Ornitz, writer, 1890–1957
Adrian Scott, writer and producer, 1912–1973
Dalton Trumbo, author and screenwriter, 1905–1976

Those Who Named Names

One of the more contemporary reminders of the long arm of the blacklist came at the 1999 Academy Awards. When the Academy of Motion Picture Arts and Sciences decided to confer a Lifetime Achievement Award upon director Elia Kazan, some actors in Hollywood showed their displeasure by refusing to clap for the Oscar-winning director of *On the Waterfront, East of Eden,* and *A Streetcar Named Desire*. The brief controversy over Kazan's award, however, is only a coda to the decision by many within the industry to "name names." Some did so because they believed that Communists had a dangerous foothold in Hollywood; others named names in a desperate effort to save their own careers.

In the first round of HUAC hearings in 1947, the committee heard from author Ayn Rand, Walt Disney, Ronald Reagan, Gary Cooper, and dozens of other witnesses. In the hearings several years later, that list included fewer major Hollywood names, but expanded to several witnesses who had previously refused to cooperate, including Edward Dmytryk, one of the Hollywood Ten. When asked about his change of heart, Dmytryk cited what he felt was the difference in the political climate between 1947 when he braved contempt of Congress charges and 1951. He went on to say, "I don't say all members of the Communist Party are guilty of treason, but I think a party that encourages them to act in this capacity is treasonable" (Navasky 2003, 236). He then encouraged Congress to outlaw the Communist Party.

Elia Kazan's position was somewhat similar to Dmytryk's; in January 1951, Kazan had refused to name names before HUAC. By April, however, he had changed his mind and appeared again before the committee. This time, he openly disclosed his experiences with various people whom he had known while briefly in the Communist Party in the mid-1930s. In the statement he submitted to the committee, he listed those names he could remember; he also briefly discussed his support for the Hollywood Ten. As their case continued, Kazan "was disgusted by the silence of the 10 and by their contemptuous attitude." After listing all of the films with which he'd been involved (and trying to gauge whether or not they were at all subversive), he went on to reassure the committee that "first-hand experience of dictatorship and thought control [as a member of the Communist Party] left me with an abiding hatred of these. It left me with an abiding hatred of Communist philosophy and methods" (Bentley 2002, 494).

The principal difference between the hearings in 1947 and 1951 was a change in the tactics used by witnesses who were reluctant to describe any history they had with the Communist Party. In 1947, those who refused to answer questions faced contempt of Congress prosecutions; by 1951, they had a legally established defense and could safely invoke their constitutional right to protection against self-incrimination. Those encounters with the committee tended to be brief and uninteresting. At the first mention of the supposed "$64,000 question," (which was a reference to the then-popular radio show of that name)—whether or not the witness was then or ever had been a member of the Communist Party—the witnesses declined to answer, citing the Fifth Amendment to the U.S. Constitution. While there are no exact statistics, approximately one-third of those who appeared before HUAC named names.

Committee for the First Amendment

Not all in Hollywood were willing to stand by or name names as they saw their peers brought under public and congressional scrutiny. One of the best-organized efforts to show industry support for the Hollywood Ten was the Committee for the First Amendment. The committee, whose supporters included several prominent actors and directors (including John Huston, Humphrey Bogart, Lauren Bacall, and Frank Sinatra), chartered a plane to Washington to lobby Congress to leave Hollywood alone. As studio support for the Hollywood Ten turned to animosity, and as the Ten themselves proved combative and

Salt of the Earth

Few films of the 1950s (science fiction excepted) were as far ahead of their time as Herbert Biberman's 1954 *Salt of the Earth.* This movie was conceived and written by one of the blacklisted Hollywood Ten, filmed with a refreshing mix of professional actors and members of a small New Mexico mining community, and produced despite open hostility from the government, many in organized labor, and the film industry. It remains a testament to the progressive attitudes of the filmmakers and to a brave struggle by Mexican American zinc miners, their spouses, and families for better wages, better conditions, and more respect from their Anglo-American peers.

Based relatively faithfully on a lengthy and bitter strike by predominantly Mexican American miners against the Empire Zinc Company from the summer of 1950 until early 1952, the film reflects both the left-leaning attitudes of its makers as well as the efforts by the miners to improve their situation. While some of the movie's stars had been in other major motion pictures, a great number of the actors came from the community itself. The story follows Esperanza, a miner's wife who breaks down gender barriers as she and other miners' wives help the male miners to win their strike. By the end of the film, and despite a variety of barriers erected in their way, unity is discovered only once the male miners accept the help of these women; the community shows the company that it will not be cowed by harassment, arrest, and intimidation.

Unfortunately, the film faced only animosity in a Hollywood that remained vigorously committed to rooting out suspected subversion, especially of the Communist variety. As a result, the filmmakers found it difficult to muster financial or technical support for the film. Even after they finished the film, it proved to be nearly impossible to find theater owners (and, even more important, union projectionists) willing to screen it. Despite the consistent support of the International Union of Mine, Mill, and Smelter Workers, which represented the miners in the Empire Zinc strike and which itself had been unceremoniously ejected from the Congress of Industrial Organizations (CIO) a few years before, few moviegoers had the opportunity to see the film. It showed commercially in only 13 theaters nationwide. Since its controversial but brief run in the United States, many agree that the film itself represents a significant achievement not only because of the forces arrayed against it, but also because its message of worker solidarity, gender equality, and the quest for social and economic justice still seems all too uncommon today (Lorence 1999, 195–203).

confrontational, much of the liberal and progressive support waned. With the announcement of the blacklist, studio heads put pressure on actors like Bogart, Bacall, and Sinatra to publicly renounce communism and distance themselves from their radical peers. Those who valued their careers and feared being blacklisted promptly did so (Radosh and Radosh 2005, 148–162).

THE IMPACT OF MCCARTHYISM ON EDUCATION

McCarthyism in its various forms had serious impacts on all levels of education. While this was particularly true in higher education, educators at all levels faced enormous pressure to conform to the anticommunist rhetoric of the day. Some effects were general, such as the constriction of dissent; in other cases, specific teachers faced dismissal and blacklisting. In many instances, teachers who refused to take loyalty oaths because of moral objections experienced the same penalties as those whose backgrounds were, in fact, more suspect.

Professors accused of having lied, concealed, or understated previous or current ties to so-called subversive groups (especially Communist Party membership) usually faced the combined weight of government, institutional, and public scrutiny and censure. In some instances, like the case of Owen Lattimore at the Johns Hopkins University, individuals with no ties to subversive organizations endured similar treatment. Only rarely were those under investigation vindicated completely; the hint of suspicion sometimes followed educators until the end of their careers. Those who escaped prosecution for perjury or contempt of state or federal investigative committees often found themselves confronted by skeptical administrators on campus. Those administrators, also under pressure from governing boards, alumni, and state and local government, frequently took the easy way out: finding ways to fire those who came under suspicion. While in several cases university officials supported the faculty members under scrutiny, more often than not they bent under public and private pressure to act.

At the federal level, and as they had done with other targets like Hollywood and organized labor, certain congressional committees (especially the House Committee on Un-American Activities and the Senate Internal Security Subcommittee) focused at various points on the degree of supposed Communist infiltration into higher education.

Despite the dramatic and negative impact that many of these investigations had on the lives of individual faculty members, it is important to address (at least briefly) the broader impact of the Cold War on American higher education. While certain fields in the humanities experienced relatively little change, many of those in the natural sciences and the social sciences were the beneficiaries of government largesse. Broad concerns about American preparedness, particularly in the sciences, provided many academic institutions with massive infusions of funding.

Educational Loyalty Oaths

As was the case for federal government employees after 1947, loyalty oaths became one of the preferred vehicles for states, university systems, and school districts to identify and excise possible Communists. In most cases, loyalty oaths at the state level mandated that all state employees (which included public school teachers, public college and university professors, as well as many others) deny membership in any organization that sought the overthrow of the government of the United States; at the time, of course, the Communist Party was thought to be the principal organization committed to that end.

A few loyalty oaths predated McCarthyism. In New York, for example, an oath had been required of all teachers since 1934; it is still a requirement for professors working in the State University of New York system. As Ellen Schrecker notes, however, that oath was an affirmation of loyalty to the constitutions of the State of New York and the United States, not a denial of membership in subversive organizations; the latter type most often comprised the loyalty oaths of the McCarthyism era (Schrecker 1986, 116). The University of California loyalty oath was more complicated than a simple affirmation; while it included language like that in the New York oath, it was fundamentally more aggressive. It required adherents to defend the constitutions of the United States and the State of California against "all enemies, foreign and domestic." Additionally, its tone bought into the anticommunist rhetoric of the era when oath takers had to confirm that they took the oath "freely, without any mental reservation or purpose of evasion." Evasiveness was considered to be a tactic employed by those with something to hide. By the same logic, Communists were the only ones with something to hide. By the mid-1950s, there was some type of loyalty oath in more than 20 states.

Either refusing to take an oath or violating its terms made academics easy targets. That was often an issue only at public universities, however. Those at private institutions were not subject to the terms of loyalty oath laws; their experiences, as one might imagine, were more complicated, although perhaps no less problematic.

New York's Feinberg Law

An example of how states used legislation to prevent the tainting of schools with Communists, New York's Feinberg Law amended New York State's education law (§3022, New York Consolidated Legal Code). New York already had the means to discipline teachers for statements deemed seditious or treasonous (§3021). The Feinberg Law went one step further, allowing the Board of Regents to make a list of "subversive" organizations; membership in any of those organizations thus became evidence of objectionable behavior. Membership resulted in "disqualification for appointment to or retention in any office or position" in public schools.

Court challenges to the Feinberg Law resulted in a lower court decision that the law denied due process to those affected. Higher appeals courts reversed the decision; the U.S. Supreme Court agreed. In its decision in *Adler v. Board of*

Education, 342 U.S. 385 (1952), and reflecting the political tenor of the time, the majority argued that due process had not been violated. Further, the Court upheld the right of public schools to be protected; its decision reinforced Cold War middle-class assumptions about schools as sacrosanct. Membership in organizations was not the only pretext for dismissal; the Court also warned of suspicious "associates." Citing precedents from "time immemorial," the decision further said that the state "may very properly inquire into the company they keep." In a common comparison of subversive belief to disease or contamination, the Court concluded that the state's right to protect schools against "pollution" outweighed the right of teachers or school employees to free speech. The term *pollution* illustrates nicely the broader societal attitude toward subversion, especially of the Communist variety.

In New York City, school administrators had an option that removed even the basic constitutional guarantees of due process under the Feinberg Law. Under a section of the city's charter, a city employee (which included all public school teachers as well as the employees of the City University of New York system) could be fired for taking the Fifth Amendment when called upon to testify.

College and University Reactions

While some universities, such as Johns Hopkins, did at times stand up to broader public and government pressure to punish or dismiss academics thought to be Communists, many schools faced more difficult decisions based on both external pressure and ideological imperatives. In many cases, those decisions resulted in demotion or dismissal for the faculty members under consideration, even those at least theoretically protected by tenure. Those without tenure lacked any basic guarantee that their cases would be handled fairly. Functioning similarly to the Hollywood blacklist, academic policy made it easier for colleges and universities to deny tenure to junior scholars without explanation than to level formal charges against more senior tenured faculty.

Outside pressure aside, there was an ongoing debate within academia about whether or not Communist beliefs were fundamentally inconsistent with academic freedom and integrity. Some of the policy reversals of the Popular Front and wartime CPUSA seemed to confirm that American Communists were beholden to the party line and not capable of the critical open-minded inquiry championed at least theoretically within higher education. To most academics, CPUSA membership was simply incompatible with the profession.

Unfortunately, administrators rarely took the time to distinguish between scholars who may have been involved in Communist activity at some point and those who engaged in a variety of other political and social activities. This included faculty members who participated in campaigns and organizations linked to progressive or subversive causes, some who objected to taking loyalty oaths on principle, and those who refused to name names.

Administrators sought ways to satisfy internal and external pressure for protecting their institutions against communism while maintaining the appearance that they were simultaneously protecting academic freedom. They sought new models for dealing with faculty under scrutiny. They got one in early 1953, when Zechariah Chafee, a law professor at Harvard, and Arthur Sutherland, a former law professor at Cornell, drafted an interpretation of the usage of the Fifth Amendment to refuse to testify about others' participation in questionable activities. Construing the constitutional protection narrowly (as did college and university presidents and trustees), they concluded that the Fifth Amendment only shielded witnesses from discussing their own activities, not those of others. Administrators around the country eagerly sought copies of the document to help guide them in their own efforts (Holmes 1989, 108–111).

Some administrators applied themselves to the process of rooting out subversive faculty members with zeal equal to that of congressional committees. They solicited information from government agencies to strengthen internal cases against suspected Communists on campus. At times, bolstered by analyses like those of Chafee and Sutherland, they even denied that faculty members enjoyed the same constitutional protections as other American citizens.

The University of California System
The loyalty oath of the University of California system exposed what Ellen Schrecker calls the "underlying fragility" of academic freedom (Schrecker 1986, 117). At least initially, a large number of faculty members refused to take the oath; in early 1950, they received an ultimatum from the administration. If they did not take the oath, they would be fired. Thirty-one faculty members refused to take the oath; the university subsequently fired them even though the regents knew none of them was a Communist. Subsequent state court action reinstated them, albeit on the grounds that California already had a loyalty oath on the books.

Rutgers University
At Rutgers University in New Jersey, the administration faced a dilemma with Moses Finley and Simon Heimlich. When appearing before the Senate Internal Security Subcommittee in 1952, Finley testified in part but took the Fifth when asked if he had ever been a member of the Communist Party. Rutgers immediately sought to protect itself; a faculty committee recognized that the Fifth Amendment was a necessary protection against possible prosecution but noted (at least implicitly supporting the idea that Communists who attempted to influence classroom politics should be fired) that neither faculty member had ever brought politics into the classroom. Despite the committee's finding, the trustees

demanded the dismissal of the two and dictated that pleading the Fifth was cause for immediate dismissal (Lewis 1988, 157–162).

Ohio State University

At Ohio State, the university's president dismissed tenured faculty member Byron Darling solely because he took the First and Fifth Amendments when called to testify before HUAC. Darling vigorously denied any connection to the Communist Party but affirmed that he had taken the position he did because of his moral objection to the questioning and because of fear that testimony could result in later legal action.

Wayne University

Often the burden of proof fell upon faculty members to prove that they were not, in fact, Communists. At Wayne (now Wayne State) University in Detroit, administrators applied Michigan's Public Act 117 that presumed (similar to New York's Feinberg Law) that refusal of public officials or employees to testify was prima facie proof of affiliation with Communism. When two faculty members, a mathematician (who had tenure) and a physicist (who did not), received notice that they were to testify, the university insisted that it was up to the two to prove that they were innocent of any suspect affiliations. Although there was little evidence against either, the fact that both refused to cooperate at various parts of the process resulted in their dismissal (Lewis 1988, 114–117).

Different Patterns in Enforcement

There were some patterns to the academic controversies. In general, public universities consistently took more punitive measures against faculty than did private universities. Fairly often, college and university administrations rejected the findings of faculty committees and imposed more drastic penalties. This was the case at the University of Washington, where six faculty members were under review for their affiliations to the Communist Party. Three admitted to prior membership in the Party; the other three refused to speak at all. A faculty committee recommended dismissal of only one of the six; the president of the university recommended that the Board of Regents fire all three who had been uncooperative, and it did.

Options for Academics

There were relatively few options for those faculty members who became targets of charges, whether they came from on or off campus. Fellow faculty members were sympathetic and often showed support for their colleagues, particularly if they perceived little or no bias for Communist causes. Few, however, challenged the premise that active Communists did not belong in the academy. Even those who disagreed with university actions rarely risked their own careers to protest firings.

In terms of professional support, the McCarthyist attacks on college and university faculties came at a time when the American Association of University Professors (AAUP), the principal organization representing the rights and privileges of faculty nationwide, was largely ineffective. While local chapters provided support for their colleagues, they relied on the national organization to investigate cases and, in cases when the association felt that faculty rights had been trampled, to censure institutions for their behavior. Unfortunately, AAUP remained silent during some of the higher-profile cases of the early 1950s. Only in 1956 would it finally announce censure of institutions for unfair treatment of faculty members.

Although anticommunist efforts in academia were rarely as visible as those of the Hollywood blacklist, many institutions were loath to take risks by hiring people who had lost their previous academic positions because of loyalty questions. Few (if any) academics thus secured jobs at what Ellen Schrecker terms "respectable" institutions (Schrecker 1986, 266). Those affected faced a decade or more of isolation from the academy. In this process, faculty members themselves played a role, removing controversial applicants from consideration in the first place. As with the decisions to deny tenure or reappointment to junior faculty, it was possible to eliminate controversial candidates without necessarily drawing attention to their previous political activities; administrators or faculty members could claim that other factors were responsible.

Owen Lattimore: The Exception to the Rule

One of the most notorious academic cases of the McCarthy era involved Owen Lattimore, a specialist on Chinese politics who taught at the Johns Hopkins University in Baltimore. Already incensed at the supposed "loss" of China to the supporters of Mao Zedong in 1949, critics of the State Department and U.S. Asian policy sought scapegoats, including Lattimore, for the fall of China to the Communists.

Some suspected that American Communists or fellow travelers were responsible for sabotaging that policy. Lattimore, who had developed a reputation as one of the nation's foremost Sinologists (experts on China) during the 1930s, became the target of such suspicion. Despite much evidence to the contrary, including his appointment by the Roosevelt administration as an advisor and liaison to China's Nationalist leader Chiang Kai-Shek before and during World War II, Lattimore was vulnerable during the hysteria of the period.

Well before McCarthyism became a prominent national issue, Lattimore had been roundly criticized for some editorial decisions made while editor of *Pacific Affairs*. From 1941 on, he became a periodic target of investigation for the FBI; according to Robert Newman, Lattimore's file eventually comprised almost 39,000 pages (Newman 1992, 53). Most of what Lattimore wrote in this period, however, promoted a pro-Nationalist agenda for China and urged the United States to pay more attention to China if it wanted to avert a civil war. Critics felt that his support for Asian self-determination symbolized a far too permissive attitude toward communism.

Throughout the post–World War II period, Lattimore continued to be an advocate of a more sensitive Asian policy and bemoaned the increasing tension between the Soviet Union and the United States. By the late 1940s, however, Lattimore was once again under the scrutiny of the FBI, this time as a result of an accusation by a Soviet defector who

Owen Lattimore testifies before the Senate Internal Security Subcommittee. Lattimore, an academic and expert on China, was accused of being a Soviet spy by Joseph McCarthy in 1950. The charge was never proven but Lattimore suffered under the indictments of McCarthy and the subcommittee. (Library of Congress)

claimed Lattimore had been a Soviet agent in China in the early 1930s. FBI director J. Edgar Hoover took the accusation seriously and expanded the investigation of the scholar. By the end of 1949, Hoover decided to prosecute.

Although familiar with the public attacks against him, Lattimore continued his daily routine unaware of the growing government investigation. He could no longer ignore it, however, after March 21, 1950, when Sen. Joseph McCarthy testified to a subcommittee of the Senate Foreign Relations Committee that Lattimore was not only a Communist, but that in fact he also headed a major spy ring in the United States. While McCarthy would soon minimize Lattimore's involvement in espionage, the initial accusation had immediate repercussions and thrust Lattimore into an undesirable limelight. Even though that committee eventually exonerated Lattimore by concluding that there was no evidence that he had any links to the Communist Party, it was only a matter of time before the government sought to link him to other questionable activities.

Indeed, McCarthy struck again in July 1950, shortly after the North Korean invasion of South Korea, when he listed Lattimore as one of those who shared responsibility for North Korean aggression. Despite his continual denials of wrongdoing, Lattimore's reputation and career suffered. His problems only worsened when Sen. Patrick McCarran (D-NV) formed the Senate Internal Security Subcommittee and almost immediately began investigating the Institute of Pacific Relations, with which Lattimore had been associated for many years.

The McCarran Committee's hearings lasted from July 1951 until June 1952. Lattimore testified before the committee for six hours in July 1951; his much longer, and more contentious, testimony took 12 days in late February and early March 1952. Much of it apparently consisted of a series of heated exchanges between Lattimore and the committee. When the committee's report appeared in July 1952, it recommended among other things that Lattimore's testimony be examined for evidence of perjury and that a grand jury be charged with evaluating whether or not he should be prosecuted.

Despite its own distaste for Lattimore, the FBI believed that only two counts of perjury would ever hold up in court. By December 1952, however, a grand jury decided to indict Lattimore on seven counts. At least partly responsible was then–Assistant U.S. Attorney for New York Roy Cohn, who later became Joseph McCarthy's principal aide.

After Lattimore's indictment, the Johns Hopkins' administration placed him on paid leave. He spent much of early 1953 preparing his defense; at least initially, the defense seemed to have a strong argument that the charges were vague and without substance. The judge agreed and dismissed four of the seven counts out of hand. Appeals subsequently delayed the outcome of the case until July 1954, when the appeals court upheld the dismissal of the central count of the indictment. Lattimore's strain increased even further when the government announced a second indictment in October 1954. After another appeals court decision that favored Lattimore, the government finally dropped its case at the end of June 1955; Lattimore himself had already left the country for a successful lecture tour in Europe.

Owen Lattimore's experience illustrated the vast resources that could be marshaled by the government to investigate disloyalty, espionage, and subversion during the McCarthy period. Yet, despite those odds, it was possible for the innocent to prevail, at least occasionally. Lattimore's case was also different from those of many other academics because of the response of the Johns Hopkins University, his employer. While some at Johns Hopkins refused to support him and sought his ouster, the university ultimately decided, more perhaps as a defense of tenure than as a sign of any affection for Lattimore, to keep him on as a lecturer in the History Department. Despite his reduced circumstances, Lattimore remained in Baltimore until 1963, when he moved to Leeds University in Great Britain to found a department in Chinese studies. He died in 1989.

THE FALL OF JOSEPH MCCARTHY

Few politicians in American history have enjoyed such a rapid rise into the public consciousness as Joseph McCarthy; even fewer have so rapidly lapsed into political and social obscurity. After less than two years as head of his oft-touted "one-man committee," McCarthy faced censure by his peers in the U.S. Senate. He would be dead less than three years later.

While there is no question that Joseph McCarthy owed much of his professional downfall to his own behavior, it is important to remember that outside forces had been seeking that same end, in some cases ever since his election to the Senate. While the Wisconsin senator still had significant support both in the Midwest and around the country, many other Americans found the Wisconsin senator a bully and his tactics reprehensible. In particular, those who had found their livelihoods or reputations threatened or ruined by McCarthy's actions waited for opportunities to strike back.

Wisconsin senator Joseph McCarthy speaks in front of a television camera in 1953. (Library of Congress)

Edward R. Murrow reports the news in 1954. Murrow began his career reporting on the radio, but quickly moved to televised reporting in the early 1950s. From 1951 to 1958, Murrow and Fred W. Friendly produced a weekly television program called See It Now, *devoted to national and international events and problems and considered the most objective, informative, and penetrating on the air. One of the most interesting episodes of* See It Now *was an attack on Sen. Joseph McCarthy that aired in 1954. (Library of Congress)*

This is not to suggest that anti-McCarthy sentiment had always been so passionate, particularly among those within his own party. But by the time of the 1954 hearings in which McCarthy had, at least in some people's opinions, the gall to question the loyalty of the U.S. Army, even fellow Republicans sought ways to undermine his support and limit his influence.

McCarthy's accusations during congressional hearings were very difficult to challenge from a legal standpoint. Not subject to the same evidentiary requirements as criminal cases, those hearings (if abused) gave witnesses few options to respond to what often amounted to slander that could have very serious repercussions for their lives. Yet some people stood up to McCarthy, as others had before similar questions from HUAC or Senator McCarran's Internal Security Subcommittee (SISS).

In addition to individual defiance, McCarthy also faced more organized opposition from both inside and outside of government. Within the government, McCarthy faced opposition most vigorously from President Truman. Even after the Republicans won the White House in 1952, McCarthy over time alienated President Dwight Eisenhower as well. Ike's antipathy for the senator grew after the 1952 elections, and his administration used the 1954 Army-McCarthy hearings to fight back, although Eisenhower never criticized McCarthy openly. A third influential factor in opposition to McCarthy was the media. Although the media rarely reacted in truly objective fashion, it did print and broadcast challenges to McCarthy's methods and decried the impacts on his victims.

Finally, it is important to mention public reaction to McCarthy. Especially because of the heavy media coverage of various hearings and the litany of accusations, Americans had strong feelings about him, feelings that over time grew more and more negative. Yet some remained faithful to the end, convinced that the Communist conspiracy McCarthy lamented had in turn sealed his fate.

Turning Point: The Army-McCarthy Hearings

Although many people had begun to question Joseph McCarthy's claims of Communist subversion within the government long before, no single moment defined how far he had fallen more than the Army-McCarthy hearings that took place from April to June 1954. Following on his hotly contested charges against the State Department and other areas of the executive branch, McCarthy eventually turned toward the Army (Bentley, 2002, 494). The conflict with the Army had several different components. The first centered on security concerns at Fort Monmouth, New Jersey. McCarthy followed up the Fort Monmouth hearings with an attack on the Army for its handling of Irving Peress, an Army dentist who had been mistakenly promoted and then honorably discharged after he failed several security checks and refused to discuss past political activities.

For its part, the Army sought the offensive by documenting the efforts by McCarthy and Roy Cohn to influence the Army career of G. David Schine, a friend (and possible love interest) of Cohn and an unpaid assistant to McCarthy's committee. Charges and countercharges led to the fateful hearings. At those hearings, the Army's counsel, Joseph Welch, managed what few others had thus far been able to do: he goaded McCarthy into a tirade that made him look like a bully on national television.

The incident involved a young lawyer named Frederick Fisher who worked for Welch's Boston law firm. Welch initially tapped Fisher to help him with the hearings but changed his mind after Fisher disclosed he had briefly been a member of the National Lawyers Guild, an organization deemed subversive by some. Cohn agreed to keep Fisher's name out of the hearings if Welch similarly buried Cohn's draft history; McCarthy was aware of the pact.

As Welch aggressively cross-examined Cohn, McCarthy broke in and cited Fisher as an example of a Communist or at least fellow traveler within Welch's own firm. Cohn was aghast; Welch was irate. His response to McCarthy became legendary. After an impassioned plea to protect Fisher's reputation from further damage, which McCarthy ignored, Welch burst out, "Have you no sense of decency, sir, at long last? Have you left no sense of decency?"

While the hearings continued for several more weeks (36 days of hearings in total), the damage had been done. McCarthy's approval ratings continued to slide as they had during the first half of 1954 (Doherty 2003, 204–214).

GOVERNMENT REACTION TO MCCARTHY

It is somewhat ironic that Joseph McCarthy faced the most serious opposition to his behavior only once his fellow party members were in control. That said, McCarthy still faced a number of challenges when Democrats held a majority in the Senate. For the first several years of his tenure in the Senate, McCarthy succeeded in alienating his peers on both sides of the aisle. Some questionable financial arrangements raised suspicions about his integrity, and his failure to secure important committee assignments in 1949 reflected his unpopularity. Few of his Republican colleagues felt any loyalty to the brash, confrontational senator.

In the wake of McCarthy's Wheeling allegations, his Democratic critics saw an opportunity to put the Wisconsin senator on the spot. They called for hearings and formed a committee headed by Maryland Democrat Millard Tydings. During the committee hearings, McCarthy made one of his larger gaffes by labeling Owen Lattimore as a top Russian agent in the United States; later evidence proved the inaccuracy of the charge. McCarthy's peers were not the only ones debating his smear tactics; the White House also got into the act. In the wake of McCarthy's Wheeling speech and subsequent disavowals by State Department spokesmen that it was harboring dozens (if not more) known Communists, McCarthy sent a telegram to President Truman demanding that Truman order Secretary of State Dean Acheson to follow through on the administration's earlier loyalty investigations. The telegram warned Truman that "failure on your part will label the Democratic Party of being the bed-fellow of inter-national Communism" (McCarthy 1950). Truman's staff drafted a response (that may or may not have been sent). It captured the indignation of the White House at McCarthy's charges. "Your telegram is not only not true and an insolent approach to a situation that should have been worked out between man and man but it shows conclusively that you are not even fit to have a hand in the operation of the Government of the United States" (Truman 1950). Truman went on to openly criticize McCarthy on March 30, 1950, in the midst of the Tydings committee hearings. He told reporters that partisan squabbling over foreign policy in the Senate (and by extension the senator from Wisconsin and his supporters) was the "greatest asset the Kremlin has" (Oshinsky 1983, 143).

In the end, McCarthy capitalized on the chaos of the hearings. With his arguments seemingly bolstered by the North Korean invasion of South Korea in the summer of 1950, his colleagues stood behind him and opposed the report that blamed McCarthy while exonerating his targets. Stuck in a bitter partisan deadlock, the Foreign Relations Committee did not approve the report, but simply sent it to the Senate floor for consideration, where it eventually passed along strict party lines. The first major effort to muzzle McCarthy had succeeded at least in theory, but the partisan fight (along with the Korean conflict) guaranteed that it would be a pyrrhic victory. Tydings himself fell victim to voter backlash (about Korea as well as other things); he lost his seat in the 1950 election.

Despite the Senate's professed emphasis on civility and restraint, McCarthy rarely abided by those imperatives. From physical assaults on critics to ad hominem attacks on all who opposed him, McCarthy continued to bully his way through American public life. In early August 1951, Sen. William Benton rashly proposed that the Senate investigate McCarthy and possibly expel him. McCarthy used his influence and his investigators to challenge the patriotism and loyalty of the committee members and their staffs. When Senator Benton agreed to waive privilege in his comments about McCarthy, McCarthy promptly sued him for slander, seeking $2 million in damages. The eventual report noted various problems with McCarthy's conduct, but recommended no action by the Senate.

With the election of a Republican majority to the Senate and a Republican president, the political calculus changed dramatically. The new occupant of the White House, Dwight D. "Ike" Eisenhower, liked Senator McCarthy little more than Harry Truman, Ike's predecessor in the Oval Office. Eisenhower, however, faced significant pressure from his staff and fellow Republicans to mute criticisms of McCarthy; that restraint largely lasted until the Army-McCarthy hearings. While in private he dismissed McCarthy, in public President Eisenhower most often only hinted at his dissatisfaction with the Wisconsin senator's conduct.

In the wake of McCarthy's behavior during the Army-McCarthy hearings, more senators recognized the need to intervene. Sen. Ralph Flanders introduced a resolution in July 1954 deploring McCarthy's actions. After spirited debate, the Senate voted to empanel a committee to investigate. It held its first hearings at the end of August. Although somewhat subdued, McCarthy continued the line that had succeeded so often in the past; he suggested that outside political forces influenced the committee's efforts. When the Senate finally met to discuss the committee's report, which quite rightly excoriated McCarthy for several of his more dramatic attacks, it became clear that many senators (even among those who hated McCarthy) were uncomfortable with the entire process. In the month that followed, the Senate dithered. It finally voted 67–22 to condemn McCarthy's actions. The resolution as passed called McCarthy's conduct "unbecoming" and "contrary to senatorial traditions." It "condemned" the Republican's actions. The broad support for the resolution showed that it was finally safe for both Republicans and Democrats to punish McCarthy without any real fear of retribution.

MEDIA REACTION

While Sen. Joseph McCarthy had his fair share of critics prior even to his Wheeling speech, the media reacted to his often-wild charges much as the public did. Depending on the political orientation of newspaper owners and editors, the concerns of television and radio sponsors, and the partisan orientation of their principal constituencies, some in the media coddled McCarthy while others regularly took him to task.

Unlike today, when many assume media bias, there was a lively debate going on in the late 1940s and early 1950s over the nature of journalism; that debate contrasted "objective" with "interpretive" journalism. Did Americans trust journalists to tell them some facsimile of the "truth"? If not, could journalists be trusted at all? These were some of the key issues surrounding media reports of McCarthy's anticommunist campaign.

To complicate matters further, the media continued to evolve, largely as a result of technology. Newspapers continued to be a powerful force, as did radio, which served as an important source of updated news during World War II and the early Cold War. Becoming more important every year, however, television added a new dimension (literally) to many people's lives.

From the Hiss and Rosenberg cases, the first big media spectacles of the Cold War 1950s, to McCarthy's self-destructive performance at the Army-McCarthy hearings in 1954, the media played an important, albeit at times irresponsible, role. In the news coverage of the government's prosecution of Julius and Ethel Rosenberg, for example, the mainstream papers refused to report discoveries that raised doubts about certain pieces of evidence and generally downplayed the prejudicial atmosphere facing the couple. While press reports in France (which as a nation had a higher tolerance for socialism and communism) led to public outrage there, few newspapers in the United States took such critical stances. Only a leftist New York weekly, *The National Guardian,* sought to investigate charges of government conspiracy. It was also responsible for helping to found an organization to support the Rosenbergs' defense (Radosh and Milton 1997, 323–326).

Perhaps unsurprisingly, editorial content in mainstream papers during the McCarthy period followed the political dictates of the papers' owners. Thus, papers owned by the Hearst newspaper corporation tended to support McCarthy and his actions. Others, however, opposed the senator's methods. Opposition to McCarthy started locally. The *Milwaukee Journal* made regular attacks on McCarthy's tactics; he responded in kind, charging (as he often did with newspapers as well as other critics) that the reporters and editors were obviously soft on communism if they disagreed with him. That opposition was not limited, however, to Wisconsin newspapers. Despite its otherwise conservative political positions, for example, the *Christian Science Monitor* challenged McCarthy's methods without denying the threat of communism.

Newspaper coverage by the *New York Times* illustrates the complex nature of reporting about McCarthy. For much of the senator's time in office, the *Times* stuck to simply reporting basic, descriptive stories of McCarthy's actions. On the one hand, this eschewed the biased editorializing of other, more anti-McCarthy papers. On the other hand, since McCarthy so regularly abused his authority and position, the lack of a critical voice meant that readers might in turn treat McCarthy's actions uncritically.

Edward R. Murrow

For many years touted as the journalist most responsible for the turn in public opinion away from Joseph McCarthy, Edward R. Murrow (1908–1965) was an internationally renowned radio and television personality. Born in North Carolina, Egbert Roscoe Murrow (he would later change his name to Edward) grew up in the Pacific Northwest. After graduating from Washington State College in 1930, Murrow became the president of the National Student Federation of America. That position included some limited radio time during which Murrow hosted famous political, scientific, and cultural figures.

In late 1931, Murrow joined the staff of the Institute of International Education (IIE). For the next several years, he barnstormed across Europe, making contacts with student groups and witnessing firsthand the impact of fascism on Italy and Germany. In 1933, Murrow signed on to help the Emergency Committee in Aid of Displaced German Scholars, which sought to assist academic refugees (many but not all of them Jewish) from Hitler's Germany.

Two years later, Murrow joined the Columbia Broadcasting System (CBS). In early 1937, he moved to London as the network's European director. For many Americans, Murrow's voice brought the war into their homes; in addition to stories coming in from around Europe, he witnessed personally the devastation of the German bombing of London. Returning to New York in 1946, Murrow became vice president of CBS's news division. An uncomfortable manager, Murrow resigned the following year. Happy to be back in the news division, Murrow spent the next several years struggling to reconcile his frank editorials with the need to keep corporate sponsors happy. He was not always successful.

By the end of the 1940s, a new medium had begun to compete with the radio. Still in its infancy, the technology was rudimentary; within several years, however, television looked more and more like the wave of the future. In 1951, Murrow started a television project with Fred Friendly. Entitled *See It Now,* the show took on important national and international topics. One episode included footage and interviews from Korea; others reported on Cold War tensions, the 1952 elections, desegregation efforts, and the lingering effects of World War II on Europe.

Murrow was arguably the most prominent radio personality of the time; *See It Now* became the most popular and respected TV news program and took Murrow's reputation to new heights. Starting in the fall of 1953, Murrow and Friendly decided to use their influence to tackle Sen. Joseph McCarthy.

For several years after McCarthy had faded into political obscurity, Murrow remained a mainstay of primetime television. Hobbled by high costs and the lack of a major corporate sponsor, *See It Now* lost its prime time slot in 1957; it went off the air in 1958.

Murrow also hosted *Person to Person,* a popular show in which he interviewed celebrities. It lasted until 1961. That year, at the request of John F. Kennedy, Murrow took over the United States Information Agency (USIA), where he remained until shortly after Kennedy's assassination. This was a particularly difficult time for American public relations; from the Bay of Pigs debacle to the growing American presence in Vietnam, Murrow faced various challenges promoting American policy abroad.

See It Now

See it Now ran four key episodes on McCarthy, portraying both directly and indirectly the pitfalls of McCarthyism. In "The Case of Milo Radulovich," the program documented the effort of the Air Force to dismiss a lieutenant not because his own loyalty had been questioned but because he refused to disavow his father and sister, who supposedly had suspect loyalties. Public outrage mounted and the Air Force relented.

"An Argument in Indianapolis" showcased the effort by a chapter of the American Civil Liberties Union (ACLU) to hold a meeting; several halls denied them space for political reasons. Murrow and Friendly juxtaposed the earnest, patriotic ACLU activists with the seemingly intolerant and ill-informed members of groups like the American Legion. In contrast to the show's claim to impartiality and fairness, both the filming and editing of the episode resulted in a sympathetic portrayal of the ACLU.

The third show, which directly attacked McCarthy, aired in early March 1954 shortly before the commencement of the Army-McCarthy hearings. The "Report on Senator McCarthy" promised viewers (somewhat disingenuously) that they would for the most part see and hear McCarthy "in his own words." The carefully selected clips showed McCarthy as an abusive, power-hungry politician using anticommunism for self-gain. In those clips, McCarthy attacked Democrats and the media, made grandiose (and inaccurate) claims about Communist subversion, and browbeat witnesses. Murrow ended the episode with an indictment not only of McCarthy, but of the society that had allowed him to become so influential.

The final McCarthy episode played the following week. "Annie Lee Moss Before the McCarthy Committee" pitted the powerful senator against a middle-aged African American woman. McCarthy alleged that Moss was a Communist sympathizer who had access to Army codes and was therefore a serious security risk. Moss testified that she was not a Communist and the Army denied she had access to sensitive material. After McCarthy excused himself from the hearing, his Democratic colleagues took over. Showing sympathy for Moss, and even questioning whether the committee had subpoenaed the right person, the senators' questions reflected the growing antipathy toward McCarthy within the Senate. Moss was the perfect foil for McCarthy; she was humble, uncertain, and denied any connections to subversion. Somewhat ironically, FBI files later suggested that Moss was indeed a Communist and had been for some time.

For the fourth and final time, *See It Now* had painted the McCarthyist crusade as an abomination. As per CBS policy, McCarthy asked for equal time to respond to the episode that showcased him directly. Aired on the April 6 *See It Now*, McCarthy faced the camera and attempted to counter the polished attack by Murrow and Friendly with yet another litany of charges. How important the *See It Now* episodes were in McCarthy's demise remains unclear; his popularity had been waning and there was growing unhappiness in the Senate with his antics. But the programs showed that McCarthy was no longer invincible, and, along with the Army-McCarthy hearings, they likely hastened his fall from grace (Rosteck 1994; Doherty 2003, 161–188).

A long-time smoker who had periodic bouts of exhaustion and other illnesses, Murrow was in failing health by the mid-1960s. Even before he left USIA, Murrow had to scale back his activities after the removal of a cancerous lung. He died in April 1965 (Sperber 1986).

POPULAR REACTION TO McCARTHY'S DOWNFALL

For many years, McCarthy's growing unpopularity seemed to have resulted largely from either the scathing attacks on the Wisconsin senator by CBS's Edward R. Murrow or from McCarthy's own missteps during the Army-McCarthy hearings. Yet, more recent studies have quite correctly noted that opposition to McCarthy had been growing for some time, even among those in his own party (like President Eisenhower) who decried his tactics. Few of them deny, however, that the hearings and *See It Now* helped to hasten that demise.

Some of McCarthy's opponents also had vested interests in hyping the significance of their attacks. CBS, for example, cited thousands of phone calls about Murrow's attack on McCarthy as evidence of shifting public sentiment. While claiming that the calls were anywhere from 10 to 15 to 1 in favor of Murrow (and against McCarthy), CBS could argue that it was accomplishing a public service as much as it was marketing a commercial product.

Newspaper editors around the country reacted to the news of McCarthy's censure predictably; those who had opposed him understandably reacted to his downfall with glee while those who had most staunchly supported him reacted with the same vitriol that characterized their earlier support. The *New York Times,* for example, which had turned increasingly against McCarthy over time, noted that the Senate "had done much to redeem itself in the eyes of the American people." The *Chicago Tribune,* on the other hand, blamed President Eisenhower and the Republicans, affirming the McCarthy rhetoric that only he recognized the real danger and was willing to fight heroically against it.

McCarthy had already discovered in the wake of the fateful Army-McCarthy hearings that without his trusty staff (many of whom left in the summer of 1954) and a quiescent Senate, he had very little official influence left. While there were certainly those who continued to support him, reporters began to ignore his pronouncements and his name all but disappeared from the columns of national newspapers. The White House even refused to invite McCarthy and his wife to formal functions.

It was among the public, however, that McCarthy saw the biggest drop in support. During his campaign to avoid censure by the Senate, for example, more than 10,000 people attended a pro-McCarthy rally in New York City. While it indicated that McCarthy still had significant public clout, the turnout disappointed organizers. He found that invitations to speak came from smaller organizations and turnouts were dramatically smaller than before. In almost every forum, McCarthy was painfully aware of how far he had fallen.

BIOGRAPHIES

Irving Adler, 1913–

Author and Teacher

Irving Adler headed the math department at a Manhattan high school; he had been working there since 1932. He became one of the early victims of New York's Feinberg Law and also became the named appellant in the 1952 Supreme Court case *Adler v. Board of Education,* 342 U.S. 485 (1952). Joining him in that appeal were three other teachers and several parents.

In the wake of the Supreme Court's decision, Adler and a growing number of other public school teachers in New York City faced dismissal for refusing to cooperate in what the *New York Times* termed "the drive against subversives." Although none were accused of subversive activity, their refusal made them guilty of insubordination according to the law.

Ben Barzman, 1911–1989

Screenwriter

Ben Barzman was another screenwriter whose American career foundered as a result of the Hollywood blacklist. One of his best-known early films was *Back to Bataan* (1945). After being blacklisted, Barzman and his wife moved to Europe, where Barzman continued to write or adapt screenplays for films in Italy, France, and elsewhere. Some of his later major films included *El Cid* (1961), *The Fall of the Roman Empire* (1964), and *The Blue Max* (1966). He became relatively well known in France as a commentator on Hollywood and the government's ongoing attack on the Left, which endeared him to the French public. He returned to the United States in 1976.

Alvah Bessie, 1904–1985

Writer, Member of the Hollywood Ten

Alvah Bessie was a writer who only worked on about half a dozen films (including 1945's *Objective Burma*) before being blacklisted. A veteran of the Abraham Lincoln Brigade (a group of American leftists who volunteered to fight for the republicans in the Spanish Civil War), Bessie had received acclaim for his creative writing (including a Guggenheim Fellowship). He wrote about his experiences in Spain in *Men in Battle* (1939); after being blacklisted, he wrote several books, including *The Un-Americans* (1957) and *Inquisition in Eden* (1965). Unlike some of his Hollywood peers, he did not try to work in Hollywood under assumed names.

Herbert Biberman, 1900–1971

Director, Member of the Hollywood Ten

Herbert Biberman directed several films from the late 1930s to the mid-1940s, including *Meet Nero Wolfe* (1936) and *The Master Race* (1941). Married to actress Gale Sondergaard, Biberman was one of the Hollywood Ten who refused to answer the so-called $64,000 question about past or present membership in the Communist Party. Later named as a Communist by Edward Dmytryk and others, Biberman (like Dmytryk) received only six months for his contempt of Congress conviction, not the year meted out to most of the others. Another victim of the blacklist, Biberman struggled heroically to make *Salt of the Earth* (1954). While it was never a commercial success, it remains a testament to the social vision of several of the blacklisted workers as well as that of the International Union of Mine, Mill, and Smelter Workers. His final film, *Slaves* (1969), also failed to reach a broad audience in the United States.

Roy Cohn, 1927–1986

Attorney

Roy Cohn was a legal prodigy; he graduated from the law school at Columbia University at the age of 20. He was too young even to practice for six months afterward. His first job was as an assistant U.S. attorney in New York. Almost immediately, Cohn's sense of self-promotion and ambition served him well. He assisted in the prosecution of several high-profile subversion cases, including that of Julius and Ethel Rosenberg. In 1952, Cohn went to Washington as a special assistant to the attorney general of the United States.

Cohn first met Sen. Joseph McCarthy at the end of 1952; his recollection was that McCarthy had heard good things about him. Shortly thereafter, Cohn accepted McCarthy's offer of a job. As the committee's work progressed, Cohn often served as a surrogate to McCarthy; he had access to confidential FBI reports and the network of often anonymous sources that provided grist for the McCarthy mill.

Cohn's aggressive prosecutorial style fit well with McCarthy's. His zeal, however, resulted in a number of highly publicized gaffes for the committee. These included an ill-advised trip to "investigate" the American information services libraries overseas. Cohn took along his confidante, G. David Schine, for whom he'd secured a position on the committee; foreign newspapers and domestic enemies of McCarthy pilloried the two for taking an anticommunist junket and calling for the burning of books, charges Cohn vigorously denied.

Cohn's relationship with Schine became an even bigger problem later during the Army-McCarthy hearings. As McCarthy's career faded after the hearing and subsequent censure, Cohn left the subcommittee and returned to private practice in New York. Little changed about his style; Cohn became a local power-broker and had many high-profile clients. Controversy continued to dog him, however. Shortly before his death, Cohn was disbarred for several types of misconduct going back to the 1970s. He died in 1986 in Bethesda, Maryland.

Bertolt Brecht, 1898–1956

Screenwriter and Playwright

Bertolt Brecht became one of the most notorious of the Hollywood Ten (technically he was the eleventh) not because of his testimony before HUAC, in which he denied ever having been a member of any Communist Party, but because of what he did shortly after his testimony; he left the country and went to Switzerland for more than a year before ending up in East Berlin. Brecht sought to read a statement before the committee, but the committee only allowed the statement to be read into the record. In it, Brecht discussed how he had used drama and his other writing to fight Nazism and Hitler but that he had specifically refrained from any political activity while in the United States. Brecht's fame stems from his work in the theater, not the cinema; his plays and other works rightly overshadow the one story he cowrote with Fritz Lang while in Hollywood (*Hangmen Also Die* in 1943). He is widely credited for being a major influence on contemporary theater.

David Fox, 1921?–1999

Physicist

The case of David Fox illustrates how easily colleges and universities could terminate those without the protections of tenure. Fox enjoyed none of them; for that matter, he did not even enjoy the protections of a faculty appointment. A teaching assistant in the Physics Department at Berkeley, Fox had testified (in very limited fashion) before HUAC in 1948 regarding his work at a Manhattan Project lab at Berkeley in World War II. While pleading the Fifth Amendment when asked about his own political affiliations and those of his coworkers, Fox insisted that he was not aware of any espionage at the facility. Late the following year, the Regents of the University of California questioned Fox and found his assurances unconvincing. They fired him.

Fred Friendly, 1915–1998

Television Producer

With a name shortened for broadcasting (his real name was Ferdinand Friendly Wachenheimer), Fred Friendly was the producer of *See It Now*. After a career as a journalist during the war, Friendly later sold audio recordings made during the war. He decided to compile many of those recordings; when seeking a narrator with a pleasant voice, he recruited Edward R. Murrow. Their first collaboration, a 1948 audio recording entitled *I Can Hear It Now, 1933–1945,* was very popular.

Friendly and Murrow released several other recordings and then decided in 1951 to try television. On Sunday, November 18, 1951, *See It Now* aired for the first time and showed the promise of a collaboration that would last much of the next decade. Even after *See It Now* ended, Friendly remained an executive producer for CBS until 1966, when he resigned in protest because the network refused to broadcast live Senate hearings on the Vietnam War.

Abraham Glasser, 1915?–?

Legal Scholar

Abraham Glasser was a law professor at Rutgers who followed in the footsteps of Moses Finley and Simon Heimlich, although he faced a much stiffer requirement: the new mandate that faculty pleading the Fifth Amendment could be immediately fired. When called to testify in early 1953, Glasser pled the Fifth Amendment. A faculty committee could do little under the circumstances given the strict wording of the Rutgers Board of Trustees. In a minor show of mercy, it suggested that he resign. Glasser complied.

Bernard Gordon, 1918–2007

Screenwriter

Bernard Gordon was not one of the Hollywood Ten, although his name came up in the first round of hearings before HUAC in 1947 when one of the "friendly" witnesses named him as a Communist. As Gordon himself ruefully notes in his memoir, that did not prevent Hollywood from adding his name to the not-yet-official blacklist only two months later. He continued to work on and off in Hollywood until 1952, when HUAC eventually subpoenaed him to testify; the committee never got around to calling him. He remained on the blacklist for a decade. From 1954 to 1965, Gordon had a successful writing career attributing scripts to other writers (and sharing the money) or using pseudonyms. Some of his films included *Hellcats of the Navy* (1957), *55 Days at Peking* (1963), *The Thin Red Line* (1964), and *Circus World* (1964). He and his wife lived in Madrid for many years, returning to the United States in 1966. He lived in Spain for several years again in the early 1970s. In the late 1990s, several film organizations decided to give proper credit to many of the writers whose lives had been affected by the blacklist and who had been forced to remove their names from scripts and films in order to eke out a living. Gordon himself notes that he was one of the few blacklisted writers who actually made a decent living despite the anticommunist frenzy.

Lillian Hellman, 1905–1984

Playwright and Screenwriter

Lillian Hellman is best known as a capable playwright but had a lucrative career in Hollywood as well. Her writing success led to work writing screenplays, adapting some of her own plays in several cases. The results were at times both critical and popular successes; the film version of *The Little Foxes,* which Hellmann produced for the stage in 1939 and adapted for Hollywood in 1941, received nine Academy Award nominations.

Lillian Hellman, a playwright and screenwriter with left-leaning politics, was called before the House Committee on Un-American Activities (HUAC). Her refusal to cooperate with the committee caused her to be blacklisted in Hollywood for over a decade. (Library of Congress)

Perhaps more significantly, Hellman was a leftist who sought to reflect her political sympathies through her art. She was involved in several films that reflected those sympathies; she wrote the story for *The Spanish Earth* (1937) about the Spanish Civil War, the screenplay for *The North Star* (1943), which was a wartime propaganda piece lionizing the Soviet Union and its people, and *The Watch on the Rhine* (1943), which was an antifascist play also made into a film.

Hellman escaped undue scrutiny in the first round of HUAC interviews; in the second round in 1952, however, she was not so lucky. As with others who appeared before the committee by then, she had the option of taking the Fifth Amendment to avoid any legal consequences. Like Arthur Miller, Hellman chose a different course; she told the committee that she was willing to testify about her own history with the Communist Party (to which she belonged for a few years in the late 1930s into 1940 or so), but that she was unwilling to "name names." If the committee asked her to do so, Hellman wrote that she would be forced to invoke her constitutional privilege against self-incrimination. While the committee did permit her letter to be read into the record, it also refused to allow her to dictate the terms of her testimony and Hellman largely took the Fifth during her committee testimony. While the committee could have charged her for her selective use of the Fifth Amendment, it chose not to do so and Hellman escaped the prison sentence that her longtime lover and detective novelist Dashiell Hammett had not. The blacklist had a significant financial impact on Hellman; she concentrated on plays for the next decade. In three separate memoirs, Hellman wove stories of persecution that reached a large audience but contained some factual inaccuracies that tarnished her reputation by the time of her death.

Ralph Himstead, 1893?–1955

Faculty Advocate

Himstead became the general-secretary of the American Association of University Professors (AAUP) in 1936; he would serve in that capacity for two decades. During his tenure, the AAUP made what was (and still remains) a strong statement defending academic freedom. The 1940 statement on academic freedom and tenure received endorsements from almost 200 other organizations.

By the late 1940s, however, the AAUP appeared incapable of meeting the challenges to tenure and academic freedom posed by antiradical campaigns. While continuing to claim that the association stood by the principles elaborated in the 1940 statement and elsewhere, Himstead seemed to be doing precious little in the face of dismissals of tenured faculty at the University of Washington, the University of California, and elsewhere.

When confronted with evidence of AAUP's apathy, Himstead cited several causes, including overwork, underfunding, and rules preventing the AAUP from intervening if faculty members had not specifically requested assistance. While granting the validity of these to a degree and acknowledging his deteriorating health, Ellen Schrecker notes that Himstead proved unequal to the managerial and administrative responsibilities of his office. He resigned under pressure in 1955, shortly before his death (Schrecker 1986, 319–332).

Lewis Jones, 1899–1975

University President

President of Rutgers University from 1951 to 1958, Lewis Jones was responsible for defining university policy in the cases of Moses Finley and Simon Heimlich. More important, perhaps, he was instrumental in crafting (like Chafee and Sutherland) a policy on the need for faculty members to prove their commitment to academic freedom by testifying before legislative committees. Some of Jones's ideas appeared in the broader policy announced in March 1953 by the Association of American Universities (AAU).

Ring Lardner Jr., 1915–2000

Screenwriter, Member of the Hollywood Ten

After dropping out of Princeton, spending time studying in Russia, and traveling in Europe, Lardner went to Hollywood as a young screenwriter in the mid-1930s. He co-wrote the screenplay for *Woman of the Year* (1942), for which he won an Academy Award. Lardner was an active member of the Communist Party and the Screen Writers Guild in the late 1930s. When subpoenaed along with the 18 other "unfriendly" witnesses to appear before HUAC, Lardner became one of the infamous Hollywood Ten. When asked whether or not he had ever been a member of the Communist Party, Lardner's sardonic reply, "I could answer it, but if I did, I would hate myself in the morning," reflected the dilemma facing witnesses; most solved it by refusing to "name names" and subjecting themselves to charges of contempt of Congress. Like several of his peers, Lardner received a one-year sentence. Although released early for good behavior, Lardner was unable to write openly in Hollywood for almost 15 years. During that period, he wrote under different names. After his public return to Hollywood, Lardner's greatest success came with the screenplay for *M*A*S*H* (1970). He died in 2000, the same year in which his autobiography, *I'd Hate Myself in the Morning,* appeared.

John Howard Lawson, 1894–1977

Playwright and Screenwriter, Member of the Hollywood Ten

Regarded by many as the most fervent Communist of the Hollywood Ten, Lawson was a founder of the Screen Writers Guild and the head of the Hollywood chapter of the Communist Party. After a promising early career as a playwright in the mid-1920s, Lawson transitioned into screenwriting for Hollywood; by the late 1930s and early 1940s, he was doing some of his best work. Films like *Action in the North Atlantic* (1943) and *Sahara* (1943) are good examples. Perhaps the most confrontational of those called to testify, Lawson was the model of an uncooperative witness; he informed HUAC that it was on trial and likened its tactics to those of Hitler. Blacklisted like many others, Lawson found work on only a few films after 1947; he did write the screenplay, however, for *Cry the Beloved Country* (1951), the film adaptation of Alan Paton's novel about race relations in apartheid South Africa.

Albert Maltz, 1908–1985

Author and Screenwriter, Member of the Hollywood Ten

Albert Maltz gained some notoriety even before being exposed publicly as one of Hollywood's Communists. In 1946, Maltz published "What Shall We Ask of Writers" in *New Masses*. The article suggested that art could not always be used for political ends. Very quickly, other Communist writers (including Alvah Bessie, Herbert Biberman, and John Howard Lawson) attacked Maltz for arguing from an anti-Marxist position. Only two months later, and under increasing peer pressure, Maltz reversed his position. In a new article for *New Masses,* he admitted the error of his ways and contended that art and politics were inseparable.

According to Victor Navasky, Maltz had been interested in leftist causes from high school onwards. At that time, he considered himself a pacifist. As he made his way through college at Columbia and then drama school at Yale, Maltz found himself increasingly attracted to communism; he joined the Communist Party in 1935. During World War II, after an award-winning career as an author and dramatist, Maltz went to Hollywood and wrote *Destination Tokyo* (1943) and *Pride of the Marines* (1945) among others.

As with seven of his Hollywood Ten peers, Maltz received a one-year prison sentence for contempt of Congress. Like some of the other writers, Maltz was able to continue to get work (using fronts and pseudonyms) after being blacklisted. He wrote or worked on almost a dozen movies following his official exile from Hollywood.

Philip Morrison, 1915–2005

Physicist

Philip Morrison was a leftist academic who continued supporting progressive causes even during the beginning of the McCarthyist crusades. Even more surprisingly, he never lost his job at Cornell. Morrison was a member of the Communist Party for six years from 1936 to 1942. Despite his affiliations, he was also a physicist working on the Manhattan Project who accepted a post in the Physics Department at Cornell after the war. He was a peace activist whose efforts over time earned the attention of HUAC, the Senate Internal Security Subcommittee, and numerous Cornell alumni who complained to the university of Morrison's activities.

By 1951, Cornell acted. At first, the administration tried to convince Morrison to rein in his activity and to dissociate himself from Cornell when engaging in political activity. It also encouraged him to limit any such activity for the good of the university. When the Senate Internal Security Subcommittee called him as a witness in 1953, Morrison (with Arthur Sutherland at his side) cooperated and, at least temporarily, quieted some of the animosity toward him.

In 1956, with the strong support of his department, Morrison won promotion to full professor despite the concerns of the Cornell trustees. In that same year, however, the board appointed a subcommittee devoted to Morrison's situation. That committee questioned Morrison at length and found no evidence of disloyalty. While perhaps not unscathed, Morrison had survived when so many others lost their reputations and/or their jobs.

Larry Parks, 1914–1975

Actor

One of the few higher-profile actors caught up in either round of HUAC's Hollywood hearings, Larry Parks made his first film in 1941, the same year he joined the Communist Party. He arguably became a star after portraying Al Jolson in *The Jolson Story* in 1946. When called before the second round of HUAC hearings in 1951, Parks recognized that although he was the first cooperative witness to testify, he would likely not work in Hollywood again. While that was not entirely true, Parks acted in only a few films thereafter.

Drew Pearson, 1898?–1969

Journalist

Pearson was a popular journalist and broadcaster whose work appeared in print, on radio, and on television. Despite being anticommunist, Pearson had regular run-ins with McCarthy and became a favorite target of the senator, at least once literally. After the senator threatened to attack Pearson, he got his chance during a confrontation at a private club in Washington on December 12, 1950. McCarthy slapped Pearson and kneed him several times in the groin; Richard Nixon forced the two apart. Several days later, McCarthy followed up the battery with a verbal assault. He read a laundry list of charges against Pearson on the Senate floor. Following the strategy McCarthy had used against Sen. William Benton, Pearson subsequently sued McCarthy for libel and assault, seeking more than $5 million in damages. He eventually dropped the suit.

Adrian Scott, 1912–1973

Producer and Screenwriter, Member of the Hollywood Ten

Adrian Scott was arguably one of those most affected by his brief stint in the Communist Party. He wrote for or produced at least 10 films between 1940 and 1947, when he became notorious as one of the Hollywood Ten. Having previously battled with John Howard Lawson over the content of a film, Scott (like Edward Dmytryk) was no longer as close to the party as many of his fellow witnesses. Like Dmytryk also, however, he went along with the strategy devised by the group to attempt to put HUAC on trial. After being blacklisted, Scott was an uncredited writer for a 1955 TV series and only participated in two other film projects thereafter.

Morton Sobell, 1917–

Engineer and Rosenberg Codefendant

Morton Sobell, codefendant of Julius Rosenberg. (Library of Congress)

Morton Sobell was part of a group of friends from City College in New York that included Julius Rosenberg. While never a significant part of Rosenberg's atomic efforts, Sobell fled to Mexico with his family to escape unwanted federal scrutiny. In August 1950, armed men kidnapped him, drove him to the border, and turned Sobell over to the FBI. Despite the fact that the government failed to link him to most of the individual incidents cited in the Rosenberg prosecution, Sobell was the principal public coconspirator whose fate hinged on that of the Rosenbergs. Unlike them, however, he avoided the death penalty. Judge Irving Kaufman sentenced him to the maximum 30 years allowable by law; he served 18 years. In September 2008, Sobell admitted to the *New York Times* that he had spied for the Soviets.

Dalton Trumbo, 1905–1976

Author and Screenwriter, Member of the Hollywood Ten

Dalton Trumbo proved one of the most decorated Hollywood personalities caught up in the blacklist scandal. Both a screenwriter and writer of fiction, Trumbo started working in Hollywood in the mid-1930s. Progressing from being a reader of scripts to a writer of them, Trumbo received an Academy Award nomination for *Kitty Foyle* (1940) and wrote several important screenplays in the mid-1940s; they included *A Guy Named Joe* (1943) and *Thirty Seconds Over Tokyo* (1944). He continued writing fiction as well. His most famous book, *Johnny Got His Gun* (1939), became a movie more than three decades later.

Like the others in the Hollywood Ten, Trumbo served time in prison for contempt of Congress. Afterward, he struggled to continue working in Hollywood, resorting to writing under pseudonyms or selling scripts using friends as fronts. Two of his films, *Roman Holiday* (1953) and *The Brave One* (1956), earned

Trumbo Academy Awards, although neither was credited to him at the time. In 1975, Trumbo finally received credit for *The Brave One;* in the case of *Roman Holiday,* he did not receive credit until 1992, more than 15 years after his death.

Trumbo was one of the first of those blacklisted who was invited to return to work in Hollywood. The fact that he received public credit for working on *Spartacus* (1960) caused controversy but proved that the power of the blacklist was beginning to erode. He worked on approximately 12 more movies before his death.

Joseph Welch, 1890–1960

Attorney

Joseph Welch was a partner in the Boston law firm of Hale and Dorr. Although Welch was a Republican, Sen. Joseph McCarthy's highly publicized and poorly substantiated attacks concerned him greatly. When the attorney general sought his counsel in the government's preparation for the Army-McCarthy hearings, Welch deftly managed the Army's case against McCarthy during the hearings. Throughout, Welch exhibited apparent humility and decency that starkly contrasted with McCarthy's own theatrics.

REFERENCES AND FURTHER READINGS

Adams, John G. 1983. *Without Precedent: The Story of the Death of McCarthyism.* New York: Norton.

American Association of University Professors. 1940. Statement of Principles on Academic Freedom and Tenure. Available at http://www.aaup.org/AAUP/ pubsres/policydocs/contents/1940statement.htm.

Bayley, Edwin R. 1981. *Joe McCarthy and the Press.* Madison: University of Wisconsin Press.

Bentley, Eric, ed. 2002. *Thirty Years of Treason: Excerpts from Hearings before the House Committee on Un-American Activities, 1938–1968.* New York: Thunder's Mouth Press/Nation Books.

Biberman, Herbert, and Michael Wilson. 1965. Salt of the Earth: *The Story of a Film.* Boston: Beacon Press.

Budenz, Louis F. 1948. *Men without Faces: The Communist Conspiracy in the U.S.A.* New York: Harper and Brothers.

Buhle, Paul, and Dave Wagner. 2003. *In Plain Sight: The Hollywood Blacklistees in Film and Television, 1950–2002.* New York: Palgrave Macmillan.

Chambers, Whittaker. 1952. *Witness*. New York: Random House.

Chomsky, Noam, et al. 1997. *The Cold War and the University: Toward an Intellectual History of the Postwar Years*. New York: The New Press.

Cohn, Roy. 1968. *McCarthy*. New York: New American Library.

Dmytryk, Edward. 1996. *Odd Man Out: A Memoir of the Hollywood Ten*. Carbondale: Southern Illinois University Press.

Doherty, Thomas. 2003. *Cold War, Cool Medium: Television, McCarthyism, and American Culture*. New York: Columbia University Press.

Gerson, Deborah A. 1994. "'Is Family Devotion Now Subversive?' Familialism against McCarthyism." In Joanne Meyerowitz, ed., *Not June Cleaver: Women and Gender in Postwar America, 1945–1960*. Philadelphia: Temple University Press.

Gordon, Bernard. 1999. *Hollywood Exile or, How I Learned to Love the Blacklist: A Memoir*. Austin: University of Texas Press.

Haynes, John Earl, and Harvey Klehr. 1999. *Venona: Decoding Soviet Espionage in America*. New Haven: Yale University Press.

Haynes, John Earl, and Harvey Klehr. 2003. *In Denial: Historians, Communism, and Espionage*. San Francisco: Encounter Books.

Hellman, Lillian. 1969. *An Unfinished Woman: A Memoir*. Boston: Little Brown.

Hellman, Lillian. 1973. *Pentimento*. Boston: Little Brown.

Hellman, Lillian. 1976. *Scoundrel Time*. Boston: Little Brown.

Herman, Arthur. 2000. *Joseph McCarthy: Reexamining the Life and Legacy of America's Most Hated Senator*. New York: The Free Press.

Hiss, Alger. 1957. *In the Court of Public Opinion*. New York: Knopf.

Hiss, Tony. 1977. *Laughing Last: Alger Hiss*. Boston: Houghton Mifflin.

Holmes, David R. 1989. *Stalking the Academic Communist: Intellectual Freedom and the Firing of Alex Novikoff*. Hanover: University Press of New England for the University of Vermont.

Krebs, Albin. 1986. "Roy Cohn, Aide to McCarthy and Fiery Lawyer, Dies at 59." *New York Times,* August 3, 1986.

Lardner, Ring, Jr. 2000. *I'd Hate Myself in the Morning: A Memoir*. New York: Thunder's Mouth Press/Nation Books.

Leab, Daniel J. 2000. *I Was a Communist for the FBI: The Unhappy Life and Times of Matt Cvetic*. University Park: Pennsylvania State University Press.

Leviero, Anthony. 1950. "A Presidential News Conference." *New York Times,* March 31, 1950, p. 1 (accessed October 15, 2005, on Proquest Historical Newspapers).

Lewis, Lionel S. 1988. *Cold War on Campus: A Study of the Politics of Organizational Control.* New Brunswick, NJ: Transaction Books.

Lewis, Lionel S. 1993. *The Cold War and Academic Governance: The Lattimore Case at Johns Hopkins.* Albany: State University of New York Press.

Lichtman, Robert M., and Ronald D. Cohen. 2004. *Deadly Farce: Harvey Matusow and the Informer System in the McCarthy Era.* Urbana: University of Illinois Press.

Lorence, James J. 1999. *The Suppression of* Salt of the Earth: *How Hollywood, Big Labor, Politicians Blacklisted a Movie in Cold War America.* Albuquerque: University of New Mexico Press.

McCarthy, Joseph. 1950. Telegram to Harry Truman, February 11, 1950. Ca.12/1930–ca.03/1955, President's Secretary's Files, The Papers of Harry S. Truman, Harry S. Truman Library. Online version accessed on October 15, 2005, at http://www.archives.gov/education/lessons/mccarthy-telegram/#documents.

Meeropol, Ivy, dir. 2003. *Heir to an Execution.* HBO Documentary Films.

Meeropol, Michael, ed. 1994. *The Rosenberg Letters: A Complete Edition of the Prison Correspondence of Julius and Ethel Rosenberg.* New York: Garland.

Meeropol, Michael, and Robert Meeropol. 1975. *We Are Your Sons: The Legacy of Ethel and Julius Rosenberg.* Boston: Houghton Mifflin.

Murrow, Edward R. 1967. *In Search of Light: The Broadcasts of Edward R. Murrow, 1938–1961.* New York: Knopf.

Navasky, Victor S. 2003. *Naming Names.* New York: Hill and Wang.

Neville, John. 1995. *The Press, the Rosenbergs, and the Cold War.* Westport, CT: Praeger.

Newman, Robert. 1992. *Owen Lattimore and the "Loss" of China.* Berkeley: University of California Press.

Nova, WBGH, Public Broadcasting System, originally aired February 5, 2002. "Secrets, Lies, and Atomic Spies." Transcript online at http://www.pbs.org/wgbh/nova/transcripts/2904_venona.html.

Olmsted, Kathryn S. 2002. *Red Spy Queen: A Biography of Elizabeth Bentley.* Chapel Hill: University of North Carolina Press.

Oshinsky, David M. 1983. *A Conspiracy So Immense: The World of Joe McCarthy.* New York: Free Press.

Prendergast, William B. 1950. "State Legislatures and Communism: The Current Scene." *American Political Science Review* 44, no. 3 (September): 556–574.

Radosh, Ronald, and Joyce Milton. 1997. *The Rosenberg File.* 2nd ed. New Haven: Yale University Press.

Radosh, Ronald, and Allis Radosh. 2005. *Red Star Over Hollywood: The Film Colony's Long Romance with the Left*. San Francisco: Encounter Books.

Rosteck, Thomas. 1994. See It Now *Confronts McCarthyism: Television Documentary and the Politics of Representation*. Tuscaloosa: University of Alabama Press.

Schneir, Walter, and Miriam Schneir. 1965. *Invitation to an Inquest*. Garden City, NY: Doubleday.

Schrecker, Ellen. 1986. *No Ivory Tower: McCarthyism and the Universities*. New York: Oxford University Press.

Schrecker, Ellen. 1994. *The Age of McCarthyism: A Brief History with Documents*. Boston: Bedford Books of St. Martin's Press.

Schrecker, Ellen. 1998. *Many Are the Crimes: McCarthyism in America*. Boston: Little Brown.

Schrecker, Ellen. 2000. "H-DIPLO/JCWS ARTICLE DISCUSSIONS: Schrecker on Haynes." In H-Diplo, h-diplo@msu.edu, December 18, 2000. Cited by John Earl Haynes and Harvey Klehr. 2003. *In Denial: Historians, Communism, and Espionage*, 151–152. San Francisco: Encounter Books.

"16 Lose Positions in City Schools." *New York Times,* April 30, 1954, p. 18 (accessed on Proquest Historical Newspapers).

Sobell, Morton. 1974. *On Doing Time*. New York: Scribner's.

Sperber, A. M. 1986. *Murrow: His Life and Time*. New York: Freundlich Books.

Strout, Lawrence N. 1999. *Covering McCarthyism: How the* Christian Science Monitor *Handled Joseph R. McCarthy, 1950–1954*. Westport, CT: Greenwood Press.

Truman, Harry S. 1950. Draft telegram to Joseph McCarthy, n.d. (February 1950). Ca.12/1930–ca.03/1955, President's Secretary's Files, The Papers of Harry S. Truman, Harry S. Truman Library. Online version accessed on October 15, 2005, at http://www.archives.gov/education/lessons/mccarthy-telegram/#documents.

U.S. Congress. House of Representatives. 1952. *Communist Infiltration of Hollywood Motion-Picture Industry—Part 7*. 82nd Cong., 2nd sess.

Weinstein, Allen. 1978. *Perjury: The Hiss-Chambers Case*. New York: Knopf.

White, G. Edward. 2004. *Alger Hiss's Looking Glass Wars: The Covert Life of a Soviet Spy*. New York: Oxford University Press.

American Workers in the 1950s

OVERVIEW: THE CHANGING FACE OF WORK IN THE 1950S

While historians very often look at the 1940s and economic and occupational changes during World War II as the critical point in establishing postwar employment patterns, occupational shifts during the 1950s illustrate perhaps even better than the immediate postwar years the ways in which the American economy, and therefore the work experiences of millions of Americans, was changing.

After losing more than two million jobs during the 1940s, the agricultural sector continued to hemorrhage, losing almost another two million during the 1950s. In terms of the overall nonagricultural economy, trends away from basic manufacturing and toward service sector, retail, and government employment accelerated noticeably during this period (see Table 2.1). While employment in several sectors like mining, transportation, and manufacturing either dropped or grew more slowly, others exploded. Construction and wholesale and retail employment increased just more than 20 percent each during the decade. Service sector employment grew even more, increasing more than 35 percent. Outpacing all other sectors was government employment, with an increase of more than 41 percent. The vast majority of that increase came at the local and state government level, where 2.5 million jobs were added during the decade.

The expansion of employment during the decade (an increase of almost 10 million nonagricultural jobs) disproportionately affected some groups more than

Table 2.1. Sector by Sector Employment Change between 1940s and 1960s

	Total Civilian Labor Force	Employed Civilian Labor Force	Agricultural Labor Force	Agricultural Labor Force (% of total)	Nonagricultural Labor Force	Nonagricultural Labor Force (% of total)	Unemployment (%)
Total							
1940	55,640,000	47,520,000	9,540,000	20.08	37,980,000	79.92	14.60
1945	53,860,000	52,820,000	8,580,000	16.24	44,240,000	83.76	1.90
1950	63,099,000	59,748,000	7,497,000	12.55	52,251,000	87.45	5.30
1953	63,815,000	61,945,000	6,555,000	10.58	55,390,000	89.42	2.90
1960	70,612,000	66,681,000	5,723,000	8.58	60,958,000	91.42	5.60
Men							
1940	41,480,000	35,550,000	8,450,000	23.77	27,100,000	76.23	14.30
1950	44,442,000	42,162,000	6,271,000	14.87	35,891,000	85.13	5.10
1953	44,194,000	42,966,000	5,496,000	12.79	37,470,000	87.21	2.80
1960	47,025,000	44,485,000	4,678,000	10.52	39,807,000	89.48	5.40
Women							
1940	14,160,000	11,970,000	1,090,000	9.11	10,880,000	90.89	15.50
1950	18,657,000	17,584,000	1,226,000	6.97	16,358,000	93.03	5.80
1953	19,621,000	18,979,000	1,061,000	5.59	17,918,000	94.41	3.30
1960	23,587,000	22,196,000	1,045,000	4.71	21,151,000	95.29	5.90

Source: U.S. Bureau of the Census. 1962. *Statistical Abstract of the United States: 1962.* 83rd ed. Washington, DC: Government Printing Office.

others. Women were the key beneficiaries; their gains were numerically greater than those of men. Perhaps more important, the number of women in the non-agricultural workforce during the decade increased by almost 30 percent versus an increase of only slightly more than 10 percent for men.

For the more than 17 million working Americans who by the end of the decade had placed their trust in trade unions to seek workplace justice, larger paychecks, and better conditions, the decade was a period of profound change in both positive and negative ways. The legacy of the 1947 Taft-Hartley Act was to stifle broad-based grassroots labor activism; many of the more successful methods of that activism, like wildcat strikes and secondary boycotts, were no longer possible without significant and potentially crippling financial penalties.

In the face of increased government and employer antagonism, the organized labor movement responded in several critical ways. First, they sought to pool their collective financial and human power in the 1955 merger of the American Federation of Labor (AFL) and the Congress of Industrial Organizations (CIO). While the AFL-CIO would retain the more conservative leadership of the larger AFL in the form of George Meany, the merger suggested that union leaders were more aggressively seeking to maintain the gains made by organized labor during the previous quarter century.

In a somewhat more controversial fashion than the merger of the AFL-CIO, the CIO engaged in a massive purge of unions in 1949 and 1950 in an effort to root out any unions whose leaders had seemingly Communist leanings. New unions set up by the AFL and CIO to recruit workers from the expelled unions engaged in bitter jurisdictional disputes that served to undermine union power. Industrial unions also shifted their negotiation strategies in key ways that guaranteed regular wage increases, generous benefits, and a prosperous future for their members in long-term contracts. In return, however, those unions sacrificed many of the more radical demands of previous decades, including participation in management decisions and the flexibility of using industrial action to force greater concessions from employers.

Many workers enjoyed significant income gains during the 1950s. As a result of higher wages, more professional opportunities, and broader prosperity, American workers moved into higher income brackets and their disposable income helped to fuel the continuing boom in consumer spending. Easier access to credit further spurred consumption. Workers also worked fewer hours per week and had more access to paid vacations and sick leave than in the past. Government spending on the Korean War in particular led to the lowest unemployment rate in the decade; it was only 2.9 percent in 1953. By the end of the decade, however, there were signs of a significant slowdown. Unemployment was almost double the 1953 level in 1960.

For workers defined by the census as "nonwhite," the picture continued to be less rosy. While more of these workers did make gains during the decade (more reported income in 1960 than in 1950, for example), they continued to lag behind their white peers. The median income of white workers continued to be double that of nonwhite workers. The percentage of nonwhite workers living below the individual poverty level (approximately $1,500 in 1960) was about 35 percent as compared to less than 23 percent of white workers. Nonwhite women fared the worst, with a median income of $909, only 21 percent of the $4,319 median income of white male workers. Nonwhite workers often suffered a variety of forms of discrimination both inside and outside of the workplace. Nor did they receive much support from unions; the organized labor movement generally failed to aggressively confront issues of racial discrimination, either before or after the merger of the AFL and CIO. The record of the federations on including women unionists in their leadership and decision-making bodies was little better.

TIMELINE

1950   CIO completes its purge of unions (that began in 1949) with Communist leaders and members in labor's own Red-Scare.

General Motors signs sweeping five-year contract with United Automobile Workers union (UAW) guaranteeing cost-of-living adjustments and pension and benefits increases to workers.

Strike begins against Empire Zinc in Bayard, New Mexico; it lasts more than a year and is eventually memorialized in the progressive film *Salt of the Earth*.

The Women's Trade Union League (WTUL) disbands its national organization; the New York City chapter lasts until 1955.

The Food, Tobacco, Agricultural, and Allied Workers Union of America (FTA) loses its bid to continue to represent workers at R. J. Reynolds in North Carolina.

1951   The National Negro Labor Council is founded.

1952   George Meany and Walter Reuther become the heads of the American Federation of Labor (AFL) and Congress of Industrial Organizations (CIO) respectively.

More than 500,000 steelworkers strike for two months after a failed effort by President Truman to seize control of the steel industry.

1954   Workers at the Kohler Company in Wisconsin go on strike; it officially lasts until 1965.

1955   After almost two decades of competition, the AFL and CIO merge into the AFL-CIO.

Westinghouse employees go on strike at more than a dozen plants nationally; the strike lasts until 1956.

1956   For the first time in American history, white-collar workers outnumber blue-collar workers.

The AFL-CIO encourages local unions to push for equal pay provisions in contracts.

1957   The AFL-CIO expels the International Brotherhood of Teamsters for corruption.

Steelworkers strike for just over a month in July.

The Trade Union Leadership Council, dedicated to improving visibility and opportunity for African American autoworkers, is founded.

1959   Steelworkers strike for almost four months; President Eisenhower intervenes aggressively in an effort to end the strike.

Congress passes the Landrum-Griffin bill, which tightens government control over financial accounting in unions and further limits union flexibility during strikes.

Table 2.2. Increase in Civilian Employment, 1940–1960

	Total Number Employed	Increase in Employment	Change (%)
Total			
1940	47,520,000		
1950	59,748,000	12,228,000	25.73
1960	66,681,000	6,933,000	11.60
Men			
1940	35,550,000		
1950	42,162,000	6,612,000	18.60
1960	44,485,000	2,323,000	5.51
Women			
1940	11,970,000		
1950	17,584,000	5,614,000	46.90
1960	22,196,000	4,612,000	26.23

Source: U.S. Bureau of the Census. 1962. *Statistical Abstract of the United States: 1962.* 83rd ed. Washington, DC: Government Printing Office.

Table 2.3 Employment in Selected Industries, 1950–1960

Employment	Total Number of Employees	Change (%)
Total nonagricultural employees		
1950	45,222,000	
1960	54,347,000	20.18
Mining		
1950	901,000	
1960	709,000	−21.31
Construction		
1950	2,333,000	
1960	2,882,000	23.53
Manufacturing		
1950	15,241,000	
1960	16,762,000	9.98
Transportation and public utilities		
1950	4,034,000	
1960	4,017,000	−0.42
Wholesale and retail		
1950	9,386,000	
1960	11,412,000	21.59
Service and miscellaneous		
1950	5,382,000	
1960	7,361,000	36.77
Government employment		
1950	6,026,000	
1960	8,520,000	41.39

Source: U.S. Bureau of the Census. 1962. *Statistical Abstract of the United States: 1962.* 83rd ed. Washington, DC: Government Printing Office.

ORGANIZED LABOR

Labor's Red Scare: The Purge of the CIO Unions

Wrangling over which presidential candidate to endorse in the 1948 election seemed to illustrate to anticommunist Congress of Industrial Organization (CIO) leaders the significant influence of Communist union leaders within the organization. The Communist Party of the United States (CPUSA) endorsed third-party candidate Henry Wallace as did some union leaders who had ties to the party. More radical unionists also criticized (as did the CPUSA) the Marshall Plan. Some CIO leaders, fearing that a defection from the Democratic Party would result in a loss for President Truman and the subsequent diminution of union influence in Washington, used a variety of internal mechanisms to try to force many of

Harry Bridges, leader of the International Longshore and Warehouse Union (ILWU), speaks at a stop-work meeting of ILWU members in San Francisco in 1952. The CIO expelled the ILWU for being dominated by Communists in 1950. (Library of Congress)

their member unions to back the Marshall Plan and the Democrats. They were largely successful as only one significant union officially endorsed Wallace. The issue confirmed in the minds of more conservative CIO leaders the need to do something about Communist influence in several of its unions (Zieger 1995, 268–277).

Those CIO leaders finally did so at their 1949 annual convention, putting into place constitutional changes that allowed the executive board to refuse to seat delegates who had ties to the Communist Party or to remove affiliate unions whose policies were similar to those of the CPUSA. In the first half of 1950, the CIO put several unions "on trial" for their leaders' political beliefs. After the expulsion of several additional smaller affiliates, the CIO had lost almost one million of its members, some of whom it promptly tried to get back by creating vigorously anticommunist alternatives like the International Union of Electrical, Radio and Machine Workers (IUE); the IUE attempted to "raid" the membership of the now-expelled United Electrical, Radio, and Machine Workers (UE). The same process had been going on between anticommunist CIO affiliates and their more radical peers for several years prior to the purge (Zieger 1995, 277–293).

Table 2.4. The Expelled Unions and Approximate Membership When Expelled

Union	Membership When Expelled
United Electrical, Radio, and Machine Workers (UE)	427,000
International Union of Mine, Mill, and Smelter Workers (Mine-Mill)	74,000
International Fur and Leather Workers Union (IFLWU)	44,800
International Longshoreman and Warehousemen's Union (ILWU)	43,900
United Farm Equipment and Metal Workers of America (FE)	43,000
United Office and Professional Workers of America (UOPWA)	31,500
Food, Tobacco, Agricultural, and Allied Workers Union of America (FTA)	22,500
United Public Workers of America (UPW)	14,000
American Communications Association (ACA)	10,000
International Fishermen and Allied Workers of America (IFAWA)	10,000
National Union of Marine Cooks and Stewards (NUMCS)	7,000
Estimates of expelled union membership	727,700
Percent of CIO membership represented	17–20

Source: Steve Rosswurm. 1992. "Introduction: An Overview and Preliminary Assessment of the CIO's Expelled Unions." In *The CIO's Left-Led Unions,* ed. Rosswurm, 1–17. New Brunswick, NJ: Rutgers University Press.

The Damage to Progressive Unions: The FTA and Local 22

While the UE and several other large unions were key targets for those seeking to end leftist influence in organized labor, several smaller unions were also the victims of anticommunist fervor. The Food, Tobacco, Agricultural, and Allied Workers Union of America (FTA) was one such example. With a base of power in Local 22, which represented workers at the R. J. Reynolds tobacco-processing and cigarette-making plants in Winston-Salem, North Carolina, the union was a politically and racially progressive organization that had done much to improve wages and working conditions in its brief existence. When the anticommunism of the AFL and CIO led to efforts by both federations to replace Local 22 as the bargaining agent for Reynolds' workers, the beleaguered FTA struggled to fight back.

Central to the process (as it was to that of union elections in the post–New Deal and post–Taft-Hartley period) was the National Labor Relations Board (NLRB), which oversaw elections to determine which union (if any) would represent the workers. With local officials and outside union organizers encouraging Reynolds workers to reject Communist influence, the outcome of a March 1950 election was ambiguous. Approximately 3,400 workers voted for the option not to have a union, while 3,300 voted for the FTA; 2,000 more voted for either the CIO or AFL alternatives. In a run-off election several weeks later, the FTA seemed to win in a close race; more than 100 disputed votes, however, hung

The UE:
The Most Dangerous Union in America?

No other large union suffered as much from the red-baiting anticommunism of fellow unionists, the federal government, and corporate officials than the United Electrical, Radio, and Machine Workers of America (usually shortened to UE). From the mid-1940s on, the union struggled against the rising tide of antiradical sentiment that targeted many of the left-leaning leaders of the large union.

For several days in late July 1947, the House Committee on Un-American Activities (HUAC) questioned several current and former UE leaders. Several of those witnesses identified fellow unionists as Communists and questioned their loyalty to the United States. Similar efforts to expose Communists in the UE leadership would continue for more than a decade (Schatz 1983, 176–178). The government took other steps as well, infiltrating the union with FBI informants and limiting union representation in defense-related plants.

The UE, like several other smaller CIO unions, was particularly vulnerable to one of the new legal burdens imposed upon the organized labor movement by the Taft-Hartley Act. One section of the act required that all union leaders take an oath disavowing membership or any connection to the Communist Party or any similar organization. If they failed to do so, their union would not be certified by the National Labor Relations Board (NLRB) and could not use government dispute-resolution mechanisms.

While many other labor leaders (Communists and anticommunists alike) initially balked at the oath as a heavy-handed attempt by the government to intervene in the affairs of the union movement and purge unions of radical leaders, most eventually did so. UE leaders refused to sign until 1949; in the intervening period, rival unions had "raided" hundreds of UE locals with varying degrees of success (Schatz 1983, 180).

Not all of the challenges to the UE's radical leaders came from outside the union; more conservative UE officials had been challenging the left-wing leadership from within for several years prior to the 1949 blowup with the CIO. In the wake of the UE's expulsion from the labor federation, many of those officials defected to the CIO's new anticommunist IUE under the presidency of former UE head James Carey.

Over the next several years, the IUE (with the help of the government and the CIO) aggressively sought to undermine the enduring loyalty of many electrical workers to the UE. Results of a few key 1950 union elections show the mixed results of that effort. In NLRB elections in early 1950 to determine who would represent workers at Westinghouse, which had many operations in the Pittsburgh, Pennsylvania, area, the UE lost a close election in which the IUE pulled out all the stops. Building on popular anticommunist rhetoric, the IUE claimed supporters ranging from Harry S. Truman to God as reason enough to vote against the UE. In

Continued on next page

The UE, Continued

Erie, Pennsylvania, however, the UE, citing its past success in securing concrete improvements for its membership and stressing worker unity, defeated the IUE in an election at one of General Electric's largest plants.

Unfortunately, the interunion competition of the late 1940s and early 1950s only worsened during the decade. By the early 1960s, the IUE was the single largest representative of GE, but another seven or eight unions (including the UE) represented tens of thousands more. This scattered and fractured system worked against efforts to craft a united front against an increasingly hostile employer; there is little question that the electrical workers suffered as a result (Schatz 1983, 226–227).

---

in the balance and would determine the final outcome. When the NLRB counted those votes for the "no union" option, the FTA lost its role as bargaining agent by 66 votes (out of more than 8,900 cast).

Recognizing its inability to continue as an effective advocate for workers' rights in the wake of its loss at Reynolds, the FTA sought to combine with several other left-wing unions; the result was the creation in October 1950 of the Distributive, Processing, and Office Workers of America. Despite these reverses, one scholar who has studied the FTA says, "hope still propelled" its leaders (Korstad 2003, 413). Union activists in the Reynolds plant faced the blacklist, but the company's fear of further organizing efforts forced it to pay competitive wages and offer benefits unheard of before the FTA.

Changes at the Top: New Blood at the Helm and the Creation of the AFL-CIO

The two major American labor federations had differed in many ways since the founding of the Congress of Industrial Organizations, which itself began in 1935 as an offshoot of the American Federation of Labor. The CIO focused principally on organizing in the mass-production industries, eschewing the more traditional trade or craft unions of the AFL. In 1938, when it became clear that the differences between the two groups were significant, the CIO became an independent entity and a number of unions decided to leave the AFL entirely.

In 1952, both William Green, the almost-octogenarian head of the AFL, and Philip Murray, who had been president of the CIO for more than a decade, died. Waiting in the wings were two labor leaders who had been expected to contend for any succession. George Meany, who became president of the AFL, had been secretary-treasurer of the federation since the late 1930s. Walter Reuther, who had headed the large and dynamic United Automobile Workers since 1946, followed Murray at the helm of the CIO but only after a relatively close election with Allan Haywood, a popular CIO official (Lichtenstein 1995, 322).

While Meany and Reuther would always have a somewhat rocky relationship, they both agreed to start discussions about a possible merger of the two labor federations. In December 1955, those talks came to fruition. In an act intended to consolidate labor's political and economic influence, the AFL and CIO agreed to merge. The new body's affiliates represented almost 15 million workers in the United States and Canada. Meany remained as the president of the merged federation; Walter Reuther chose to lead the new Industrial Union Department rather than serve as Meany's second-in-command. Reuther talked about how the new department would soon lead a brash new organizing campaign; the newly merged federation, however, never funded the department adequately for anything bold or particularly innovative.

George Meany became president of the American Federation of Labor (AFL) in 1952, then unified the labor movement by overseeing the merger of the AFL with the Congress of Industrial Organizations (CIO) in 1955. He was president of the AFL-CIO until 1979. (Library of Congress)

Reuther would continue to maintain a higher profile both at home and abroad than Meany, but would never equal Meany's influence within organized labor. Because of the numerical superiority of the AFL and Meany's virtual stranglehold over the increasingly important foreign policy agenda of the federation, Reuther remained largely on the periphery through the rest of his life. One of Reuther's biographers argues that Reuther had expected that Meany, already 61 at the time of the merger, would retire in the not-too-distant future, thus allowing Reuther to ascend to the presidency of the federation (Lichtenstein 1995, 334). This proved far from prescient as Meany stayed at the helm of the AFL-CIO until 1979, almost a decade after Reuther himself had perished in a small plane crash.

Contests at Home and Abroad: Meany vs. Reuther

In addition to disputes over the form and funding of domestic organizing efforts, few arenas illustrated the divide between George Meany and Walter Reuther better than the international efforts of the separate federations before 1955 and in the international activities of the AFL-CIO thereafter. To a great degree because of its suspicions about the fledgling World Federation of Trade Unions (WFTU), which had been formed in Europe in 1945, the AFL refused to take part. That body, which included representatives from federations in Western and Eastern Europe (as well as the Soviet trade union federation), was not acceptable to the AFL; the CIO, however, tended to have a more flexible attitude toward socialism and social democratic union movements. Yet even the CIO had to admit by the late 1940s that the influence exerted by the Communist union movements had made it difficult if not impossible to continue participating in the WFTU.

Thus, both the AFL and CIO became affiliates in the newly created International Confederation of Free Trade Unions (ICFTU). The term *free* referred to the anti- or noncommunist nature of the affiliates; the AFL didn't consider union movements in Communist countries as *free* of government control. Each also maintained offices in Europe in the postwar years. The AFL's representative in Paris was Irving Brown, a confidante of AFL foreign policy head Jay Lovestone (who over the course of his career had gone from being the head of the Communist Party in the United States to one of its most savage critics). Walter Reuther's foreign-policy advisor was even closer to him; Walter's brother, Victor, would serve as the main architect of CIO foreign policy (and UAW foreign affairs after the merger of the AFL and CIO) for decades.

Generally, the pattern that emerged in the first half of the decade placed the AFL and CIO on opposite sides of the table in Brussels, where the ICFTU had its headquarters. Despite having joined the new organization, the AFL consistently criticized the body for being soft on communism and indecisive in its policies toward the burgeoning Cold War. The CIO, on the other hand, had relatively warm relations with the social democratic unions of Western and Northern Europe; it also was sympathetic toward developing and newly independent nations, such as India, and their respective union movements.

After the merger, the head of the AFL-CIO Foreign Affairs Department was initially Michael Ross of the CIO; the power behind the throne, however, was still Jay Lovestone, who relied on his closeness with George Meany to guide the federation's efforts overseas. The conservative policies that resulted ensured that the federation would generally support the Cold War aims of the U.S. government. At its worst, the union movement collaborated both with the government and with multinational corporations to undermine leftist union movements, especially in Latin America. Later, the union movement would also be a stalwart supporter of U.S. intervention in Vietnam.

New Stability and Prosperity Come at a Price

Labor historians often refer to the period in the late 1940s and early 1950s as one in which the leaders of organized labor's largest unions effected a paradigm shift in labor negotiations with some of the country's largest employers. Some of the bigger industrial unions, like the United Automobile Workers and the United Steelworkers, had historically counted upon the militancy of their members and their ability to paralyze their respective industries—or at least the factories of the companies with which they were engaged in conflict. This strength provided key leverage in contract negotiations. This proved harder during World War II when an official CIO no-strike pledge had greatly lessened (although not entirely eliminated) industrial unrest.

In the postwar period, union leaders pushed for significant wage increases to counterbalance creeping inflation and sustain the consumer products boom that accompanied the return to civilian production. While the UAW's Walter Reuther and some others desired government participation in a kind of tripartite bargaining structure (labor-employer-government), the AFL sought to return to business as usual in which individual unions negotiated contracts directly with employers without the intervention of the state (Lichtenstein 1995, 226). It also became clear, with a turn toward a more conservative Congress in the postwar period, that the government was unlikely to allocate funds for increased social security or other societal protections.

Employers were no more cooperative with Reuther's postwar vision. As had been the case in the wake of World War I, employers chafed under the production, wage, and price limits established by the government during World War II. They eagerly anticipated a return to relatively uncontrolled markets in which their own influence was paramount. This led almost immediately into a UAW strike against General Motors in 1945 as well as a series of large strikes (especially in the steel industry) that followed in late 1945 and 1946. The outcome of those strikes was not any revolutionary change, but a significant wage increase and little else. The accompanying price increases led to significant inflation in the first several years after the war and did little to provide any broader labor peace.

Several key UAW contracts during the 1950s, however, indicated that organized labor was willing to sacrifice key parts of its previous demands in order to ensure regularly increasing wages and some protections against layoffs and the corrosive impact of inflation on take-home pay. The first, a 1950 contract with General Motors, followed along the lines of a 1948 agreement in terms of periodic cost-of-living adjustments to pay based on changes in the Consumer Price Index (CPI) and regular annual wage increases. It added pension benefits and subsidized health insurance. It came to be known, because of the sweeping implications both of the corporate concessions and the five-year length, as the "Treaty of Detroit" (Lichtenstein 1995, 280).

A subsequent contract between the Ford Motor Company and the UAW in 1955 further expanded corporate benefits to workers, guaranteeing supplementary unemployment benefits to employees laid off by the company; this

Dangerous for Different Reasons:
The Ejection of the Teamsters

In 1960, the single-largest union in the United States was the International Brotherhood of Teamsters. With almost 1.5 million members, it eclipsed its next largest peer (the United Steelworkers of America) by more than 300,000 members. And this was despite the fact that the Teamsters was an independent union, having been unceremoniously expelled from the AFL-CIO in 1957 in the wake of government accusations of corruption against former Teamsters president Dave Beck (who had been removed from office by the AFL-CIO) and his successor, James "Jimmy" Hoffa.

The size of the Teamsters union was a testament to its organizing prowess and its aggressive (indeed often physical) style that had won gains from trucking companies around the country and pulled members from other unions with which the Teamsters competed. By the mid-1950s, however, there were significant questions about the means used to enrich the union's coffers as well as the pockets of its leaders. Jimmy Hoffa had been investigated several times during the 1940s for malfeasance of various sorts. After a succession of highly publicized congressional hearings that targeted organized crime and other forms of corruption, both the AFL and CIO and others in government shifted the spotlight onto the Teamsters.

At the head of the anti-Teamsters crusade was Robert Kennedy, then chief counsel to the Senate's Permanent Subcommittee on Investigations (the vehicle through which Sen. Joseph McCarthy had his rise to infamy). The AFL-CIO joined in, passing executive resolutions that gave them the power to remove union leaders who pled the Fifth Amendment in order to protect themselves. After the Senate expanded Kennedy's inquiry (under the chairmanship of Sen. John McClellan), Dave Beck eventually appeared before the committee and sought refuge behind the Fifth Amendment more than 60 times in one day of testimony (Russell 2001, 186–187). In addition to being removed from the AFL-CIO leadership, Beck eventually went to prison for larceny and tax evasion.

Hoffa became Kennedy's next target. Previous investigations had linked Hoffa to various figures in organized crime in the East and Midwest. After being acquitted on charges of bribery, Hoffa went on to win the election to the presidency of the Teamsters. As the federal government sought new ways to catch Hoffa doing something untoward, the AFL-CIO wasted little time in acting against the entire international union. At its December 1957 convention, the federation cited organized labor's public image as one of the key reasons why something had to be done. In the end, delegates who represented 10.5 million workers voted to expel the Teamsters against those who represented 2.2 million (Russell 2001, 199–200).

precedent took root in steel and several other industries. By the end of the decade, millions of workers had some coverage under such agreements.

The cost of this new corporate largesse, however, was significant. By agreeing to the various contracts in the 1950s, some scholars argue that the UAW (and other unions subsequently) had essentially abdicated any right to intervene in managerial decisions. The companies could lay off or hire workers at will, they could conceal their profitability from unions, and they could raise prices in order to offset increased labor costs. As one scholar noted, in its agreement with the UAW, Ford had "paid the union off" (Brody 1993, 177–178). In combination with the draconian nature of the Taft-Hartley law, some unions found themselves hostages of lucrative, long-term contracts and with little recourse to the direct pressure or broader solidarity that had earned them critical gains before the war.

James "Jimmy" Hoffa went from an impoverished childhood to the leadership of the International Brotherhood of Teamsters, which he helped make one of the largest and wealthiest labor unions in the world. Much of his success was due to his connections to organized crime. He served more than four years in prison and disappeared in 1975. (Library of Congress)

Hours and Vacations Continue to Improve

While the most dramatic decreases in hours worked per week occurred earlier in the century (from 60 hours per week in 1900 to 45 hours per week in 1930), American workers continued to see a slow but steady diminution in hours worked. In 1950, American workers labored for 42.5 hours per week; by the end of the decade, that number was 40.8 hours. While Americans worked fewer hours on average, they also enjoyed better benefits like paid vacations. This was especially true for unionized workers, whose contracts included increasingly long vacations. In 1950, six days of paid vacation was the norm in "major" contracts, with 58 percent of the agreements containing such provisions. In that same year, only 14 percent of contracts mandated eight days or more. In 1960, 25 percent of contracts provided eight days of vacation and another 11 percent offered nine days or more of paid vacation (Kreps and Spengler 1966, 356–358).

NOTABLE STRIKES OF THE 1950s

While many of the significant strikes of the 1950s lacked the militancy of those that occurred during and immediately following World War II, there were a number of large and lengthy strikes that illustrated how American workers continued to struggle to define their roles in increasingly powerful corporate organizations. Much of that struggle occurred in their attempts to secure some of the benefits that seemed to be promised by the liberal New Deal Keynesian models of full employment and unending prosperity. To that end, unions in the late 1940s sought guarantees from employers that expanded upon the traditional demands relating to wages and hours; these new demands included pensions, guaranteed incomes for laid-off workers, and cost-of-living adjustments that would soften the impact of inflation. Employers resisted those demands more or less vigorously depending on the general prosperity of the economy and on the federal government's willingness to allow price increases. In hard times, unions faced a hard sell; when things were flush, the likelihood of a more advantageous contract improved significantly. Major (and multiple) strikes occurred in the steel and electrical industries during the decade. Their outcomes reflected the economic realities of the 1950s. In general, however, the total number of work stoppages declined significantly during the decade, suggesting that the combination of restrictive government legislation and new contracts that obligated union leaders to quell rank-and-file unrest had succeeded in lessening worker militancy.

The Empire Zinc, or *Salt of the Earth,* Strike, 1950–1952

The International Union of Mine, Mill, and Smelter Workers was one of those hounded out of the CIO in 1949 and 1950 because of its leftist union leaders. A union with a proud radical tradition springing from the Western Federation of Miners and the even more radical Industrial Workers of the World (IWW), Mine, Mill became an obvious target for the red-baiting of the era.

The union was successful in organizing both the white and Hispanic workers from several mines in the Southwest; the Empire Zinc mine in Bayard, New Mexico, was no exception. Given the national antipathy toward their union and the depressed economic conditions in the region, however, the strike promised to be an uphill battle for Local 890. In addition to an end to race-based wage differentials, benefits and pensions also played a role in the talks. When the company refused to resume negotiations in the fall of 1950, the workers went on strike. After months of stalemate, and as workers increasingly struggled to make ends meet despite a modest strike fund, the company announced it would re-open one mine in the area.

Tensions rose, and, as it was portrayed in the movie *Salt of the Earth,* the community responded to a judicial order by replacing male picketers with their wives and children, who were not mentioned in the injunction. Facing violence, intimidation, and the at-times aggressive efforts to get strikebreakers through the picket lines, both male strikers and the women who had become the heart of the picket line stood firm. Despite their efforts, the cost of maintaining the strike and fighting the legal battles associated with it wore down the local. Because of its suspected leftist sympathies, the union also faced jurisdictional "raids" from the anticommunist United Steelworkers of America in the area. The CIO condoned raiding—or trying to lure union members away from one union to another—against those affiliates kicked out of the federation for supposed Communist ties.

After 15 months of striking, the company and union agreed to end the strike. The company conceded small gains in wages and benefits, along with some other issues; the wage differential between the largely Hispanic miners at the Empire mine and their white peers was reduced, but had not disappeared. Furthermore, criminal charges against union members and organizers remained, and some would be dogged by legal action for years to come.

Steel Strikes, 1952, 1956, 1959

The steel industry suffered a series of strikes through the 1950s. Each seemed to feature slightly different issues and they had varied outcomes. Both the 1952 strike and that of 1959 saw aggressive intervention by the federal government in an effort to get the mills running again. The 1959 strike, like many others in the latter part of the decade, reflected the growing desire by companies and corporations to end union intervention (in this case the United Steelworkers of America or USWA) in managerial decisions and to erode union expectations in contract negotiations.

1952 Steel Strike

While the American economy generally boomed during the Korean War, with low unemployment and high production, American workers faced higher prices and inflationary costs of living, as they often had during other wars in American history. Since the CIO had not made any sort of no-strike pledge similar to the one offered during World War II, workers felt empowered to confront their employers and demand that wage increases match any increases in inflation.

President Truman shared many of the concerns about both increasing prices and wages; his administration utilized a variety of agencies, including the Wage Stabilization Board (WSB), to try to keep inflationary pressures under control. Workers viewed those controls with distrust because they appeared to favor industry and the government at the expense of the working class.

A steel worker taps a blast furnace at the M. A. Hana Steel Co., near Buffalo, New York. A series of strikes swept the steel industry in the 1950s. (National Archives)

While wages were certainly part of the 1952 dispute, one of the most important issues turned out to be the question of the union (or closed) shop. A "closed shop" is one in which all workers in a specific workplace must belong to the union that is the legal bargaining agent. United States Steel, the single-largest employer in the industry and the one that set the standard that informed many other labor agreements, sought to reinforce that employment was a contract between individuals and their employer, not between a union and a company. Closed shops remained controversial throughout the decade.

In the negotiations that began in late 1951, the union sought significant wage increases (to reflect the booming market for steel during the Korean War), while the company sought government promises that prices could increase to compensate for the higher labor costs. The WSB, however, recommended significant wage increases without corresponding Office of Price Stabilization guarantees of price increases, thus ensuring that the companies would reject the plan. The union voted to strike in early April 1952 if no agreement could be reached.

President Truman had limited options to stop the strike. He chose one of the most draconian, announcing shortly thereafter that the government would take control of the steel industry. The union instantly called off the strike and the disgruntled steel owners sought legal relief. The case, eventually heard before the Supreme Court in *Youngstown Co. v. Sawyer,* 343 U.S. 579 (1952), agreed with an appeals court that the president had exceeded his constitutional authority; the majority opinion argued that Congress, not the president, had the constitutional right to intervene in such a case. President Truman immediately ended the seizure and the USWA began to strike the next day.

The strike involved more than 500,000 steelworkers and lasted almost two months. U.S. Steel continued to reject the union shop, but Bethlehem Steel, one of the other major companies involved, effectively conceded the union shop, thus setting the pattern for the 1952 agreement and significantly increasing the number of union members throughout the industry. In the end, the government pushed for significant wage and benefit increases and allowed the companies to raise the price of steel, thereby ending the strike at the end of July. Many analysts saw the outcome as a symbol of the influence of organized labor in the Democratic Party; that alliance resulted in significant contractual benefits and protected the union from the possible backlash of striking a critical industry during wartime (Zieger 1995, 294–295).

1956 Steel Strike

The shorter steel strike in 1956 shared some of the major issues of the strike four years before. And, once again, the government conceded that wage hikes would be paired with price increases, thus permitting an inflationary outcome to the dispute. There were some differences, however.

In 1956, both the USWA and U.S. Steel had different leaders. Even before the 1952 strike, popular union head Philip Murray had died; David McDonald, whose own support never rivaled that of Murray, replaced him. U.S. Steel had a new leader as well. Roger Blough, who later became famous for a public dispute with President John F. Kennedy in 1962, sought to restrain union demands and ensure corporate profitability.

Negotiations broke down during the early part of the summer. While the company had agreed to significant wage increases, it also sought a long-term contract that implied increased stability but limited options for the union if economic conditions altered substantially. The union struck on July 1, 1956, and the stoppage lasted 36 days.

With pressure from the Eisenhower administration, the industry conceded large wage increases and accepted a three- (rather than five-) year contract. The contract also included what E. R. Livernash called "for all practical purposes a full union shop" (Livernash 1961, 111).

1959 Steel Strike

By 1959, the economic tides of the industry were turning; foreign steel imports were larger than domestic steel exports for the first time (Filipelli 1990, 515). Given the pressure from cheaper competitors overseas, the steel industry sought a new united front against the USWA. For the first time, negotiators for the 12 largest steel employers gathered to bargain with the union rather than relying on the largest companies to provide the models for other agreements. Not only did the companies seek a short-term contract with no wage increases, but they also sought to limit or end union control over what were known as "local practices" or "work rules," in which unions were able to determine staffing levels for specific tasks. Companies saw this as an unreasonable intrusion in managerial prerogative.

Somewhat surprisingly, the union shop was not a particular source of dispute during the negotiation. Nor were wages the critical issue; the USWA asked for a small increase in fringe benefits but no wage increase. The companies, however, pushed a number of smaller issues, including seniority, local practices, and others that combined to alienate the union and guarantee that no agreement would be reached.

When the strike began in the middle of July, the Eisenhower administration seemed unsure of how to proceed. It had intervened very little in the negotiation process, but viewed with concern the prospect of a long strike. As the strike dragged on into its third month, President Eisenhower used another legal weapon against the strike: the injunction. Under the Taft-Hartley Act of 1947, the president could invoke national emergency provisions. When government mediators failed to secure an agreement, the U.S. attorney general sought an injunction that forced the workers to go back to work for an 80-day "cooling off" period during which negotiations could resume. In the end, with hostile employees unlikely to accept the proposed contract, and with government pressure to end the strike, the companies dropped some of the more offensive issues (like many of the local practices points) and compromised on a contract. In the end, the lengthy strike lasted roughly four months and paralyzed the vast majority of steel production in the United States; it is considered one of the longest industrial strikes in American history. Ironically, it may have opened U.S. markets even further to foreign imports, thus continuing the decline of the domestic steel industry that would eventually harm both the steel companies and their workers.

Kohler Strike, 1954–1965

While the strike against the Kohler Company by the United Automobile Workers of America (UAW) was not a particularly large one (involving only several thousand workers), its longevity and its violent nature suggest not only that anti-union employers were still willing to aggressively fight unionization, but also that their union opponents responded with equal force to secure bargaining rights in the workplace.

Prior to the efforts by several AFL and CIO unions to organize Kohler, the company entered the 1950s with an agreement only with the Kohler Workers' Association, a company union with no affiliations to national federations like the AFL or CIO. By 1951, however, even the officials of the company union realized that they needed such an affiliation to put pressure on the company to make concessions in contract negotiations. The company union voted overwhelmingly to affiliate with the UAW in early 1952.

Negotiations between the new UAW local and the company dragged on for more than a year when the local agreed on a contract that fell short of what they had hoped for but provided key guarantees of some benefits, union security, and arbitration. Almost immediately, both sides sought to renegotiate the contract; they began discussions in February 1954. The union authorized a strike if it became necessary, while the company continued to stockpile weapons (it had already increased its own "special police" force dramatically since the UAW had become the bargaining agent for Kohler workers two years before). The key issues were wages, union security, provisions that permitted union dues to be withheld directly from workers' paychecks, and rules on whether or not non-union subcontractors could be hired. By April, it was clear that no agreement was likely. On April 5, 1954, a picket line appeared in front of Kohler's gates (Uphoff 1966, 117–144).

For almost two months, mass picketing prevented replacement workers from entering the plant; after that, the Wisconsin Employment Relations Board ordered that the number of pickets be reduced to permit the company to operate the plant. As the strike continued, various acts of petty violence marked the tense relationship between company and workers. The company claimed in 1958 that more than 800 acts of violence against people and property had occurred in the strike's first three years. The union countered with a list of dozens of alleged acts against strikers' property (Uphoff 1966, 187–191).

The Kohler strike is also interesting because it coincided with the hearings of the so-called McClellan Committee (the Senate's Permanent Subcommittee on Investigations), which examined the Kohler strike; testimony on the Kohler strike eventually filled more than 2,000 pages. The committee earned its greatest notoriety for its campaign against corruption in the Teamsters union. Facing Republican accusations that they were shielding the UAW's Walter Reuther from scrutiny, both Robert Kennedy (the committee's counsel) and his brother and future president Sen. John F. Kennedy (D-MA) pushed for hearings on Kohler. More than 70 witnesses testified. As might be expected, the committee members disagreed about what the testimony proved (Uphoff 1966, 262–292).

After five years without any meaningful bargaining, talks resumed in 1962. Some of the issues that had previously held up negotiations were apparently no longer important, and the company conceded several without any apparent protest. The union subsequently signed a series of one-year agreements with Kohler. While the strike had technically been called off in 1960 to take advantage

Boulwarism

One of the new tactics taken by company owners in the 1950s to limit concessions to labor unions was the brainchild of Lemuel Boulware, who had become a vice president for General Electric (GE) in the wake of World War II. Despite a background in marketing, GE put Boulware in charge of a project to analyze employee relations. The study concluded that GE had been trying to give employees what they wanted, but that it had failed to impress that fact upon their employees. Thus, the study concluded that in addition to some other management changes, GE needed a new collective-bargaining strategy as well (Northrup 1964, 25–28).

After 1948, GE adhered to this new policy, which came to be known as "Boulwarism." After talks with union representatives and after careful research, GE would make one offer to the union and, in the absence of additional information that would affect that offer, not vary from it. According to one scholar of the practice, the company thus "denies unions the political victory of proving that it forced the company to accede to union demands" (Northrup 1964, 29). Since GE also publicly disclosed details of the offer, it put additional pressure on the union to come to terms. Another scholar quoted a union official who said that GE had "turned negotiations into theatre" (Schatz 1983, 173–174). This new model informed much of General Electric's bargaining strategy over subsequent decades and was a symbol of the reluctance of even the appearance of granting concessions to organized labor.

of a National Labor Relations Board (NLRB) ruling that favored the union, company resistance to concessions and its unwillingness to abide by the NLRB decision resulted in the conflict lasting another five years. At the end of 1965, the company finally reached an agreement with the UAW on a new contract and on back pay for the reinstated workers.

Southern Bell Strike, 1955
In early 1955, the Communication Workers of America struck Southern Bell for more than two months; the strike involved more than 50,000 workers in nine states. Despite opposing arbitration, the company eventually agreed to a contract that earned the workers wage increases, the recognition of the right to strike, and several other concessions.

Westinghouse Strike, 1955–1956
The Westinghouse strike of 1955 and 1956 was not one, but two distinct work stoppages. The first, a shorter strike by the IUE, started in August 1955 at the large plant in East Pittsburgh, Pennsylvania. According to the union, "Westinghouse was in bad trouble in 1955." After losing several government contracts,

and with sluggish sales of consumer products, the IUE claimed that Westinghouse's "solution was to take it out of the hide of its employe[e]s," especially those at the massive plant in Pittsburgh (IUE n.d., 1).

The union cited the shift from incentive pay to day-work pay and the expected drop in wages that would accompany it as a principal grievance. It also criticized the infamous "speed-up," in which a company insists on speeding up production without changing compensation. At the time, the union still had a significant part of its two-year contract remaining, but Westinghouse management clearly decided that it needed to rework some of the basic ground rules of managerial prerogative and the power of the union. In response to a seemingly inflexible five-year contract offer (and perhaps a sign that Boulwarism had spread beyond General Electric contracts), the entire IUE went out on strike on October 16, 1955; more than 50,000 workers left Westinghouse facilities nationwide.

Just as negotiations were under way to merge the AFL and CIO, the IUE struggled to fend off the determined efforts of the company, which they claimed was "determined to smash the IUE" (IUE n.d., 1). The union stated that the company used violence, intimidation, and harassment to try to push the strikers back to work or to allow strikebreakers into Westinghouse plants. Both sides cited the GE contract as an important benchmark. Westinghouse claimed its offer was almost identical, while the IUE countered that the benefits in the Westinghouse contract were dramatically less than those in the GE contract.

After determined negotiation and a variety of efforts at mediation, the two finally reached an agreement in March 1956; the strike ended after 156 days. The union earned the right to renegotiate the contract (despite its five-year length), some small wage increases, and expanded pension benefits.

An even longer strike against Westinghouse, this one by members of the now-independent United Electrical Workers (UE), which had been driven out of the CIO over its Communist leadership, occurred in the same time period. UE members of Local 107 at Westinghouse's Lester, Pennsylvania, plant went out on strike in October 1955, a day or so before their IUE peers.

Workers at the Lester plant (near Philadelphia) stayed out at least in part because they demanded the reinstatement of more than a dozen workers who had been fired during the strike and also because they claimed that Westinghouse was seeking to cut their wages by as much as 20 percent. As the Lester strike dragged on into the summer, many of the striking workers found other jobs. Finally, in August 1956, federal mediators, company officials, and local union leadership agreed on a new five-year contract similar to the one signed earlier with most of the company's other workers. News reports said that the new contract mandated the reinstatement of the fired unionists. After 296 days, Westinghouse's labor troubles in 1955 and 1956 finally came to an end. Estimates of lost revenue varied, but the unions suggested that they were in the hundreds of millions of dollars.

Police and United Auto Workers pickets battle at a Westinghouse jet engine plant in Kansas City, Missouri, after an attempt was made to move a Missouri-Pacific freight train into the strikebound plant, 1958. (Bettmann/Corbis)

GE Strike, 1960

Technically not occurring during the 1950s, the 1960 strike at General Electric characterized the transformed landscape of collective bargaining in the post–World War II period and showcased the weakening ability of formerly powerful industrial unions to challenge employer supremacy. After the policy of Boulwarism instituted by General Electric came into force, the IUE often faced difficulties in securing improvements in what union leaders termed as GE's "take it or leave it" offers. The contract in 1955 was an exception; relatively flush economic times, coupled with GE's desire to expand, resulted in an unusually good contract for the union. As business slowed in the late 1950s, however, it became clear that both the IUE and GE management expected some sort of turmoil at the end of the decade.

IUE president James Carey had unsuccessfully tried to secure a strike vote several times in previous years. Championing an AFL-CIO campaign to secure certain basic guarantees, like the guaranteed annual wage implicit in some of the agreements in the automobile industry, the IUE instead faced a GE demand that the union's expensive cost-of-living-adjustment clause be eliminated from the contract. A strike vote in September barely rejected the contract offer and authorized a stoppage. Several of the largest IUE locals, however, voted not to strike, including the historically militant local at GE's plant in Schenectady, New York (Schatz 1983, 226–228).

General Electric capitalized on the tensions in the IUE and promised the original contract offer to those who returned to work; many did so after less than a day on the picket lines. Within less than two weeks, many workers had returned to work and Carey was forced to accept GE's contract, which remained very similar to what the company had originally offered. The company thus appeared in control and magnanimous in victory. The increasingly ill-tempered Carey, on the other hand, seemed surly in defeat and his union appeared weak and divided.

AFRICAN AMERICAN WORKERS IN THE 1950S

African American workers had mixed experiences during the 1950s. On the one hand, their income went up significantly, while continuing to lag behind that of their white peers. African American workers also joined trade unions in increasing numbers (even in the American Federation of Labor, which had a poor reputation when it came to enforcing egalitarian principles among its affiliates). At the same time, however, race continued to be a powerfully divisive force; predominantly white unions remained so and African Americans were still often subject to discrimination by their employers, fellow workers, and many in the organized labor movement. There were also significant disparities between the incomes of African American men and women; the latter continued to earn on average the least of any group. The types of employment for African Americans also changed notably during the decade. More African Americans left rural farms and headed for towns and cities and away from agricultural work. More African Americans got professional jobs, a result at least in part of better educational opportunities; it was also a function of a segregated society in which African American professionals ministered to, treated, taught, and represented the African American community almost exclusively.

African American Workers and Organized Labor

Historians continue to debate the degree to which African American workers suffered racial discrimination in the organized labor movement after World War II. There is little doubt that African American workers, like other groups, enjoyed some of the material gains of a booming post–World War II economy and the new wartime economy of the Korean War. The merger of the American Federation of Labor (AFL) and Congress of Industrial Organizations (CIO) also seemed to usher in the possibility of more progressive racial practices, particularly with some unions that sought historically to exclude African Americans entirely from membership.

Through much of the 1950s, and particularly after the merger of the AFL and CIO, African American workers looked to unions for better treatment than they had historically received. Early in the decade, little seemed to have changed. As before the war, the CIO had a better record in terms of welcoming African American members, but its track record of elevating them to executive roles and other positions of responsibility was limited. In some cases, African American workers were given token positions, thus limiting their ability to press for real change within their international union. The ongoing unwillingness of their unions to push for racial equality made some African American workers consider leaving their unions entirely; they felt that the union had become at least as much of the problem as segregationist employers (Nelson 2001, 238–239). There were some exceptions, however; African American women made some gains through the lobbying of some relatively hidebound unions as well as some of the more progressive ones. In some cases, they gained access to positions previously reserved for white women (Cobble 2004, 81).

The AFL, on the other hand, had many more African American members than the CIO, but a much longer tradition of racial exclusion and discrimination. In some cases, this had the strange effect of allowing African American workers greater agency. For example, African American workers in segregated local unions were able to control their own affairs and gain critical leadership experience. Thus, however paradoxically, some African American workers benefited (at least at the local level) from segregation.

It was in the AFL, too, that African American workers had one of their most visible champions. While an ardent anticommunist and a fierce Cold Warrior, A. Philip Randolph, the longtime head of the Brotherhood of Sleeping Car Porters and the one African American executive vice president of the federation, consistently prodded the AFL-CIO to live up to its promises of a color-blind labor movement. In that quest, he often found himself in conflict with AFL head (and later AFL-CIO president) George Meany. At the 1959 AFL-CIO convention, Randolph openly attacked the slow pace of progress. Meany, who had been pushing for changes in the few remaining whites-only unions and those with segregated locals, responded with characteristic impatience. According to a news report of the exchange, Meany exploded, "Who the hell appointed you as the guardian of all the Negroes in America?" (Raskin 1959, 1).

In an effort to avoid a more permanent schism within organized labor, Randolph continued to work within the movement's limits but did not abandon the broader goal. In 1960, he and several others founded the Negro American Labor Council (NALC); the organization's goal was to continue to seek racial parity and equality for African American unionists.

The National Association for the Advancement of Colored People (NAACP) pushed organized labor to take more proactive steps to realize its stated commitment to racial equality. Here, the San Francisco NAACP branch demanded that the American Federation of Labor (AFL) "smash the color line in its own interest," San Francisco, California, ca. 1954–1960. (Library of Congress)

The National Negro Labor Council

African American unionists and political activists founded the National Negro Labor Council in 1951 in response both to the oppressive nature of recent government legislation (especially the 1947 Taft-Hartley Act) and a recognition that the organized labor movement had fundamentally failed to address issues of importance to African American workers. The CIO's move against several "left-led" unions in 1949 and 1950 had critically undermined at least one union, the Food, Tobacco, and Agricultural Allied Workers Union, which had been a boon for African American tobacco workers in the South. Its Local 22 in Winston-Salem, North Carolina, had been a key incubator for African American workers and leaders in the post–World War II period. This was especially true for African American women, who comprised approximately one-third of those who gathered to organize the council.

The council, then, was an effort to reverse the trends that seemed to isolate African American workers (many of whom were already formally excluded from protective government legislation) and ensure that they would remain second-class citizens in unions as well as in American culture more broadly. Their "'militant struggle'" against the entrenched racial order in organized labor, while progressive in many ways, never reached the level of success they desired (Zieger 1995, 348). It, too, fell prey to red-baiting both from within organized labor and from federal government efforts to harass left-leaning organizations out of existence (Jones 1995, 266–267). The group disbanded in 1956 after it had been determined by the federal government to be a "subversive" organization. Despite its relatively short life, the council was responsible for pushing companies to agree to contractual language that mirrored that of the federal government's fair employment practices during the war, thus reducing or removing race-based wage differentials and job discrimination.

The Trade Union Leadership Council

A group of African American unionists within the United Automobile Workers Union formed the Trade Union Leadership Council (TULC) in 1957. They sought to publicize issues related to race in the industry and to pressure the leadership of the union to promote or elect African American autoworkers to positions of greater responsibility and prestige. This was a particularly sensitive issue for African American UAW members. Their union supported a progressive civil rights policy, but the industry had a long tradition of racial discrimination and all of the members of the International Executive Board were white.

Shortly after the incident in which George Meany publicly upbraided A. Philip Randolph for his efforts, UAW president Walter Reuther found himself in a similar position at the 1959 UAW convention. When pushed to get an African American on the executive board of the union, Reuther responded defensively, arguing that when an African American was qualified enough, he or she would be put on the board (Lichtenstein 1995, 375–377).

African American Income during the 1950s

As with most Americans, African American workers enjoyed significantly improved income during the decade. The median income of Americans who worked in 1950 was approximately $1,900 (all figures in this section are in 1950s dollars); in 1960, that amount (adjusted for inflation) was approximately $2,275, an increase of more than 18 percent. Perhaps not surprisingly, white workers fared the best in this regard; white workers' median income in 1960 was $2,458, up from approximately $2,000 in 1950.

Those whom the U.S. Census categorized as "nonwhite" did not fare as well as their white peers. The Bureau of the Census defined nonwhites as African Americans, East and South Asians, Pacific Islanders, and American Indians. Those

Were American Unions Discriminatory in the 1950s?

Herbert Hill, a longtime critic of the shortcomings in the trade union movement's efforts to bring racial equality to organized labor, wrote in the mid-1960s that the movement had essentially failed African American workers. As he put it, "the tradition of racial discrimination within trade unions is the great historic failure of organized labor. . . . If the failure of organized labor to introduce the spirit of equality and democracy into the workplace has been a heavy burden for Negroes, it is also the tragedy of American labor as a social institution" (Hill 1967, 397). Hill rightly noted that a number of unions maintained racially exclusive memberships and that many of the federation claims for a racially progressive policy were largely rhetorical. Hill is certainly not alone in this argument; more contemporary scholars of the AFL-CIO like Robert Zieger agree. Zieger argues that many of those in the CIO failed to aggressively confront shop floor racism or make any efforts to help create a more racially egalitarian society (Zieger 1995, 374).

Others, however, see some qualified progress for African American unionists in the same period. In a recent book, Paul Moreno cites the significant increase in income for African Americans, as well as their gains in membership in trade unions, to suggest that many prospered during the decade. While conceding that employers certainly used racist appeals to frustrate union campaigns and fan community fears of African American domination, miscegenation, and other potent images, Moreno discounts the arguments of Hill and Zieger. He contends that their view "exaggerates the commitment of the federations to fair employment before the 1950s and understates it afterward." He agrees, however, that the seemingly glacial pace with which the union movement seemed to address racism within its affiliates caused "increased disillusionment among civil rights advocates," including those within the labor movement itself (Moreno 2006, 225, 235). Given many unions' emphasis on seniority, African Americans who had faced discrimination in the past were locked into an inflexible system that would keep them behind their white peers even if their union locals had since disavowed racism.

thus classified continued to earn a fraction of the income of their white peers. The median income of nonwhite workers over the age of 14 was approximately $970 in 1950 (or just less than 50 percent of the median income of white workers); their median income of $1,220 in 1960 represented a slight percentage gain against white workers but only a minor one.

African Americans, numerically dominant in the nonwhite category, enjoyed an even lower median income than their peers. In 1960, African American workers earned a median income of approximately $1,220; those listed as coming from "other races" earned more than $1,585. Thus, while African American workers' median income was up almost 22 percent during the decade, the gap between white workers and African American workers remained the same as 10 years previous.

The median income disparity is useful to illustrate that gap; looking at income groupings shows even more explicitly that few African Americans were "fully" enjoying the American Dream. African Americans were closing that gap in the higher income levels. An income of $10,000 in 1950 was worth approximately $83,000 in 2006. In 1950, more than one million white Americans, 1.7 percent of the white population, earned $10,000 or more annually. In that same year, only 6,000 African Americans, or 0.1 percent of the African American population, were in the same income bracket. Ten years later, however, more than 23,000 African Americans were in the same income range; that still only represented 0.3 percent of the African American population.

One of the reasons that African American workers earned significantly lower incomes than those from other groups was that their jobs continued to cluster in service and agricultural occupations. Farm work was one of the nation's lowest-paying occupations. For the more than 500,000 African American farm workers, this meant even lower income levels. Median income for African American farm workers was only $554, barely one-third of the more than $1,521 median income of African Americans working in urban areas.

Greater incomes were by themselves no guarantee of financial stability or symbols that African Americans were necessarily realizing greatly increased living standards. Statistics on poverty and welfare reflect this reality. In 1960, three out of every four welfare recipients in New York City were either African American or Hispanic (Walkowitz 1999, 216).

Trends in African American Employment

African Americans, reflecting broader population shifts away from rural, farm employment, left farms in droves between 1940 and 1960. In 1940, the census reported almost 1.5 million African American farmers and farmworkers; by 1950, that number had dropped to just more than one million and in 1960 had dropped again by almost 50 percent to just over 500,000. Many of those leaving agricultural employment moved to cities and towns.

Shifts in employment for African American workers mirrored many of the social and economic changes in the American population more broadly. While those shifts were often largest between 1940 and 1950, largely a product of the wartime boom and general prosperity thereafter, many of the trends continued during the 1950s as well.

By 1960, more African Americans than ever before were going to school and staying in school longer. The 1960 census reported that African American men and women were staying in school for an average of almost nine years; this was a significant improvement over 1950. The 1960 census reported more than

300,000 African Americans over the age of 14 who had gone through four or more years of college.

With better education, more African Americans entered what some studies termed professional or semi-professional employment; that number almost doubled between 1950 and 1960. Certain fields showed significant growth as well. The numbers of school teachers, lawyers, and judges, for example, increased by almost half, while the number of African American physicians (not surprisingly given the difficulty of breaking racial barriers in medical school) increased much more modestly. This is an area in which segregation may have played a slightly positive role; African American professionals principally served an African American clientele, thus ensuring a need for their services and motivating some to seek advanced education.

After the relative prosperity during the Korean War, workers of color (like Americans more generally) faced a weakening economy and more uncertain prospects for the future. Often victims of the "last hired, first fired" syndrome, African Americans faced growing unemployment after 1953. Unemployment in 1960 in the civilian labor force for nonwhite workers was almost 9 percent, four percentage points higher than that of white workers. Other statistics suggest that nonwhite unemployment in 1950 was over 10 percent; it would continue to rise until 1964. More African American workers also worked in part-time rather than full-time employment than their white counterparts, further complicating the unemployment picture. Some historians and economists have referred to this as a problem at least as much of underemployment as unemployment.

Victims of Double Discrimination: African American Women Workers in the 1950s

African American women workers entered the 1950s (as they had many other decades) in one of the least enviable positions because of a combination of factors: they earned the least of any major group, they lacked the government protections granted to many other workers, and their gains during the decade failed to address some of the structural inequalities they faced.

On paper, African American women seemed to be doing significantly better during the period. That increase in income, however, was small when compared to almost all of those other groups. As with other demographic groups, their income had risen during the decade. They spent more time in school; there were also more jobs for teachers. Teaching and nursing were among the few professional occupations that were relatively accessible to African American women. Median income went up from $703 in 1950 to $735 in 1960, an increase of approximately 5 percent while white women enjoyed a slightly smaller increase of 3 percent. African American men's average income by contrast increased on average 30 percent or more during the decade. African American

An African American teacher leads her students in the pledge of allegiance, 1958.
Teaching was one of the few professional occupations available to African American
women. (Library of Congress)

women also continued to trail white women in median income; their $740 was about 60 percent less than the median $1,170 of white women workers. Given that the median income of white men in 1960 was $3,511, African American women's incomes were shockingly low.

There are a number of reasons for these lower incomes. African American women workers in 1950 continued to cluster in a relatively limited number of occupations. More than 40 percent of those working in 1950 labored as domestics (Jones 1995, 257–258). Domestic work paid very little, especially compared to the factory work that some African American women had been able to secure during the war. It also lacked some of the basic guarantees of minimum wages, overtime guarantees, and other protections offered by federal labor legislation. These problems were not unique to African American women, but because racial discrimination had effectively limited them to the lowest-paying jobs in domestic or agricultural work, their burden was disproportionately heavy.

Thus, driven out of unions deemed too radical for the political climate of the day, and facing ongoing discrimination because of both their race and their sex,

African American women continued to struggle against often overwhelming odds. As labor historian Philip Foner noted, "the African American woman worker was 'doubly exploited'" (Foner 1980, 396).

Women Workers in the 1950s

Shifts in Women's Work

While some historians disagree about the exact nature of what happened to women workers in the post–World War II period, they all agree that many of the women who had gained relatively high-paying (and often unionized) jobs in manufacturing during the war lost those positions in the wake of victory over the Axis powers. What happened to them then, however, has been a little harder to trace. Many stayed in manufacturing jobs, albeit not those that had produced some of the bonanza of the war years.

Recent research suggests that women who remained in manufacturing continued to capitalize on the increasing societal acceptance of unionization and flocked to trade unions in even greater numbers. For example, many remained prominent in the United Electrical Workers Union, even after its ouster from the CIO. Those forced out of manufacturing, into what Dorothy Sue Cobble, Eileen Boris, and others have called the "'pink collar' ghetto," joined the burgeoning service sector unions like the Hotel and Restaurant Employees Union and the National Federation of Telephone Workers (Cobble 1994, 59).

Attitudes about women's work seemed to have changed during the decade. In 1958, for example, the National Manpower Council argued benevolently for the desirability and necessity of women working outside of the home. There were still, however, many social pressures on women to work only in occupations that were "acceptable" for women. One study notes that by 1960, 80 percent of working women occupied positions "stereotyped as female" (Hartmann 1994, 93: Kessler-Harris 1982, 303).

While previous opponents of women's work had often argued that women worked only to provide themselves with luxuries or frivolities, the trends of the 1950s suggest that in order to realize the American nuclear family dream (and the consumer goods and more expensive homes that came along with it), more and more women had to contribute to the family economy in order to supplement their husband's income. In 1950, approximately 22 percent of wives worked for wages and that number was even higher for African American women. Ten years later, that number of working wives exceeded 30 percent (Kessler-Harris 1982, 302). Women who were the sole or principal breadwinners in their families still faced the limits of an economy all too often segregated by sex and race or ethnicity.

Shifts in Home-Work

Home-work had been a staple for many women since the 19th century. From cigar rolling to garment finishing (or even the sewing of whole garments), women faced many of the same challenges (e.g., poor conditions, piece rates, the speed-up) as their male and female peers who worked in workshops or factories.

As more and more garment manufacturing started to happen overseas, however, there was a shift in the postwar environment toward a different kind of home-work. Mirroring some of the broader employment shifts toward clerical work, women began doing more and more clerical home-work (as typists or as workers for the direct mail industry). During the 1950s and after, this was increasingly the case. What is most striking about this very different kind of home-work is how similar many of the other dynamics of this type of employment were to those that defined home-work earlier in the century. Women still received piece-rates, they still faced the equivalent of the speed-up, and they still faced some of the same health challenges (e.g., repetitive motion disorders) of women workers of a previous generation. Despite government efforts to root out child labor, the burden of clerical home-work often fell not just on the woman worker, but also on her children (if she was a mother) (Boris 1994, 314).

For some women, however, home-work made sense. If they had children or could not work full-time, home-work was one option for bringing often much-needed income into the household. As had been the case for several decades, some Americans questioned whether working mothers (whether in the home or outside of it) were working out of necessity or out of a desire for luxury goods. Those critics believed that such women endangered their families and the existing social order but refused to recognize that many working women had little choice.

Even for those who condoned women's clerical home-work (very often the contractors who employed them), women's status in the home workplace was still defined by their sex. Employers fought vigorously to keep state and federal government agencies from defining home-work as industrial work and therefore subject to basic hours, health, and safety regulations. With some rare exceptions, it would be the 1960s before there was significant change to this status quo.

Women and Organized Labor

There was little question that the number of women who joined trade unions rose dramatically during the war years and thereafter. Since the late 19th century, trade unions had conflicted reactions about women working in more industrialized environments; these conflicts only increased as mechanization and automation made it more and more possible for women to compete with men

A mother waves good-bye to her family as she leaves for work, 1953. The issue of women working outside the home continued to be a controversial subject during the 1950s, although many women had no choice. (Library of Congress)

for manufacturing jobs. In some cases, women were preferred because some perceived their manual dexterity to be significantly greater than that of men.

Since that time, women had been knocking on the doors of the union hall; they used two types of arguments to justify their admittance. The first, and more idealistic, argument came from class conflict and worker solidarity. According to it, women on the shop floor were no less proletarianized than men and that, by "allowing" women into unions, men only increased their collective-bargaining power. The second, and much more cynical, argument was that if women were organized, they would sign contracts guaranteeing them higher (if not equal) wages, thus protecting men's jobs by reducing the likelihood of competition between men and women.

As employers and men asserting their prewar seniority pushed women out of the higher-paying manufacturing jobs after the war, women still clustered in some sections of manufacturing; this was particularly the case in the burgeoning electrical industry. Organizing women in the service sector was somewhat more challenging than in manufacturing, but several unions (like the Communication Workers of America) made significant strides in the late 1940s and 1950s. Perhaps not surprisingly, the unions that had the most success organizing women (like Local 1199 and the Communication Workers) were in those industries that reflected an increasing percentage of women workers.

For women whose ambitions included leadership positions in their local unions or even as organizers or administrators in the national offices, there continued to be significant gender barriers. Prior to its merger with the AFL, the CIO had a dismal record on women in leadership positions. The situation actually worsened between 1946 and 1954 as the number of female convention delegates went down (Zieger 1995, 350). Few women worked as CIO organizers, and only one woman, Katherine Ellickson, worked in a professional position at CIO headquarters.

The Double Bind of Seniority

The concept of seniority (how much time a worker had in a particular plant or working for a particular employer) became a critical guarantor for union workers in the post–World War II period. It protected those who might be temporarily laid off from having to start over again in terms of wages and benefits, and it protected workers somewhat from the actions of arbitrary foremen. At the same time, however, seniority obviously protected those who had been there the longest. Given past patterns of sexual and racial discrimination, seniority privileged white male workers in most manufacturing environments.

With the shifts in employment during the war, however, many women (and to a lesser degree African Americans) had gained several years of seniority, thus theoretically qualifying them to be called back to work before males of lower seniority. Thus women began to have a stake in the seniority system; while they often could not surmount discrimination by employers who decided not to hire women in many sectors of their respective industries or compete against men who had more seniority than they did, women workers developed a vested interest in the seniority system, which was often a principal union demand in postwar labor negotiations.

The End of the WTUL

The Women's Trade Union League, often identified by scholars as one of the most important labor organizations of the early 20th century, finally disbanded in 1950 after almost a half century of activism committed to improving conditions for women workers nationwide and urging them to organize. In some sense, it may have been a victim of its own success. With approximately three million women union members nationally, and with many of its functions increasingly taken over by the organized labor movement, the league had fallen on hard times. Philip Foner reports that the WTUL could no longer reliably pay the salaries of its own executive secretary. It had also lost much of its influence with the organized labor movement; one CIO official urged WTUL activists to leave organizing to unions and to shift its efforts to encouraging housewives toward consumer and political activism. The local chapter of the WTUL in New York City was the last to disband; it finally did so in 1955 with members continuing to argue over whether or not the WTUL still had a mission in American society (Foner 1980: 405–406).

Equal Pay Campaigns

In a pattern that repeated itself over and over in the history of American organized labor, federation policy was often driven by the militancy of the rank-and-file workers. Equal-pay campaigns were no exception. UE activists pushed for the removal (or at least diminution) of sex-based wage differentials in its strike against GE in 1946. The issue came up again in 1951 when more than 15,000 workers demonstrated at GE's Schenectady, New York, plant to push for more progress on sex-based discrimination.

In 1956, the newly merged AFL-CIO finally took up the baton and committed itself to a three-year campaign in which it encouraged local unions to require contractual language guaranteeing equal pay for "comparable work." While the federation did make some progress toward reducing those differentials, it wasn't until 1963 that the federal government stepped in to address the issue with the Equal Pay Act. Even then, the legislation fell short of activists' hopes; rather than demanding equal pay for "comparable" work, it mandated equal pay for "equal" work, thus limiting the likelihood that women workers could achieve greater parity in wages.

Sign of Things to Come: Local 1199

One of the best examples of the shifts in service-sector unionism came with the significant expansion of New York City's Local 1199, a union comprised almost exclusively of druggists and drugstore workers. Local 1199 started a campaign in the late 1950s to organize hospital workers at the so-called voluntary hospitals in New York City. Those hospitals were nonunion, and their workers were denied federal labor law protections. Starting at Montefiore Hospital in the Bronx, Local 1199 quickly organized a majority of the almost 1,000 service workers at the hospital (Freeman 2000, 135–139).

Local 1199's success represented a symbolic victory for local AFL-CIO officials who knew all too well the federation's spotty record when it came to organizing

African American and Hispanic workers. It also was a real victory for the non-professional workers, the majority of whom were African American and Hispanic women. Yet, the quickly growing union faced the intransigent hostility of the hospitals; their administrators relied on their exemption from NLRB rules to refuse to hold recognition elections or bargain with the union.

After organizing six of the hospitals, and with administrators continuing to refuse to negotiate, Local 1199 decided to strike. In May 1959, more than 3,000 workers struck; they included kitchen workers, porters, and housekeeping staff. Despite arrests and ongoing efforts by hospital officials to force them into going back to work, the workers stayed out for 46 days. At the end of the strike, Local 1199 had not won recognition, but had secured an agreement from management that those joining the union would not face discrimination and some concessions on minimum wages and seniority rules. Yet it would be four more years before New York State passed a law granting collective-bargaining rights to hospital workers in New York City.

High-Flying Employment

Many of the shifts in women's employment mirrored the broader occupational shifts that were taking place. Thus, with many new jobs in the retail sector or in service-sector jobs, more women went to work in those fields. One of the highest profile of these in the 1950s was that of the burgeoning airline industry. As passenger travel increased dramatically during the decade, so too did the need for flight attendants to serve their needs while en route.

Flight attendants, reminded by the sign above the mirror, check their appearance before a flight, 1956. (Bettmann/Corbis)

Known at the time as stewardesses, female flight attendants endured some of the most restrictive limitations on their appearance and behavior in the workplace. Airline standards dictated clothing, makeup, hairstyles, and an omnipresent smile. Flight attendants were not permitted to marry, thus guaranteeing significant turnover as women sought to realize the 1950s' dream of the "nuclear" family. Weight requirements mandated that flight attendants lose weight or lose their jobs. Until the 1960s, the supervisory purser on flights was always male (Barry 2007, 45–49).

Flight attendants sought to improve their situation by organizing a union. Like many of their unionized, albeit less glamorous, peers, flight attendants leapt at the chance to seek better contractual terms through organizing in the period immediately following World War II. By 1950, and after merging with a union subsidiary organized by the airline pilots' union, the Air Line Stewardesses Association had organized two-thirds of flight attendants in the United States. By the end of the decade, it represented approximately 9,000 flight attendants (Barry 2007, 80).

The advent of jet travel by the late 1950s helped to change the nature and pace of flight attendant work. Already chafing at their subsidiary position within the pilots' union, flight attendants sought to change work rules to reflect the greater workloads caused by larger and more efficient planes. They also came into conflict with the pilots' union, setting the stage for a conflict that would grow during the 1960s and negatively affect the ability of flight attendants to fight for better pay and conditions as one effective group.

BIOGRAPHIES

Robert "Buddy" Battle III, 1917–1989

Autoworker, Unionist, TULC Member

Battle was a longtime official in Local 600 of the UAW. One scholar referred to him as the "Mayor Daley of the Rouge," in recognition of Battle's political acumen (Lichtenstein 1995, 376). Along with Horace Sheffield, Battle was responsible for helping to push Walter Reuther to improve African American representation at all levels of union administration. Battle led the group of African American UAW delegates who walked out of the 1959 UAW convention after the union refused to consider seriously the appointment of an African American vice president. The dramatic move helped to shift UAW president Reuther's opinion on the matter, and his aides arranged for an African American vice president to be elected almost three years later at the next convention.

Lemuel Boulware, 1895–1990

Corporate Executive and Labor Negotiator

A graduate of the University of Wisconsin, Lemuel Boulware was a veteran of World War I and played a significant role in World War II as a civilian appointee. During that war, he was operations vice chairman of the War Production Board, the government agency responsible for managing production and procurement. In the wake of its tumultuous 1946 strike, General Electric offered Boulware the opportunity to help to reshape their labor relations department. During his tenure at GE, Boulware became known as the innovator of a new style of negotiation with organized labor; appropriately enough, it became known as Boulwarism.

This strategy guided General Electric's (as well as several other corporations) negotiations with unions during the 1950s. Boulware later served as vice president of employee and public relations from 1956 to 1961, when he retired.

Katherine Ellickson, 1905–1996

CIO Labor Official

A New Yorker by birth, Katherine Ellickson graduated from Vassar College in 1926. From the early 1930s until the early 1940s, when Ellickson joined the research department of the Congress of Industrial Organizations (CIO), she taught at both the Women's Summer School at Bryn Mawr College and the Brookwood Labor College. Ellickson migrated to the AFL-CIO research staff after the merger of the two federations but found the new atmosphere even less congenial for women than it had been under the CIO. Ellickson not only served the labor movement directly; she also participated in a variety of activities that sought to bring women workers' issues into the spotlight. She participated in the Labor Advisory Committee set up by the federal government's Women's Bureau in the early 1950s.

Ellickson became the director of the AFL-CIO Department of Social Security in the late 1950s and started to be asked to be on a variety of government commissions; in 1959, for example, the secretary of Health, Education, and Welfare appointed Ellickson to be on a committee examining the issue of public assistance. This led to an invitation to be the executive secretary of the influential President's Commission on the Status of Women set up by President Kennedy at the end of 1961. She was later involved in helping to establish the Equal Employment Opportunity Commission. She died in 1996.

Clinton Jencks, 1918–2005

Union Organizer

Clinton Jencks, a Colorado native, graduated from the University of Colorado in 1939. Shortly thereafter, he volunteered to go to war and returned from the Air Force with the Distinguished Flying Cross. Soon after starting a job for the American Smelter and Refining Company, Jencks joined the International Union of Mine, Mill, and Smelter Workers. He rose within the union and became one of its international representatives in 1947.

Jencks and his wife, Virginia, played a key role in the strike that inspired *Salt of the Earth* that began in 1950; Jencks would later go to jail for his activities, along with several strike leaders. While Jencks first came to public attention during that strike, he gained greater fame as a victim of the anticommunism of the period. As a condition of the 1947 Taft-Hartley Act, Jencks had signed an affi-davit disavowing membership in the Communist Party. In fact, there is no evi-dence that he was ever in the party, although he was certainly sympathetic to many of its aims.

After the testimony of Harvey Matusow, one of the so-called professional anticommunists who often fabricated testimony about alleged membership in the Communist Party, Jencks was thought to have lied. Jencks did his own cause little good by pleading the Fifth Amendment when called before Sen. Pat Mc-Carran's Senate Internal Security Subcommittee in the fall of 1952 (Lorence 1999). In the spring of 1953, Jencks was accused of perjury and a long legal ordeal ensued. Early the next year, a court convicted Jencks, sentenced him to 10 years in prison, and fined him $20,000.

Jencks's role as appellant perhaps proved his most important performance in helping to put to rest the aggressive anticommunism of the early 1950s. In 1957, when the Supreme Court responded to Jencks's appeal, in *Jencks v. United States,* 353 U.S. 657 (1957), it was clear that the jurists were no longer willing to sit idly by. Justice Brennan, delivering the decision for the Court, wrote that the gov-ernment's refusal to produce the informers' allegations that had implicated Jencks originally denied Jencks the ability to mount an effective defense. Ac-cording to Brennan, the government had to choose between protecting alleged "state secrets and other confidential information" and prosecuting the accused. While the Supreme Court did not pardon Jencks, the government chose not to pursue another trial. Jencks eventually earned a Ph.D. in economics and taught at San Diego State University prior to his retirement (Lorence 1999, 181–186).

Alice Leopold, 1906–1982?

Republican Politician, Head of the Women's Bureau

Alice Leopold, a graduate of Goucher College in the late 1920s, transitioned from a career in business to that of a state legislator. She won election to the Con-necticut legislature in 1949. Two years later, she became one of Connecticut's first female secretaries of state; she served in that office from 1951 to 1953, when President Eisenhower tapped her to run the Women's Bureau in the U.S. Depart-ment of Labor. She would serve in that capacity until the Kennedy administration.

As a Republican appointee in a largely antilabor administration, it would have been surprising had Leopold been more liberal than she was. Leopold's tenure in office was not without controversy; she changed Women's Bureau policy on an equal rights amendment, which sought to guarantee equality under the law regardless of sex. Originally, in order to maintain protective legislation for women workers, the Women's Bureau had opposed the amendment, but un-der Leopold that position changed, thus angering many women in the labor movement. Under her watch, the bureau also reconfigured several bodies like its Labor Advisory Committee (Cobble 2004, 197). The bureau supported equal pay legislation, albeit not with the comprehensive language preferred by union women. Yet, the Women's Bureau served as an important locus of action and policymaking for feminist labor activists, even under Leopold's control.

Esther Peterson, 1906–1997

Union Activist, Head of the Women's Bureau, Assistant Secretary of Labor

Peterson, who would eventually become the highest-ranking woman appointee in the Kennedy administration, was one of the key "labor feminists" of the 1950s and 1960s; indeed, Dorothy Sue Cobble has described her as having "perhaps the greatest impact of any labor feminist of her generation" (Cobble 2004, 34). A graduate of Brigham Young University, Peterson worked in a variety of capacities for the Amalgamated Clothing Workers of America from the late 1930s to the late 1940s. She took a hiatus from the labor movement to travel with her diplomat husband but returned in 1958 to work as a lobbyist for the AFL-CIO's Industrial Union Department. Throughout the 1950s, Peterson supported equal pay legislation and legislative guarantees of protections for working women. A key supporter of the candidacy of John F. Kennedy, Peterson used newfound leverage to press the newly elected Democrat for a study of women; his response was to make Peterson head of the Women's Bureau. In that position, she sought to reverse what she perceived to be the misdirected approach of the bureau under her predecessor, Alice Leopold. Peterson later served as executive vice chair of the President's Commission on the Status of Women and in several later administrations.

Horace Sheffield, 1916–1995

Autoworker, Unionist, TULC Member

Horace Sheffield was a UAW official and founding member of the TULC. He served as a UAW international representative for 25 years. Like Robert "Buddy" Battle (see above), Sheffield played an active role during the 1950s in pushing the UAW leadership to elevate African American unionists to higher leadership positions. Against the wishes of the leadership, Sheffield nominated longtime UAW organizer Willoughby Abner, who (apparently by arrangement) promptly declined the nomination. The nomination (and the events surrounding it) prompted the UAW to pay greater attentions to issues of equity for African American members. Sheffield would later be involved in the Coalition of Black Trade Unionists.

J. Ernest Wilkins, 1894–1959

Attorney, Assistant Secretary of Labor

While J. Ernest Wilkins's tenure in the Eisenhower administration was relatively brief, his appointment as assistant secretary of labor for International Labor Affairs from 1954 to 1958 was significant. He was the first African American to be appointed to a sub-cabinet level post in American history. He also served for a time as an Eisenhower appointee to the Civil Rights Commission and was active in the Methodist Church. In his capacity as assistant secretary of labor, Wilkins attended International Labor Organization meetings in the midst of Cold War tensions in that organization. His

J. Ernest Wilkins, assistant secretary of labor, 1954–1958. Wilkins was the first African American in American history to be appointed to a sub-cabinet level post. (U.S. Department of Labor)

performance there prompted the *New York Times* to reflect on June 4, 1954, "In making real the guarantees of equal opportunity embodied in the Constitution, we are not only giving vitality to our democracy but opening up vast benefits for all of us."

REFERENCES AND FURTHER READINGS

Barry, Kathleen M. 2007. *Femininity in Flight: A History of Flight Attendants.* Durham, NC: Duke University Press.

Boris, Eileen. 1994. *Home to Work: Motherhood and the Politics of Industrial Homework in the United States.* New York: Cambridge University Press.

Boyle, Kevin. 1995. *The UAW and the Heyday of American Liberalism, 1945–1968.* Ithaca, NY: Cornell University Press.

Brody, David. 1993. *Workers in Industrial America: Essays on the Twentieth Century Struggle.* 2nd ed. New York: Oxford University Press.

Cobble, Dorothy Sue. 1994. "Recapturing Working-Class Feminism: Union Women in the Postwar Era." In *Not June Cleaver: Women and Gender in Postwar America, 1945–1960,* ed. Joanne Meyerowitz, 57–83. Philadelphia: Temple University Press.

Cobble, Dorothy Sue. 2004. *The Other Women's Movement: Workplace Justice and Social Rights in Modern America.* Princeton. NJ: Princeton University Press.

Filipelli, Ronald L. 1990. "Steel Strikes of 1956 and 1959." In *Labor Conflict in the United States: An Encyclopedia,* ed. Ronald L. Filipelli, 514–516. New York: Garland.

Foner, Philip S. 1980. *Women and the American Labor Movement.* New York: Free Press.

Freeman, Joshua B. 2000. *Working Class New York: Life and Labor since World War II.* New York: New Press.

Hartmann, Susan M. 1994. "Women's Employment and the Domestic Ideal in the Early Cold War Years." In *Not June Cleaver: Women and Gender in Postwar America, 1945–1960,* ed. Joanne Meyerowitz, 84–102. Philadelphia: Temple University Press.

Hill, Herbert. 1967. "The Racial Practices of Organized Labor." In *Employment, Race, and Poverty,* ed. Herbert Hill and Arthur M. Ross, 365–402. New York: Harcourt, Brace and World.

International Union of Electrical, Radio and Machine Workers (IUE), AFL-CIO. n.d. *The Westinghouse Strike, October 16, 1955–March 20, 1956: A Crucial Test, a Great Victory.* N.p.: IUE.

Jones, Jacqueline. 1995. *Labor of Love, Labor of Sorrow: Black Women, Work, and the Family from Slavery to the Present.* New York: Vintage.

Kessler-Harris, Alice. 1982. *Out to Work: A History of Wage-Earning Women in the United States.* New York: Oxford University Press.

Korstad, Robert. 2003. *Civil Rights Unionism: Tobacco Workers and the Struggle for Democracy in the Mid-Twentieth-Century South.* Chapel Hill: University of North Carolina Press.

Kreps, Juanita, and Joseph Spengler. 1966. "The Leisure Component of Economic Growth." In National Commission on Technology, Automation, and Economic Progress, *The Employment Impact of Technological Change. Appendix Volume II: Technology and the American Economy, The Report of the Commission.* Washington, DC: Government Printing Office, 1966.

Lichtenstein, Nelson. 1995. *The Most Dangerous Man in Detroit: Walter Reuther and the Fate of American Labor.* New York: Basic Books.

Lichtenstein, Nelson. 2003. *State of the Union: A Century of American Labor.* Princeton, NJ: Princeton University Press.

Livernash, E. R. 1961. *Collective Bargaining in the Basic Steel Industry.* Washington, DC: Department of Labor.

Lorence, James J. 1999. *The Suppression of* Salt of the Earth: *How Hollywood, Big Labor, and Politicians Blacklisted a Movie in Cold War America.* Albuquerque: University of New Mexico Press.

Marshall, Ray. 1965. *The Negro and Organized Labor.* New York: John Wiley and Sons.

Moreno, Paul. 2006. *Black Americans and Organized Labor: A New History.* Baton Rouge: Louisiana State University Press.

Nelson, Bruce. 2001. *Divided We Stand: American Workers and the Struggle for Black Equality.* Princeton, NJ: Princeton University Press.

Northrup, Herbert. 1964. *Boulwarism: The Labor Relations Policies of the General Electric Company, Their Implications for Public Policy and Management Action.* Ann Arbor: Bureau of Industrial Relations, University of Michigan.

Raskin, A. H. 1959. "Meany, in a Fiery Debate, Denounces Negro Unionist." *New York Times,* September 24, 1959.

Ross, Arthur M. 1967. "The Negro in the American Economy." In *Employment, Race, and Poverty,* ed. Herbert Hill and Arthur M. Ross, 3–48. New York: Harcourt, Brace and World.

Russell, Thaddeus. 2001. *Out of the Jungle: Jimmy Hoffa and the Remaking of the American Working Class.* New York: Knopf.

Schatz, Ronald. 1983. *The Electrical Workers: A History of Labor at General Electric and Westinghouse, 1923–1960.* Urbana: University of Illinois Press.

Stewart, James B. 2005. "Civil Rights and Organized Labor: The Case of the United Steelworkers of America, 1948–1970." In *African Americans in the U.S. Economy,* ed. Cecelia Conrad, John Whitehead, Patrick Mason, and James Stewart, 66–82. Lanham, MD: Rowman and Littlefield.

Uphoff, Walter. 1966. *Kohler on Strike: Thirty Years of Conflict.* Boston: Beacon Press.

Walkowitz, Daniel J. 1999. *Working with Class: Social Workers and the Politics of Middle-Class Identity.* Chapel Hill: University of North Carolina Press.

Zieger, Robert. 1995. *The CIO, 1935–1955.* Chapel Hill: University of North Carolina Press.

Urban Life

OVERVIEW

America's cities underwent a period of great change in the 1950s. Of the 15 largest American cities in 1950, only Los Angeles and Houston gained population during the decade. Metropolises of the Midwest and Northeast experienced population losses within the city limits, while suburban areas boomed. Pittsburgh, St. Louis, and Boston each lost more than 10 percent of its population between 1950 and 1960; Detroit, Minneapolis, and Buffalo dropped between 7 and 10 percent; and New York, Chicago, Philadelphia, Cleveland, Baltimore, and Cincinnati saw their populations decline by less than 5 percent (Teaford 1990, 123). Only a few economically depressed urban areas, such as Scranton, Pennsylvania, and Lowell, Massachusetts, had recorded population losses in the previous decade (McKelvey 1968, 153).

During the 1950s, cities experienced an 11 percent growth in population, while suburbs ballooned 46 percent in the true blossoming of white flight (Ebner 1985, 380). Twelve Standard Metropolitan Statistical Areas (SMSAs)—New York, Los Angeles–Long Beach, Chicago, Philadelphia, Detroit, San Francisco–Oakland, Boston, Pittsburgh, St. Louis, Washington, Cleveland, and Baltimore—each had populations of 1.7 million or more, and roughly one-quarter of the nation's population lived in one of these metropolitan areas. While central cities were home to more than twice as many people as the suburbs that ringed them in 1930, the outer rings and the central cities had become almost equal in population by 1960 (Sharp and Schnore 1962, 171). There were a total of 162 SMSAs

Map 3.1 *The nation's 12 most heavily populated urban areas in 1960.*

in 1950, and they were home to 56.8 percent of the nation's population (Bogue 1955, 480).

Clearly, metropolitan areas were not in danger, but the cities at their core faced a variety of complicated threats that required bold changes in city government operations and widespread involvement by concerned citizens. With a laundry list of expensive projects, city leaders had to be innovative. Political bosses' old bags of tricks no longer worked in the changing city landscape. A new type of reformer arose during the postwar years. Like earlier advocates of urban improvements, these activists opposed political bossism; however, they differed from their predecessors in one obvious way. Instead of viewing the business community as the enemy, they often worked hand in hand with business leaders to improve the city as a place to live and a place to work.

In the postwar years, as many members of the white middle class moved to outlying suburbs, African Americans became the largest population group in old and increasingly dilapidated inner-city neighborhoods. The families of these city dwellers had roots in the rural South, and their urban existence was the product of a migration wave that began during World War I. Unlike immigrant groups who had settled in cities for one generation before prospering and moving on to better (and often suburban) homes, African Americans struggled for generations to overcome poverty. Hispanics—whether they were Puerto Ricans or Mexicans seeking work, or Cuban exiles seeking safety—also crowded into some cities. And cities became home to a largely hidden gay subculture as well as an increasingly rebellious Beat Generation counterculture.

Growing awareness of urban problems also marked this decade, and aggressive measures to address these problems gained new momentum. Factory fumes, water pollution, overcrowding, and physical deterioration of old neighborhoods were some of metropolitan America's biggest problems, and none could be easily resolved. Cities also faced great challenges as transportation hubs. As much as they may have hated traffic jams, most Americans who could afford cars refused to give them up, and some families became two-car families in the postwar years. As a result, road construction played a key role in cities' survival strategies, but public transportation and airports also demanded attention.

At a time when cities had a rapidly declining property tax base, the cost of running city governments was expanding. For example, in Philadelphia, where the city's physical size was the same as it had been since 1854, the cost of serving the city's population was rising rapidly. The proliferation of automobiles created new demands for highways, bridges, and parking lots. Public transportation was essential for a dense population in the inner city without the money to purchase cars or the space to park them. Moreover, city government began making contributions to employee health and welfare plans and financing group life insurance. These changes, which drove the city's expenses on employee benefits up 1,629 percent, were natural outgrowths of the New Deal welfare state and labor unions' continuing emphasis on employers' obligations to workers. The city's population declined during the 1950s, but the ranks of full-time city workers rose by 20 percent between 1952 and 1958.

At the same time, Philadelphia's tax base lost value. Like many cities, Philadelphia historically had relied on property taxes as the city's top source of revenue. However, as buildings aged, they depreciated, and with much new construction occurring in the suburbs, cities lost potential property taxes as members of the white middle class moved. Thus, at the very time when cities needed to launch infrastructure work that would ease traffic problems, minimize pollution, and stop neighborhood blight, municipal governments suffered from declining property tax bases.

Table 3.1. Fifteen Most Populous Cities in 1950 and 1960

1950	1960
1. New York	New York
2. Chicago	Chicago
3. Philadelphia	Los Angeles
4. Los Angeles	Philadelphia
5. Detroit	Detroit
6. Baltimore	Baltimore
7. Cleveland	Houston
8. St. Louis	Cleveland
9. Washington	Washington
10. Boston	St. Louis
11. San Francisco	Milwaukee
12. Pittsburgh	San Francisco
13. Milwaukee	Boston
14. Houston	Dallas
15. Buffalo	New Orleans

Source: U.S. Bureau of the Census, "Population of the 100 largest Urban Places: 1950," http://www.census.gov/population/documentation/twps0027/tab18.txt (accessed January 25, 2007); "Population of the 100 largest Urban Places: 1960," http://www.census.gov/population/documentation/twps0027/tab19.txt (accessed January 27, 2007).

This forced cities to think more creatively about how to raise money; possibilities included bond issues, income taxes, and license fees. Philadelphia stood at the forefront of the effort to develop other sources of revenue to support city initiatives. The city had first levied an income tax on all who worked in the city in 1939. By 1950, property taxes accounted for just 44 percent of its revenues; by 1958, it was 34.3 percent (Teaford 1990, 76–77).

Unlike Philadelphia, some cities saw a cure to their money problems in expansion. They swallowed suburbs, transforming almost five million suburbanites into instant city dwellers. This type of augmentation was responsible for much of the 1950s growth of cities in the South and West, but the troubled old industrial centers of the Midwest and Northeast seldom had this option because they were surrounded with long-established suburban towns. Phoenix grew from 9.6 square miles in 1940 to 187.4 square miles 20 years later (Ebner 1985, 381). Census figures from 1960 show an increase of 5.6 million people in the nation's 212 SMSAs, but most of that growth came through such annexations. When this kind of synthetic expansion is discounted, growth in suburban areas during the decade is shown to be 40 times as high as in urban areas (Polenberg 1980, 128).

TIMELINE

1950   Sixty to 65 percent of the nation's population is characterized as urban.

National car registrations reach a new high—40 million in a nation of 149 million people.

An amendment to the Social Security Act makes impoverished single parents eligible for relief payments.

The average African American family's income is 54 percent of the average white family's income.

The chairman of the United Smoke Council reports that Pittsburgh's actions against air pollution have allowed city residents to see 39 percent more sunshine than in the previous winter.

1951   Cities receive expanded taxing powers in 14 states.

The American Municipal Association urges federal aid to cities for highways, airports, pollution, schools, public health services, and recreational facilities.

Harry Hay founds the Mattachine Society, a gay organization formed in cells to protect members' identities.

1952   Ralph Ellison's award-winning *The Invisible Man,* which traces one African American's exodus from the rural South and adaptation to inner-city life, is published.

Kemmons Wilson opens the first Holiday Inn in Memphis.

1953   Gateway Center, comprising three stainless steel office towers, becomes a symbol of urban renaissance in Pittsburgh.

1954   Metropolitan Regional Organizations hold their first conference in Philadelphia.

Ray Kroc begins the process of building the McDonald's restaurant chain.

1955   Annual production of passenger cars rises to eight million.

Democratic boss Richard Daley is elected mayor of Chicago.

October poetry reading in San Francisco provides launching pad for Allen Ginsberg's role as a leader of the Beat Generation.

1956   Mayor Robert F. Wagner starts the New York Metropolitan Regional Council.

Novelist James Baldwin publishes *Giovanni's Room,* which was initially rejected because of its gay theme.

Dr. Evelyn Hooker presents a study to the American Psychological Association demonstrating that trained clinicians cannot differentiate between personality test results of heterosexual and homosexual men.

The Interstate Highway Act becomes law.

1957   *West Side Story,* a musical about true love and violent deaths among Anglo and Puerto Rican youths, opens on Broadway and holds special resonance for gay Americans.

Fifty-three million Americans fly on passenger airlines, four times as many as in 1946.

Chicago declares its Midway Field as "the world's busiest airport"; a larger O'Hare Airport is already on the drawing boards.

1958   The Nation of Islam attracts national attention through Elijah Muhammad's calls for African American separatism.

African American modern dancer Alvin Ailey starts the Alvin Ailey American Dance Theater in New York City.

"Beatnik" becomes a common term for youthful non-conformists. The "nik" was taken from the name of the Soviet satellite *Sputnik*.

1959   Fidel Castro's successful effort to overthrow Fulgencio Batista increases Cuban migration to the Miami area.

Malcolm X travels to the Middle East as a representative of the Nation of Islam.

URBAN DECAY

The struggle to improve living conditions in the nation's central cities gained momentum and achieved some success during the 1950s. With a new group of civic leaders willing to push for better conditions in urban areas, individual communities witnessed significant improvements and learned some lessons from costly failures. Efforts to replace poor neighborhoods with public housing projects often failed; however, these fiascos demonstrated that wiping out a neigh-borhood was not likely to revitalize it. At the same time, ambitious city governments managed to reduce pollution in some areas and to direct the national spotlight toward this problem. Activists began to realize that two key groups—urban residents and downtown businessmen—approached redevelopment with conflicting agendas, each demanding consideration in urban planning.

Opponents of redevelopment form a picket line in opposition to the planned destruction of New York City's Lincoln Square neighborhood to make way for a cultural arts venue, Lincoln Center, 1956. (Library of Congress)

The new urban leaders were predominantly Democrats, and as a result, Republicans lost urban power at a time when they held the White House. Bosses in both parties also suffered losses at the hands of reformers, with only Chicago's Richard Daley and Pittsburgh's David Lawrence working as both traditional bosses and mayors. Renewed interest in the city manager form of municipal government in some places also reflected the desire for more professional and less politically oriented leadership. Jon C. Teaford contends in *The Rough Road to Renaissance: Urban Revitalization in America, 1940–1985* that "the Republican Party was meaningless in most of the major central cities, and repeated anti-boss campaigns had badly battered the Democratic party organizations" (Teaford 1990, 65). At least in part, the Republicans' loss reflected the continuing growth of the predominantly Democratic African American urban population and middle-class white flight to the suburbs, which moved many GOP votes outside older cities.

Democratic leaders developed partnerships with downtown leaders, real estate interests, and civic organizations. Often, business needs received more attention than residential concerns. Because many redevelopment efforts were dependent on investments by business interests or on business-driven efforts to win passage of bond issues, even the most liberal civic leaders could not turn their backs on the opportunities that these alliances offered. In St. Louis, Civic Progress Inc., the moving force behind a $110.6-million bond issue, was composed of top executives from McDonnell Aircraft, Ralston-Purina, Anheuser-Busch, and Monsanto Chemicals. The 25-member group also included department store owners and bank presidents. In Cleveland, 100 businesses united to form the Cleveland Development Foundation, which won promises from banks to finance private investment in housing construction and set up a $2-million revolving fund to address urban problems, especially those related to housing (Teaford 1990, 48).

There was also a growing push for regional organization to coordinate actions within central cities and among the suburbs that surrounded them. Often, these efforts faced strong opposition from non–city dwellers. Pittsburgh and St. Louis each attempted to consolidate city and county governments so that a single entity would oversee both the urban and suburban sectors; however, these efforts failed. Some metropolitan areas found it easier to consolidate services. Kansas City, for instance, established a contract to supply water to suburban areas, and Grand Rapids, Michigan, established an "urban services district" that encompassed both the city and surrounding townships. In all, 72 cities provided library services to suburbanites, 24 provided trash collection for outlying areas, and 36 offered fire protection to suburban areas. In May 1954, the American Planning and Civil Association spun off a separate Association of Metropolitan Regional Organizations to support cooperation when consolidation was not possible (McKelvey 1968, 1960).

Social Critics and Urban Policy

Some social commentators believed that the decay of American cities was a by-product of middle-class prosperity. They bemoaned the lack of interest in urban deterioration among those enjoying newfound opportunities, and they condemned the federal government for not taking greater responsibility for relieving urban poverty. However, these were voices in the wilderness, and as historian Richard Pells noted in *The Liberal Mind in a Conservative Age,* liberal dissent was stifled in the 1950s by McCarthyism, Cold War fears, overreliance on experts, too much focus on the middle class, and a tendency to embrace established approaches to economic and political questions (Pells 1989, ix).

Nevertheless, a few spoke up, mostly in intellectual and liberal magazines such as *Dissent* and *Commentary.* Among the most eloquent liberal spokesmen was economist John Kenneth Galbraith, who saw prosperity as the direct cause of many of the nation's problems. Noting urban decline, environmental contamination, and limited attention to important issues such as mass transportation, Galbraith argued that "expansion of economic output" was not "a test of social achievement" or a "solvent of all social ills." Scoffing at the idea that the United States could be considered an "advanced" civilization, he contended that prosperous Americans demonstrated their deficiencies by turning a blind eye to America's problems (Pells 1989, 169).

Michael Harrington, author of the 1962 landmark study of poverty, *The Other America,* argued that Americans embraced a myth in which poverty was declining, but he contended that 50 million Americans continued to live below "the standards we have been taught to regard as the decent minimums for food, housing, clothing, and health." Many of these poor Americans were isolated in central cities or scattered in rural areas of the South and, in a way, that made them invisible to the nation's majority. Intellectual Irving Howe argued that the nation's two major political parties were "utterly without principle" and that "neither party was willing to confront the problems of modern American life" (Pells 1989, 385, 396).

Discussion of urban decay, racism, and poverty was muted in political circles during this decade of middle-class expansion. However, interest in urban affairs was growing among civic leaders, laying the groundwork for a more open debate and a more activist government approach to urban problems. Within a few years, these simmering issues would reach a boiling point that necessitated fuller attention to their causes and more inventive approaches to finding solutions. The problems that plagued inner cities would mutate, but they would not disappear.

White Flight

Despite the postwar baby boom, cities were losing people—in a trickle in some places, in a flood elsewhere. The white middle class was scurrying away to suburbs, leaving municipal governments with the problem of serving a less prosperous population with a less robust tax base. At the same time, many of America's poorest citizens found themselves locked within the decaying cores

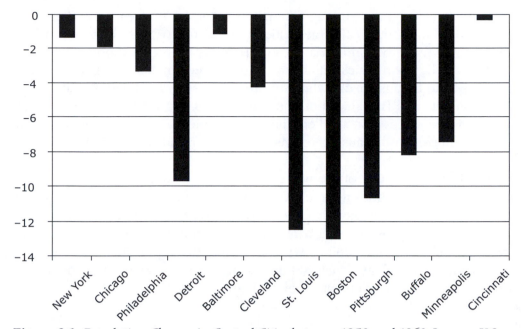

Figure 3.1 *Population Change in Central Cities between 1950 and 1960.* Source: *U.S. Bureau of the Census. U.S. Censuses of 1950 and 1960. Washington, DC: Government Printing Office, 1952 and 1961.*

of the nation's metropolises. White departures helped to create a situation in which the nonwhite population accounted for nearly one-fifth of the 112 million people living in central cities (McKelvey 1968, 154). The United States' 12 biggest cities acquired 4.5 million new nonwhite residents and lost 3.6 million whites in this decade (Ebner 1985, 380). The only central city among that group that did not suffer a loss of whites was Los Angeles–Long Beach, and even there the growth of the white population fell (Sharp and Schnore 1962, 176). While central cities did gain some white residents, many of the new additions were poor people fleeing economically disadvantaged areas, such as Appalachia, Puerto Rico, and Mexico. (A late 1940s court ruling had declared that Hispanics were white.) Appalachian refugees were more likely to migrate to the Midwest, while Puerto Ricans favored New York and Mexicans most often settled in the Southwest.

Looking at the 12 largest SMSAs as a group, whites' share of the central city population fell from 86.4 percent in 1950 to 78.6 percent in 1960. The white population's share of the population in suburban rings held steady at 95.6 percent, and the total white share of the metropolitan population slid from 89.9 to 87.1 (Sharp and Schnore 1962, 178). The percentage of the white population living in the suburban rings rose from 40.9 percent in 1950 to 54.9 percent 10 years later (Sharp and Schnore 1962, 179).

Jobs often fled the city along with much of the white population. Suburban jobs around the nation's 25 largest cities increased by 61 percent between 1948 and 1963, while urban industrial jobs dropped by 7 percent (Ebner 1985, 380). Declining job opportunities within the city guaranteed higher unemployment and poverty. And because many white suburbs found ways to keep African American residents and Hispanics out, these minorities had little access to the new suburban jobs. It is also unlikely that they would have been welcomed into suburban positions because of efforts to maintain racial segregation in all facets of suburban life.

The loss of so much of the white middle class in urban areas added to instability and vacant housing stock. Civic involvement was lower in areas where impoverished residents saw little means of escape and little hope of improving their surroundings. As a result, white flight bolstered urban blight. White voters who had moved to the suburbs were less likely to support initiatives aimed at improving the lot of city dwellers. And because urban residents were not organized to fight for improvements, they had little clout.

Slum Clearance and Housing

Deterioration of inner-city neighborhoods created a complicated web of problems. Poor residents often could not afford to make the improvements necessary to upgrade their neighborhoods. In addition, because their political voice was muted, decisions often were made without full consideration of their impact on residents. There were a few exceptions to this pattern, but they were rare. The Housing Act of 1949 provided financial aid for public housing projects. Philadelphia launched a 174-unit public housing project early in the decade, and San Francisco followed with an even larger complex. St. Louis, Boston, Providence, and Cincinnati quickly began development of their own projects, and these efforts met with problems. Rather than placing public housing structures in areas where they would cause little disruption to daily life, decision-makers typically acted under the belief that they could kill two birds with one stone by tearing down slum areas and replacing them with new projects. As a result, these projects as well as highway planning often splintered existing neighborhoods and created a temporary housing shortage for the poor who were ousted by demolition.

In 1954, the Eisenhower administration acted to reform this process. New legislation required those planning redevelopment projects to offer a program that included resettlement of poor residents. The federal government established regional offices to administer this process; however, these offices were understaffed and ill-equipped to handle a flood of requests. By late 1954, 76 cities had received federal support. A total of 340 projects in 218 cities were in the works under the 1949 and 1954 acts. Cities had launched 216 demolition projects that

A girl stands in front of a wooden well and two run-down houses occupied by African Americans in Washington, D.C., during the 1950s. The buildings were demolished in 1958 and replaced by a housing project. (Library of Congress)

would destroy 108,000 substandard residences; however, only a few minor projects had been completed (McKelvey 1968, 170–171). Although some projects were intended to attract middle-class residents, few wanted to move into deteriorating neighborhoods, and when these projects displaced poor families, they often crowded into areas around the proposed project, thus worsening neighborhood conditions. The Philadelphia Redevelopment Authority reported in 1956–1957 that some projects transformed "what was sometimes only somewhat bad into totally bad sections" (Teaford 1990, 116). As a result, the authority decided to try to focus on neighborhoods beginning to show the early stages of decline.

It is worth noting that the terms *slum* and *ghetto* sometimes were applied too broadly to minority neighborhoods when urban developers sought to demolish entire areas to make way for new construction. Sometimes these neighborhoods had viable economies and were homes to working-class people; however, some poor and deteriorating neighborhoods were caught in a downward spiral, and the big question was how to improve them without worsening the lives of their residents.

Pollution

The urban environment of the 1950s featured many potential sources of pollution. Factories, homes, public transportation, and automobiles contributed to an unhealthy atmosphere in many cities. Civic leaders during the decade attacked both air and water pollution with varying degrees of success. Noise pollution received less attention, but as rattling trolleys were replaced by motorized buses in most cities around this time, traffic sounds eased slightly. Incinerators—industrial, residential, and municipal—were large contributors to air pollution. Home heating systems, trains, and automobiles powered by leaded gasoline also emitted waste that filled the air and sometimes blocked the sunlight in urban areas. These emissions came in a variety of forms, including gases, liquid droplets, and solid particles. Some pollutants were confined to the area in which they were created; others drifted away with passing air currents. As a result, air pollution threatened livestock, vegetation, and people outside the city. Steel mills, oil refineries, and smoke stacks often received the blame for urban air pollution; however, individual automobiles, trucks, and household chimneys acted cumulatively to worsen the problem.

Americans' affinity for cars made many drivers unwilling to address the possibility of reducing their use. Moreover, trucks were becoming an important asset to many businesses. Some experts recommended changing work hours so that workers would drive to and from work at varying times. This would reduce pollution because cars emitted more pollutants while idling and decelerating in traffic jams. Similar suggestions called for staggering factory hours of operation to avoid concentrations of industrial waste during certain hours.

Air quality did show improvement in the 1950s but not because of dramatic lifestyle changes. Several cities had produced antismoke ordinances in the 1940s and began to reap the benefits in the early 1950s. Pittsburgh, the nation's top producer of steel, became a leader in reducing air pollution through a smoke ordinance that went into effect in 1949. The ordinance, which covered smoke emissions from private homes, trains, and industries, increased visibility in the city by almost 70 percent in its first three years of operation. Cincinnati, which had begun fining those who violated smoke

Thick smog hangs over New York City in 1953, obscuring a view of the Chrysler Building from the Empire State Building. (Library of Congress)

regulations in 1948, found that by 1950 infractions had dropped 77 percent. Philadelphia's Bureau of Municipal Research reported in 1950, "There appears to have been real progress toward smoke elimination" (Teaford 1990, 85–86). The first important federal legislation on air pollution was the Clean Air Act of 1955, which authorized assistance to state and local government fighting pollution. Congress appropriated a mere $12.5 million for this purpose over the following five years.

Philadelphia was a leader in ongoing efforts to reduce water pollution. The city's Delaware and Schuylkill rivers were badly polluted when the decade began. Philadelphia opened three sewage-treatment plants in 1955—and they had a dramatic effect. Only one-fifth of the city's sewage had undergone treatment in 1947, but by 1960, 96 percent of city sewage was processed through a treatment plant. Improved water-treatment facilities also improved tap water's smell and taste. In other cities, water pollution would remain a big problem for decades to come (Teaford 1990, 89).

Downtown Businesses

Businessmen who operated retail establishments or hotels in central cities often participated in redevelopment planning, sometimes to the detriment of neighborhoods and their residents. Hotels suffered in the 1950s as the motel phenomenon began to gain strength. Many travelers chose to stay outside of the downtown areas. In Minneapolis, for example, the occupancy rate plummeted between 1951 and 1960, from 87 percent to 70 percent (Teaford 1990, 134). Retail business also declined. U.S. Census data shows a drop in sales in most major northeastern or midwestern cities' downtown retail areas between 1958 and 1963. Many of the nation's largest cities suffered losses. Buffalo's sales showed the biggest decline—23.5 percent. Detroit, Baltimore, Cleveland, St. Louis, and Cincinnati also showed losses of more than 10 percent. Boston was an exception, showing a 0.9 percent increase in sales (Teaford 1990. 130). Moreover, many downtown areas lost important sales outlets. In New York, eight major retailers closed. Faced with big financial losses, downtown merchants often promoted an agenda that overwhelmed residential concerns. They wanted dramatic changes in a city's appearance that would draw more people into the downtown area, and sometimes these changes wiped away the homes of the poor. These attempts at problem solving were part of a process that would extend into the 21st century.

Drug Use

Drug use was a significant issue among those who feared urban blight and corruption of the nation's youth. Congressional hearings in 1948–1951 showed increased abuse of narcotics and specifically cited heightened use among young people. Many experts drew a strong connection between drug use and potential increases in other crimes. Authorities saw opiates such as morphine and heroin as the biggest threats. Some politicians argued that the migration of African Americans and other minorities to urban centers had broadened the market for drugs within densely populated areas. Others contended that drugs were being supplied by the nation's Communist enemies as a Cold War initiative.

In this era, the most convenient drug for people to obtain was Benzedrine, an amphetamine sold over the counter in pharmacies as an inhaler to increase the size of nasal and bronchial passages. It also offered the cheapest way to achieve a "high." Users typically cracked an inhaler open and swallowed the Benzedrine-treated paper strip inside. In 1959, the Federal Drug Administration attempted to end abuse of the drug by requiring a prescription for purchase.

Marijuana, often brought into the country from Mexico, was the most popular drug among the young, but possession of the drug carried penalties as severe as those facing users of more heavily addictive drugs. During this decade, the argument that marijuana served as a gateway to more serious drug abuse first surfaced. The Boggs Act of 1951 set mandatory sentences for possession of any narcotics, including marijuana: 2 to 5 years for a first offense, 5 to 10 years for a second offense, and 10 to 20 years for three or more offenses. In addition, each offense carried a $2,000 fine. In 1956, the Narcotics Control Act raised maximum fines to $20,000 and increased mandatory sentences.

Help for City Dwellers

The existence of urban problems was never up for debate in the 1950s. The problems were clear, but there were no easy answers about how to address them or how to pay for them. The American Municipal Association had pleaded for federal aid on a wide array of urban issues in 1951, but there was little support in Washington for widespread intervention. Although the administration of Harry S. Truman had sought to offer aid, much of Truman's legislative package was stifled as concerns about the Korean War grew early in the 1950s. Republican Dwight D. Eisenhower took office in 1953 with every intention of limiting federal aid to state and local governments because he opposed the concept of big government. However, he was bound to carry out the Housing Act of 1949, which ordered federal aid to urban housing. The law committed the federal government to paying two-thirds of local governments' net costs in buying and preparing blighted areas for residential construction. By March 1958, the total amount allocated to the nation's largest cities ranged from New York's $34,064,229 to Buffalo's allocation of $0 (Teaford 1990, 107). Much more federal money was invested in highways and airports. Eisenhower's Commission on Intergovernmental Relations recommended in 1955 that federal grants-in-aid should be reduced and favored "greater self-reliance at local and state levels" (McKelvey 1968, 161). However, the best efforts of Eisenhower and his administration could not stop the flow of federal money to troubled cities. In 1956, Congress passed a Federal Water Pollution Control Act that allocated $50 million to match local funds in efforts to clean up the water in small cities. A year later Eisenhower announced that he would support federal assistance for school construction and would not try to reduce housing aid. Nevertheless, he proposed reductions in federal water and sewer assistance programs and vetoed legislation increasing federal aid to depressed areas in 1958. Congress went on to pass a 1959 bill mandating federal grants to local airfields and increased support to local programs such as libraries.

As the tug of war occurred in Washington, most central cities faced state government's reluctance to allocate aid, too. City dwellers were underrepresented in many state legislatures, a reality that greatly limited their clout and their prospects of acquiring state aid. With districts still drawn as they had been decades earlier before urban growth, rural areas had a disproportionate share of power. Even when courts issued orders demanding reapportionment, as they did in Wisconsin, antiurban forces in the legislature managed to obstruct changes. Some cities were forced to pursue other avenues. The *National Municipal Review* heralded Minneapolis's federal suit for fair apportionment as "a real milestone" (McKelvey 1968, 186).

The many obstacles to urban change led some writers to call for renewed consideration of some kind of democratic socialism that would stop national business leaders from discouraging federal aid and would place social needs above the desire for profit. In fact, local governments had scored many victories during the decade by appealing directly to the voters. Philadelphia promoted bond issues for 12 consecutive years beginning in 1952, and the measures were approved in every year except 1953. Cleveland voters supported 69 percent of $345 million in proposed bond issues from 1946 to 1958 (Teaford 1990, 71). The decade's most heralded redevelopment projects—Pittsburgh's Gateway Center and Philadelphia's Penn Center—both replaced shabby railroad operations with shimmering high-rises. Each reflected the city government's ability to work with private enterprises to rebuild areas in a way that served big business and downtown interests without remaking deteriorating residential neighborhoods. The federal government had little impact on either project.

MINORITIES AND AMERICAN CITIES

Growing African American and Hispanic populations contributed to the steady flow of social change in American cities during the 1950s. Many members of minority groups experienced poverty in the inner city because of poor educational backgrounds and an often-segregated job market. As African Americans found the stigma of skin color was difficult to overcome even in northern cities, Hispanics struggled to minimize the handicap of a language barrier.

During this era, a growing divide developed between urban whites and urban African Americans. The African American urban population exceeded 9,393,000 in 1950, which made African Americans the largest minority group in American cities, outdistancing the combination of all foreign-born residents. Despite expanded immigration from foreign lands, the urban African American population exceeded the foreign-born population by more than 5 million at the decade's end. More than 13,792,000 African Americans, a majority of the minority group, lived in the nation's cities at that time. Only one-third of the nation's white population could be found in urban centers. In the suburbs, there were 35 times as many whites as African Americans (Polenberg 1980, 150). By 1960, more than 75 percent of the African American population was urban, and just 60 percent still lived in the South. African Americans still made up 23.86 percent of the Southeast's population (Koslow 1999, 101).

Census figures show that the percentage of nonwhite residents in the nation's largest cities grew significantly during the decade. Nonwhites, a category that included most descendants of Africans and Asians, made up 9.8 percent of New York's population in 1950 and 14.7 percent in 1960. Similarly, Chicago's nonwhite population grew from 14.1 to 23.6 percent; Philadelphia's, from 14.1 to 26.7 percent (Teaford 1990, 126). By 1960, it became clear that the nonwhite population in the 12 largest metropolitan areas was expanding at a much higher rate than the white population. The white growth rate from 1930 to 1960 was 46.5 percent, while the nonwhite population grew by 215.2 percent. In individual metropolitan areas, nonwhite growth was two to four times as large as white growth (Sharp and Schnore 1962, 172–174). Nonwhites had made up 44 percent of the incoming migrants in the previous decade (Bogue 1955, 477). However, in more than 60 percent of southern metropolitan areas, the nonwhite population actually declined during the 1950s (Schnore and Sharp 1963, 252). This decade marked the end of the population drain from southern states. In future decades, migration into the South would exceed outmigration, with industries relocating in the South and taking jobs with them.

A growing Hispanic population—some of whom self-identified as black and others as white—also played a significant role in urban life. Puerto Ricans came to mainland American cities in search of work. Mexicans also migrated for economic reasons, and while many favored agricultural work, some pursued blue-collar jobs in urban areas. Cuban refugees, who arrived in relatively small numbers early in the decade, had a very different social profile. They came in a steadier stream after Fidel Castro took control of their island in 1959 and instituted a socialist regime. Unlike Puerto Ricans and Mexicans, the Cuban immigrants of the 1950s and 1960s primarily were political refugees from the more affluent propertied class. Because of their refugee status, Cubans who came in the late 1950s and early 1960s received government help unavailable to Puerto Ricans and Mexicans. As a group, Cubans experienced greater social mobility because of government assistance and because many of them were better educated than migrants from Puerto Rico and Mexico. Each of these Hispanic groups tended to settle in a particular geographic area. Chicanos made the biggest inroads in the Southwest, although Chicago had a significant Mexican population. Puerto Ricans favored urban areas in the eastern half of the mainland, especially the New York metropolitan area. And Cubans favored the Miami area.

African Americans Trapped in the Inner-City Neighborhoods

As cities attempted to address the problem of inner-city decay in the 1950s, many African Americans and Hispanics moved to cities only to find themselves locked in impoverished urban neighborhoods that offered little hope of escape. Over the years, various immigrant groups had passed through the city slums, living and working there until they earned enough money to move to greener pastures in more polished working-class or middle-class neighborhoods. In a sharp contrast to the immigrant experience, there was little opportunity for African Americans to escape in the 1950s. In the United States, a slum is typically an economically depressed area suffering a drain of resources. The extent of that drain broadens to include "savings, physical capital, human resources, and incomes," according to economists Daniel R. Fusfeld and Timothy Bates (1984, 136). As these neighborhoods grow, professionals and service companies depart along with more prosperous residents whose neighborhoods are being nibbled away by expanding population of the urban poor. Residents place their meager savings in banks that invest them in businesses located in more prosperous neighborhoods, not in local housing or redevelopment projects. As white residents flee, jobs, money, and services all flood out of the neighborhood. The residual minority population usually lacks political clout and, as a result, the area's physical infrastructure is allowed to degenerate. Those left behind in the poor neighborhoods are typically poor members of minority groups with little education or job training. Because of cultural differences, they cannot mesh with the dominant population group, and they end up anchored in their poor neighborhoods.

Although impoverished African Americans often shared their neighborhoods with low-income whites and with newcomers like Mexicans and Puerto Ricans, they had limited opportunities to rise from their poor roots in the 1950s. Moreover, no group waited in line to replace them at the bottom of the economic ladder. Just as the mythical melting pot never was expected to consume African Americans, old inner-city residential patterns did not hold true for most African Americans. In their previous incarnations, poor urban enclaves had provided a starting place for new immigrants, with successive groups achieving enough success to move elsewhere and then being replaced in the neighborhood by newcomers. However, many African Americans in the 1950s found that for them, the economically challenged neighborhood represented the end of the road. Aid was available, but in many cases solid jobs were not.

Government policy had a direct effect on the lives of struggling inner-city dwellers. For instance, some policies favored poor single-parent households, thus discouraging maintenance of homes with two strong parents. During the Great Depression, Aid for Dependent Children went only to needy children, but a 1950 amendment made it possible for a single parent, usually a woman, also to receive aid if the family's income fell below a certain level. More and more African American family units were headed by women, and in the 1950s, when the stereotypical family had a father, a mother, several children, and perhaps a pet, this represented one more way in which the urban African Americans in poor neighborhoods did not match middle-class expectations.

African American Exodus from South Nears Its End

The African American urban population grew by approximately 1.6 million during the 1950s. Statistics show that 23.2 percent of the Alabama and Mississippi African American populations left their home states. White poverty was high in Kentucky and West Virginia at this time, but only 15 percent of whites made an exodus from their rural homes. This represented 1.45 million white migrants versus 1.36 million African Americans (Kirby 1983, 594). Chicago's African American population grew by 77 percent in the 1940s and by another 65 percent in the 1950s (Price-Spratlen 1998, 519). The decade's postwar prosperity raised the hopes of many African Americans in the South, drawing them away from the rural roots as the number of agricultural jobs continued to decline. Some moved to urban areas in the South, and after spending a while in those cities, some moved to metropolitan areas outside the South, following often-vain hopes of finding better opportunities. Others migrated directly to cities in the North and West. They escaped Jim Crow laws that demanded segregation; however, they frequently found themselves confined to segregated neighborhoods and a racially structured and shrinking job market.

The Nation of Islam

The Nation of Islam became widely known in the 1950s for its aggressive stand on African American nationalism. Founded quietly in 1930 as a religious organization, the group increasingly stressed the need for African Americans to separate themselves from whites. Leaders encouraged their followers to challenge racism by acting under a simple directive: Do for Self. Under the leadership of Elijah Muhammad, the Nation of Islam evolved to include several urban temples, the Clara Muhammad Schools, and the Fruit of Islam, a paramilitary organization. Based in Chicago, members of the Nation of Islam differed from most Muslims because they believed their group's founder, Wallace Fard, was Allah himself. In 1959, Malcolm X, one of Elijah Muhammad's two leading disciples, traveled to the Arab world to meet with other Muslims. He visited Egypt and Saudi Arabia, where he was surprised to see African American slaves. Although Islamic leaders in the Middle East refused to recognize Fard's holy status, Malcolm celebrated his trip as a triumph in hopes of counteracting negative publicity generated by a televised documentary called *The Hate That Hate Produced*, which focused intensely on Malcolm's antiwhite sentiments.

Malcolm X, an advocate of black nationalism, emerged in the 1950s as a leader of the Nation of Islam. The movement, led by Elijah Muhammad, received increasing visibility in American cities during this era. (Library of Congress)

Puerto Rican Immigration Gains Speed

Placed under U.S. jurisdiction after the 1898 Spanish-American War, the island of Puerto Rico became an American commonwealth in 1952. This designation made all Puerto Ricans citizens of the United States. Although they could not vote and had no voting representative in Congress, their citizenship removed any restrictions on migration to the mainland. The availability of cheap airline fares added further incentive to move. Passenger records show that arrivals from Puerto Rico peaked in 1953 when 74,603 arrived on the mainland (Fitzpatrick 1971, 12). While most Puerto Rican immigrants moved from an urban area on the island to an urban area on the mainland, a much smaller number traveled from rural areas to be seasonal farm workers, much like Mexican agricultural workers.

The youth and inexperience of the Puerto Rican population on the mainland affected their status in the workforce. Between 1957 and 1961, 46 percent of Puerto Rican migrants were between the ages of 15 and 24, and 53 percent had no work history. In a decade when migration totaled almost 400,000, the number of children born to Puerto Rican parents more than tripled, further diminishing the average age of Puerto Ricans on the mainland (Hernández-Alvarez 1968, 43, 51).

Tenements in a Puerto Rican neighborhood in New York City. (Library of Congress)

When Puerto Rican migrants left the island, they typically settled in densely populated, urban enclaves. Most chose to stay in the city where they first arrived—New York. The 1960 census showed that about 70 percent of Puerto Ricans on the mainland lived in New York, but enclaves also existed in Philadelphia, northeastern New Jersey, Connecticut's Bridgeport, and the Chicago–Gary, Indiana, area. In New York, they expanded the ranks of impoverished residents: More than half of the city's families with annual incomes of less than $4,000 were Puerto Rican, according to the 1960 census. In 1950 and 1960, most Puerto Rican–born workers in the state of New York were low-paid operatives, but by 1960, the majority of people with Puerto Rican parentage could be found in somewhat better-paying sales and clerical jobs (Cortés 1980, 60–61).

Mexican Immigrants Find City Role

Chicano neighborhoods in America's urban areas faced many threats during the 1950s. Redevelopment projects nearly destroyed Mexican "barrio" neighborhoods in several cities. In some cases, new highways sliced through the center of Mexican enclaves, and city governments seldom provided adequate replacement housing. In both Denver and Chicago, universities used their right of eminent

Table 3.2. Puerto Rican–Born Population Growth, 1950 to 1960

	1950	1960
Total U.S. mainland	226,110	615,484
Ten-year U.S. increase	223.2%	172.2%
New York City	187,420	429,710
New York City, mainland total	82.9%	69.8%

Source: U.S. Bureau of the Census.

domain to seize land from Mexican neighborhoods to make way for campus expansion. (Eminent domain allows government-financed operations to appropriate private land for public use.) Elsewhere, Chicano neighborhoods were chosen for slum clearance projects. Often, those barrio residents with the highest incomes moved out as a result of these construction projects, and the loss of housing frequently led to the consolidation of several households within a single-family dwelling. The use of eminent domain by government forces robbed residents by seizing their land or making their businesses untenable. At least in part as a result of these processes, a growing number of Chicano families slid below the poverty line. Devastation of Chicano neighborhoods in East Los Angeles continued for three decades as a result of interstate highway construction, beginning in the early 1950s with the Santa Ana Freeway. Chicano neighborhoods suffered similar fates in San Jose, El Paso, San Antonio, San Diego, and Phoenix.

Among all nationalities, Mexicans were most likely to immigrate to the United States illegally. In the 1950s, the U.S. government set up Operation Wetback to reduce Mexicans' illegal entries into the United States. (The term "wetback," now considered an ethnic slur, referred to the fact that many Mexicans entered the United States by swimming across the Rio Grande River.) The program, which ran from 1953 through 1955, had expelled almost four million Mexicans by 1954 (Acosta-Belén 1988, 91). It has been estimated that 6,841 Mexicans came to the United States legally in 1950, while 469,581 entered the country illegally. Illegal immigration reached a peak in 1954, when more than a million Mexicans crossed into the United States. The number of illegal immigrants fell steadily after that year as government efforts to block illegal immigration increased (Del Castillo 1984, 114).

Revolution Sparks Cuban Flight to Miami

Political upheaval in Cuba prompted thousands to travel to the United States. In the mid-1950s, most immigrants were trying to escape the dictatorship of authoritarian Fulgencio Batista; late in the decade, the majority of Cuban refugees were people who had thrived during Batista's reign and saw their prospects declining after Fidel Castro seized control of the nation on New Year's Day 1959 and began to institute a socialist regime. Between 1946 and 1950, a yearly average of 2,161 Cubans immigrated. During the 1951–1955 period, immigration more than doubled, and as political unrest grew, rates were even higher in 1956–1958 when 40,267 Cubans arrived (Pérez 1986, 128). An additional 26,527 immigrated in the first six months of 1959, followed by 60,224 in 1960. Heavy anti-Castro immigration would continue through late 1962, and most refugees would settle in south Florida.

That last wave of 1950s immigration included significant numbers who were wealthier and better educated than their predecessors. Thirty-seven percent of family heads had held professional, managerial, or ownership positions. The 1953 Cuban census had revealed that less than 10 percent of Cuban workers fell within that category. About 12.5 percent of these late immigrants had finished four years or more of higher education—an achievement only 1 percent of the broader Cuban population could claim in 1953 (Pérez 1986, 129). Given the choice between hiring one of these Cubans and an African American, many Miami-area employers demonstrated favoritism toward Cubans.

African American Families' Economic Challenges

Most African Americans who moved from the South to major urban centers experienced a less rigid form of segregation, but they also discovered that the cost of living outside the South was higher. Housing, in particular, was much more costly. By 1960, 77 percent of the African American population lived in areas designated as Standard Metropolitan Statistical Areas. Only 66 percent of the white population had that distinction (Maloney 1994, 367). Many central areas of big cities were in a state of decline in the 1950s as white residents and some industries exited. Most of the newest urban African Americans had been educated in the poor, segregated schools of the South and trained to carry out only agricultural tasks. As a result, they arrived in cities with great disadvantages and came face to face with a declining job market for unskilled workers. At this time, compensation began to reward those who held high school diplomas. With many African American youths leaving school before graduation, they had no chance to cash in on this new dividend. Many employers also favored white migrants from rural areas over African Americans with similar backgrounds, a reminder that both in the North and the South, African American workers continued to face race discrimination.

Despite tough economic conditions during much of the decade, African Americans did achieve some successes. Early in the decade, employment conditions were good. The nationwide nonwhite unemployment rate in 1953 was just 4.1 percent, and among teenaged job seekers, 7.3 percent were unemployed. Urban African Americans in the 1950s also enjoyed greater access to clerical jobs as many downtown offices expanded operations. A significant number of women profited from this change. A study of the central city areas of Chicago, Baltimore, Cleveland, Detroit, and Philadelphia showed that the percentage of African American women in clerical jobs more than doubled over the course of the decade. While only 7.5 percent had clerical jobs at the beginning of the decade, 16.9 percent performed clerical work in 1960. In those cities, African American women's share of all white-collar jobs expanded from 16 percent to 29.5 percent during the decade. African American men's advances were not quite as impressive. Study findings showed the number of African American men with clerical jobs grew only from 6.4 percent to 9.7 percent over the 10-year period. African American men held 18.5 percent of white-collar jobs in 1960—an increase of 5.2 percentage points over 1950. Unfortunately, African American unemployment also began to grow after the end of the Korean War as economic growth slowed. The United States' gross national product had increased at an annual rate of 4 percent between 1946 and 1953; however, that growth slowed to just 2.4 percent per year from 1953 to 1960. The nonwhite jobless rate rose to 12.6 percent in 1958 and held steady between 10 and 13 percent until 1964 (Fusfeld and Bates, 115–117, 118).

Wage disparities between whites and African Americans grew during the 1950s, and African Americans also enjoyed less job security (Maloney 1994, 374). In industrial plants, African American men were typically limited to unskilled departments with little opportunity for promotion, and because newly arrived migrants had low seniority, they often were the first workers to lose their jobs in layoffs. African Americans constituted 8 to 9 percent of all automobile workers during the decade, but African Americans of this era never held more than one-half of 1 percent of skilled jobs in the industry. Among more than 11,000 skilled workers at General Motors, fewer than 100 were African American (Fusfeld and Bates 1984, 118–119). A comparison of African American and white incomes in the South shows that in 1953 the typical African American male earned 46 percent of a white man's income; that dropped to 33 percent in 1959. The female African American worker's income was 45 percent of a white working woman's income in 1953, and that dropped to 42 percent in 1959.

In the North and West, African American workers faced less wage inequity but still struggled to keep up. In these areas, an African American man made 74 percent of a white man's income in 1953 and 73 percent in 1959; African American women earned 85 percent of a white woman's income in 1953 and actually surpassed white women in 1959 with a typical income that was 6 percentage points higher than the income of an average white woman worker. These figures compare the median African American income with the median white income, and they are a bit misleading because they do not reflect unemployed persons, a group in which African Americans held a disproportionately large share. Even among college graduates, African Americans received lower pay. African American male college graduates between the ages of 25 and 34 could expect to earn just 59 percent of what their counterparts in the white community received in 1959 (Fusfeld and Bates 1984, 106, 110). Throughout these years, African American family income was a bit more than half as large as white family income, and the African American family's standing actually slipped in the decade's final years.

Hispanic Education as an Issue

New Hispanic arrivals faced educational hurdles, many of which sprang from their ignorance of English. Although a court had ruled in the late 1940s that Hispanics were white, school systems often used tortured logic to justify segregation of Hispanic children. In many cases, educators explained segregation by citing Hispanic children's language difficulties, and some school systems put African Americans and Hispanics in schools together as they maintained white Anglo-only schools. Leading educators of the era opposed the concept of bilingual education. As political refugees, Cubans eventually received educational aid, but Chicanos and Puerto Ricans largely fended for themselves. The issue of educating Hispanics did not receive great attention, except in the New York City school system, where a Mayor's Advisory Committee on Puerto Rican Affairs began studying the issue in 1951. A four-year undertaking from 1953 to 1957 resulted in *The Puerto Rican Study,* which examined the best ways to teach English to Hispanic students, to help parents and children adapt to the community, and to identify Puerto Rican students within the school system. The study reached few conclusions. It did, however, recommend integrating vocabulary lessons, structured grammar studies, and lessons in language used in everyday life. It also concluded that Puerto Rican parents were too preoccupied with their own adjustment to make their children's education a high priority (Cortés 1980, 15).

The Catholic Church and Hispanic Immigrants

In addition to linguistic challenges, many Hispanic immigrants faced a period of adjustment in their religious affiliations. While many previous immigrant groups had brought priests, ministers, or rabbis with them from their native lands, Hispanics seldom did. Most Hispanics grew up in a Catholic culture, but those who arrived before 1950 had not found a welcoming Catholic Church in the United States. The Church did not reach out to offer social or financial aid to Hispanics. Consequently, Protestant churches stepped in to convert small numbers of Hispanic migrants. In the 1950s, the Catholic hierarchy began urging parishes to address the needs of these migrants more fully. Although the Catholic Church managed to retain most of the migrant population, the rigid orthodoxy of Catholicism in the United States was at odds with the mixture of Catholicism and folk religion common among these immigrants.

Limited Progress and Ongoing Minority Challenges

Urban African Americans experienced some advances in the 1950s, along with many disappointments. A growing trend toward establishment of interracial community organizations, particularly in southern cities, provided more equal facilities for schools and recreation, although segregation was still common in the South. In addition, some cities outside the South had begun embracing fair employment and housing regulations that made it more difficult to victimize African Americans. These changes provided small openings for a fortunate minority of African American city dwellers to enjoy better lives and escape the poverty of inner-city neighborhoods with few resources. African Americans who had moved out of the South welcomed the possibility that their children would receive a better education in integrated schools. Many hoped that their children might be able to pursue a college education in inexpensive public universities or traditionally African American universities and colleges. For some, scholarships or job opportunities provided a route out of urban poverty. There was an African American middle class that enjoyed a better life in more prosperous city neighborhoods or in predominantly African American suburbs. These people were often professionals, such as doctors, lawyers, and college professors, who somehow managed to escape the worst facets of African American urban life. While they were significantly better off than many poor African Americans, they typically did not enjoy all of the luxuries available to the white middle class.

By the decade's end, the rate of migration from the South was losing momentum, and in the coming years, an increasing number of nonsoutherners began moving into what would become known as the Sunbelt. A pair of demographers concluded that by the 1960s, "the counterstream . . . [became] the dominant migration stream" (Kirby 1983, 593). Clearly, some African Americans chose to remain in the South because it was their home, and dissatisfaction with life outside the South inevitably diminished the old pattern in which one family member migrated, found success, and encouraged others to follow. "The dreams embodied in the Great Migration eventually collapsed under the weight of continued racial oppression and the failure of industrial capitalism to distribute its prosperity as broadly as expected," concluded historian James R. Grossman (1989, 265). Outside of the South, urban African Americans also found that de facto segregation, which was an undeniable part of American life in the 1950s, could be as harmful as the legalized segregation policies that prevailed in the South. Within the nation's poor African American neighborhoods, a sense of hopelessness grew and opened the door to the rage that would fire the violent riots of the 1960s.

The Hispanic share of the United States' overall population rose from 2.7 percent in 1950 to 3.9 percent in 1960 (Davis, Haug, and Willette 1988, 11). More Mexicans immigrated to the United States legally or illegally in the two decades following World War II than had arrived in the previous 100 years. Puerto Ricans represented the largest group of legal Hispanic migrants, but they garnered little attention nationally because European immigrants still outnumbered them. Hispanics found that long-held cultural traditions, such as the husband's role as breadwinner, were challenged by job markets that sometimes allowed women to find jobs when their husbands could not. In other places, skilled women earned more than their unskilled husbands. This was true in New York and Chicago, where many women entered the needlework trades. Children of Hispanic immigrants enjoyed broader opportunities to move into white-collar jobs such as clerical work if they had opportunities to learn English; however, dependence on Spanish remained a handicap for migrants seeking economic success.

URBAN LIFE AND TRANSPORTATION

Pivotal changes in transportation, both within and between urban areas, had a profound impact in this decade. The nation's attachment to automobiles came into full blossom with the 1956 decision to establish an expensive interstate highway system, which would bolster businesses' use of trucks and promote national tourism. In addition, Americans flew more, and the introduction of passenger jets late in the decade promised to enhance the popularity of air travel. These events contributed to a decline in railroads' share of both the passenger and the freight business.

Some of these transportation changes contributed to the changing look of American cities. Declining use of railroads allowed cities like Philadelphia and Pittsburgh to redevelop their central cities and put towering office buildings where ugly rail yards and loading docks once stood. Railroad commerce no longer was profitable enough to justify allowing trains and tracks to detract from the urban environment. Moreover, improvement and expansion of urban expressways, as well as the introduction of interstate highways, facilitated the movement of people and industry out of the city. Expanded use of trucking on interstate highways enabled some industries to move to suburban areas; others settled in small towns where union activity was low.

Most metropolitan jobs remained in central cities, although many had moved to the suburbs or to neighborhoods near the city's outskirts. As a result, many people commuted to and from work each day—and a great number of those workers used their cherished automobiles for their daily journeys. Some cities tried to buttress public transportation and protect urban areas from becoming massive parking lots. Philadelphia, for example, worked hard to maximize its commuter train service; however, by the mid-1950s, it became clear that many suburban Philadelphians were unwilling to consider mass-transportation options. The city's Urban Traffic and Transportation Board warned in 1956 that the Philadelphia area was "becoming mired in a traffic problem so intense that the region's livability, its efficient functioning and its competitive power to attract population and industry [were] all seriously impaired" (Teaford 1990, 95). Daily traffic jams belied American romanticism about automobiles, which were the subject of rock 'n' roll songs and American dreams. Every week on her television variety show, Dinah Shore invited Americans to "see the U.S.A. in your Chevrolet." And if anything, Americans' yen for cars was growing.

Motor vehicles and Americans' use of them were changing. Station wagons became a hit in the 1950s, especially among families who liked road trips. By 1956, one in eight cars sold was a station wagon, and pickup trucks also enjoyed growing popularity among footloose Americans. There were more two-car families, too. The nation was on its way to developing a drive-in culture. Many Americans in the upper and middle classes saw driving as the best way to travel within a metropolitan area. Some members of the working class owned a motor vehicle, too, but for those in major cities, cars were often impractical because of their expense and their need for parking spaces. Poor residents of inner city neighborhoods only experience with the travel revolution might have come in riding city buses that replaced most trolleys in this era. The Space Age was just beginning, and while dramatic change may have seemed tangible to suburban drivers of two-tone cars with flashy fins, inner-city travelers seemed light-years away from the glistening new transportation options of the 1950s.

Little Money for Public Transportation

Faced with limited budgets and infrastructure options, the federal, state, and local governments made choices in the 1950s that encouraged automobile travel and consequently discouraged the further development of mass transportation. By funding a national interstate highway system, the federal government gave a boost to local and state efforts already under way to improve roads connecting suburbs to central cities. Government support of the national road network indirectly subsidized the automobile and suburban housing industries at the same time that it facilitated and reinforced white flight to the suburbs.

Road builders made driving easier, thus limiting the appeal of mass transportation to potential commuters. Civic leaders still supported public transit as a means of minimizing traffic jams and limiting the amount of parking lot construction necessitated by so many cars coming into the city daily. As Philadelphia leaders emphasized maintenance of public transportation between 1950 and 1955, the city achieved mass-transit improvements costing $42.9 million, while only $34.7 million was spent on highways and bridges and $29.7 million on airports. Philadelphia mayor Richardson Dilworth was able to work out an arrangement with the Pennsylvania Railroad to expand commuter rail service, and he offered the railroad company a city subsidy to lower fares on experimental routes. However, in 1959, Dilworth hit a brick wall when he tried to unite with other urban leaders and railroad companies in a plea for federal subsidies to broaden commuter rail service nationwide. At a meeting of railroad executives and mayors, he found that western railroads opposed the idea of subsidies. Northwestern Railroad's chairman argued that subsidies were unnecessary because Chicago's commuter train service was profitable. The Southern Pacific, which provided commuter service in San Francisco, opposed the idea of federal

New York City's subways represented one of the most successful models of urban mass transportation in the 1950s. (Library of Congress)

involvement, portraying it as an invitation to federal regulation. Some analysts also argued that providing commuter train service was too expensive given the brief period of peak use each day and the cost of building stations. A National League of Cities study in 1959 showed that a collapse of rail commuter service in New York, Chicago, Boston, Philadelphia, and Cleveland would necessitate $31 billion in additional highway construction. Dilworth's quest for federal subsidies was not satisfied until President Lyndon B. Johnson signed legislation in the summer of 1964 to bolster urban rail projects by providing matching funds to cities and states (Healy 1974, 211–214).

Despite the lack of federal aid, many cities expanded their mass-transit systems in the 1950s. Cleveland, which made mass transportation its top spending priority from 1951 to 1956, established its first rapid-transit line, and Chicago expanded its subway system. Many cities reduced or eliminated trolley car systems and replaced them with buses, providing more flexibility by using vehicles not restricted to a track system. By mid-1954, Chicago had discontinued all but four trolley lines, and the last went out of service in 1958. Detroit stopped trolley service in 1956. While cities attempted to modernize public transit, commuters continued their growing dependency on automobiles. Mass-transportation ridership dropped 51 percent in Philadelphia and 66 percent in Detroit between 1945 and 1958. Despite New York's expansive subway system, the city lost 34 percent of mass-transit passengers between 1947 and 1958 (Teaford 1990, 104–105).

Rail Travel Decline

Railroad passenger service, which had provided the best long-distance transportation for decades, also experienced a decline during the 1950s. When the decade began, trains carried more than 75 percent of long-distance travelers, but by 1960, trains retained only about 39 percent of those passengers (Young and Young 2004, 263). The primary reason for this decline was heightened competition from other forms of transportation. Construction of new highways and the proliferation of nicer motels and inexpensive restaurants along roadways made car travel a more appealing option for Americans traveling regionally. Airliners offered shorter travel times on long-distance trips, especially late in the decade when major airlines introduced passenger jet service. Census data shows that railroads carried 57.4 percent of intercity freight in 1950, while motor vehicles handled just 15.8 percent of that business. By 1960, the railroads' share of freight transportation had dropped to 44.7 percent, and trucks carried 21.5 percent. (Inland waterways, oil pipelines, and airlines were the other key means of freight transportation.)

Faced with declining revenues, railroad companies made major cutbacks in passenger train service. Over the course of the decade, more than 53,000 miles of railroad tracks lost passenger train service. That represented about one-fourth of the passenger train network that existed in 1950. At the same time, the total miles traveled by passenger trains dropped 40 percent. The number of passenger train cars in service declined by 34 percent from 43,585 to 28,396. Annual passenger miles on Class I railroads, which did 99 percent of freight hauling, dropped from 31.8 billion in 1950 to 20.1 billion in 1961—a decline of about 1 billion passenger miles per year (Berge 1964, 1). The heavily unionized railroad industry found it difficult to cut costs without slashing services; airlines of the same era, which lacked strong labor organizations, had much lower labor costs. Railroad companies reported that they lost $1.44 for every $1 they collected in dining cars, but they continued to experiment with new ways to lure riders, including glass-domed observation cars and Slumbercoaches, which offered eight double-room sleeper compartments per car (Young and Young 2004, 263).

The sad truth for railroads was that the federal government was giving a boost to the competition. Congressional spending buoyed both highway and airport construction in the 1950s. Railroad advocates pointed out that riding a train remained 22 times as safe as automobile travel and almost four times as safe as the domestic air travel of that period. They also noted that train travel remained less expensive than flying. The average per-mile rail coach fare was only a little over 50 percent of the cost of making the same trip by plane. Nevertheless, for people in a hurry, what often mattered was getting there quickly. The train, which had led a transportation revolution and shortened the psychological distance from coast to coast, now offered travel at a leisurely pace for those who were willing to set aside the time to enjoy it.

Airline Growth

The number of airline passengers in the United States quadrupled between 1946 and 1957, when 53 million American airline tickets were sold (Teaford 1990, 99). In 1955, air passengers exceeded train passengers for the first time. And all of that increase occurred when airliners were powered by four piston engines instead of jet engines. TWA became the first airline to offer a nonstop flight from

New York to Los Angeles in 1953, and just four years later, Pan Am began providing nonstop flights from New York to London. In both cases, other airlines quickly matched these achievements. As ridership grew, airlines also started to establish different classes of service, copying the railroad industry's division of first-class and coach accommodation.

Dynamic growth within the industry led American cities into a competition for air routes. Deteriorating older cities of the Midwest and Northeast saw a new source of revenue. Good airline service could attract businesses to a city and generate tourism. Cleveland, Baltimore, Philadelphia, and St. Louis gamely joined the fray, but officials at Chicago's Midway Field happily proclaimed that it was the "World's Busiest Airport" in 1957 when the city's three airports handled 11 million arriving and departing passengers. Planning for Chicago's gigantic O'Hare Airport, which began as World War II ended, led to a 1958 sale of $120 million in revenue bonds (Teaford 1990, 100). Congress supported airport development through federal grants, and in 1958, the Federal Aviation Administration (FAA) was created to regulate air travel.

Jets, which traversed the skies at unprecedented speeds, debuted in December 1958 when National Airlines scheduled its new jetliners for international routes. Less than two months later, American Airlines inaugurated the nation's first domestic jet service. Pan Am began providing a round-the-world jet route in October 1959. The introduction of jets boosted the number of Americans traveling abroad, which reached a total of almost two million during the decade. American airlines' adoption of jets led to a worldwide jet-buying spree by international airlines, and that expanded the opportunities for international travel while it bolstered American companies such as Boeing and the two companies that would merge to form McDonnell-Douglas in the 1960s.

Cars and More Cars

Americans had loved cars since their introduction early in the century, but in the postwar years, automobile production spiraled upward. The eight million cars manufactured in 1955 reflected a quadrupling of 1946's production. Car registrations similarly skyrocketed. There were 25 million registered cars in 1945, 40 million in 1950, 51 million in 1955, and 62 million in 1960. Almost 90 percent of suburban families owned at least one car, while only 60 percent of urban families owned an automobile (Polenberg 1980, 130). Truck registrations in 1955 stood at just over 10 million. There was roughly one truck for every five cars. The truck-to-car ratio had been one-to-six in 1935 (Jackson 1985, 162). In the 1950s, trucks were taking a bigger share of the freight-hauling business away from railroads.

The existence of so many cars, not to mention trucks and buses, increased demand for smooth highways. During the early 1950s, many highways were widened, lengthened, or reinforced; however, many industries wanted the government to make a much bigger commitment. State highway departments, bus companies, the American Trucking Association, the Automobile Manufacturers Association, and the American Parking Association were among the top promoters of an interstate highway system in the mid-1950s. The gargantuan project also received support from a variety of groups likely to profit from road construction, including car dealers and renters, labor unions, advertising agencies, banks, real estate groups, and homebuilders as well as the oil, rubber, and asphalt industries. Faced with growing pressure, Eisenhower ordered a study in 1954 to determine the extent of highway needs. The panel considered no options other than initiating a massive highway-construction project.

Even before the interstate highway system received congressional consideration, America's old central cities in the Northeast had 184 miles of expressways in operation and 94 miles of similar highways under construction. By this time, cities and state highway departments already had invested a considerable amount of time and money in planning urban transportation corridors. Many pieces of land had been bought, and to the extent that their budgets would allow, construction had been completed. Nevertheless, traffic remained a serious problem in urban areas and contributed to the popular conception of cities as crowded and unpleasant necessities. Parking was another huge urban issue. Once commuters reached cities, they needed a place to store their cars for the day. As a result, cities displayed a seemingly insatiable appetite for parking facilities, which often were considered to be eyesores in the urban environment. "When people find it too much trouble to park downtown, they stop coming downtown," Cleveland's planning commission reported in 1951 (Teaford 1990, 97–98).

The Interstate Highway System

The Interstate Highway Act won approval in 1956. It entailed a federal commitment to finance 90 percent of interstate highway construction, including 5,300 miles of expressways in metropolitan areas. By 1960, the federal government was paying out more than $1 billion a year for urban highways (Teaford 1990, 94). After the bill's passage, several cities quickly made proposals for projects within their metropolitan areas. St. Louis was the first urban area to claim a grant, which was used to build one section of the Mark Twain Expressway.

After Congress approved the project, American social critic Lewis Mumford said, "the most charitable thing to assume is that they hadn't the faintest notion of what they were doing" (Jackson 1985, 250). The federal government generated its contribution through new taxes on cars, trucks, and buses, as well as new levies on automotive necessities, such as tires, gasoline, and oil. Money was no problem because the Highway Trust Fund's tax revenues could not be diverted to cover other government expenses. Sen. Gaylord Nelson of Wisconsin

New York City's Major Deegan Expressway opened in 1956 as part of the Interstate Highway System. (Library of Congress)

said that 75 percent of government's spending on transportation in this era went to highways, while only 1 percent was devoted to mass transit (Jackson 1985, 250).

One of the Eisenhower administration's rationales for this big expenditure sprang from the Cold War threat of nuclear attack. Administration spokesmen assured lawmakers that better roads would facilitate evacuation of American cities if nuclear war seemed imminent; however, by the late 1950s, the introduction of ballistic missiles capable of carrying nuclear weapons made city evacuation plans obsolete because U.S. forces could expect only about 15 minutes' warning before a missile launched by the Soviet Union hit its target.

As part of construction of the nationwide system, the government set into motion a quality-control test. A seven-mile strip of highway was built near Ottawa, Illinois, to test which types of construction survived wear and tear. The $27-million road was built with a combination of government funds and business contributions. The Pentagon provided members of the armed services to drive large and small vehicles on the track from November 1958 until 1960. At the end of the test period, experts judged which construction materials and techniques showed the most durability. Signs were one of the system's big expenses. The typical sign cost $10,000, but some cost as much as $50,000. Tests showed that a driver moving at the assigned highway speed had about 10 seconds to respond to a sign 1,000 feet away.

Some bureaucratic details were settled at the start. East/west highways would get even numbers, while north/south highway numbers were odd. The lowest numbers would be assigned along the Pacific coastline, and the numbers would rise until the highest numbers were allotted to highways along the East Coast. The maze of highways would become more complicated in urban areas as many long-distance travelers favored bypassing congested urban expressways. Most of the nation's interstate highways were built between 1956 and 1966, although some remained unfinished when the projected closing date—1972— arrived (McNichol 2006, 114, 115–122).

Transportation Changes Alter American Lifestyles

The expansion of U.S. highways begun in the 1950s was a direct reflection of the nation's love affair with cars. Along with cars, these new superhighways helped to change the way Americans traveled, ate, and conducted business. As highways spread, businesses popped up at highway junctions to appeal to busy drivers and to make motorists' lives more convenient. Service stations were the most obvious new additions, but other parts of the economy were affected as well.

Now that many jobs offered one week of paid vacation per year, more and more Americans were traveling, and more than 80 percent of travel entailed automobile trips within the continental United States. Often, trips lasted one to two weeks and provided families with the opportunity to explore national parks and other recreation facilities. Almost half of American families engaged in a summer trip at least once in the 1950s. As a result, the nation's stock of motels changed dramatically and doubled in number from 30,000 to 60,000 during the decade. Roadside motor inns traditionally had been unassuming shelters, but the new age required more comfortable accommodations for the millions of American families now making road trips. Holiday Inns originated in 1954 and quickly spread across the nation (Young and Young 2004, 260–262). And Howard Johnson's, which had a successful nationwide chain of restaurants, entered the motel business in the same year. Among the luxuries offered by new motels were free ice, in-room telephones, and air conditioning. Most of the nation's new motels were owned by franchisees of nationwide chains.

The 1950s also marked the real beginning of the drive-in business phenomenon. Drive-in movie theaters probably had the biggest impact on American culture because of teenagers' habit of using them as semi-private venues for sexual experimentation. Moreover, drive-through restaurants, such as the McDonald's chain, started a fast-food revolution that would change the way Americans ate. Food on the run became a popular option for busy Americans, and drive-in windows simplified the process. Drive-through banks also began to appear, making business dealings easier.

Meanwhile, transportation for poor city dwellers did not reflect significant effort by government at any level. Building highways for prosperous suburbanites took a higher priority, both because of the suburban traveler's financial clout and because the voices of these commuters were more likely to be heard than those of the poor. Some public-transit improvements were made during the 1950s; however, spending for that purpose was dwarfed by highway construction expenditures.

Not all Americans stayed down to earth. Improvements in air travel attracted more passengers, and because airports were located in metropolitan areas, cities became destinations for some travelers and way stations for others. Longer trips now seemed more manageable for business travelers as well as tourists. While many Americans viewed New York as an example of everything that was wrong with American cities, the convenience of air travel reinforced its position as a tourist destination.

THE BEAT GENERATION

The Beat Generation, which only fully emerged in the late 1950s, represented both a subculture and a literary movement. The Beats, also known as beatniks and hipsters, took a stand against the conformity and regimentation that they associated with middle-class life. These 20th-century bohemians demonstrated disdain for the behavior that surrounded them but did not go a step further by embracing social activism as a means of curing the problem. Like method actors and jazz musicians of the era, they favored displays of emotional freedom and rebellion against the status quo. While they lived within what was typically an urban counterculture, the Beat Generation reached out to young people to join them, but they offered no well-defined model to replace the world they disdained. In his 1959 book *The Holy Barbarians,* Lawrence Lipton called them "the swinging, sex-free, footloose, nocturnal, uninhibited, nonconformist genus of the human race" (Moore 1960, 376).

Author Jack Kerouac first coined the term *Beat Generation* in a 1948 interview. There has been debate about the true meaning of "Beat" in this context. Some have contended that it suggests members were beaten or tired; others have claimed that it identified members as beatific. The writer Hettie Jones has argued that the size of the group was exaggerated by its label "because at one point everyone identified with it could fit into my living room, and I didn't think that a whole generation could fit into my living room" (Charters 2001, xvi). As she asserted, relatively few Americans became active participants, but the group's ideals captured the imaginations of thousands of disaffected young Americans.

Poet Allen Ginsberg and Kerouac became the front men for the movement. Other important Beat writers or hipsters included novelists William Burroughs and John Clellon Holmes and poet Lawrence Ferlinghetti. They opposed the materialism of American society and the limitations placed on personal independence in a Cold War culture. As they rejected traditionalism, the Beats encouraged youths to abandon the cultural establishment's framework and to exercise individuality, spontaneity, and nonconformism. They also endorsed sexual freedom, including homosexuality.

Politically, members of the movement rejected both the right and the left. Neither communism nor anticommunism made sense to these young people, although the antimaterialism that animated them did give the movement a left cast that would be drawn upon by cultural radicals in the next decade. Freedom from societal constraints was at the heart of their philosophy. Many members of the Beat Generation also embraced Asian theology—an interest enhanced by Alan W. Watts's Sunday night radio broadcasts of "Philosophy East and West" on Berkeley, California's KPFA radio station. Zen Buddhism, in particular, won over many devotees among those who were seeking alternatives to everything associated with the seemingly buttoned-down American culture of the 1950s.

The Beat Environment

The Beat movement was heavily influenced by a negative response to the Cold War, nuclear weaponry, and what was seen as the empty life of prosperity enjoyed by people like them—the predominantly white middle class. Forsaking the culture of their parents, hipsters demonstrated an affinity for African American culture and, particularly, African American music. Bebop, one form of jazz, provided an unconventional model for the expression of emotions, the demonstration of creativity, and the art of living in the moment. Members of this subculture opposed conformity, and yet they had a dress code of sorts. The men typically grew beards and wore turtleneck sweaters with jeans or chinos. The women around them often dressed in black leotards and wore dramatic eye shadow. Gathering in coffeehouses or bars, the Beats created their own realm.

Young women among the Beats adopted their lifestyle as a means of avoiding the domestic life that awaited many white middle-class girls, according to author Wini Breines. By aligning themselves with the Beats, girls demonstrated dissatisfaction with the role of suburban wives that they had been encouraged to pursue. In doing so, they achieved a bit more freedom than their suburban counterparts, but the Beat writers often demonstrated sexist behavior. A young woman's primary means of joining this subculture was through romantic or sexual involvement with a male beatnik.

Members of the Beat movement could be found in cities all over the world, but New York City's Greenwich Village and San Francisco became the movement's two primary focal points. Both areas had a history of accommodating alternative lifestyles. Author Rudyard Kipling once described San Francisco as "a mad city—inhabited for the most part by perfectly insane people" (Raskin 2004, 9). Far from the nation's staid capital, San Francisco provided a forum for off-beat Americans.

While the Beats offered a critique of the dominant American culture, they also profited from exposure in the era's mass media. Some mainstream writers ridiculed them; however, movies, television, and magazines introduced many Americans to their writing or to the jazz that served as background music for their work. Much of the Beats' literary output was produced to be consumed through hearing rather than reading. As a result, writers often held readings or led discussion groups at cafés and galleries as well as in the streets.

Howl

Allen Ginsberg quickly rose to stardom among the Beat Generation with his long poem *Howl*. Author Jonah Raskin has argued that this particular poem had an unusual impact on its writer. "The poem created the poet," he contends, and that reversed the typical pattern (Raskin 2004, 18). The emotional poem bemoans the loss of "the best minds of my generation destroyed by madness, starving hysterical naked," and its footnote repeats "Holy!" 15 times—another proclamation of the movement's "beatific" status. *Howl* first attracted attention at one of the Beat Generation's big events—an October 1955 poetry reading at San Francisco's Six Gallery. At the time, Ginsberg had few published writings, but his emotional reading captivated the audience. The large and rowdy session introduced the work of six poets who defied "the system of academic poetry," according to Ginsberg (Raskin 2004, 13). The gathering, which was hosted by poet Kenneth Rexroth, generated strong emotional displays by the poets as well as their audience. A

Allen Ginsberg, pictured in 1958, was the poet laureate of the Beat Movement and is best known for his poem Howl. *(Bettmann/Corbis)*

year later, Ginsberg said that he had written the poem to free readers and to make them realize that they were angels. In 1957, controversy over the poem sparked a trial in which Lawrence Ferlinghetti of City Lights Books, which published *Howl,* was tried in San Francisco for selling obscene and indecent writing. He was acquitted, and the Beat movement gained further momentum. Ginsberg became one of its biggest stars through cathartic poetry readings often fueled by intoxication. He stripped off all of his clothes at one.

On the Road

Jack Kerouac's restless novel *On the Road* garnered widespread attention when it hit the market in 1957 at around the same time that the *Howl* trial was capturing national headlines. It quickly became what writer Peter Tamony has called "the hip-pocket bible of the beat generation" (Tamony 1969, 274). Like Ginsberg and some other Beats, Kerouac had attended Columbia University, where malcontents shared their complaints about existing cultural norms. The semiautobiographical novel, which he wrote in three weeks, chronicled a trip across the United States and back. At the end of his actual trip, Kerouac reportedly arrived at his mother's New York residence and felt the need to walk around the block several times because he could not accept the fact that there was no more American land to traverse. While mimicking the spontaneity of jazz, his writing style mirrored the frenzy of his post-trip emotions. Part of the author's appeal to young American readers was his sense of isolation, which was conveyed through his frequent references to loneliness. During a 1959 appearance on *The Steve Allen Show,* Kerouac rejected the mainstream media's tendency to identify him as a Beat icon rather than a serious writer. Unlike Ginsberg, Kerouac found no allies among the leadership of the New Left in the 1960s; instead, he became known as a political conservative who isolated himself from his former colleagues and succumbed to chronic alcoholism. Despite the success of *On the Road,* Kerouac did not produce a broad literary legacy. When he died in 1969, he had written more than 20 books, but only *On the Road* remained in print.

Beatnik

The term *beatnik* did not become a familiar part of the English language until 1958. During the 1950s, "beat" had become a common term among jazz musicians, and *San Francisco Chronicle* columnist Herb Caen coined the term *beatnik* to define members of the Beat Generation. Caen built on Kerouac's choice of the word "beat" to define his generation and added "nik," a word fragment tied very specifically to the late 1950s, when the Soviet Union launched Earth's first artificial satellite, *Sputnik.* Use of "-nik" as a suffix was not new; Al Capp's contemporary comic strips had adapted the Slavic word for humorous purposes, referring to nogudnik, McNooknik, and Liddle Noodnik. Just two months after Caen's creation of the term, the *San Francisco Examiner* published two articles about "Life and Love among the Beatniks." Within weeks, the term had gained a place in the national and international vocabulary. The stereotypical beatnik frequented coffeehouses, liberally used slang, wore sunglasses indoors, and sported a beard.

Beat Talk

The Beat Generation introduced many slang terms that became a part of the American vernacular. This was especially true in the way Americans talked about illegal drug use. Thanks to the Beats, drug sellers became known as *dealers* who *pushed* drugs. Similarly, Americans followed the Beats in defining a dose of a drug as a *fix* and in labeling marijuana users as *heads*. A marijuana butt became widely known as a *roach*. When something disturbed someone, the Beats described that person as *bugged*. They also used *cop out* to indicate abandonment of one's ideals to conform with the majority and *far out* to express something's spectacular nature. By the close of the 1950s, some of these terms had worked their way into the language of American teenagers; others would gain common use in the next decade.

A Culture of Dissatisfaction

Unlike most Americans in the 1950s, the Beats had little trust in the nation's democracy. Disillusionment was central to their message. They had deep concerns about the state of the nation, and they voiced their feelings often. In *On the Road,* Kerouac wrote about "the end of America" and openly contradicted the image of the United States as a great nation. In *Naked Lunch,* William Burroughs wrote that "America is not a young land: it is old and dirty and evil" (Raskin 2004, 21).

The Beats raised concerns among some Americans of their era. Their anti-intellectualism put them at odds with many liberal commentators who shared their discontent with governmental and economic policies. Worried educators expressed fears about young people who chose to revolt against society instead of contributing to it. In a 1958 *Partisan Review* article, Norman Podhoretz described the Beat Generation as a group of "know-nothing" iconoclasts, and he voiced the belief that they were "hostile to civilization." He argued that they viewed the English language as "enemy territory" (Pells 1989, 277).

While much of the Beats' message was picked up by the student protest movement of the following decade, the Beats differed from their successors in many ways. They lacked the hope of the flower children, who called for a cul-

Were the Beats Spiritual?

Most historians have categorized the Beat Generation as a literary movement that challenged the ideas guiding American culture, and while their interest in Zen Buddhism has been noted, it has received little serious consideration. Most explorations of the Beat Generation can be found in literary analyses rather than religious studies. Religious historian Carl T. Jackson and Zen expert Alan Watts both characterized the Beats' religion as something less than authentic Buddhism. Watts, in fact, called it "phony zen." Nevertheless, religious historian Stephen Prothero argues that the Beats represented a spiritual movement often maligned because it rejected the Judeo-Christian religious establishment. He contends that much of the Beats' work was driven by a search for a new divinity and that they shared what John Clellon Holmes called "a perfect craving to believe . . . the stirrings of a quest." He suggests that they attempted to turn the streets of American cities into holy places. To support his argument, Prothero draws heavily on the Beats' writings, but he also notes their choice to see "Beat" as a shortened form of beatific, which gave their work a holy resonance. Prothero acknowledges a certain eclecticism in the Beats' spiritual beliefs, but he concludes that "in the Beat cosmos God is both absent and everywhere." Prothero rejects the narrow analysis of the Beats as literary adventurers and casts them as religious explorers (Prothero 1991, 207, 210, 219).

ture of peace and love, and they showed no eagerness to take their protests to the streets or to play an active role in the nation's political system. More than anything, anger, frustration, and disillusionment shaped the Beats' message. They did not seek a cure to the problems they saw.

GAYS IN THE CITY

Homosexual Americans experienced a transitional period during the 1950s. As a group, they made no great strides forward and won no new rights; however, by making efforts to establish networks, they began to develop a sense of community. It was a first step on a long and difficult road toward acceptance, and that first step often meant simply feeling pride in one's identity instead of accepting the shame that society assigned to them. Most still hid their homosexuality to avoid derision, job loss, or criminal charges. One of the movie industry's biggest stars, Rock Hudson, was a gay man who became the prototype of the tall, dark, and handsome romantic heterosexual leading man in films. Like gays all over the country, Hudson practiced subterfuge to hide the truth about his sexuality because he knew that his movie career would collapse if the public knew he was gay. Most homosexuals remained "in the closet" during this decade, but for many, that closet became a less lonely place as organizations and publications opened up a forum for the exchange of ideas and feelings among gay Americans.

At that time, San Francisco and New York offered the most comfortable homes for gay Americans. As magnets for nonconformists of all types, the two cities offered a refuge of sorts, where small enclaves of gays could gather in friendly bars and clubs. Those who came into these cities during the postwar years have been called "invisible immigrants" by historian Charles Kaiser. Typically, they were veterans or recent college graduates looking for a place to live where society's restrictions on gay life were a bit less rigid. Typically, they found gay and lesbian bars clustered in discrete neighborhoods. In other cities around the nation, similar establishments could be found but in smaller numbers.

Early in the decade, publication of *The Homosexual in America* marked a milestone for a group long hidden from public view. This 1951 book, written by Edward Sagarin under the pseudonym Donald Webster Cory, spoke up for the nation's gay community and called for an end to laws that attempted to criminalize homosexual behavior. The author urged Americans to stop practicing discrimination that forced gays to lead secret lives. Arguing that gays were in no way inferior, he also pointed out the growing weight of evidence that homosexuality was an inborn trait, not a choice. This intelligent, unemotional, and well-structured argument for gay normality may not have brought a swift change in heterosexual opinion, but it offered homosexual Americans an anchor in the storm.

Another important 1950s event for homosexual Americans was Dr. Evelyn Hooker's study of personality tests given to similar groups of heterosexual and homosexual men. When she asked three clinicians to separate the two groups' tests, they could not do it (Kaiser 1997, 124). Hooker's study triggered a series of studies that would show that, despite what many Americans assumed to be the case about gays and lesbians, there were no basic personality differences between heterosexual and homosexual Americans. Hooker's colleagues greeted her findings with derision, but she had laid the foundation for a more conclusive argument that gay Americans suffered from no basic personality flaw. Hooker provided one more piece of validation for self-doubting gays who dared to crack the closet door, although homosexuality remained classified as a psychiatric sexual disorder until 1973.

Public Conservatism about Sex

Sex was a carefully guarded subject for discussion in the 1950s. Although Alfred Kinsey's 1948 and 1953 reports on male and female sexuality had shown that plenty of Americans were participating, the nation embraced a prim public attitude toward the subject. On television, even heterosexual married couples slept in separate beds to avoid any sexy connotations that might arise from the presence of a double bed in the bedroom. TV executives allowed Lucille Ball's popular character, Lucy Ricardo, to have a baby, but they concluded that use of the word "pregnant" to describe her condition would be too graphic for primetime viewers. Given this discomfort with discussing sex in general, aversion to homosexuality was hardly surprising.

Homophobia was a part of American life. Analytic psychiatrists in the United States abandoned Freud's teachings and labeled homosexuality as an illness in 1952. Some saw homosexuals as a threat to the then-dominant middle-class view of normality—the nuclear family. Even in New York City, which was home to millions of people with diverse backgrounds, most newspaper references to homosexuals referred to "perverts" or "deviants." News coverage of gay life was generally limited to reports on sweeps of gay bars and the

James Baldwin, author of the semi-autobiographical Go Tell It on the Mountain *in 1953, encountered resistance when he sought a publisher for* Giovanni's Room *because of its homosexual subject matter. Nevertheless, the book was published in 1956. (Sophie Bassouls/Corbis Sygma)*

Times Square area where gay hustlers looked for customers. Although those arrested in a 1954 clean-up campaign pleaded guilty to disorderly conduct and paid only a $2 fine, the sense that the city was policing this allegedly strange behavior was news.

African American author James Baldwin had little difficulty getting Alfred A. Knopf to publish his semiautobiographical first novel, *Go Tell It on the Mountain,* in 1953. In it, he wrote about life as an impoverished boy in Harlem. However, Knopf refused to publish his second book, *Giovanni's Room,* which had a homosexual theme. "I guess they were scared. . . . Homosexuality wasn't on the books in those days and they turned it down," said the company's publicity director at the time, William Cole (Kaiser 1997, 73). Another publisher produced the book in 1956, and Baldwin continued to be one of the nation's leading African American writers for decades.

Gay Scare in Government

Homosexuals became a target of anticommunist government purges to eliminate potentially subversive people within the federal government. The U.S. Senate ordered a study of gays in government in June 1950, and the results were released by the Senate Subcommittee on Investigations in December of that year. The panel's report concluded that homosexuals and other people considered to be sexually deviant were not acceptable federal government employees for two reasons. First, the report argued, their very nature cast doubt on their moral rectitude; second, as potential blackmail victims, they could be security risks. Committee members accepted the theory that homosexuals were sick people in need of medical care. They believed that gay behavior symbolized diminishing moral fiber and that a homosexual employee was likely to surround him- or herself with other gays who shared the same weaknesses. In addition, Alfred Kinsey's *Sexual Behavior in the Human Male* had contended that homosexual activity was more common than previously thought. And Kinsey's controversial findings suggested that stereotypes of gay Americans did not apply to all of those who engaged in such activity. As a result, the panel members saw the threat of homosexuality as being even greater than they had feared.

The committee praised Civil Service Commission actions to block employment of homosexuals—a process that had uncovered 382 "sexual perversion" cases over the preceding seven months. The Civil Service Commission's position on homosexuals was explained in this way: "Regulations of the Civil Service Commission have provided that criminal, infamous, dishonest, immoral or notoriously disgraceful conduct, which includes homosexuality or other types of sex perversion, are sufficient grounds for denying appointment to a Government position or for the removal of a person from the Federal service" (Cory 1951, 269). In response to the government purge, Lee Mortimer, a *New York Daily Mirror* columnist, wrote several books on the topic, alleging that 10,000 gay federal employees remained on government payrolls. More than 60 suspected homosexuals had been ousted from government jobs each month between April and September 1950, compared with an average of five per month over the previous three years. Separations from the military for alleged homosexuality also rose by almost 100 percent in the 1950s, averaging 2,000 each year (D'Emilio 1983, 43–44).

The ongoing hunt for gays became an offshoot of McCarthyism. Some zealous investigators concluded that because gays were different, it was necessary to identify them and remove them from positions of influence. Mortimer's allegation that thousands of gays remained in government posts was not unlike Sen. Joseph McCarthy's famous and ever-changing mythical lists of Communists in the State Department. Ironically, one of McCarthy's most ruthless henchmen was Roy Cohn, a man who happened to be a homosexual.

Policing the Gay Community

Across the country, police focused on homosexuals as targets for arrest during the 1950s; however, enforcement of laws against "sexual perversion" was spotty. Wichita, Memphis, Dallas, Salt Lake City, Philadelphia, and Seattle were all the scenes of heightened police activity against homosexuals. Raids on gay bars spread panic in the homosexual community within several cities. An Institute for Sex Research study showed that one-fifth of gay men had experienced some negative interaction with police.

In Boise, Idaho, police conducted a 15-month investigation of the city's gay community after three men were charged with engaging in sexual activity with teenagers. The Boise police force interviewed 1,400 residents and pressured acknowledged gays to name other homosexuals. The probe led to an exodus of gay men from the city (D'Emilio 1983, 50–51). In most cities, action against gays was intermittent.

Homosexuality in Public Discourse

The Delaware River Port Authority (DRPA) decided in 1955 to give one-time Philadelphian Benjamin Franklin's name to an existing bridge between Philadelphia and Camden, New Jersey. To provide balance, the authority chose to name a new bridge connecting Philadelphia and Gloucester, New Jersey, after a famous person from southern New Jersey. The authority's choice, the 19th-century poet Walt Whitman, set off a loud debate led by the Camden Diocese of the Roman Catholic Church. The Reverend Edward Lucitt, speaking on behalf of several Catholic groups, wrote to the DRPA, saying that Whitman had been described in a recent biography as "homo-erotic." The Reverend James Ryan wrote three articles published in the *Catholic Star Herald* on the subject. The first, which appeared in November 1955, merely labeled Whitman as "unworthy" and did not identify him as gay. Instead, Ryan described Whitman using then-current code words such as "saccharine," which conveyed Whitman's true nature to the savvy reader. In his second article, he claimed that while some of Whitman's works were uplifting, others contained "baser, irreverent passages." Finally, in his third article, Ryan stated that Whitman used "revolting homosexual imagery" (Stein 2001, 138–144). The Church convinced many members to write letters protesting the name, and others wrote letters condemning a religious denomination's attempt to affect public policy. The DRPA reportedly considered renaming the bridge in honor of poet Joyce Kilmer. In the end, the bridge took Walt Whitman's name and became a staple in traffic reports without the slightest suggestion of sexual preference.

The 1950s Broadway play West Side Story *and its portrayal of an impossible romance between a white boy and a Puerto Rican girl found great resonance in the nation's gay community, which remained predominantly closeted in the 1950s. This photo shows Richard Beymer and Natalie Wood in the 1961 film version of the musical. (John Springer Collection/Corbis)*

West Side Story

The musical *West Side Story,* which debuted on Broadway in 1957 and went on to become an Academy Award–winning film in 1961, became an instant favorite among gay Americans. The play was based on the tragic love story of Shakespeare's *Romeo and Juliet;* however, in the updated version, the doomed lovers came from different cultures—Anglo and Puerto Rican. To many homosexual Americans, the play's impossible love story had a subtext that spoke about a time when gay love could be celebrated in the open.

The production was put together by three openly gay men—Jerome Robbins, Arthur Laurents, and Stephen Sondheim—and a fourth, Leonard Bernstein, who was conflicted about his sexuality. Robbins directed and choreographed the show; Laurents produced the book; Sondheim wrote the lyrics; and Bernstein, a married man who reportedly had gay sexual relationships, composed the music (Kaiser 1997, 214). Knowledge that the show's creators understood gay life led audience members to draw a different message from the story. For example, the song "Somewhere" can easily be read as a gay anthem. Below is an excerpt.

> There's a time for us,
> Some day a time for us,
> Time together with time to spare
> Time to learn, time to care,
> Someday!
> Somewhere,
> We'll find a new way of living,
> We'll find a way of forgiving
> Somewhere . . .

Author Charles Kaiser wrote that "thousands of gay Americans fell in love with *West Side Story* when they were children in the fifties. . . . To many gay adults coming of age in the sixties, the romance, violence, danger, and mystery so audible on the original cast album all felt like integral parts of the gay life they had embraced" (Kaiser 1997, 93).

Organizational Efforts

In the 1950s, gay Americans began organizing and communicating with one another at unprecedented levels. Groups often were secretive about their membership, and publications sometimes were passed along surreptitiously. Nevertheless, these developments marked an important step toward establishment of a gay rights movement. As gays began to see themselves as a minority group deserving of the same rights given to the majority community, they found broader grounds for discussion. However, it would be wrong to suggest that a separate gay community or gay culture existed across the United States. Instead, gays connected with one another through a loose network of contacts that often was limited by the threat of exposure. In addition to fearing that they might be identified as homosexual and suffer legal or social condemnation, gay Americans, like many others in the 1950s, feared that their organizations might be linked to radical politics, such as communism.

Against this background of fear, gays took their first tentative steps toward political and social organization on a national level. The most well-known organization was the Mattachine Society, which originated in Southern California. (The name seemed fitting because a medieval mattachine was a masked figure, hiding his true identity as many homosexuals hid their homosexuality in the 1950s.) Organized in secret cells like the Communist Party, the group promoted discussion of topics related to gay life, and at the same time, its cell-like structure guaranteed that no one member would know the names of all members. Establishment of the West Coast organization in 1951 was quickly followed by formation of a New York chapter. One of the organization's primary goals was to improve the gay American's self-image through development of pride in homosexuals' contributions to the nation's social and cultural achievements. At its founding, the society identified most gays as unaware of their minority group status. The society enabled isolated gay Americans to meet dozens of others who shared their orientation. While the organization continued to function in secret, it spun off a Citizens Committee to Outlaw Entrapment after one of its original members was arrested in 1952 by a plainclothes police officer. The committee distributed flyers on the case, which eventually ended with a hung jury. A year later, Mattachine cells began operation in San Francisco, Berkeley, and Oakland. In 1953, more conservative leadership took hold, replacing some of the original leaders who had links to the Communist Party. Mattachine now eschewed use of collective action to affect public policy. Instead, such action was considered to be an individual choice. Membership declined; only 42 people attended its annual convention in 1954. However, by the end of 1955, membership had begun to rise again.

Because the Mattachine Society was dominated by gay men, lesbians found little support there. The Daughters of Bilitis, founded in San Francisco in 1955, provided an opportunity for lesbians to meet and to discuss ways of educating society about lesbian life. It worked closely with the Mattachine Society in the "homophile movement." The Daughters of Bilitis placed its emphasis on self-help to achieve success in the working world and in society at large.

Gays Maintain Hidden Lives, Open Secret Dialogues

The efforts at organization within the gay community in the 1950s made very little impression on the majority population, which continued to define gays as "perverts" and to treat them as shadowy threats to the nation. To most Americans, homosexuals remained in the shadows, but among themselves, they began to establish a sense of community and a list of shared goals. Many probably expected to live their entire lives as closeted gay Americans, but contact with counterparts made it possible to promote pride that could replace decades of shame.

Gay organizations touched the lives of a relatively small group of homosexuals in urban areas during the 1950s, but publications spread newly emerging ideas across the country. *ONE*, which sprang from the early and more radical membership of the Mattachine Society, was produced beginning in January 1953 by a team of men and women who promoted an aggressive form of gay pride. It offered a forum for gays with a broad array of ideas about gay identity and gay culture. The *Mattachine Review*, produced by the organization's San Francisco chapter, first appeared in 1955. The *Ladder*, which began publication in late 1956, was produced by the Daughters of Bilitis. It featured a "Lesbiana" column that was an annotated list of literature—both fiction and nonfiction—about lesbianism. *ONE* openly attacked police harassment of gays, but the other two publications adopted a more low-key approach. They endorsed gay life without becoming confrontational. Because few homosexuals wanted to have gay publications mailed to their homes, circulation figures are not indicative of readership. A single issue may have passed through many hands. *ONE* could claim sales of more than 5,000 per month; the *Mattachine Review*, 2,200; and the *Ladder*, only 500. Nevertheless, the range of letters to the editor made it clear that these publications were reaching a nationwide audience, apparently passing through an invisible network.

BIOGRAPHIES

Catherine Bauer, 1905–1964

Public Housing Advocate

For most of her life, Catherine Bauer was a strong advocate of adequate housing for the poor. She believed that "modern housing" could be attainable for middle- and low-income Americans if it was planned carefully, constructed slowly, and offered only a minimum of amenities. Bauer, who had worked to establish public policy since her days as executive secretary with the Labor Housing Conference during Franklin Roosevelt's presidency, wrote about the growing struggle between different metropolitan agendas during the 1950s. She believed that urban planners, redevelopers, and housing experts had developed many useful tools by 1955 but had not yet settled on how to make good use of those devices because of local dependence on federal aid and federal regulations. She argued that those who were working to improve urban life needed to fight for federal aid without sacrificing local initiative and control (Bauer 1955, 102). Moreover, she contended that each city needed to adopt a unified vision of what it hoped to achieve for all of its residents. In the early 1950s, she believed urban programs had been unwisely driven by different goals. Housing interests sought to obey federal regulations to get aid, while redevelopment largely was ceded to downtown business interests, which placed a low priority on issues such as life in poor urban neighborhoods. She also asserted that jealousy between different city departments hampered the work of urban planning. She believed that local activism had the potential to create a more effective approach. Bauer provided housing advice to five presidents of the United States and served as a member of the faculty in the University of California at Berkeley's Department of City and Regional Planning.

William S. Burroughs, 1914–1997

Beat Generation Novelist

William S. Burroughs used his fiction to explore the themes of his own life, including homosexuality and drug addiction. For a while, he escaped the urban scene and farmed marijuana in Texas and then Mexico. In 1951, a drunken Burroughs attempted to shoot a glass off the head of his common-law wife, Joan Vollmer, and killed her. Tried in absentia, Burroughs received no prison sentence. The author, who had befriended Allen Ginsberg and Jack Kerouac in the 1940s, published his first semiautobiographical work, *Junkie,* in 1953. He wrote part of a sequel, *Queer,* in the early 1950s but did not publish it until 1985. His greatest success came with *Naked Lunch,* published in Paris in 1959 and in the United States in 1962. The book chronicled a drug addict's slide into Hades.

Burroughs wrote much of the manuscript in bits and pieces in a Tangiers hotel room between 1954 and 1957. Ginsberg helped to provide a structure for Burroughs's disjointed writing. The notorious book's publication in the United States sparked an obscenity trial in 1966, but the book later was transformed into a 1991 motion picture. Burroughs intermittently experimented with writing for the rest of his life.

Evelyn Hooker, 1907–1996

Psychologist

Evelyn Hooker was the first American psychologist to present empirical data countering the era's common assumption that homosexuality was a mental disorder. She became interested in the subject after befriending a gay man, and she applied for a six-month grant from the National Institute of Mental Health in 1953. She received the grant, and it was renewed through 1961. She tested 30 gay men and 30 straight men with similar IQs, ages, and levels of education. By using three standard personality tests, including Rorschach inkblots, she demonstrated that three expert clinical psychologists could not differentiate between the tests results of gay men and those of straight men. Hers was the first clinical project conducted with gay men who were not patients of some kind. In an era when most gays were closeted, she was able to get a healthy sample group with the help of the Mattachine Society. Her goal was to reveal that typical psychological tests recognized no disorder among the men who were gay. Her research drew skeptical responses at the 1956 American Psychological Association meeting; however, her conclusions soon were confirmed by the work of other researchers.

Irving Howe, 1920–1993

Intellectual, Writer, and Editor

As a cofounder and editor of *Dissent* magazine and a frequent contributor to *Commentary* and the *New Republic,* Irving Howe became one of the leading voices of leftist dissatisfaction with the urban policies of Dwight D. Eisenhower. Howe, who had a Ph.D. in English, joined the Brandeis University faculty in 1953 and remained there until 1961. During the 1950s, he authored *Sherwood Anderson: A Critical Biography, William Faulkner: A Critical Study,* and *Politics and the Novel during the 1950s.* As a widely recognized social critic, Howe argued against government policy aimed at reducing the federal government's involvement in urban life. He opposed Eisenhower's efforts to give state and local governments a bigger role in financing their own existence. Howe, who was a democratic socialist, wrote that President Dwight D. Eisenhower had too much confidence in continuing prosperity and that he overlooked the gaps in that prosperity. Howe often joined other left-wing intellectuals in the chorus of complaints about the decay of the nation's cities.

Ray Kroc, 1902–1984

Founder of McDonald's

Ray Kroc got the idea for a chain of drive-in restaurants in 1954 when he saw an efficiency-oriented restaurant in San Bernardino, California. That eating establishment was owned by Dick and Mack McDonald. With a limited menu and eight Multimixers milkshake machines that ran all day, the McDonald brothers had created a fast-moving, hamburger-producing operation that offered consumers quick service and low prices. Kroc, who was then the exclusive distributor of Multimixers, initially saw this sort of restaurant as a perfect customer for his product. Then, recognizing the opportunity for drive-in restaurants offered by the nation's continuing infatuation with automobiles and roads, Kroc went into business with McDonald's. He opened the first franchised restaurant in Des Plaines, Illinois, in 1955. Soon, restaurants began to spring up across the nation. Kroc bought out the two brothers in 1961. McDonald's later became the largest restaurant company in the world.

Richard C. Lee, 1916–2003

"Mr. Urban America"

Mayor Richard C. Lee of New Haven, Connecticut, was elected in 1953 on a platform that promised to revitalize the city. Soon after taking office, he organized a Citizens Action Commission to help him turn his promises into reality, and he became known in the 1950s as a leading opponent of urban blight. By the end of 1958, the relatively small city became the sixth-largest recipient of federal rehabilitation grants and the top per capita recipient. Lee also achieved an unusually good record in carrying out the projects once money had been received. He quickly drove projects through the phases of relocating inner-city populations, demolishing outmoded buildings, and erecting new structures in their place. Nicknamed "Mr. Urban America," Lee was a New Haven native who served as mayor from 1954 through 1970.

Robert Moses, 1888–1981

New York City Urban Planner

Robert Moses, who was neither an architect nor a planner, became the guiding force behind the redevelopment of New York City from the 1930s through the 1960s. Although he was responsible for construction of many major projects in

Urban planner Robert Moses was a leading proponent of urban redevelopment, often at the expense of poor neighborhoods. He contributed to many projects in the New York City area. (Library of Congress)

the nation's most populous city, Moses lost a battle in 1956 when he sought unsuccessfully to replace a forested play area in Central Park with a parking lot. In 1959, he again was defeated when he tried to prevent free presentations of Shakespearean plays in city parks; however, in that same year, he successfully resisted neighborhood complaints about the course of the Cross Bronx Expressway, which would eliminate at least 1,500 existing apartments. A strong advocate of public works, he held many public offices—often simultaneously. Among them were New York City parks commissioner, head of the State Parks Council, chairman of the Triborough Bridge and Tunnel Authority, and head of the State Power Commission. Moses's imagined New York was a striking collection of glittering towers with lush, expansive green parks. He envisioned efficient highways to avert traffic congestion and glorious beaches. Critics asserted that Moses's New York was not a city of neighborhoods where people lived; it was an object to be seen and admired from inside an automobile. After a long legal battle in the 1950s, Moses was able to seize 556 acres of land from the Tuscarora Indians for a New York State Power Authority hydroelectric project to serve the needs of proliferating urbanization. He is credited with leading development of the Triborough Bridge, the Verrazano-Narrows Bridge, the West Side Highway, the Jones Beach State Park, and the Long Island parkway system. He was nudged out of his city positions in 1959, and he became president of the upcoming 1964 World's Fair in New York. He held his state posts until 1968.

Edward Sagarin, 1913–1986

Author of *The Homosexual in America*

Using the pseudonym Donald Webster Cory, Edward Sagarin wrote the first significant book on the gay community in the United States. *The Homosexual in America* was published in 1951, and its publication was one of the key events in the 1950s that led to a more open gay community in New York City. "For the thousands of gay readers who discovered it at stores across the country, it was a revelation," according to historian Charles Kaiser (1997, 125). Declaring that homosexuality was an involuntary trait, Sagarin, a closeted homosexual with a wife and children, argued that gays comprised a minority group without leadership. He called for an end to all attempts to legislate rules governing sexual activity. In addition to authoring the book, Sagarin joined with Brandt Aymar, his editor, to operate a gay bookstore, Book Seller, in New York. Gore Vidal was one gay author who held a book signing in the store. Sagarin and Aymar also began a short-lived gay book club known as the Cory Book Service, which lasted about a year before running out of titles.

Kemmons Wilson, 1914–2003

Founder of Holiday Inn

Kemmons Wilson founded the Holiday Inn chain of motels in the 1950s. When he was on a family vacation to the nation's capital, it occurred to him that rapidly increasing car ownership and highway construction would create a market for a new kind of motel that offered tidiness, good service, and delicious food. Previously, motels had been rather rustic, and Wilson decided to change that. Already a millionaire, Wilson opened the first four Holiday Inns in Memphis in 1952. He appropriated the name from a 1942 Bing Crosby/Fred Astaire movie musical, *Holiday Inn*. In 1955, Wilson founded the International Association of Holiday Inns, a group of franchisees and employees with the goal of maintaining the same standard of hospitality in motels around the world. When interstate highways began to spread through the country late in the decade, his franchisees followed the well-traveled roads, planting Holiday Inns across the nation over the years to come. At the phenomenon's peak, a Holiday Inn opened every 2.5 days somewhere around the world.

REFERENCES AND FURTHER READINGS

Acosta-Belén, Edna. 1988. "From Settlers to Newcomers: The Hispanic Legacy in the United States." In *The Hispanic Experience in the United States: Contemporary Issues and Perspectives,* ed. Edna Acosta-Belén and Barbara R. Sjostrom. 81–106. New York: Praeger.

Bauer, Catherine. 1955. "Housing, Planning and Public Policy." *Marriage and Family Living* 17 (2): 101–102.

Berge, Stanely. 1964. "Why Kill the Passenger Train?" *Journal of Marketing* 28 (1): 1–6.

Bogue, Donald J. 1955. "Urbanism in the United States, 1950." *American Journal of Sociology* 60 (5): 471–486.

Breines, Wini. 1994. "The 'Other' Fifties." In *Not June Cleaver,* ed. Joanne Meyerowitz. 229–262. Philadelphia: Temple University Press.

Charters, Ann. 2001. "Introduction." In *Beat Down to Your Soul: What Was the Beat Generation?,* ed. Ann Charters. New York: Penguin Books.

Cortés, Carlos E., ed. 1980. *Regional Perspectives on the Puerto Rican Experience.* New York: Arno Press.

Cory, Donald Webster (pseudonym for Edward Sagarin). 1951. *The Homosexul in America: A Subjective Approach.* New York: Greenberg.

D'Emilio, John. 1983. *Sexual Politics, Sexual Communities: The Making of a Homosexual Minority in the United States, 1940–1970.* Chicago: University of Chicago Press.

Davis, Cary, Carl Haug, and Joanne Willette. 1988. "U.S. Hispanics Changing the Face of America." In *The Hispanic Experience in the United States: Contemporary Issues and Perspectives,* ed. Edna Acosta-Belén and Barbara R. Sjostrom. 3–56. New York: Praeger.

Del Castillo, Richard Griswold. 1984. *La Familia: Chicano Families in the Urban Southwest, 1848 to the Present.* Notre Dame: University of Notre Dame Press.

Diaz, David R. 2005. *Barrio Urbanism: Chicanos, Planning, and American Cities.* New York: Routledge.

Ebner, Michael H. 1985. "Re-Reading Suburban America: Urban Population Deconcentration, 1810–1980." *American Quarterly* 37 (3): 368–381.

Fitzpatrick, Joseph P. 1971. *Puerto Rican Americans: The Meaning of Migration to the Mainland.* Englewood Cliffs, NJ: Prentice-Hall.

Fusfeld, Daniel R., and Timothy Bates. 1984. *The Political Economy of the Urban Ghetto.* Carbondale: Southern Illinois University Press.

Geospatial and Statistical Data Center. University of Virginia Library. http://www2.lib.virginia.edu/geostat/index.html (accessed May 21, 2006).

Grossman, James R. 1989. *Land of Hope: Chicago, Black Southerners, and the Great Migration.* Chicago: University of Chicago Press.

Healy, Patrick. 1974. *The Nation's Cities, Change, and Challenge.* New York: Harper and Row.

Hernández-Alvarez, J. 1968. "The Movement and Settlement of Puerto Rican Migrants within the United States, 1950–1960." *International Migration Review* 2 (2): 40–52.

Jackson, Kenneth T. 1985. *Crabgrass Frontier: The Suburbanization of the United States.* New York: Oxford University Press.

Kaiser, Charles. 1997. *The Gay Metropolis: 1940–1996.* Boston: Houghton-Mifflin.

Kirby, Jack Temple. 1983. "The Southern Exodus, 1910–1960: A Primer for Historians." *Journal of Southern History* 49 (4): 585–600.

Koslow, Philip, chief ed. 1999. *The New York Public Library African American Desk Reference*. New York: Stonesong Press.

Lane, James B. 1973. "Underground to Manhood: Ralph Ellison's *Invisible Man*."
Negro American Literature Forum 7 (2): 64–72.

Maloney, Thomas N. 1994. "Wage Compression and Wage Inequality between Black and White Males in the United States, 1946–1960." *Journal of Economic History* 54 (2): 358–381.

McKelvey, Blake. 1968. *The Emergence of Metropolitan America*. New Brunswick, NJ: Rutgers University Press.

McNichol, Dan. 2006. *The Roads That Built America*. New York: Sterling Publishing Co.

Moore, Harry T. 1960. "Enter Beatniks: The Boheme of 1960." In Albert Parry, *Garrets and Pretenders, a History of Bohemianism in America,* rev. ed. New York: Dover Publications.

Muhammad, Mother Tynetta. 1996. "A Brief History on the Origin of the Nation of Islam in America: A Nation of Peace and Beauty." NOI.org, http://www.noi.org/history_of_noi.htm (accessed February 1, 2007).

Pells, Richard H. 1989. *The Liberal Mind in a Conservative Age: American Intellectuals in the 1940s and 1950s*. Middletown, CT: Wesleyan University Press. Orig. pub. 1985.

Pérez, Lisandro. 1986. "Cubans in the United States." *Annals of the American Academy of Political and Social Science* 487, Immigration and American Public Policy: 126–137.

Polenberg, Richard. 1980. *One Nation Divisible: Class, Race, and Ethnicity in the United States since 1938*. New York: Viking Penguin.

Price-Spratlen, Townsend. 1998. "Between Depression and Prosperity? Changes in the Community Context of Historical African American Migration." *Social Forces* 77 (2): 515–539.

Prothero, Stephen. 1991. "On the Holy Road: The Beat Movement as Spiritual Protest." *Harvard Theological Review* 84 (2): 205–222.

Raskin, Jonah. 2004. *American Scream: Allen Ginsberg's* Howl *and the Making of the Beat Generation*. Berkeley: University of California Press.

Schnore, Leo F., and Harry Sharp. 1963. "Racial Changes in Metropolitan Areas, 1950–1960." *Social Forces* 41 (3): 247–253.

Sharp, Harry, and Leo F. Schnore. 1962. "The Changing Color Composition of Metropolitan Areas." *Land Economics* 38 (2): 169–185.

Stein, Marc. 2001. *City of Sisterly and Brotherly Loves: Lesbian and Gay Philadelphia, 1945–1972*. Philadelphia: Temple University Press.

Tamony, Peter. 1969. "Beat Generation: Beat: Beatniks." *Western Folklore* 28 (4): 274–277.

Teaford, Jon C. 1990. *The Rough Road to Renaissance: Urban Revitalization in America, 1940–1985*. Baltimore: Johns Hopkins University Press.

U.S. Census Bureau. 1975. *Bicentennial Edition Historical Statistics of the United States Colonial Times to 1970, Part 1*. Washington, DC: Government Printing Office. Also available at http://www2.census.gov/prod2/statcomp/documents/CT1970p1–01.pdf (accessed October 10, 2007).

Young, William H., and Nancy K. Young. 2004. *The 1950s*. American Popular Culture through History Series. Westport, CT: Greenwood Press.

The Nuclear Family and the Baby Boomer Home

OVERVIEW

The American family and the American home experienced dramatic transformations in the post–World War II years. Change occurred at all levels of the social ladder; however, it was most evident among the white middle class in the 1950s. As Americans launched into the century's second half, an unprecedented boom in childbirth was accompanied by an equally impressive boom in the construction of new homes. Home ownership came within reach of many middle-class and working-class families. And for the first time, many families experienced sufficient affluence to spend a significant amount of money on entertainment and other leisure activities.

Compared with their parents' generation, Americans in the 1950s married at a younger age, had more children, and spaced the births closer together. The number of children under five years old per 1,000 white American women rose from 419 in 1940 to 580 in 1950 and to 717 in 1960 (U.S. Census Bureau 1975, 54). Although many married women worked outside the home, most did not.

In the nation's early years, the family operated as an economic unit, with all family members working, often on a farm, in a workshop, or in a store. At that time, women took on specific responsibilities, and children began working at an early age. To an extent, this model survived in the working class after industrialization. Often, youths left school and took jobs to augment family income. However, during the late 19th century, the birth rate began to decline. Big families were no longer an economic asset and, in fact, could be an added drain on family income. Attempts to limit reproduction became common among the evolving middle class as white-collar employment expanded early in the 20th century. Not surprisingly, the birth rate declined even more under the stresses of the Great Depression.

As veterans returned from World War II and the nation experienced growing prosperity, many women continued to work outside the home, but the growing cohort of middle-class women found their households had no need for a second income. As a result, while many working-class women had little choice but to work, pursuing a career typically was an option chosen by middle-class women for their own fulfillment—an often-difficult choice in a house full of children. Frequently, new parents established a child-centered culture at home, but parents of older children sometimes found that rebellious teenagers caused cracks in the façade of peaceful domesticity.

In the booming postwar economy, prosperity touched the lives of most white Americans. The nation's income climbed more than 60 percent between 1947 and 1961, and the number of families with discretionary income increased by more than 100 percent during the same period (May 1988, 165). Managers' pay had risen 45 percent between 1939 and 1950, and production workers experienced an increase of more than 100 percent in the size of their paychecks (Palladino 1996, 101). Per capita income rose 35 percent between 1945 and 1960 (Breines 1992, 3). Though prevalent, this new affluence was by no means universal. The median income for white families was $3,445 in 1950, and it rose to $5,643 by 1959. However, for African American families, comparable figures showed a median income of just $1,869, creeping up to $2,917 at the end of the decade. In 1959, African American family incomes had not risen to the level white families enjoyed in 1950. The vast majority of African Americans were trapped on the economy's lowest rungs (U.S. Census Bureau 1975, 297).

Nevertheless, it was the white middle-class stereotype that shaped the public perception of American families and their values. Members of the African American middle class and the white working class had opportunities for occasional tastes of the life enjoyed by the white middle class, and they aspired to have more. However, life in the white middle class had its challenges, too. As women struggled with conflicting messages about the value of having a career and the importance of being stay-at-home mothers, men found that they faced new expectations as well. "Togetherness" became the watchword of many families.

Prosperity also changed the material world of many Americans as they became consummate consumers. New cars replaced used ones. New kitchen and laundry appliances changed daily routines, and televisions played an expanding role in the hours that Americans spent at home. By 1952, slightly less than 50 percent of American households owned televisions (Palladino 1996, 101), and by 1960, that number had risen to 87 percent (Englehardt 1995, 133). Even some poor families invested in new tokens of prosperity like televisions.

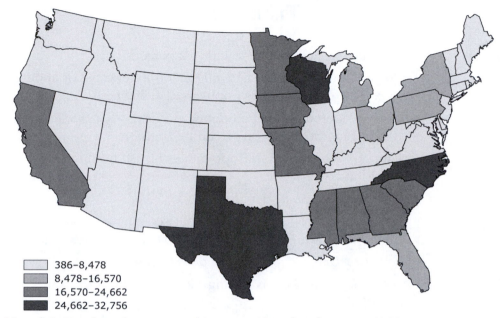

Map 4.1 *Number of women working unpaid in their homes in 1950.*

386–8,478
8,478–16,570
16,570–24,662
24,662–32,756

At the same time, more Americans became owners of their own homes. While only 55 percent of families were homeowners in 1950, 61.9 percent of families lived in their own homes by 1960. More than 78 percent of families living in detached homes owned them in 1960, an increase of more than 5 percentage points over 1950 (U.S. Census Bureau 2004). Many of these new homeowners bought houses in the burgeoning suburbs, some of which rose virtually overnight because they were constructed with prefabricated materials. In 1950, 84 percent of households reported less than one person per room—a far cry from crowded life in small farmhouses and urban tenements of earlier generations (Jackson 1985, 243).

From all appearances, Americans were prospering and enjoying the fruits of their labors. However, there were voices of warning in the United States. *The Lonely Crowd,* a 1953 study by three social scientists, argued that Americans were losing their individuality in postwar "togetherness" and becoming anonymous figures in a silent and faceless crowd. David Reisman, Nathan Glazer, and Reuel Denney contended that Americans once had set their own course through life as inner-directed individuals. However, in the middle of the 20th century, they concluded, Americans had become other-directed conformists who followed a course set by their peer group. Lost in a corporate bureaucracy or isolated in the repetitive cycle of suburban housework, Americans faced the possibility that they were losing something vital as their material wealth grew.

TIMELINE

1950   Illiteracy reaches all-time low of 3.2 percent.

Movies attract approximately 60 million Americans, or about 40 percent of the nation's population, each week.

Marilyn Monroe makes film debut in *The Asphalt Jungle;* Marlon Brando debuts on screen in *The Men.*

Stand-up comedian Bob Hope moves his act from radio to television.

The Steve Allen Show debuts on TV.

Television networks broadcast Senate committee hearings on crime, which were led by Tennessee Democrat Estes Kefauver.

Betty Crocker's Picture Cook Book is released.

The Diners Club begins issuing the first credit cards in the United States.

First *Peanuts* comic strip appears.

1951   Health experts promote the use of fluoride in drinking water to diminish tooth decay.

CBS broadcasts the first color show in the history of commercial television in June.

Newsman Edward R. Murrow's televised *See It Now* debuts.

I Love Lucy, which would become a prototype for family-oriented situation comedies, joins CBS's television lineup.

Earl S. Tupper begins marketing Tupperware kitchen storage products.

J. D. Salinger releases his novel *The Catcher in the Rye.*

Cleveland disc jockey Alan Freed begins spotlighting rock 'n' roll music.

1952   Republican vice-presidential candidate Richard Nixon delivers his famous "Checkers" speech—the first use of television for political damage control.

Jonas Salk starts testing of polio vaccine.

A show that would become Dick Clark's *American Bandstand* premieres in Philadelphia.

The crime drama *Dragnet* makes the leap from radio to television.

A housing development in St. Louis becomes the first to advertise central air-conditioning in all units.

1953

Lucy Ricardo, played by actress Lucille Ball, gives birth on *I Love Lucy* in one of the most widely viewed TV episodes ever.

Compared to 1950, three times as many television stations now schedule regular programming.

The total number of television stations now stands at 300.

Alfred Kinsey publishes his second sex study, *Sexual Behavior in the Human Female.*

Marlon Brando stars in *The Wild One.*

1954

Sun Records releases Elvis Presley's first commercial recordings in July.

Tupperware executive Brownie Wise becomes the first woman to appear on the cover of *Business Week.*

1955

Dr. Jonas Salk's polio vaccine is declared safe, and millions of children are vaccinated.

Disneyland opens in Anaheim, California, in July.

The August release of Chuck Berry's "Maybelline" attracts interest in rock 'n' roll.

RCA Victor buys Elvis Presley's contract.

Actor James Dean, star of this year's *Rebel Without a Cause,* dies in a September motor vehicle accident. He becomes a cult hero.

Mad magazine begins publication.

Squeaky-clean Pat Boone, sometimes seen as the anti-Elvis, has his first No. 1 single, a remake of Fats Domino's *Ain't That a Shame.*

1956

Presley makes his first TV appearance on *Stage Door.* Based on public response, Ed Sullivan signs Elvis to appear three times on his variety show.

U.S. Senate Judiciary subcommittee releases critical findings on the dangers of comic books, television, and motion pictures to young Americans.

Bill Haley and His Comets portray themselves in *Rock Around the Clock,* a film based on their 1955 hit record.

1957   *West Side Story,* the acclaimed musical about opposing youth gangs, debuts on Broadway.

Sixteen-year-old singer Paul Anka scores a hit with "Diana," a song he wrote as an ode to his babysitter.

1958   Presley joins the U.S. Army as a private.

American Express expands affluent consumers' buying power with new credit cards.

Hula Hoops become gigantic youth fad.

Stereophonic records go on sale.

1959   The baby boom, which peaked in 1957, helps to boost the U.S. population to 179 million. That reflects an 18 percent jump from 1950's total and demonstrates the most rapid population increase since the 20th century began.

The number of youths attending school jumps to 79 percent of the population between the ages of 5 and 19—an increase of more than 50 percent over 1950.

A typical worker's pay reaches nearly $5,000—an increase of 61 percent over 1950.

Richard Nixon and Nikita Khrushchev debate the value of U.S. consumer goods versus Soviet missiles in a U.S. exhibition in Moscow. The debate takes place in a model American kitchen.

A federal investigation uncovers corruption in television quiz shows.

BABY BOOM FAMILIES

Family life changed in fundamental ways in the 1950s. Marriage became a stronger expectation, and more Americans exchanged wedding vows than at any time in history. Only 27.4 percent of women between the ages of 20 and 24 remained single in 1960. Instead of waiting to marry, many young people tied the knot when they were still in their teens. By 1950, the median marriage age for men, which stood at 26.7 in 1890, had dropped to 22.8. For women, the median age had declined from 21.3 in 1930 to 20.3 in 1950. By the end of the 1950s, 24 percent of 18-year-old girls were married (Palladino 1996, 169). At the same time, the divorce rate had slowed to a trickle; among the ranks of females over the age of 14, only 8.9 women per thousand were divorced. The divorce rate had risen in the 1920s, declined during the economic hardships of the 1930s, and climbed again during and immediately after World War II. In 1946, a record

17.9 divorces per 1,000 married women were recorded, but a decline began the following year and continued through 1958, when divorces hit a postwar low (Weiss 2000, 4, 179).

Some couples married early in response to memories of the insecurity and separation brought on by the Great Depression and World War II. The Korean conflict also contributed to this trend as couples rushed to the altar before young men's deployment on the Asian peninsula. Another factor that probably contributed to early marriages was societal opposition to premarital sex. Alfred Kinsey's 1948 report on male sexual activity and his 1953 work, *Sexual Behavior in the Human Female,* offered new insights on the role of sex in American private lives and showed that about 75 percent of males had sexual intercourse in their teens (Reiss 1961, 55–56). In addition, 50 percent of surveyed women admitted to engaging in sexual intercourse before marriage (Mintz and Kellogg 1988, 201). However, marriage had a practical value to young Americans: It gave society's stamp of approval to an active sex life.

Historian Elaine Tyler May has argued that a new ideology specifically aimed at controlling sexual activity promoted marriage, large families, and togetherness in the 1950s (May 1988, 174). Obviously, societal pressure to keep women in the home meshed with the concept of having multiple small children within a mother's care. Moreover, the baby boom sprang from greater prosperity, including a 30 percent rise in real wages during the 1950s (Young and Young 2004, 5).

Racial conflict, Communist subversion, and nuclear war lurked in the shadows outside white suburbanites' split-level homes. The prospect of a family and togetherness promised stability in a time of change when homes became fortresses where Americans took shelter from the rapidly morphing outside world. Newly married middle-class couples often began their families immediately while the husband was still pursuing a college degree. Almost one-third of American women had their first child while in their teens (Mintz and Kellogg 1988, 178). Giving birth every year was not considered unreasonable during the era, although it did place a heavy strain on the family's financial position. Women who became adults during the 1930s gave birth to an average of 2.4 children, while their counterparts in the 1950s had 3.2 children (May 1988, 136–137). Families with three, four, or five children were becoming more common. Women's magazines were filled with jeremiads on togetherness. Family vacations, backyard barbecues, and shared meals were important steps toward that goal.Women who chose to give up careers so that they could be housewives faced the prospect of a short period of intense mothering followed by years with time on their hands. Those who married early faced the reality that they probably would live for at least 40 years after their children had reached school age (Kaledin 1984, 36). In addition, they were likely to spend years as widows because men were more vulnerable to accidents and to diseases such as heart disease and cancer (Mintz and Kellogg 1988, 173).

New Ideal Family

The family model of the 1950s did not follow previous or subsequent patterns; however, its development was not accidental. Parenting manuals and marriage guides offered countless examples of expert advice on the importance of marriage and families and reinforced the trend toward earlier marriages and larger families. In fact, unmarried women as young as 21 sometimes were labeled "old maids," and a husband and wife without children were considered pitiful or aberrant.

In the *Modern Pattern for Marriage,* Walter Stokes argued that "emotionally mature and responsible young couples who are deeply in love may often feasibly enter marriage at an early age, perhaps seventeen or eighteen" (Weiss 2000, 23). Many young wives worked while their husbands went to college or vocational school under the GI bill. In both 1950 and 1960, the average man between 25 and 29 had some education beyond high school, a significant jump from 1940 when the average man in that age group had a little more than a 10th-grade education. And many young wives were affected by husbands' educational pursuits (U.S. Census 1975, 381). Marriage provided these young people with recognition as adults, even though they often had to depend on money from their parents to make ends meet. Having children contributed to a healthy society in the eyes of many Americans. Marriage advocate Louisa Randall Church contended that parenthood represented a part of good citizenship. And some experts, such as psychiatrist O. Spurgeon English and coauthor Constance J. Foster, urged parents to share parenting more equally.

The best-known source of parenting advice was Dr. Benjamin Spock, whose 1946 book, *Baby and Child Care,* remained popular among parents in the 1950s. He strongly supported women's choice to stay in the home. While not encouraging outright permissiveness, Spock urged parents to avoid developing strict, rule-laden households in which children faced the challenges of authoritarian parents. He also advocated an expanded role for fathers, beginning in the child's infancy. "He'll feel more bashful about pushing his way into the picture later," Spock explained (Weiss 2000, 88).

This new role for fathers changed their perceived position in the family. Because men generally interacted with children on weekend projects or vacations, fathers became less associated with family leadership and more closely tied to the idea of family fun, according to Newburn Sedam. A study by sociologists Theodore Johannis Jr. and James M. Rollins found that most respondents saw men as family leaders but not family bosses (Weiss 2000, 43–44).

Some advisers on family life counseled parents not to lose sight of each other as they developed a child-centered household. Helen P. Glenn warned that inattention to the marriage itself could lead to trouble. Although divorce rates were low, dissolution of unhappy marriages was seen as a positive step by some. In the advice manual *Marriage Is for Two,* Frances Strain supported divorce, saying,

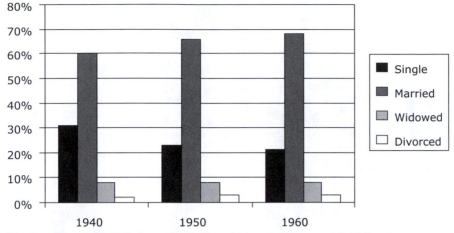

Figure 4.1 *Marital Status of U.S. Population 14 Years and Older. Source: U.S. Bureau of the Census. 1975. "Marital Status of the Population, by Age and Sex: 1890–1970."* Bicentennial Edition: Historical Statistics of the United States Colonial Times to 1970, 20. *Washington, DC: Government Printing Office. Also available at http://2www.census.gov/prod2/statcomp/documents/CT1970p1-01/pdf.*

"Human life is too short, happiness too rare, unhappiness too destructive in this troubled world to ask any man or woman to live out together an empty and unproductive existence" (Weiss 2000, 183). Marriage and family were intended to bring happiness and stability; when they did not, couples faced a choice between staying unhappily married or accepting the stigma of divorce in a marriage-happy culture. The pressure to conform and remain married ran counter to the trend that placed greater emphasis on fulfillment and satisfaction in the lives of both men and women.

Housewives and Mothers

Young women of this era confronted both subtle and all-too-obvious pressures to marry and have children. About one-fourth of all female college students married during the mid-1950s, and many of them dropped out of school (Weiss 2000, 28). For most of these women, an early pregnancy marked the dividing line between a life of individual endeavors and life largely devoted to the communal needs of a family. Surveys at this time showed that middle-class women demonstrated a clear preference for working at home, and among women working outside the home, only 60 percent enjoyed self-esteem from their work life (Breines 1992, 53).

In the modern home, mothers faced new, time-consuming duties that often intensified the drudgery of their daily lives. New appliances, cookware, and food

A photo from a Westinghouse advertisement shows a stereotypical mother and child in a spotless kitchen equipped with a variety of electric appliances, ca. 1950. (National Archives)

products made food preparation less time-consuming than it had been in the previous generation; however, the typical housewife now faced more demands for cleaning and higher expectations than her mother had encountered. Prosperity brought larger houses, which increased opportunities for women to demonstrate their cleaning and organizational skills. In some places, the development of all-white suburbs isolated from urban mass transit also made it difficult for married women to hire domestic servants, although large numbers of African American women still earned an income in these jobs, particularly in the South. As they faced the challenge of making housekeeping a career, women raised their standards. Because many homes now had washing machines, clothes were washed more often, usually after being worn only once. Vacuum cleaners demanded frequent use to banish dust. Newly bought freezers were grand additions, but they added to women's workload because of the need to defrost them regularly. For mothers with school-aged children and access to an automobile, part of the day was consumed by chauffeuring duties as they delivered their youngsters from school to ballet lessons and Little League games. Increased automobile traffic made skittish mothers less likely to ask their children to walk to their after-school activities. Many women had two or three children still wearing cloth diapers. And a study by William Dyer and Dick Urban on the roles of parents found that although many chores were shared, women remained re-

Did Media Limit Women's Choices?

Looking back at the 1950s, many historians have accepted an argument that Betty Friedan made in her 1963 book, *The Feminine Mystique.* Based on an examination of fiction in women's magazines, Friedan argued that the era's mass media, particularly American magazines, pressured women to restrict themselves to life as housewives. However, Friedan's assertion has been challenged in recent years. Subsequently, historians have examined magazines' nonfiction offerings and found no evidence that magazines as a group opposed outside careers for women.

Historian Joanne Meyerowitz made a systematic study of "middlebrow" magazines, such as *Reader's Digest,* "highbrow" publications, such as *Harper's,* African American periodicals and women's magazines. Her examination of 489 nonfiction articles found a wide range of articles that supported working women, although the magazines also published articles that cast a positive light on those who chose to be stay-at-home mothers. Meyerowitz discovered many articles that praised working women and expressed admiration for their efforts to overcome obstacles and achieve career success. She also found that only 15 percent of articles profiling women placed their focus largely on women's roles as wives and mothers. Many articles also promoted the idea of marriage as a partnership (Meyerowitz 1993, 1461). Historian Jessica Weiss reported similar findings in a study of 34 articles published between 1950 and 1972. What she uncovered was support for women whose wages helped their families to lead a better life. Some articles backed outside jobs only after all of the children had reached school age, but as long as there was no sign that a woman was ignoring her children's needs to satisfy her own, working women received encouragement. Both of these studies concluded that magazines, which played a significant role in the middle-class home, were not a monolithic, antifeminist force in the 1950s.

sponsible for addressing youngsters' physical needs (Weiss 2000, 39). In other words, most fathers dodged diaper duty.

To cope with the rigors of housework and the mental toll of following a boring routine, some women "professionalized" the job of housewife. By setting high ideals for themselves and investing their self-esteem in the quality of their work, they were able to declare themselves satisfied with life as a homemaker. However, once their children reached school age, these women faced a potential crisis as their full-time profession became only a part-time job. One solution was having more children; another was seeking part-time or full-time work outside the home. By 1960, more than one-third of women between the ages of 25 and 34 worked outside the home (Weiss 2000, 50). Some married women returned to work to seek new challenges, but others just hoped to earn money for their children's college tuition. A 1957 survey of 247 married white homemakers in a southern town showed that most approved of women working unless they had small children at home (Shapiro 2005, 135). Some middle-class women also found fulfillment in community activities.

Many marriage guides reported greater equality in marital decision making. Psychiatrist Edmund Bergler wrote, "The relationship between the sexes is at present in a period of transition—between the full emancipation of women and man's smoldering rebellion against that emancipation." Indeed, while women still scrubbed bathrooms, the Institute for Human Development at the University of California at Berkeley conducted a study that confirmed women did share a larger role in household decisions (Weiss 2000, 18–20, 40).

Breadwinners and Fathers

Like mothers, fathers felt new pressures from parenting gurus during the 1950s. Many marriage experts advocated an expanded role for men in family life and in daily household chores. *Life* reported "the domestication of the American male" in 1954 (May 1988, 146). Indeed, men were beginning to share more household chores on an occasional basis, but most husbands consistently performed only three tasks—yard work, locking the house each night, and repairing broken household items.

In the workplace, most men experienced greater prosperity than they could have imagined in their youth; however, if that prosperity led to establishment of a suburban home, fathers also spent a great deal of time commuting to and from work. As a result, fathers sometimes found it difficult to live up to the ideal of family "togetherness." Men who became deeply committed to career advancement often had trouble finding any time even for this kind of shared activity.

Fatherhood was supposed to bring fulfillment to men, but fathers also had an important role to play in protecting society, according to psychiatrists and others concerned about the next generation of men. The dominant role of women in the home could result in a generation of "sissies," some argued, and therefore, the importance of a strong father figure was especially vital for boys. Many fathers attempted to establish close relationships with their children, although significant contact with their offspring often was limited to the weekends. Firing up the backyard barbecue was one common way in which fathers drew the family toward them. The kettle version of charcoal grills arrived in the marketplace in 1952, just in time for fathers to use them as tools in their effort to bolster family togetherness.

Baby Boomers

As a result of scientific and technological advancements, baby boomers were born in a safer world than their predecessors. They were the first babies to crawl within the protective walls of a playpen, introduced in 1955. And because of heightened understanding of infections and greater cleanliness in the home, they were less susceptible to diseases than the children who had come before. For most, illness was only a distant threat. However, thousands fell victim to polio in the decade's first half. Fortunately, many experienced a full recovery, and the successful effort to develop a polio vaccine provided an even more care-free existence for youngsters who lived beyond poverty's reach.

In the child-centered, middle-class home, many youngsters enjoyed early life in the bright sunshine of prosperity. With no requirement to work in the home or in a factory, they experienced a life with few responsibilities and numerous material treasures. As standards of living improved, working-class children also got a share of the toy bonanza. Whether they wore coonskin caps and pretended to be Davy Crockett or lovingly played mommy to a plastic doll, many children lived in a world filled with playthings. One best-selling book warned: "Mobile people have adopted the notion that you must eternally give to your children; otherwise, you are not a loving parent" (Mintz and Kellogg 1988, 185). In November 1955, Mattel introduced the new Burp Gun, which became so popular that President Dwight D. Eisenhower had to write to the company requesting one as a Christmas gift for his grandson. Mattel promoted the cap guns as being "modeled after the machine guns used in WWII jungle fighting." A million Burp Guns were given to eager boys and girls during that holiday season alone (Englehardt 1995, 148).

Often as children watched their TV heroes or read about valiant comic-book figures, they unknowingly became targeted as consumers. Many characters in popular culture created merchandising booms. TV Western hero Hopalong Cassidy promoted a radio show, a comic strip, cowboy outfits, guns, spurs, and holsters, as well as pajamas, towels, rugs, bedspreads, and candy, all of which bore the hero's name or image. Mothers often decorated children's rooms with likenesses of their heroes. Among the popular innovations in children's products during the 1950s were Hula Hoops, Matchbox toys, Silly Putty, and Mr. Potato Head. The Slinky, a simple coil of wire, had been introduced in 1945, but it gained popularity during the succeeding decade. The popular and fashionable Barbie doll arrived on the scene in 1959.

Polio Epidemic

By the 1950s, a killer and a crippler had stalked the United States for many years, striking hundreds of thousands of American children. New York City had come to expect a serious summer outbreak at least every five years. Parents lived in fear of seeing the first symptoms appear among their children. With little warning, the disease transformed healthy youngsters into handicapped Americans in a matter of days—a fact that was unacceptable even before so many American families adopted child-centered cultures. In the postwar years, polio was an enemy feared almost as much as the Soviet Union. The United States had experienced widespread outbreaks in the summers of 1944 and 1946. Then three rough years—1949, 1950, and 1951—came consecutively. In 1952, a record number of Americans fell victim to polio. Approximately 58,000 Americans contracted the disease in a year when it began striking down its victims in May and remained a threat until October (Mintz and Kellogg, 1988, 188).

In one Iowa family, 11 of 14 children contracted polio in short order. It began simply when a 16-year-old girl developed a fever. Her doctor recommended ice packs and she showed some improvement, but within two days, she reported a stiff neck as well as muscle and joint pain, the most telling symptoms of polio. Her parents had taken precautions to protect the children: They had not allowed them to swim in the community swimming pool; they had insisted that the youngsters wash up before eating; and they had tested their well water. Out of the 11 stricken children, 9 fully recovered, and 2 remained paralyzed. None died. However, in a Milwaukee family, 4 of 6 children were stricken, and all 4 died (Oshinsky 2005, 162).

The National Foundation for Infantile Paralysis conducted a yearly fundraising campaign called the March of Dimes, and in January 1954, the drive raised $50 million, breaking all previous records. News that Dr. Jonas Salk and others were trying to develop a polio vaccine helped to increase donations. While competing scientists continued to work, Salk conducted a clinical trial in 1954 in which 400,000 children were vaccinated. In the spring of the following year, the vaccine received approval for massive use. Millions of children were vaccinated, and public swimming pools were reopened that summer. By 1957, the United States suffered only 7,000 polio cases (Oshinsky 2005, 161, 189).

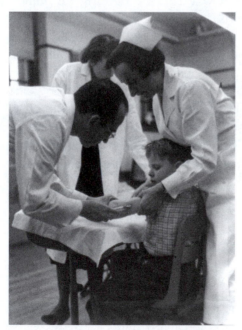

Dr. Jonas Salk, who created the first vaccine to stop polio's rampage among America's children in the 1950s, vaccinates a child in 1954. (Library of Congress)

After development of the vaccine, middle-class families could celebrate the slaying of a monster that had threatened their children; however, poor children remained vulnerable. In many cases, routine doctor visits were not a part of their lives. Because each child had to get three shots with intervening intervals for the initial vaccination and a booster shot every year, those without access to regular medical care were unlikely to undergo the full regimen required for the Salk vaccine to work properly.

Disneyland Opening

For children in the late 1950s, Disneyland was synonymous with dreams come true. Walt Disney's gigantic amusement park opened in July 1955. It promised imaginative visitors, both young and old, a memorable expedition into other worlds. Whether they chose Adventureland, Frontierland, Tomorrowland, or Fantasyland, visitors to the Anaheim, California, park took home memories of something rare. Disney attempted to transform the magic of his motion pictures and TV shows into something tangible—an interactive experience unlike anything else of that era.

On opening day, July 17, the line began to form at 2 a.m. Most of the eager visitors were not young baby boomers but adults eager to see what the park had to offer. Disney himself greeted the first two youngsters in line, a seven-year-old boy and a five-year-old girl. Some social critics condemned the park as a crass example of thinly camouflaged, raw capitalism, but others reveled in the midst of Wild West fights, water adventures, and robotic crocodiles that seemed to smile as they showed off sharp plastic teeth. Some reviewers complained that the prices were excessive, but attendance at Disneyland passed the 10-million mark by New Year's Eve 1957, and about two-fifths of the park's visitors had come from outside California (Marling 1991, 174). The nation's first theme park was a huge hit that earned a place high on children's wish lists.

Everyone entering the park had to walk through Main Street, Disney's nostalgic reproduction of the town where he grew up—Marceline, Missouri. As young visitors' minds raced ahead to the fun that awaited them, Walt Disney drew their parents' minds back to the days before much of America became a maze of suburbs, expressways, and parking lots. His affection for America's simpler days shone through Disneyland's razzle-dazzle. Recapturing a treasured past as he offered glimpses of imagined worlds, Disney created a prime example of 1950s culture—a mixture of technological wizardry, traditional values, and shared family fun.

Impact of 1950s Family Life

Family life in the 1950s laid the groundwork for change over the rest of the 20th century. The birth rate had begun to drop by 1957. None of the decade's other statistical marvels—a high marriage rate, early median age at marriage, and low divorce rate—would be long-lasting phenomena. The ideal of a protective fabric created by family togetherness never came to fruition, and despite popular memory of the fifties as a happy time of unquestioning conservatism, the short life span of this family ideal was predicted by some analysts of that era.

Late in the decade, the news media and women's magazines had begun to examine frustration, isolation, and restlessness among women. These articles ran under headlines like "The Mother Who Ran Away," "Is Boredom Bad for You?" and "Why Young Mothers Are Always Tired?" Already, women were beginning to play a bigger role in family choices, a fact that marketers acknowledged in advertisements showing women as decision makers or at least decision-making partners on big purchases such as cars and household appliances. A study of Florida teenagers found that 63 percent viewed their parents as a "joint decision making team" (Weiss 2000, 44). And in *Making the Most of Marriage,* Paul H. Landis predicted "increasing sex equality and role sharing in the relationship of men and women and greater cooperation and sharing in the experience of parents and children" (Weiss 2000, 17–18). In retrospect, some historians have seen the spark of feminism in the eyes of daughters who saw their mothers constrained by household drudgery. Social scientists have noted that parents during this decade treated boys and girls more equally than previous generations, thus raising girls' expectations.

At the same time, a great volume of literature criticized suburban family life. Among works of fiction and nonfiction were *The Split-Level Trap, The Man in the Gray Flannel Suit,* and *The Organization Man.* These books blamed suburban affluence and the bureaucratic workplace for perpetuating both isolation and conformity. Some authors even condemned what they saw as a dangerous matriarchy.

Despite outward signs of normality, adults of the 1950s saw intermittent glimpses of serious problems. Connecticut mothers reportedly were using alcohol and drugs to get through the day, and wife swapping was reported in San Francisco. Investigators were bringing child abuse and other evils into the light of day. For many adults, this was an age of anxiety that set the stage for a period of dramatic change.

For the children of the 1950s, toy purchases marked just the beginning of a decades-long shopping spree. Heroes like Davy Crockett and Hopalong Cassidy would fade from memory among a generation with a hearty appetite for change, but competition for the best "toys" would not end with childhood. The consumer culture and the information age would continue to expand as baby boomers aged and the generation's size would remain a factor in social change. Within a decade, many baby boomers would turn into rebels who no longer trusted authority figures.

EMERGENCE OF YOUTH CULTURE

The 1950s represented an important period when a youth culture began to evolve as something totally separated from adulthood. In the past, young people had seemed to pass almost seamlessly from childhood through adolescence and onward into adult roles. However, the growing number of students who finished high school, as well as expanding college attendance, created a strong delineation between often free-wheeling youth and the responsibilities of adulthood. The discrete boundaries between the stages of life made it easier for youths in their teens and early twenties to develop a culture of their own in which adults played little role. The shift toward a service economy, which created many part-time jobs for teenagers, allowed more teens to finish high school and maintain enough pocket money to partake in a youth culture that encompassed fashion, lifestyles, music, literature, movies, and language.

Alienation from adults was the culture's clearest theme. Young people in the 1950s sometimes were characterized as the "Silent Generation," and clearly most young people did not challenge the older generation in the streets by adopting radical fashions or radical politics. Nevertheless, the generation that came to maturity in the 1930s exhibited uneasiness with the role models chosen by their children. Some saw Elvis Presley's swiveling hips and James Dean's brooding rebelliousness as threats to domestic tranquility. During the 1950s, the older generation's discomfort often came to the fore in fears about juvenile delinquency's potential impact on the culture at large. At times, parental concern exaggerated the breadth of the problem, and these adult anxieties indicated fault lines between the generations.

The Beat culture of the 1950s represented an intellectual challenge to the established parameters of literature. Novelists and poets promoted a movement that rejected institutional culture and functioned outside its bounds. Allen Ginsberg was a leading poet in this loosely connected group of free spirits. Jack Kerouac, best known for his book *On the Road,* used a stream-of-consciousness writing technique to project spontaneity and valued instinctive actions above carefully honed crafts. There is some question about how many people in the youth culture truly absorbed the Beats' art, but bearded, sloppily dressed "beatniks" became a part of the urban scene in many cities.

The automobile, which young amateur mechanics often transformed into a personal fashion statement, played a significant role in the youth culture. Often, youths bought cheap models or used cars, which immediately provided an independent sphere free from adult intrusion. Young people liked to cruise areas where they could see and talk with their contemporaries. In drive-in movie theaters, the car, whether it was a souped-up hot rod or a generic economy car, became the site of sexual liaisons between young people who had no other place where they could be alone and away from adult supervision.

As Americans became more dependent on automobiles in the 1950s, drive-in businesses, such as this movie theater, gained popularity. Drive-in movie theaters became the venue of choice for sexual experimentation among many American teenagers. (Library of Congress)

Many diverse elements became part of the 1950s' youth culture. From the poetry of the Beats to the mumbling defiance of Marlon Brando in *The Wild One,* this culture became a piece of sovereign territory that young people controlled, often away from the prying eyes of worried parents. Within its confines, they determined their own tastes and their own mores, which is exactly what adults feared.

Teens as Consumers

The continuing expansion of the mass market helped in the development of a unique youth culture. A wide variety of magazines from *Seventeen* to *Hepcat* appealed specifically to teenagers and 20-somethings. Books, television programs, and movies targeted the new market of consumers who lived in the space between the playful days of childhood and the anxious years of adulthood. More than anything else, what became emblematic of this generation was its music. The blossoming of rock 'n' roll music in the 1950s established a genre that would continue, with variations, beyond the century's end. A product of African American rhythm and blues, what was once called "race music" captured the attention of white youths as they spun the radio dial and landed on urban African American stations. After white teens showed an interest, Alan Freed and other disc jockeys began featuring the music on stations appealing to a general audience of young listeners. Soon, Elvis Presley and other white performers helped to bring rock 'n' roll into the mainstream of youth culture. Their success opened the door for African American singers and musicians to cross the color divide and step out onto center stage within the era's mainstream youth culture.

Unlike the bland records their parents liked, this music, both subversive and sexy, led to dancing—and like Elvis, American youths often writhed with more than a hint of seduction in their steps. Rock 'n' roll was provocative, stimulating, and very different from what Doris Day and Perry Como were singing for adult audiences. Teenagers were explorers on a quest for new experiences. An adult favorite like "Doggie in the Window" offered no challenges and promised no discoveries. And it did not tempt listeners' hips to sway to the rhythm. Another part of rock 'n' roll's appeal was the simple fact that the singers often were no older than their listeners. This music was new—and it was theirs. As the beat made them dance, the lyrics helped to foster a language that was unique to Americans of their age group. In addition to undisguised sexuality, the songs often explored the pain of rejection and disillusionment, both of which were felt deeply by many adolescents in a culture that placed so much emphasis on young marriage. In previous decades, adults had set the rules for teen culture by sanctioning group activities and establishing media outlets, such as *Seventeen,* which were intended to prepare young people for adulthood. Teens' adoption of rock 'n' roll marked the end of adults' control over adolescent culture and the beginning of more widespread rebellion.

Young stars like Presley and Dean wore their hair long in "ducktails" and instead of sporting respectable khakis they wore tight jeans and leather jackets. When their fans imitated these outfits, some schools imposed dress codes. Seeing the way teenagers responded to the new stars alarmed adults, too. When Elvis sang, girls screamed and entire audiences stomped their feet to the music. He seemed dangerous, and that was a big part of his appeal. Many adults thought Presley's dancing was indecent, and seeing white crowds enthralled by African American performers also worried some parents who had never before considered themselves racist.

Television soon joined the bandwagon and staked a claim on youth culture. Several variety shows featured Elvis early in his career, and a Philadelphia television series became a national sensation featuring teenagers dancing to the music they loved. Under Dick Clark's orders, the dancers on his *American*

Table 4.1. Number One Hits at Beginning of Each Year

1955	"Mr. Sandman" by the Chordettes
1956	"Sixteen Tons" by Tennessee Ernie Ford
1957	"Singing the Blues" by Guy Mitchell
1958	"Let Me Be Your Teddy Bear" by Elvis Presley
1959	"The Chipmunk Song" by The Chipmunks and David Seville

Top Debuting Singles

1955	"Sixteen Tons" by Tennessee Ernie Ford
1956	"Love Me Tender" by Elvis Presley
1957	"Jailhouse Rock"/ "Treat Me Nice" by Elvis Presley
1958	"Twilight Time" by the Platters
1959	"I Need You Tonight" by Elvis Presley

Source: Joel Whitburn. 1991. *Billboard Top 10 Singles Charts,* Menomonee Falls, WI: Record ResearchWhitburn. The growing popularity of rock 'n' roll music is clearly evident at the decade's end.

Note: Billboard charts not available before 1955.

Bandstand dressed like perfect ladies and gentlemen. Clark made rock 'n' roll wholesome, and like a masquerading stowaway, the music moved into American households.

Catcher in the Rye

One of the sharpest portraits of teenagers' alienation toward adult society came in J. D. Salinger's landmark 1951 novel, *The Catcher in the Rye.* Although Salinger was in his thirties when he wrote the book, he captured young people's angst and ambivalence with remarkable clarity. The book, which has been compared to Mark Twain's *Huckleberry Finn,* revealed "the yearning for authenticity and innocence that marks the picaresque quest," according to historian Stephen Whitfield (1997, 574). Both *Catcher in the Rye* and *Huckleberry Finn* won critical praise and provoked calls for censorship among conservatives. One observer noted that *Catcher in the Rye,* which quickly earned a place in high school classrooms, "had the dubious distinction of being at once the most frequently censored book across the nation and the second-most frequently taught novel in public high school" (Salzman 1991, 15). Those who sought to ban the book expressed outrage about its crudeness and profanity, and they believed it was an attack on the American way of life. In 1956, the National Organization for Decent Literature condemned the book, but there was little chance of keeping young readers away from this novel. Despite widespread criticism, it became part of a middle-class tradition by being designated as a Book-of-the-Month-Club offering. Young readers found resonance in the words of the book's narrator, Holden Caulfield, as he voiced contempt for "phony" elements of bourgeois middle-class culture. His sentiments had the ring of authenticity, and yet it was clear that Caulfield would take no action to improve his environment because he was trapped in a tangled web of futility and apathy. Caulfield's alienation from society was not unlike the point of view expressed by the Beats.

Movie Rebels

More than a few movies in the 1950s focused on juvenile delinquency, a reflection of the decade's romanticization of rebellion. Although these works generally failed to make a clear statement about this dreaded scourge, many of the movies were condemned for their content. Among the most notable were 1953's *The Wild One,* starring Marlon Brando and Lee Marvin as leaders of competing motorcycle gangs, and 1955's *The Blackboard Jungle,* which chronicled teenagers' defiance within a high school in a poor New York City neighborhood. The star who became the most recognized symbol of youthful alienation was James Dean. The handsome Dean starred in only three films and received Academy Award nominations for two of those roles. In 1954, his second role on the Broadway stage helped him to win a starring role in the film *East of Eden,* which premiered in April 1954. He next starred in *Rebel without a Cause* in 1955. Dean, who liked to race cars, was killed in an automobile accident in September 1955, when he was 24. His third major film, *Giant,* debuted in 1956, more than a year after his death. Almost immediately after his demise, Dean became a cult figure among young people. In his biography of Dean, Joe Hyams wrote, "There is no simple explanation for why he has come to mean so much to so many people today. Perhaps it is because, in his acting, he had the intuitive talent for expressing the hopes and fears that are a part of all young people" (Hyams 1992, 270).

Elvis Presley's Debut on National Scene

Though he made his first commercial recordings in 1954, Elvis Presley really burst onto the national stage in 1956. During that year, he appeared on the mainstream television variety program *The Ed Sullivan Show* and churned out a string of hit records, including "Heartbreak Hotel," "Blue Suede Shoes," "Hound Dog," "I Want You, I Need You, I Love You," and "Love Me Tender." Presley's oily ducktail and gaudy clothes were as much a part of his image as his rhythm-and-blues singing style. Some viewers of Sullivan's show complained about Presley's dancing in his first two appearances on the program, so cameramen for his third appearance focused on the often-pugnacious Elvis from the waist up. Even with his hips deleted, Elvis drew record audiences to Sullivan's show, and he made his mark on the big screen with his first movie that year, too. His im-

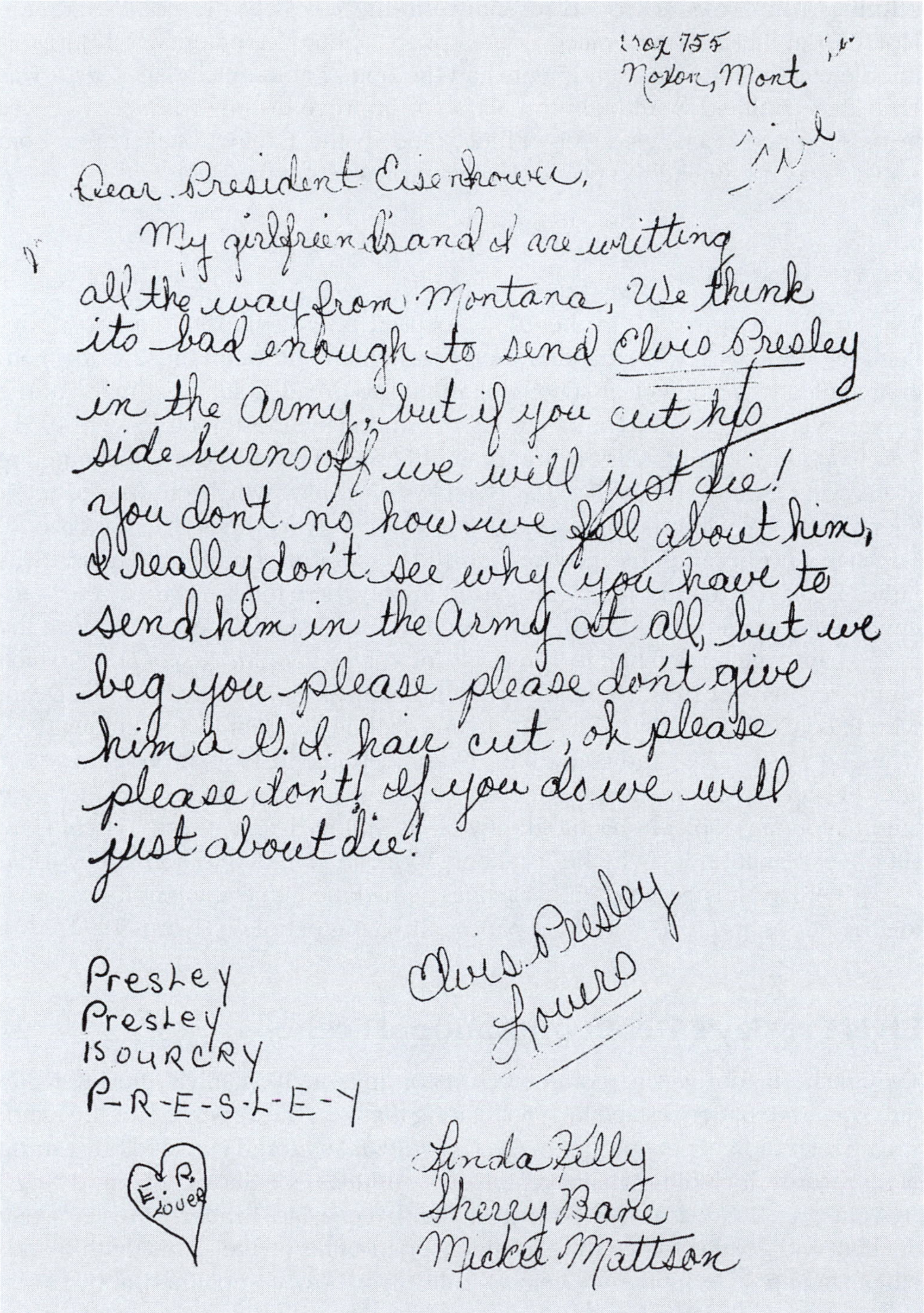

Box 755
Noxon, Mont.

Dear President Eisenhower,

My girlfriend and I are writting all the way from Montana. We think its bad enough to send Elvis Presley in the Army, but if you cut his side burns off we will just die! You don't no how we feel about him, I really don't see why you have to send him in the Army at all, but we beg you please please don't give him a G.I. hair cut, oh please please don't! If you do we will just about die!

PresLey
PresLey
Is ouR cRy
P-R-E-S-L-E-Y

Elvis Presley Lovers

Linda Kelly
Sherry Bare
Mickie Mattson

When Elvis Presley was drafted, some frantic girls appealed to President Dwight D. Eisenhower to intercede. In this 1958 letter, a fan asks the president to spare Elvis's distinctive sideburns. (National Archives) pact on youth culture was huge: He sold 10 million records in 1956—more than 10 percent of all units sold in the entire recording industry (Palladino 1996, 129). He became a fashion icon for teenage boys, and girls wore skirts decorated with his portrait. Presley's career hit a detour in March 1958 when his draft board called. Elvis got a buzz-cut and donned a uniform as a member of the U.S. Army. He served in the United States and West Germany until 1960. Afterward, he made millions of dollars through recordings, movies, and spinoff products; however, he never regained the singular status that was his in the mid-1950s.

Folk Music

Rock 'n' roll was not the only form of modern music to strike it rich at this time. Folk music experienced a revival during the late 1950s, with the Kingston Trio's "Tom Dooley" selling nearly four million copies in 1958–1959. This genre of popular music often reached its fans through the work of independent record companies. Newsletters, magazines, and folk clubs of various types added solidarity to this movement, which continued growing into the early 1960s with the ascendance of groups such as Peter, Paul, and Mary.

Traditional ballads provided the foundation for folk music, but songs with an old-fashioned style often were used to voice quite modern and sometimes subversive political opinions. Folk music found wide acceptance on college campuses, where a growing number of students favored fundamental political change that would support individuality and peace. Folk-music groups popped up on many college campuses. These folksingers followed in the footsteps of artists like Woody Guthrie and the African American Leadbelly, who were folk artists in the 1930s. Some early folk artists, including Guthrie, used traditional music as a form of protest. Guthrie was blacklisted under McCarthyism. Pete Seeger, a member of the 1940s' folk quartet known as the Weavers, was called before the House Un-American Activities Committee in 1955 and experienced a declining audience; by the end of the decade, his performances were limited to college campuses and urban coffeehouses. Similarly, actor and singer Paul Robeson, who included African American folk ballads in his concerts, found his rights and his career restricted in the 1950s because he had embraced leftist politics.

Folk music was not limited to protest music. Some urban folk fans developed affection for bluegrass music in the 1950s. This form of music, which relied heavily on fast-playing banjo and guitar artists, had debuted in the 1940s with Bill Monroe's band, the Blue Grass Boys. Bluegrass college concerts became popular during this era. While bluegrass music of this era was not widely featured on radio stations, traditional country music survived on the air in the polished "Nashville Sound" that featured a lead singer performing on a sound stage supported by a chorus and string instruments.

New Terms in the Teen Vocabulary of the 1950s

Dig = Understand

Bread = Money

Hip = Up to date

Square = Not hip

Cool = Nonchalant and/or
  admirable

Stoned = Intoxicated

Getting carded = Having your
  age checked

Six-pack = A package of beer
  bottles or cans

Fear of Juvenile Delinquency

Many adults in the 1950s wrongly believed that the nation was in danger of falling victim to widespread juvenile delinquency. Marynia Farnham spoke for many people in her 1951 book, *The Adolescent,* when she wrote that young people "seem to be out of gear with the rest of society. They have become a problem" (Cohen 1997, 254). Some people believed that prosperity had spoiled American teenagers. While the fearful envisioned gangs of violent youths, teenagers were more likely to commit crimes of defiance than crimes of violence. A 1957 report of juvenile crime in several American cities showed that violent crimes did not top the list in any city. Property crimes were at the top of the list in New York, while the leading crime of teenagers in Chicago was curfew violation. Teens arrested in San Francisco were most often charged with disorderly conduct, and incorrigible behavior was the most prominent crime in Jacksonville, Florida. Although many thought juvenile crimes were skyrocketing, statistics from the Children's Bureau show that children's court cases rose only 20 percent in the fifties. The increase was not surprising because some police departments set up special units to target teen crime, and the reallocation of personnel naturally tallied up more arrests. In the following decade, the rate of increase in court cases would be three times as high. Still, the subject garnered unprecedented attention. Historian James Gilbert examined the *Readers Guide to Periodical Literature* to chart the amount of attention given to juvenile delinquency between 1932 and 1968. He found that articles on the subject reached a low point in 1949 followed by a steep climb in the early 1950s. The number of articles remained high for several years, and then, a decline began in the decade's final years (Gilbert 1986, 65, 70, 71).

Censorship

Adult fears about juvenile delinquency surfaced in various arenas. One was the comic-book scare that arose in the decade's middle years. The Subcommittee to Investigate Juvenile Delinquency of the Senate Judiciary Committee began an investigation in April 1954 after numerous sources publicly had condemned horror comics. In his testimony, one comic-book publisher defended a cover showing a man holding a woman's severed head and described how it could have been made more objectionable by holding the head higher and showing blood dripping from it. In response to public uproar generated by the hearings, the Comics Magazine Association of America was established that year with a New York juvenile court judge as its czar. Companies that accepted a new publication code and presented their comic books for prior approval received a seal showing that their products contained no objectionable material. Many wholesalers refused to handle comic books that did not carry the seal.

Sexual Codes

Dating took on new seriousness after World War II as the age at marriage began to decline. Increasingly, instead of dating many members of the opposite sex, teenagers chose to "go steady" with one person and maintain a monogamous relationship. Among high school students heading for college, these relationships were unlikely to lead to marriage; however, steady relationships were much more likely to lead to marriage when the boy and girl were not college-bound. Studies of teen sexual behavior in the 1950s showed that steady relationships enabled teens to connect mutual affection with sexual behavior, according to sociologist Ira L. Reiss. Drawing from the research of Alfred Kinsey and others, Reiss concluded that steady relationships made teens adopt a sexual code in which girls allowed "petting with affection," even when they publicly supported the practice of abstinence. Most boys had engaged in sexual intercourse during their teen years; however, they often used a double standard, condemning girls known to allow "petting with affection" and viewing them as unsuitable marriage prospects.

Teen Consumerism

American businesses first recognized teenagers and slightly older college students as a significant market in the 1950s. Teenagers' average weekly income soared from $2.50 in 1944 to $10 in 1958. The typical youth spent $3.03 per week in 1951. As a group, teens consumed 190 million candy bars, 130 million soft drinks, 230 million pieces of chewing gum, and 13 million ice-cream bars every week (Gilbert 1986, 207). Teens were inclined to make impulse purchases, and their total spending rose to $9.5 billion in 1958 (Englehardt 1995, 134). In 1959, three-quarters of moviegoers were teenagers (Breines 1992, 92). Members of the youth culture flocked to movies chronicling teen life, often with romantic or sexual overtones. They also became big fans of cheaply made B movies, frequently in

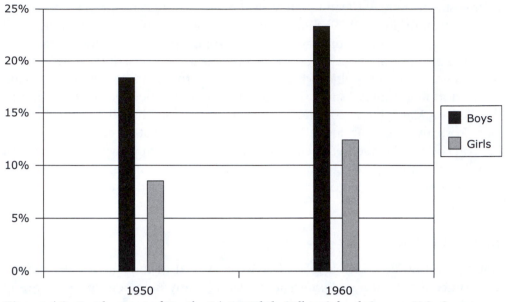

Figure 4.2 *Employment of Youths 14–17 While Still in School. Source:* U.S. Census Bureau.

the form of science fiction or horror films. By the end of the decade, the first baby boomers were entering their teen years and expanding the teen market. "In its kids," a *Life* cover story proclaimed, "U.S. has a recession remedy. . . . The first of the postwar babies are beginning to constitute a huge market for teenagers' goods and services" (Englehardt 1995, 145).

Seeds of Change

The youth culture of the 1950s planted seeds of rebellion that would flower much more fully in the succeeding decade. Looking over the distance of time, young people's behavior in the fifties seems relatively innocuous. Even Elvis, who represented social decline in the minds of many adults, wore a sports jacket when he appeared on *The Ed Sullivan Show*. Because winning adult acceptance was important, the teenagers on *American Bandstand* also dressed and behaved conservatively. Members of this Silent Generation did not engage in social warfare with their parents, but they did test the boundaries of acceptable individual behavior.

In many ways, the youth culture of the 1950s represented a paradox. While sexually active boys sometimes looked down on sexually active girls, youths who practiced great conformity in dress and behavior often believed that their very conformity with other teenagers constituted a stand for individuality. To teenagers, making a fashion statement that conflicted with their parents' tastes

Top Teen Movies of the 1950s

Glen or Glenda (1953)

The Wild One (1953)

Blackboard Jungle (1955)

Rebel without a Cause (1955)

Hot Rod Girl (1956)

Love Me Tender (1956)

Rock Around the Clock (1956)

The Girl Can't Help It (1956)

April Love (1957)

Attack of the Crab Monsters (1957)

I Was a Teenaged Werewolf (1957)

Not of This Earth (1957)

Tammy and the Bachelor (1957)

High School Confidential (1958)

The Blob (1958)

Hound Dog Man (1959)

King Creole (1958)

Gidget (1959)

Girls Town (1959)

A Summer Place (1959)

Teenagers from Outer Space (1959)

represented rebellion against the possibility of losing themselves in an adult society that they felt robbed them of their individuality. At their core, they wanted to be sure that when they looked in the mirror, they did not see their parents looking back.

Sociologist Wini Breines argues that the two narrow and yet exaggerated prototypes of women available to young women—the prim housewife and the glamorous Marilyn Monroe—led teenaged girls to seek a more workable model for their own lives. As young women navigated between the virtual gender equality of their childhoods toward the clear-cut inequality facing adult women, they became tangled in a web of contradictions. The choice between being a sex object or a workhorse following a dreary routine did not offer the kinds of options young women wanted.

It comes as no surprise that many members of the 1950s' youth culture had no interest in becoming the anonymous man in the grey flannel suit or a housewife whose days were filled with drudgery and tedium. Most had been born during a time of hardship—either because of the Great Depression or World War II—and they had absorbed some of their parents' anxieties. However, with the United States now prospering, they wanted more from life than what their parents had experienced. Even as they stood in the gloom associated with Cold War mushroom clouds, teens could dare to dream. The rapidity of sociological and technological change made almost anything seem possible. Broader frontiers were opening for education and social advancements among working-class youths, and even girls could see the prospect of a career outside the home. Even African Americans had new role models for success within the ranks of music industry stars. Some goals may have been beyond their grasp, but they could feel that change was in the air.

To a larger degree than their baby boomer siblings, teenagers of the 1950s felt the pressure of adult standards and the reality of their status as a much smaller group than the baby boom generation that protested in the streets a decade later. As a result, many experimented with rebellion without engaging in all-out battles. Although they took their stands on issues that were not earth-shattering, these teens made a first step in the emancipation of teenagers. Their rebellion of manners opened the door to young people's later involvement in the civil rights movement and politics.

THE NEW HOME

Though they were not all wealthy, young married couples of the 1950s often spent money to make their lives easier or more entertaining. Evidence of prosperity's widespread effects can be found in data that shows three-quarters of American families had both a car and a washing machine by 1960 (Englehardt 1995, 133). A variety of forces supported the tendency to buy. Of course, the strongest element in this phenomenon was the growth in real wages, but less obvious events also contributed to consumers' adoption of new products. For instance, credit was readily available and acceptable to consumers. Installment plans had been in use since the 1920s, and while the Great Depression had made many Americans wary about borrowing, this new generation of married couples was less hesitant to buy on credit. Installment-plan credit climbed from $4 billion in 1954 to $43 billion in 1960. Over the course of the decade, credit became even more accessible with the introduction of credit cards. The Diners Club card arrived on the scene in 1950 in New York City and quickly spread across the nation. American Express began issuing cards in 1958, and the BankAmeri-card, which later became Visa, found its way into many wallets just a year later. By 1960, total consumer credit had skyrocketed to $56.1 billion, more than six times as high as consumer credit in 1946 (Breines 1992, 3). In addition, married couples of this era faced less pressure to save for their old age because of the presence of the Social Security system, which had come into being in the late 1930s. Consequently, Americans used cash or credit to stock their homes with appliances that changed their daily lives. Advances in technology created kitchen appliances that made food preparation easier and fueled the creation of newly expanded product lines, such as frozen foods.

Although it did not transform housework in a direct way, the television probably played the biggest role in changing American homes and weekly routines. As network programming began to mature in the early years of the decade, television offered a new source of entertainment, a new perspective on the workings of government, and a new babysitter for children. At the decade's start, only 3.1 million television sets had made their way into American homes. Just

James S. Thomas and his family gather around the television in their Vienna, Virginia, home. (National Archives)

three years later, more than 20 million televisions had been purchased. At that point, television sets were taking up space in half of American households. By 1955, the total was 32 million, and about 10,000 Americans bought a television set every day (Whitfield 1996, 153). As family members of all ages discovered television's ability to entertain them, the wooden box became the centerpiece of many living rooms or family rooms. Some Americans developed the habit of eating while they watched. To satisfy that need, both TV trays and frozen TV dinners debuted. *TV Guide*'s circulation increased 99 percent in 1954 alone (Halberstam 1993, 154). General Electric produced the first portable TV in 1955, and another convenience—the remote control—became available in 1957. Television ownership would surpass refrigerator ownership early in the next decade.

Changing Household Environment

The changing American home and its new appliances became the subjects of social and political commentary during the 1950s. Looking at the impact of 1920s' innovations, Robert Lynd and Helen Lynd had concluded in their landmark "Middletown" study of Muncie, Indiana, that change threatened the residents' sense of community; three decades later, the greatest concerns about modernization focused on its potential negative impact on the family and the sanctity of the home. The 1950s' discourse revealed the central role of the family in the culture of that era and the prevalent use of suburban family norms to provide a model for all families. Not surprisingly, television sparked the greatest amount of commentary. Boston University president Daniel L. Marsh commented in 1950 that "if the craze continues with the present level of programs, we are destined to have a nation of morons." However, at around the same time, a school principal in Essex, Maryland, reported the results of a survey made at his school. His findings showed that the shared experience of watching TV had made families closer. He also asserted that the possibility of watching television had made housewives work more swiftly, reduced the number of children involved in auto accidents, and improved the behavior of teenagers ("Morons" 1950).

Many parents worried not that television would make their children stupid but that it could make them violent. Adults often expressed concerns about the prevalence of "action shows" on television. One television watchdog counted 167 murders, 356 attempted murders, and 167 justifiable homicides in a single week of Los Angeles television in 1952; however, no strong steps were taken against television violence. The medical profession warned the public about a variety of TV-related ailments, including "TV squint"; "TV bottom"; "bad feet," caused by lack of movement while in front of the TV; "frogitis," a leg ailment caused by awkward viewing postures; "TV jaw," a result of resting one's head on one's knuckles while viewing, a habit that reportedly pushed the eyeteeth inward; and "tired child syndrome," which could be recognized by symptoms of fatigue, headaches, and nausea (Englehardt 1995, 148–149).

Other household appliances generated little public debate in the United States, but many Americans were well aware that the most famous 1950s' debate about the American home occurred in a model kitchen in Moscow. The 1959 "kitchen debate" between Vice President Richard Nixon and Soviet Premier Nikita Khrushchev revealed a great deal about the importance of postwar prosperity and the convenient home life it provided. "There are 44 million families in the United States," Nixon said. "Twenty-five million of [them] live in houses or apartments that have as much or more floor space than the one you see in this exhibit. Thirty-one million families own their own homes and the land on which they are built. America's 44 million families own 56 million cars, 50 million television sets, and 143 million radio sets. And they buy an average of nine dresses and suits and fourteen pair of shoes per family member per year."

Khrushchev, echoing the commentary of some American traditionalists, scoffed at Nixon's assertions. Pointing to a television, he said, "This is probably always out of order. . . . Don't you have a machine that puts food into the mouth and pushes it down?" (May 1988, 163). Khrushchev believed that the Soviet Union's rockets carried far more importance than the higher standard of living in the United States, but Nixon made a strong case for the importance of a comfortable home in American life.

Television Becomes a Powerful Force Bringing News into American Living Rooms

Network news broadcasting was relatively primitive throughout the 1950s. Even at the decade's close, the large networks offered only once-nightly 15-minute reports; however, through live reports, television played a growing role in bringing the workings of American government and politics into the lives of ordinary Americans. Former World War II correspondent Edward R. Murrow of CBS was the era's leading television journalist.

Congressional hearings on a variety of subjects, including organized crime and Communist subversion, brought the real-life drama of American public affairs into the nation's living rooms. Throughout the decade, the television networks aired nuclear tests live, thus opening up a corner of American living rooms to the ominous mushroom cloud. Beginning in 1952, television enabled viewers to watch the major parties' presidential nominating conventions, and in that same year, Republican vice-presidential nominee Richard Nixon directly and melodramatically appealed to the American people via television to ignore charges of corruption against him. Denying accusations that he had accepted bribes, Nixon not only mentioned his wife's simple "cloth coat," but he claimed the only gift he had ever accepted from a backer was the family dog that his six-year-old daughter Tricia named Checkers.

America Loves Lucy

At a time before the term *situation comedy* had become a part of the American vernacular, Lucille Ball set the standard. *I Love Lucy* was one of the biggest hits of the 1950s. In the show, Ball and her real-life husband, Desi Arnaz, played a married couple living in New York. Arnaz's Ricky Ricardo was a Cuban bandleader, just like Arnaz himself. The series, first aired in 1951, attracted almost 11 million viewers by April 1952, and on the night of January 19, 1953, perhaps as many as 44 million Americans watched to see the antics surrounding the birth of Lucy's TV son, Little Ricky. That represented 68 percent of the possible viewing audience. *I Love Lucy* ran on CBS until 1957. For the following three years, the couple starred in one-hour specials, and then Lucy and Ricky disappeared from television as Lucy and Desi decided to end their marriage. Syndicated re-runs of *I Love Lucy* were sold to independent stations, where they found new audiences, especially among children. Looking back, some scholars have seen Lucy Ricardo's frequent efforts to get into show business as a reflection of women's boredom with their role as housewives. Others have characterized Lucy's daffiness as a 1950s' effort to equate women with empty-headed infants.

The NAACP Meets *Amos 'n' Andy*

Amos 'n' Andy was among several early TV comedies that focused on ethnic working-class characters. The comedy, which perpetuated gross stereotypes of African Americans, had been a hit on radio, with white actors playing the foolish characters; however, when it moved to television in 1951, African American theater performers took over the roles. The series focused on the conniving work of "the Kingfish," who was head of the Mystic Knights of the Sea Lodge. The NAACP had opposed the radio show and went to federal court to have the CBS series ousted from the TV lineup. In response, the show's stars defended their work as mild satire. However, by 1954, the show's sponsor, Blatz Beer, was tired of complaints and dropped the show. The series remained in syndication until 1966.

Like *Amos 'n' Andy, The Goldbergs* and *I Remember Mama* focused attention on the ethnicity of the characters and used differences as plot elements that drove stories. All of these programs had left the airwaves by the late 1950s and had been replaced by family comedies more like *The Adventures of Ozzie and Harriet,* which had been on the air since 1952. Among the newcomers that reflected more homogenized, white middle-class family life were *Father Knows Best, Leave It to Beaver,* and *The Donna Reed Show.* Film and television scholar Vincent Brook has shown that *The Goldbergs* ironically lost its audience when the show's producers moved the family to an upscale suburb and took them away from their working-class roots (Brook 1999, 46).

The Western

Variety shows played a big role in television broadcasting's early years during the late 1940s and early 1950s, and situation comedies and simple adventure shows had soon joined them. However, by the end of the decade, Westerns and other action dramas dominated nighttime television programming. Of 103 series in the 1958–1959 season, 69 fell into the "action-crime-mystery" category. Within that category, the dominant series format was the "adult Western." Programs in this genre made up 25 percent of all network nightly offerings in 1959 (Englehardt 1995, 89). Though many Western series were short-lived, *Gunsmoke* was

Most Popular TV Series

October 1950–April 1951: *Texaco Star Theater*
October 1951–April 1952: *Arthur Godfrey's Talent Scouts* (talent contest)
October 1952–April 1953: *I Love Lucy* (situation comedy)
October 1953–April 1954: *I Love Lucy*
October 1954–April 1955: *I Love Lucy*
October 1955–April 1956: *The $64,000 Question* (quiz show)
October 1956–April 1957: *I Love Lucy*
October 1957–April 1958: *Gunsmoke* (Western drama)
October 1958–April 1959: *Gunsmoke*
October 1959–April 1960: *Gunsmoke*
(Brooks and Marsh 1999)

on the air for 20 years, setting a record for the longest-running series with continuing characters. Historian Richard Slotkin has explored the popularity of the Western in the 1950s and early 1960s, and he has concluded that Western showdowns fit the temper of the times. The Cold War ideological conflict between the United States and the Soviet Union often brought analogies to a brave hero facing a dastardly villain at high noon. Both scenarios involve a world divided between good and evil, black and white.

Children's Programming

In television's early years, the late afternoons belonged to children. Puppets were the most visible figures in the children's programming of the early 1950s. They included Howdy Doody, Rootie Kazootie, and the Kuklapolitan Players. By the end of the 1950s, children's programming had expanded to dominate Saturday mornings and to claim a niche on weekday mornings. Over time, children lost interest in the puppets that had captivated their older siblings a few years earlier. Adult entertainers, such as comic Soupy Sales and the deceptively grandfather-like Captain Kangaroo, captured part of the spotlight. However, cartoons probably played a bigger role in children's changing tastes. In 1950, *Crusader Rabbit* was the only cartoon on the air, but by the end of the decade, a broad array of cartoons provided children with many choices. Walt Disney's *Mickey Mouse Club,* which featured real youngsters and showcased dramas about youthful adventures, debuted in 1955. The series, which attracted both children and young teenagers, was broadcast Monday–Saturday afternoons for three years. Disney Studios aired updated versions of the *Mickey Mouse Club* in the 1970s and the 1990s. Annette Funicello experienced the biggest career boost

Buffalo Bob Smith introduces TV's most popular marionette, Howdy Doody, to two young victims of cerebral palsy in 1950. (Library of Congress)

from the original *Mickey Mouse Club* series. Among the children on the 1990s series were future singing stars Britney Spears, Christina Aguilera, and Justin Timberlake and future actors Ryan Gosling and Keri Russell.

Quiz Show Scandal

Nighttime television quiz shows were very popular among adult viewers in the 1950s. By showcasing individuals with unusual mental skills and by paying winners large amounts of money, these shows captured the imaginations of ordinary people. *The $64,000 Question* was the most memorable hit, but there were many more, including *The $64,000 Challenge, Tic Tac Dough, High Finance, The Big Surprise,* and *Treasure Hunt.* In 1956, a losing contestant on *The Big Surprise* generated publicity by claiming that the contest was rigged. This led journalists to begin talking to contestants and investigating the honesty of various shows. At least one show was canceled to avoid embarrassing revelations. The following year, on NBC's *Twenty-One,* an unpopular champion named Herbert

Stempel was ordered to forget the answer to a question so that the more-telegenic contestant Charles Van Doren could become champion, raising the show's ratings and winning $129,000 over 14 weeks. In August 1958, two newspapers reported Stempel's story, and Van Doren quickly assured his fans that he was unaware of any fraud on *Twenty-One*. He later admitted his guilt and disappeared from the public eye.

Advertising

As television ownership spread, interest in TV advertising grew. In the late 1940s and early 1950s, a single sponsor actually packaged the television program it was using to sell its products, and advertisements sometimes ran for a minute or more. Within a few years, however, television offered opportunities for advertisers to buy single or multiple spots from the television networks or from local TV stations instead of paying for an entire production. And with minute-long ads costing as much as $20,000, many commercials shrank to 30 seconds. In 1951, TV ad revenues totaled only $41 million. Eight years later, revenues had surpassed $1.5 billion. Among the media, only newspaper advertising revenues exceeded those of television at that time. Ads featuring celebrities were especially popular on television, and placement of products in television episodes was a more subtle way to profit from the appeal of TV stars. Classic commercials from the 1950s can be viewed online in the Prelinger Collection (2007).

Two Advertising Icons

Betty Crocker (1921–) and Aunt Jemima (1890–) were two of the advertising icons who helped to cement the public image of women as domestic creatures who belonged in the kitchen. Ironically, during a period in which women often were discouraged from seeking career success, these fictional women were among the best-known female figures in American culture. In this era, only glamorous movie stars exceeded their fame. Played by a variety of actresses over the years, both were enduring icons representing specific brand names.

The fictional Betty Crocker became a best-selling author in the 1950s, when 97 out of 100 American women recognized her name (Marling 1994, 209–210). As a representative of General Mills, she debuted in 1921; however, her greatest success came in the 1950s, when her *Betty Crocker's Picture Cook Book* was the decade's most popular cookbook. The recipe collection, which debuted in 1950, had a first printing of almost a million copies. In reality, Betty Crocker was a composite figure representing the women who worked in General Mills' test kitchens, and she was largely the creation of home economist Marjorie Child Husted. As the decade began, Betty had a regular radio show that offered cooking tips for eager housewives, but the new medium of television created

Other Advertising Icons of the 1950s

Valleydale Sausage's marching pigs
Speedy Alka-Seltzer
The Jolly Green Giant
Charlie the Tuna
Mr. Clean
The Marlboro Man
The Pillsbury Doughboy
The Men from Texaco
Tony the Tiger from Kellogg's
Old Gold Dancing Packs (of cigarettes)
The Budweiser Clydesdales

a problem for her creators at General Mills. If she was portrayed by an actress who did not resemble the picture on General Mills' Betty Crocker advertisements and products, her creators feared that she would lose credibility. As a result, she did not appear on television until 1952. At that time, she was portrayed by actress Adelaide Hawley, but the camera devoted most of its attention to Betty's working hands. The series lasted only two seasons. In 1955, Betty received a new face after six well-known artists produced new portraits to be judged by a jury of 1,600 General Mills customers. Norman Rockwell was among the contestants, but Hilda Taylor won, dressing Betty as a maternal suburban housewife with slightly graying hair. When cake mixes became popular, Betty gave them her stamp of approval, making cooking shortcuts an acceptable part of home economics.

While Betty remained out of the public's reach in the 1950s, one of her fictional colleagues, Aunt Jemima, flipped pancakes in the nation's new playground —Disneyland. Wearing a red bandana traditionally associated with slavery, Aunt Jemima had hawked pancake mix since the late 19th century when she was created by entrepreneur Chris L. Rutt; however, in the 1950s, she was increasingly viewed as an unflattering and stereotypical representation of African American women. As a result of complaints in the 1950s and 1960s, Aunt Jemima later was remade, a choice that has enabled her to become one of the few advertising icons to survive more than 100 years. Many actresses have played Aunt Jemima over the years, although she never had her own television program. Quaker Oats, owner of her brand name since 1926, sent Aunt Jemima around the country to perform cooking shows for many years. This tradition ended in 1967, but the trademark survives. Today, Aunt Jemima's smile remains on her products, but the slave bandana has been replaced by the well-coifed look of a modern African American woman.

Home Appliances

Because mobilization for World War II had stopped production of household appliances, many Americans struggled along with old models, many of them bought in the 1920s. However, by 1950, the manufacturing of appliances was back in full swing, and Americans were eager to buy. New refrigerators came in a variety of sizes with different kinds of storage compartments, and for buyers, having a choice of colors was an innovation of the 1950s. In a nation of 155 million people, there were 33 million working refrigerators in 1952; in other words, almost every family had one.

A woman uses a vacuum cleaner to remove crumbs from a toaster in this 1955 photo. (Bettmann/Corbis)

The average refrigerator offered only a small freezer compartment, but by 1952, about four million households had invested in a stand-alone freezer. Most freezer owners at that time were farmers who filled them with fresh-grown produce. International Harvester began selling separate refrigerators and freezers in 1953, and the appliances came with plaid slipcovers and matching plaid curtains. *Quick Frozen Foods* magazine asked a designer to demonstrate various ways to camouflage large freezers, and that generated ideas such as laminating the appliance with wood veneer to make it look like an office credenza or using it as the base for a drop-leaf table. As more Americans moved to the suburbs, where they had more space, freezer sales rose. Often, if a large top-loading freezer did not fit neatly into the kitchen, it was placed in an out-of-the-way location, such as the basement.

Electric stoves were not new in the 1950s, but popular built-in ranges were a novelty. Also entering American households for the first time were clothes dryers, which complemented the work of clothes washers. Other popular appliances included dishwashers, vacuum cleaners, electric fans, electric irons, toasters, radios, and hot-water heaters. During this decade, Americans bought 75 percent of all appliances manufactured around the globe.

Innovations in Cooking

Appliances were not the only new arrivals in American kitchens. Cake mixes had debuted toward the end of the previous decade, but manufacturers experienced a boom in sales during the 1950s. Cake mix sales had reached only $79 million in 1947, but just six years later, they had climbed to more than $158 million. In 1953, General Mills' icon, Betty Crocker, gave her word to everyone who picked up one of her cake mixes: "I guarantee a perfect cake, every time you bake—cake after cake after cake." As a novelty, cake mixes, which were packaged in boxes with pictures of unbelievably appetizing treats, had found enthusiastic consumers; however, many cooks ultimately chose to stick with baking "from scratch." Although cake mix sales continued to increase, the rate of growth was a paltry 5 percent between 1956 and 1960. A Michigan State University study showed that using a cake mix saved exactly 13 minutes of a baker's time. General Mills claimed that 50 percent of homemade cakes were made from mixes in 1955, and Pillsbury raised that estimate to 70 to 80 percent. In reality, most cooks apparently continued to make cakes from scratch, even at the decade's end. Cookbooks for novices also were quite popular during this era when teenagers were becoming wives in record numbers (Shapiro 2005, 195, 743–745).

As freezer sales increased, frozen foods played a bigger role in the American diet. Frozen orange juice became a hit in the late 1940s, and by 1950, 25 percent of Florida's orange crop was going into concentrates for frozen sales (Shapiro 2005, 12). A year later, the Swanson Company introduced the concept of TV dinners with its turkey potpies. In 1954, the company added a turkey dinner to its lineup. Sitting alongside the turkey in a sectionalized aluminum pan were dressing, peas, and potatoes. Swanson trademarked the name "TV dinner," and its annual sales reached 25 million dinners by 1955, when Campbell Soup Company bought the company (Young and Young 2004, 102). Another new frozen phenomenon that changed American habits was the 1952 introduction of Birdseye fish sticks. These heavily breaded filets often were eaten with ketchup to hide any lingering evidence of their fishy nature. Birdseye sold 7 million in 1953 and 30 million in 1954 (Shapiro 2005, 15).

Science also played a role in the most up-to-date kitchens. Tupperware began selling polyethylene products that made the storage of leftovers easier, and Formica became a popular plastic laminate for easy-to-clean kitchen countertops. Moreover, for the first time, kitchen sinks offered a mix of cold and hot water from a single faucet. Nonstick Teflon-coated pans hit the market late in the decade.

Commercial Innovations Alter American Life

A variety of new inventions and a period of successful mass merchandising remade the American home in the 1950s. And as homes were replicated in suburbia, many of the new devices became standard appliances that seemed to fit as neatly as the prefabricated houses' walls. None of the appliances popular in the 1950s were short-term fads. The TV became an indispensable part of almost every home. In these early days, when most homes had only one television, it undoubtedly brought families together physically, with or without conversation. Merchandising of portable TVs, which began in the mid-1950s, opened the door to the next stage of TV viewing, when family members would scatter to separate rooms to watch the programs of their choice without interaction with other members of the family. As television became an important part of daily life, some worried about the glazed-over looks they saw on the faces of TV viewers. They feared that this form of entertainment, which required only passivity from its consumers, would have unhealthy results. More than 20 years before the term *couch potato* was coined, some people worried that the innocent-looking television in their living rooms might cause harm to Americans' mental or physical health, not to mention American culture.

Television already had prompted about 580 movie theater closings by 1950, despite relatively low television ownership at that time. In 1950–1951, more than 250 movie theaters closed nationwide, and a 20 to 40 percent drop was reported in 1951 movie attendance, even in cities with only one television station. Fewer people listened to radio, too. Even in its early days, television news represented a long-term threat to the daily habit of newspaper readership. Statistics showed that about 70 percent of New York televisions were tuned to live coverage of Senate hearings held in New York on organized crime in March 1951 (Halberstam 1993, 185, 192).

Meanwhile, some new products made the family cook's job easier, while others merely encouraged housewives to work harder. Innovations in the kitchen made food preparation easier, and family cooks, who were almost always women, had new options for saving leftover food or preserving food to be served at a later date. As of 1952, the number of women who squeezed fresh oranges for juice each day sank below the number who served frozen orange juice from concentrate. The amount of time saved in the kitchen probably meant a great deal to women who worked outside the home during this era because they, like their housewife neighbors, still bore most of the burden for domestic chores. They needed quick answers, and General Mills even marketed Betty Crocker's Answer Cake, which it said was produced to meet the urgent needs of "27 million working women, the majority of them married" (Shapiro 2005, 140). However, new efficiencies outside the kitchen did not significantly lighten the burden of housewives. As new products created new standards of cleanliness, housewives continued to run on a seemingly endless domestic treadmill with little end in sight. While these time-saving devices did not free the typical middle-class mother from life as a housewife in the 1950s, they did lay the groundwork for future decades when more women entered the job market, thus reducing the amount of time parents could invest in keeping the household running efficiently.

SUBURBANIZATION

The American suburbs underwent dramatic growth during the 1950s. As the decade began, the rate of suburban growth in the United States was 10 times as high as the growth rate in the nation's cities. Nine million people flooded into the nation's suburbs between 1944 and 1954, according to *Fortune* magazine. Suburbanization was a direct outgrowth of increasing family income, and expenditures of that money to buy new homes. There were more than 1.6 million housing starts in 1950 compared with only 114,000 in 1944 (Palladino 1996, 101). And by 1955, subdivisions represented more than 75 percent of metropolitan areas' new housing construction (Jackson 1985, 233).

Although America's suburbs have long been considered avenues of cookie-cutter houses for the white middle class, the suburbs of this era defied that stereotypical image. The suburbs themselves ranged from very exclusive upper-class enclaves, such as Grosse Point Farms outside Detroit, to the prefabricated identical tract housing of young couples just beginning their lives together in the various Levittowns in the Mid-Atlantic states. There were working-class suburbs like Compton, California, outside many cities. And despite the vision of suburbs as all white, members of the African American middle class were able to establish a relatively small number of their own subdivisions, even around some southern metropolises, where African Americans still faced legally mandated segregation in daily life.

Obviously, the atmosphere found in an upper-class suburb with large estates differed greatly from what could be found in a working-class environment with houses aligned as rowhouses or spaced just feet apart. Working-class neighborhoods generally were shaped by more interaction between neighbors, stricter division of gender roles, and a more authoritarian approach to parenthood. Also, although they could scarcely afford it, many working-class men insisted that their wives stay at home rather than supplementing the family income with their own work. By emulating the middle-class custom of women living as housewives, they demonstrated an aspiration to join the middle class and experience the advantages of that rank.

Typical suburbs were characterized by a couple of factors, in addition to the most obvious—their proximity to a city. Most had relatively low population density. Roughly 97 percent of new single-family houses were detached between 1946 and 1956. Each suburb also tended to offer houses with similar architectural styles because developers saved money by limiting floor plans to a few designs (Jackson 1985, 238). Although the suburbs began as individual housing projects, additional housing typically filled in the gaps that separated one project from the next.

As it changed individual lives, suburbanization expedited changes in the nature of the housing industry. Before the end of World War II, the average building contractor constructed no more than four houses each year, but by 1959, the median single-family builder produced 22 buildings in a year. Domination of the industry by those who built quickly and cheaply continued through the 1950s. Just a year before the decade began, 10 percent of construction companies already built 70 percent of all new homes in the United States.

Postwar Building Boom

When U.S. soldiers began returning to the United States and leaving the military after the end of World War II, it became clear that the nation faced a severe housing shortage. The need for massive construction of new homes lingered into the 1950s because of demand for a greater supply of suburban homes. At first, the housing shortage become obvious in very particular places—near colleges where veterans were attempting to cash in on the GI Bill; however, it quickly became clear that the housing shortage was a national problem. A staggering 98 percent of American cities reported a housing deficit in 1945, and as they waited for new homes to be built, more than six million families were crowding into the homes of friends or family (May 1988, 168). Making matters worse was another problem that sometimes was overlooked; by 1952, 40 percent of the nation's housing would be more than 30 years old. That was a significant increase over 1930, when only 30 percent of housing units were that old. On top of these factors, the unexpected baby boom was a key factor in changing the nation's housing needs. Many of the first houses built after the war were small—too small for a family of five or six (O'Neill 1986, 18). All of these issues combined to make the housing shortage a critical problem for the United States.

By 1950, the construction industry had built 2.5 million new apartments and houses, and *Fortune* magazine boldly declared that the housing shortage had been conquered. The government had tried various methods to spur housing construction, but the most powerful mechanisms for achieving this goal were the Federal Housing Administration's 30-year mortgages at 4.5 percent interest. With these loans, many people were able to do something they had scarcely imagined: own their own home. The suburban boom got another lift from the federal government because interest payments on mortgages were tax-deductible—and that made owning seem more economical than renting. As a result, the demand for new homes continued well beyond *Fortune*'s declaration that the nation's housing problem had been solved.

The building industry had attacked the housing shortage by envisioning and planning subdivisions outside major cities rather than investing in a great deal of new housing within the cities. The tendency of affluent residents to move from the center of cities into the hinterlands was an old one in the United States, and its only limits always had been the presence of easy transportation routes to make it feasible for people to work in the concrete-clad cities and live in the blossoming countryside. Again, the federal government gave suburbia a boost by giving approval in 1956 to the Interstate Highway System, which created better automobile routes to and from cities.

In the end, both the supply and the demand increased. Filling the housing shortage was one step. The next was building suburban homes for all of those who had houses but preferred to live in a new suburban house.

Levittown

William J. Levitt was the Henry Ford of home construction. He turned construction into a step-by-step timed process, and that enabled him to produce houses inexpensively. Young white married couples, in particular, bought them almost as quickly as he could build them. These inexpensive homes represented fulfillment of a dream, especially for newlyweds and members of the working class who could not afford more expensive housing. Others may have shuddered at the thought of living in a community of identical houses, but these new homeowners did not. After establishing his first community on Long Island in the late 1940s, he directed his attention to a large project in lower Bucks County, Pennsylvania, near Philadelphia. Work began on the site in 1951. Levitt had chosen a site just a few miles from the Fairless Works of U.S. Steel Corporation, and many Levittown homebuyers were employees at the plant. When the construction was completed in the late 1950s, Pennsylvania's Levittown had 16,000 ranch houses, a 55-acre shopping center, and some light industry. About 70,000 people lived in the development, which consisted of eight large blocks, each measuring about one square mile (Jackson 1985, 237). Each block had its own recreational facilities, primarily consisting of a swimming pool. Every home had steel kitchen cabinets and a washing machine.

To lower housing costs, Levitt eliminated basements and initially restricted all of the houses in one area to the same floor plan. A two-tone color scheme on interior and exterior walls also limited expenses. As Levitt applied the techniques of mass production to home building, he broke down the construction process into 26 steps, and 100 houses were constructed at a time. His workmen used inexpensive materials such as plywood, particle board, and gypsum. In addition, they painted with spray cans instead of brushes and used powered saws, nailers, and routers. Some parts of the houses, such as interior partitions, doors, and windows arrived from a factory fully ready for installation. Every step in the construction procedure occurred at the same time each day.

In 1958, Levitt began work on his third project in Willingboro, New Jersey, also in suburban Philadelphia. This development had 11,000 houses. Because Levitt's houses cost just $9,500 with no down payment required and no closing costs, his competitors found it difficult to match him. Nevertheless, they adopted many of his practices. During these years, the National Homes Corporation made it easy for home builders to build prefabricated, modular structures. The com-

An aerial view of Levittown, Pennsylvania, shows the regimentation accomplished through mass production of reasonably priced and often-identical homes, ca. 1959. (National Archives)

pany, founded in 1940 in Lafayette, Indiana, enabled builders to complete a house within two to five weeks after the foundation had been laid.

Westlake, California

Pioneering builder Henry Doelger had a major impact on the development of suburban homes outside San Francisco. Many of his houses still stand, and their appearance has changed little since their construction in the 1950s. Doelger produced Westlake, a development of detached houses now part of the coastal city of Daly City, California. He started construction in the 1940s on land that consisted of 600 acres of sand dunes and cabbage patches. Doelger then bought more land west and south of the original site and expanded Westlake in the 1950s. The development eventually doubled the population of Daly City and was named one of the 10 best suburban communities by one national magazine. Doelger also was responsible for building many attached homes in San Francisco's Sunset District. Between the late 1920s and the early 1960s, he constructed thousands of tiny stucco houses in the San Francisco area. Some of them were separated by only two inches of space. Doelger's houses always prominently placed the garage at the front of the house, and to avoid having block after block look identical, he varied the houses' style in Westlake to include touches of Moderne, French Provincial, and Colonial architecture.

Types of Homes

Americans buying new homes in the 1950s favored houses with a new look. Many abandoned more traditional styles and embraced ranch houses and split-level homes. Both architectural types had relatively simple floor plans that made building them easy and economical. The ranch house first began appearing in the San Francisco area, which is why it was originally called a California ranch. However, some have suggested that the ranch is derivative of Frank Lloyd Wright's earlier Prairie-style homes. Ranch houses were simple rectangles with a long side of the rectangle facing the front. Because the house was essentially horizontal, residents seldom had to climb stairs unless they were exploring a basement or attic. Often, a luscious carpet of green grass separated the house from the street, and each house had either an open carport or an enclosed garage. In the front of the house, many featured one large picture window with a 15- to 20-foot-square piece of tempered glass. Heat and cold often seeped into these houses through the picture windows, so their construction created a boon for heating and air-conditioning businesses. Ranch houses seldom had large front porches, and although they gave the illusion of roominess, ranches frequently offered less square footage than many older houses.

The split-level home had two stories on one side and just one story on the other. The central entrance was on the landing of a staircase. Downstairs were a family room and kitchen, where children often congregated. The upstairs was divided between private bathrooms and bedrooms in the two-story section and a formal living room and dining room in the one-story section. This style of architecture neatly divided the formal and informal areas of the house as well as the public and private areas. Despite the option of choosing one of these new home models, some families selected the Cape Cod model, which had a modern boxy shape and enjoyed great popularity in the preceding decades. Others chose a traditional Colonial Revival home. Many newly built homes came with central heating, and some even had central air-conditioning. One innovation in many new homes was the two-car garage; ownership of two family cars represented further proof of a household's prosperity.

On the Move

Americans' mobility in the 1950s was unprecedented in the nation's history. Often families moved from one suburb to another after only a few years in their original home. After earning promotions or pay raises, men often relocated their families in suburbs that were one step up on the demographic ladder. This transience resulted in community instability and sometimes maintained the isolation of the nuclear family. In New York's Levittown, more than 15 percent of residents moved every year. In addition, less than 6 percent of suburban residents within the New York metropolitan area were living in the same house in 1960 that they had occupied in 1955. Movement occurred not just within a single metropolitan area, but also between suburbs in different regions of the country. A major moving company, Atlas Van Lines, estimated that the average manager in the corporate world changed homes about 14 times over the course of his lifetime (Weiss 2000, 185). Statistics show that Americans between the ages of 25 and 35 were the most mobile in this era, and more than 45 percent of college graduates were likely to live outside their home states. Employees of the government, the armed services, or large corporations were most likely to be moved long distances (May 1988, 24–25). Some Americans also moved to different regions of the nation for reasons of climate or lifestyle. Military service had exposed thousands of veterans to the warmer climates of California, Texas, and the rest of the Southwest. With expanded use of air-conditioning, warm southern locales became more appealing to people from other parts of the country.

African Americans and the Suburbs

African Americans and other ethnic groups often were excluded from suburbs in the 1950s. Although prohibitions on Jewish occupancy were no longer as common, whites found many ways to exclude African Americans, despite a 1948 court ruling in the case of *Shelley v. Kraemer* that ruled it was unconstitutional for state courts to enforce restrictive housing covenants because that action violated the Constitution's Fourteenth Amendment. Ethnic groups often were isolated in the central core of urban areas, but some old suburbs became spillover areas for urban ghettoes. African Americans' entrance into newer suburbs was blocked on several fronts. Discrimination by developers, landlords, and real estate agents quietly prevented African Americans from residing in white enclaves. In addition, some zoning ordinances explicitly excluded their residence, and the Federal Housing Administration helped to maintain white-only areas through discrimination in the distribution of mortgages.

There were subdivisions in some metropolitan areas that served as suburbs for the African American middle class. As their pay rose, upwardly mobile African Americans sometimes united in an effort to carve out a place for themselves in

Demonstrators protest an African American family's arrival in a formerly all-white neighborhood during the mid-1950s. (Library of Congress)

the suburbs. They wanted a greater share in American prosperity and an opportunity to live in "luxury homes" that only the suburbs could provide. The Dallas Interracial Committee was set up by the Citizens Council and the Chamber of Commerce in the early 1950s to locate sites for the possible use of the African American middle class. A nonprofit corporation then bought and developed a 179-acre area that was situated about eight miles north of downtown Dallas. Eventually, Hamilton Park encompassed 730 suburban homes for African American families. Most of the original buyers were blue-collar workers who saw themselves as part of a growing middle class. In the Atlanta metropolitan area, the Urban League helped to set up Fair Haven, a working-class suburb of ranch houses in 1950. Houses in the subdivision cost about $6,500. When the first residents moved in, the streets were unpaved; however, the new residents managed to pressure the county into paving the streets and installing curbs, streetlights, and storm drains. By the decade's end, wealthier African Americans could move into Collier Heights Estates, which opened in 1959. It was advertised as "Atlanta's newest and most exclusive subdivision," and it offered homes with up to 1,800 square feet. Four split-level designs were available, and the houses cost up to $18,500. Each home featured built-in ranges, sliding glass doors, and paneled family rooms. After hundreds of years in which it was nearly impossible for an African American family to claim the trappings of the wealthy, this now became possible for a privileged few (Wiese 2004, 189, 191, 203).

Despite suburbia's incredible growth during the decade, fewer than a million suburbanites were nonwhite in both 1950 and 1960. During this period, African American population growth occurred mainly in the cities, while white growth was predominantly in the suburbs. Simultaneously, as rural areas declined, the white poor, who could not afford to live in the suburbs, increasingly were joining the African American poor in urban slums.

Suburbs Take the Lead

By 1960, upwardly mobile suburbanites already outnumbered city dwellers. Glitches in U.S. Census data camouflaged this turning point, but later analyses made it clear (O'Neill 1986, 288). Census figures show that the "urban fringe," or suburbia, housed 20.8 million people in 1950 and at least 37.8 million just 10 years later. The value of owner-occupied nonfarm housing grew from $12.3 billion in 1950 to $28.7 billion in 1959. Furthermore, Americans were spending a greater share of their income on housing. Statistics indicate that housing costs represented 11.1 percent of consumer expenditures in 1950, but nine years later, housing costs consumed 14 percent of American expenditures (U.S. Census Bureau 1975, 13, 317–318). For those who were striving to join the middle class, suburbs offered a piece of the American dream and provided tangible recognition of their dignity and their value to society. This kind of advancement made it easier to accept long working hours so that they could hold on to their small slice of the suburbs.

Suburbia in 1950s America often was the subject of ridicule by intellectuals. John Keats's 1957 book, *The Crack in the Picture Window,* characterized the builders of suburbs as wily and disreputable businessmen, and it portrayed the residents of those same suburbs as idiots. Keats's portrait of suburbia won praise from book reviewers in several cities, including one who concluded "as common as the picture windows which confront development houses are the monotonies and tragedies of the cracked lives within" (O'Neill 1988, 23).

Many suburbanites hoped that life in their new ranch houses would provide the perfect environment for family happiness. They believed they were claiming a piece of the American dream. In W. D. Wetherall's novel *The Man Who Loved Levittown,* one character expresses this view clearly: "Thanks to Big Bill Levitt, we all had a chance. You talk about dreams. Hell, we had ours. We had ours like nobody before or since ever had theirs. Seven thousand bucks! One hundred dollars down. We were cowboys out there. We were the pioneers" (Wetherall 1989, 7). However, 1957's *Americans View Their Mental Health* demonstrated an argument made later by Betty Friedan—that this life often was the source of unhappiness, particularly for women. The mobility of the middle class intensified women's isolation and had negative effects on the family as a whole. Uprooting a household could remove its members from a support network of friendly neighbors and extended families, and at the same time, the likelihood of future moves discouraged development of strong friendships between the new arrivals and their neighbors.

BIOGRAPHIES

Alan Freed, 1921–1965

Radio Disc Jockey

Alan Freed, working under the nickname "Moondog," was among the pioneers who brought African American rhythm and blues music to white audiences. He also is credited with coining the label "rock 'n' roll." In 1951, after getting reports from record-store owners about white teenagers' interest in African American music, he decided to spotlight rhythm and blues in his show on WJW Radio in Cleveland. Three years later, he moved to WINS in New York, where he found a broader audience. Among the guest performers in his New York studio were African American singers Chuck Berry, Bo Diddley, and Frankie Lymon. He later moved to WABC, also in New York. Freed briefly had a television series in the late fifties, but it was canceled after public outrage over one scene in which Lymon danced with a white girl—a nightmarish image to many of Freed's detractors. Because he promoted rock 'n' roll, Freed became a hero to both African American and white teenagers, but his career began a sharp decline near the decade's end when he was accused of accepting bribes to play certain records.

Betty Furness, 1916–1994

Actress, Advertising Spokeswoman, Consumer Advocate

Movie actress Betty Furness became a familiar face on television in the 1950s. Furness, whose film credits included the critically acclaimed *Magnificent Obsession* and *Swing Time,* was the spokesperson for Westinghouse shortly after World War II. Furness became a widely recognized promoter of home appliances after the 1952 national political conventions, which were broadcast under Westinghouse's sponsorship. She appeared in every advertisement, and by the time the conventions were completed, she had accumulated more air time than any individual in either party. Like many American women in the 1950s, Furness seemed to be stranded in the kitchen. She became famous for the slogan, "You can be sure if it's Westinghouse." In 1953, she briefly had her own talk show, *Meet*

Betty Furness, sponsored by Westinghouse. She also hosted *Best of Broadway,* financed by Westinghouse. Her contract with Westinghouse ended in 1960, and she later served as President Lyndon Johnson's special assistant for consumer affairs. Subsequently, she directed the consumer affairs departments in New York City and the state of New York.

Lillian Moller Gilbreth, 1878–1972

Engineer, Author, Mother of Twelve

Lillian Moller Gilbreth was called the world's greatest woman engineer in 1952 because of the time and motion studies she conducted with her husband, Frank, early in the century and because of her own achievements in industrial design and in humanizing the principles of good management. In 1954, she published *Management in the Home,* her third book, advising homemakers on how to use management techniques to run a home more efficiently. In it, she wrote, "The businessman or industrial worker has one job. The housewife has a dozen" (Shapiro 2005, 132). Gilbreth's mechanical innovations included attaching a foot pedal to a trash can to open it, adding shelves inside a refrigerator, and creating the electric food mixer. Despite her achievements as an engineer and a management consultant, she was best known in the 1950s as the real-life inspiration for the mother of 12 in the book *Cheaper by the Dozen,* written by two of her children and published in 1948 and turned into a film starring Myrna Loy (as Lillian Gilbreth), Clifton Webb, and Jeanne Crain in 1950. Although Gilbreth had worked as her husband's partner in the studies he made before his death in 1924, she found after his death that businesses were hesitant to hire a female consultant. Nevertheless, she thrived, authoring four books on her own and teaching management theory at the college level. She also was a leader in efforts to make the world more accessible to the handicapped.

Harvey Kurtzman, 1924–1993

Founder of *Mad* Magazine

Harvey Kurtzman had a profound effect on the comic-book industry in the 1950s. As the decade began, Kurtzman authored a spoof of Westerns called *Pot-Shot Pete,* and he became a writer and an editor for Entertaining Comics (EC) in 1950. A cartoonist since childhood, Kurtzman demonstrated his versatility by producing 32 horror, fantasy, adventure, war, and science-fiction tales from 1950 to 1952. Because he was juggling a great deal of editorial work, Kurtzman began limiting his cartooning work in 1951, when he drew only covers. A year later, he set out to create a comic book like no other. Using satire, he took jabs at horror and science-fiction comic books. With Wally Good and Will Elder working as cartoonists, *Mad* became EC's top seller in 1952, and Kurtzman began broadening his lampoons to take shots at newspapers and movies. However, when censors began evaluating comic books, *Mad* became one target, and it was canceled in 1954. Kurtzman transformed the comic book into a black-and-white magazine the following year. He edited five issues of the magazine before disagreements with EC's management made him end his association with EC. The magazine proved to be a long-lasting success, but Kurtzman's future attempts at satire failed. He never regained the success he had achieved with *Mad*.

Charles Van Doren, 1926–

Quiz Show Contestant

Charles Van Doren, son of Pulitzer Prize–winning poet Mark Van Doren, became the central figure in one of the 1950s biggest scandals. Americans had welcomed television and television quiz shows into their homes, and they were shocked

Quiz show host Jack Barry turns toward contestant Charles Van Doren during a 1957 episode of Twenty-One *as another contestant looks on. Van Doren later became the central figure in a scandal involving cheating on televised game shows. Americans soon learned that Van Doren had been provided with the answers to questions on* Twenty-One, *and a less charismatic previous champion had been ordered to let Van Doren win. (Library of Congress)*

to learn late in the decade that the producers of some of these programs cheated to increase the drama of the competition or the likeability of their contestants. Van Doren became a celebrity when he appeared on NBC's *Twenty-One* in early 1957. His total winnings were more than 30 times his salary as an English professor at Columbia University. After he had won, Van Doren also got a $150,000 three-year contract with NBC. Despite allegations that Van Doren's predecessor as champion had been forced to pretend ignorance to facilitate Van Doren's rise, the professor testified to a New York grand jury that he knew nothing about fraudulent practices on *Twenty-One*. After he later admitted his participation in fraud to a congressional committee, Americans were stunned to learn that he had been coached on answers and given acting instructions. Van Doren rationalized his role by saying that he was contributing to the intellectual life of the nation. Both NBC and Columbia canceled his contracts. After pleading guilty to perjury and receiving a suspended sentence, Van Doren shunned further publicity. He adopted an alias, which he used in all cases, except when he wrote a book about his experiences in the 1980s.

Brownie Wise, 1913–1992

Businesswoman

Brownie Wise, who had been a clerk in a clothing shop, a secretary at an aviation company, and a door-to-door vendor of Stanley Home Products, achieved remarkable success in the business world by using women to sell products to other women. In 1950, she set up a Florida business known as Tupperware Patio Parties and very quickly achieved success, selling more polyethylene Tupperware containers than retail stores. Earl Tupper, who had created the kitchenware, had tried unsuccessfully to use parties as sales venues, and Wise's success attracted his attention. He made her a company vice president and while he kept the design and manufacturing divisions of the company in New England, he moved the sales division to Florida. At that point, Tupper withdrew his products from department stores and hardware stores and sold them exclusively through at-home Tupperware parties. With women as salespeople and customers, Wise's strategy was so successful that she landed on the cover of *Business Week,* an achievement that no other woman had matched. At first, Tupper was happy to give Wise the spotlight, but differences between them grew, and in 1958 he fired her after she had helped to turn his company into a multimillion-dollar success. Tupper subsequently sold the company, which expanded into an international phenomenon. Wise attempted to establish several home party companies in the cosmetics field, but all failed.

REFERENCES AND FURTHER READINGS

Bowden, Sue, and Avner Offer. 1994. "Household Appliances and the Use of Time: The United States and Britain since the 1920s." *Economic History Review* 47 (4): 725–748.

Breines, Wini. 1992. *Young, White, and Miserable: Growing Up Female in the Fifties*. Boston: Beacon Press.

Brook, Vincent. 1999. "The Americanization of Molly: How Mid-Fifties TV Homogenized 'The Goldbergs' (and Got 'Berg-Larized' in the Process)." *Cinema Journal* 38 (4): 45–67.

Brooks, Tim, and Earle Marsh. 1999. *The Complete Directory to Prime Time Network and Cable TV Shows*. New York: Ballantine.

Carter, Paul A. 1983. *Another Part of the Fifties*. New York: Columbia University Press.

Cohen, Ronald D. 1997. "Delinquents: Censorship and Youth Culture in Recent U.S. History." *History of Education Quarterly* 37 (3): 251–270.

Cuddy-Keane, Melba. 1994. "Conflicting Feminisms and the Problem of Male Space: Joyce Cary and the Fifties." *Cultural Critique*, no. 28: 103–128.

Daniel, Pete. 2000. *Lost Revolutions: The South in the 1950s*. Chapel Hill: University of North Carolina Press.

Darden, Joe T. "Black Residential Segregation since the 1948 *Shelley v. Kraemer* Decision." *Journal of Black Studies* 25 (6): 680–691.

Englehardt, Tom. 1995. *The End of Victory Culture: Cold War America and the Disillusioning of a Generation*. New York: Basic Books.

Geospatial and Statistical Data Center. University of Virginia Library. http://www2.lib.virginia.edu/geostat/index.html (accessed April 21, 2008).

Gilbert, James. 1986. *A Cycle of Outrage: America's Reaction to the Juvenile Delinquent in the 1950s*. New York: Oxford University Press.

Gurin, Gerald Joseph Veroff, and Sheila Feld. 1975. *Americans View Their Mental Health: March–August 1957*. Ann Arbor: ISR Social Science Archive.

Halberstam, David. 1993. *The Fifties*. New York: Fawcett Columbine.

Hyams, Joe. 1992. *James Dean: Lost Little Boy*. New York: Warner Books.

Jackson, Kenneth T. 1985. *Crabgrass Frontier: The Suburbanization of the United States*. New York: Oxford University Press.

Kaledin, Eugenia. 1984. *Mothers and More: American Women in the 1950s*. Boston: Twayne Publishers.

Kloosterman, Robert C., and Chris Quispel. 1990. "Not Just the Same Old Show on My Radio: An Analysis of the Role of Radio in the Diffusion of Black Music among Whites in the South of the United States of America, 1920–1960." *Popular Music* 9 (2): 151–164.

Lipsitz, George. 1986. "The Meaning of Memory: Family, Class, and Ethnicity in Early Network Television Programs." *Cultural Anthropology* 1 (4): 355–387.

Lund, Jens, and Serge Denisoff. 1971. "The Folk Music Revival and the Counter Culture Contributions and Contradictions." *Journal of American Folklore* 84 (334): 394–405.

Marling, Karel Ann. 1991. "Disneyland, 1955: Just Take the Santa Ana Freeway to the American Dream." *American Art* 5 (1/2): 168–207.

Marling, Karel Ann. 1994. *As Seen on TV: The Visual Culture of Everyday Life in the 1950s*. Cambridge: Harvard University Press.

May, Elaine Tyler. 1988. *Homeward Bound: American Families in the Cold War Era*. New York: Basic Books.

Meyerowitz, Joanne. 1993. "Beyond the Feminine Mystique: A Reassessment of Postwar Mass Culture, 1946–1958." *Journal of American History* 79 (4): 1455–1482.

Mintz, Steven, and Susan Kellogg. 1988. *Domestic Revolutions: A Social History of American Family Life*. New York: Free Press.

Morantz, Regina Markell. 1977. "The Scientist as Sex Crusader: Alfred C. Kinsey and American Culture." *American Quarterly* 29 (5): 563–589.

"Morons and Happy Families." 1950. *Time*. http://www.time.com/time/magazine/article/0,9171,858841,00.html (accessed September 5, 2006).

O'Neill, William L. 1986. *American High: The Years of Confidence, 1945–1960*. New York: Free Press.

Oshinsky, David M. 2005. *Polio: An American Story*. Oxford: Oxford University Press.

Palladino, Grace. 1996. *Teenagers: An American History*. New York: Basic Books.

Prelinger Collection. 2007. Internet Archive. http://www.archive.org/details/prelinger.

Reiss, Ira L. 1961. "Sexual Codes in Teen-Age Culture." *Annals of the American Academy of Political and Social Science* 338 (November): 53–62.

Rose, Lisle A. 1999. *The Cold War Comes to Main Street: America in 1950*. Lawrence: University Press of Kansas.

Salzman, Jack. 1991. "Introduction." In *New Essays on* The Catcher in the Rye, ed. Jack Salzman. New York: Cambridge University Press.

Shapiro, Laura. 2005. *Something from the Oven: Reinventing Dinner in 1950s America*. New York: Penguin Books.

U.S. Census Bureau. 1975. *Historical Statistics of the United States Colonial Times to 1970, Part 1, Bicentennial Edition.* Washington, DC: Government Printing Office. Also available at http://www2.census.gov/prod2/statcomp/documents/CT1970p1-.01.pdf (accessed September 5, 2006).

U.S. Census Bureau. 2004. "Census of Housing." http://www.census.gov/hhes/www/housing/census/historic/ownerchar.html (accessed September 5, 2006).

Weiss, Jessica. 2000. *To Have and to Hold: Marriage, the Baby Boom, and Social Change.* Chicago: University of Chicago Press.

Wetherall, W. D. 1989. *The Man Who Loved Levittown.* Pittsburgh: University of Pittsburgh Press.

Whitfield, Stephen J. 1996. *The Culture of the Cold War.* 2d ed. Baltimore: Johns Hopkins University Press.

Whitfield, Stephen J. 1997. "Cherished and Cursed: Toward a Social History of *The Catcher in the Rye.*" *New England Quarterly* 70 (4): 567–600.

Whitburn, Joel. 1991. *Billboard Top 10 Singles Charts.* Menomonee Falls, WI: Record Research.

Wiese, Andrew. 2005. *Places of Their Own: African American Suburbanization in the Twentieth Century.* Chicago: University of Chicago Press.

Young, William H., and Nancy K. Young. 2004. *The 1950s.* American Popular Culture through History Series. Westport, CT: Greenwood Press.

Migrations, Western Development, and Environmental Change

OVERVIEW: WHAT'S DIFFERENT ABOUT THE WEST?

While the region known as the West arguably exhibits many different environmental and topographical characteristics from its peers, it is also socially constructed as part of a historical trajectory unique from the rest of the country. Its frontier past continues to inform the ways in which people inside and outside of the West define it. Since the 19th century, the West has symbolized the potential for economic and demographic expansion. Not all of that potential is symbolic, however; the phenomenal growth of the 1950s fulfilled some of the earlier promise while also providing a glimpse of the problems that would plague the region and the entire United States into the 21st century. By its very nature, the West presented both opportunities and challenges for new arrivals. The region's environment and wide-open spaces seemed to propel its population toward choices that generated both social and environmental obstacles. Conflicts among an increasingly multicultural population seemed inevitable, and population increase created new demand for a scarce resource—water. In addition, the ever-expanding highways that provided access to ever-expanding suburbs contributed to air pollution. The West was not the only region to feel the impact of population shifts, but because it is, in many ways, unique, the region's experiences warrant special attention.

Migration is a constant in human history and the 1950s are no exception. In the first full postwar decade, immigration into the United States by both documented and undocumented immigrants increased dramatically over the previous decades. In even greater numbers, Americans were also on the move; increasing numbers were leaving the Northeast for the Midwest, South, and West. Migrants moved for many reasons. They perceived economic opportunities or left straitened economic circumstances. They moved to be closer to migratory family and friends or to flee cold northeastern winters. Whatever their reasons, these migrations were made possible by federal support for economic and residential development and improved transportation networks.

There continued to be concerns about the effect of immigration on American society and its economy. This was particularly the case with the influx of Mexican migrants, most of whom worked in agricultural jobs in the Southwest, West, and Northwest. Employers first sought great numbers of temporary Mexican workers during World War II, when labor shortages were endemic. The government later extended the program for temporary labor; it eventually lasted 22 years. This program had its critics; they challenged whether or not Mexican workers were necessary and argued that imported labor drove down wages and conditions for their "American" peers. Even more controversial was the fact that the scale of undocumented immigration spiked rapidly during the decade. There were major government efforts to control that influx and to impose comprehensive immigration reform.

Migration put not insignificant pressure on the communities that people were leaving and on the communities to which they were going. Urban populations in the West and South increased greatly and suburban populations did so at an even faster clip. Suburbs were already having some adverse environmental consequences; conservationists and urban planners worried about the toxicity of supposedly healthy suburbs. The presence of so many new residents in the parts of the country that were arguably less hospitable for human habitation posed further environmental questions. How would cities, for example, get adequate supplies of water while avoiding the catastrophic effects of moments when they had too much? Building in arid environments was a risky proposition; as a result, water conservation and reclamation were key factors in political decision making at the local, state, and federal levels. The self-interested campaigns for the all-electric house denied opportunities for some more creative, and environmentally friendly, alternatives.

By examining the experiences of the residents of several communities in the West and Southwest, it is possible to see how these pressures affected people's lives and also how people responded to the various environmental, economic, and social challenges to their new lives. In Los Angeles, less-affluent residents struggled to find safe and affordable housing. At various points, both advocates of public housing projects and private commercial and residential developers sought to displace those residents from neighborhoods for the purposes of reinventing modern Los Angeles. Protests and political conflicts ensued; generally, public housing was either scaled back or phased out while private developers received access to premium land that was often heavily subsidized by city leaders anxious to anchor businesses and middle-class residents in the city. Simultaneously, they struggled to deal with the consequences of living somewhere that had become all too popular; smog, for example, presented unique challenges to officials as more and more automobiles clogged Southern California freeways.

In the case of Las Vegas, located in an even more arid region, the city's explosive growth represented its rise as a center of both wartime and Cold War military production as well as its higher-profile presence as a resort city for Americans seeking leisure and Lady Luck in new casinos. Las Vegas, however, symbolized many of the limits of the racial and economic progress sought by African Americans who had moved there in droves. Working in the casinos or defense plants was often better work than they had left behind, but segregation prevented even famous African Americans from eating or staying at casinos; when the African American residents of Las Vegas's Westside sought help with municipal sanitation and urban redevelopment, it came only when city officials had the need to build a highway through the neighborhood. Only the determined pressure by high-profile African Americans and the efforts to provide multiracial alternatives to the all-white Strip finally opened Las Vegas to people of color.

In migration, development, and environmental change, many of the patterns that became pronounced in the 1950s have only intensified since then. As population shifts continue, the cities and states of these popular regions struggle to find solutions for many of the same problems.

TIMELINE

1950   Los Angeles begins acquiring property in Chavez Ravine for the Elysian Park Heights.

1951   Atomic testing begins at the Nevada Test Site, only 60 miles from Las Vegas.

1952   Congress passes the Immigration and Nationality Act of 1952 (McCarran-Walter Act) over President Truman's veto.

1954   Federal government begins Operation Wetback to round up and deport illegal Mexican immigrants.

1955   Disneyland opens.

Nevada forms Gaming Control Board to tighten regulation of gambling and reduce the influence of organized crime in Las Vegas.

The Moulin Rouge, the first integrated casino/resort in Las Vegas, opens.

1956   Construction begins on the Glen Canyon Dam in Arizona.

Congress approves plans for the Colorado River Storage Project.

William Whyte's anticorporate study, *The Organization Man,* appears for the first time.

1957   Los Angeles County bans use of backyard incinerators in an effort to reduce air pollution.

City of Los Angeles officials and Brooklyn Dodgers agree to bring team to city.

Minsky's Follies, Las Vegas's first topless revue, begins at the Desert Inn.

1959   William Pereira prepares a plan for the future University of California Irvine campus.

The Changing Face of the West: Immigration and Demographic Change

Both internal and external migrations have characterized American history from the years of first contact between Europeans and American Indians. At various moments, external immigration has eclipsed smaller internal migrations and vice versa. By the early 20th century, the federal government imposed significant restrictions on external immigration, providing preferential treatment for immigrants from Western and Northern Europe. Two world wars had dramatic impacts on migration, but it was in the 1950s that immigration numbers began to go upwards significantly after 30 years of strict limits.

Internal migrations also experienced various ebbs and flows. While some of the most significant internal migrations of the 20th century occurred during the so-called First and Second Great Migrations of African Americans out of the South in the first half of the century, another pattern of internal migration was occurring. Largely a result of economic change and massive government development in regions previously less desirable for habitation, many Americans were leaving the industrialized Northeast for the South and West.

Internal and External Migrations: Population Shifts South and West

While the population of the United States continued to be more heavily concentrated in the northern and eastern states, population shifts during the 1950s illustrated trends that would continue for the next several decades. While it was still numerically smaller in population than its three larger counterparts, the region defined by the census as the West grew by almost 39 percent during the decade. In that period, it added (through either birth or migration) more than 7.8 million people, more than any other region. The South experienced the second-largest percentage change; its population increased by almost 7.8 million people, a 16.5 percent change.

Certain states experienced disproportionate gains in population. The population of California increased by 48.5 percent as more than five million more people called California home by 1960. The population of Florida grew even faster in percentage terms; it changed by almost 80 percent. Texas and Nevada grew by 24.2 percent and 78.2 percent, respectively.

Most of the people moving into states in the South and West were moving into urban or suburban areas; the population changes in cities and what were

Aerial view of suburban housing developments sprawling into the distance, Los Angeles, 1954. (Library of Congress)

defined as "urban fringes" reflect this. The urban fringe of Denver, Colorado, for example, expanded by more than 270 percent in the 1950s. The urban fringe of Los Angeles and Long Beach, California, got bigger by more than 80 percent. Of the 5.1 million additional people living in California by 1960, more than 1.6 million of them were in the suburbs of Los Angeles.

People moved west and south for many different reasons. Some had positive experiences there while in the military during World War II. Others sought new jobs enabled by federally sponsored development in places like Orange County, California. Some simply sought warmer climes; with the arrival of air-conditioning in homes, factories, and offices, they could counteract the worst excesses of temperature and create climate-controlled oases, even in the desert. This rapid growth had economic, social, political, and environmental consequences.

Immigration and Nationality Act of 1952

The Immigration and Nationality Act of 1952 (or McCarran-Walter Act) was an effort to streamline and consolidate what had been up to that time an assortment of different laws regarding immigration and naturalization. It also built upon the pre-existing law and reflected how much attitudes and public policy had shifted since some of the earlier immigration statutes had been implemented. It eliminated racial language from naturalization requirements and gendered language from immigration policy.

The new legislation arguably created higher barriers for some potential migrants while somewhat increasing protections for those at risk of expulsion. Historian Mae Ngai notes that consular decisions on visas were final and citizenship decisions would no longer be subject to judicial review (Ngai 2004, 207). The act also established new immigration quotas based on different formulas than those of earlier immigration restriction acts while maintaining extremely low quotas (as few as 100 people per year) from colonial countries. It also increased the grounds upon which aliens could be barred from entry or deported while simultaneously improving "procedural safeguards" for those facing deportation. In what would become a trend in terms of targeting potential immigrants, the law also created preferential standards for skilled migrants whose talents were perceived as useful in the United States.

Cold War pressures certainly affected the tenor of the legislation (which sought to improve the ability of the government to deny entry to political radicals) and the opposition to its passage. Some legislators with constituencies that contained large numbers of immigrants protested the injustice of the colonial policy (which disproportionately affected colonies like Jamaica versus other independent Caribbean nations). Some worried that the restrictive policies would become integrated into anti-American Cold War propaganda. President Truman vetoed the legislation, but Congress overrode his veto (Pastor 1984, 43).

American Immigration during the 1950s

After decades of very limited immigration (largely a result of strict immigration quotas established by the federal government in the 1920s), immigration to the United States grew significantly in the 1950s. Statistics tracking those who obtained permanent residency status show a significant jump over the 1940s when 856,909 immigrants received permanent residency status. During the 1950s, that number increased to almost 2.5 million; this represented growth of almost 200 percent over the immigration of the 1940s.

Immigrants to the United States during the 1950s came from some of the usual places. More than half came from Europe, with the single-largest group coming from Germany. Both Italy and the United Kingdom had large numbers of nationals gaining permanent residency as well, although nowhere close to Germany in number.

Migration was relatively limited from Asia, although it too was dramatically higher than it had been in the 1940s (more than one-third of which was spent in a war with Japan). After Europe, the region with the second-highest number of migrants achieving permanent residency was the Americas. Canada contributed the single-largest number from this region, with more than 350,000 migrants becoming residents. Mexico was close behind, with more than 270,000 migrants.

The number of Mexican migrants winning residency status, however, is only a small percentage of the numbers of Mexicans who crossed the border each year in search of employment and a better life for themselves and their families, who often remained behind. Under a federal government program, often referred to as the "bracero" (or farmworker) program, a large number of Mexican migrants were allowed temporarily into the country. The numbers also fail to account for the huge numbers of undocumented Mexicans who entered the country illegally.

Mexican Americans

One analyst who bemoaned the dearth of scholarship on the Mexican American community wrote in 1951 that the "group is so old that it has been forgotten and so new that it has not yet been discovered" (McWilliams 1951, 301). Referring simultaneously to the historical legacy of Mexican habitation of what became part of the United States and the more recent influx of migrants from Mexico, Carey McWilliams shrewdly situated Mexican Americans in the broader historical context of the West. He noted that despite their great numbers and cohesive communities, Mexican Americans had as yet been unable to break through discriminatory barriers to formal political power in places like Texas and California. He noted with satisfaction that a Mexican American man (Edward Roybal) was elected to the city council of Los Angeles in 1948, the first to serve since 1881.

Table 5.1. Immigration between the 1940s and 1960s

Immigration Statistics	1940s	1950s	1960s
Total number granted permanent residency	856,608	2,499,268	3,213,749
Percentage change		191.76	28.59
Region of origin			
Europe	472,524	1,404,973	1,133,443
Asia	34,532	135,844	358,605
Americas	328,435	921,610	1,674,172
Country of origin			
Germany	119,506	576,905	209,616
Italy	50,509	184,576	200,111
Canada	160,911	353,169	433,128
Mexico	56,158	273,847	441,824
China	16,072	8,836	14,060
Japan	1,557	40,651	40,956

Source: U.S. Department of Homeland Security. 2006.

Table 5.2. Voluntary Departures in the 1940s and 1950s

Aliens expelled	Formal	Voluntary
1950	10,199	572,477
1951	17,328	673,169
1952	23,125	703,778
1953	23,482	885,391
1954	30,264	1,074,277
1955	17,695	232,769
1956	9,006	80,891
1957	5,989	63,379
1958	7,875	60,600
1959	8,468	56,610
Total 1950–1959	153,431	4,403,341

Source: Yearbook of Immigration Statistics: 2005. Washington, DC: U.S. Department of Homeland Security, Office of Immigration Statistics.

Note: "Voluntary" departures means that illegal aliens agree to be deported. DHS identifies the majority of voluntary deportations as those of Mexican nationals.

Chinese Immigration and Ongoing Discrimination

There was a long tradition of anti-Asian sentiment in the United States dating back to the middle of the 19th century. The Chinese Exclusion Act of 1882 and its subsequent renewals prohibited Chinese immigration for six decades; only during World War II when China was an ally did the federal government end the restriction. Despite the theoretical right of Chinese nationals to apply for immigration, strict quotas initially allowed only a few more than 100 immigrants annually. This was a symbolic relaxation of Chinese exclusion at best.

The rise to power of Mao Zedong and the increase of Cold War tensions further complicated the efforts by some Chinese migrants to seek permission to enter the United States. The American Consulate in Hong Kong used tactics that one scholar likened to a "severe interrogation" (Ngai 2004, 207). Because of problems obtaining the required birth and identity documentation or the testimony of Americans who would vouch for them, visa applicants often faced an impossible standard.

Federal immigration authorities were zealously seeking those Chinese immigrants whom they believed had entered the country fraudulently. In 1956, grand juries in San Francisco and New York investigated the matter. Their efforts explicitly challenged the various Chinese cultural and "family" associations that federal officials believed were complicit in immigration fraud. Chinese groups responded with legal and political strategies, as well as using the media to criticize the government's actions. A judge eventually quashed the subpoenas (Ngai 2004, 212–216). Compared to the sensationalism of its efforts, the government succeeded in uncovering relatively few cases of organized immigration fraud.

The following year, the government tried a new tactic. In exchange for government assistance in applying for documented status to some undocumented or fraudulent Chinese immigrants, the immigrants were encouraged to "confess" their immigration sins. Between 1957 and 1965, more than 11,000 confessed to false claims while another 19,000 were "implicated . . . by the confessions of others." Mae Ngai argues convincingly that while the confession program illustrated some relaxation of historical anti-Asian sentiment, the way the government handled the process "reproduced racialized perceptions that *all* [emphasis added] Chinese immigrants were illegal and dangerous" (Ngai 2004, 221–223).

Mexican Migrants: The Bracero Program

Documented and undocumented immigrants from Mexico had experienced low wages and discrimination since the early 20th century. During the Great Depression, hundreds of thousands of Mexican immigrants had been deported back to Mexico, much to the chagrin of the Mexican government, which felt that its citizens had been sadly misused. The Mexican government was thus suspicious when mounting pressure for low-wage labor spurred a request from the United States to discuss a new contract labor program in the early 1940s. At the same time, the government was reluctant to deny the United States assistance in wartime; according to one scholar, they were also mindful of the close economic

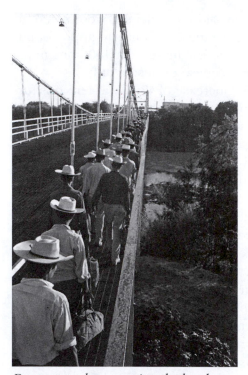

Bracero workers crossing the border from Mexico into Hidalgo, Texas, in 1956. They were among the roughly five million Mexicans who toiled on U.S. farms and on railroad lines during the 22-year temporary worker project dubbed the "bracero program." This program became notorious for its abuses of Mexican workers, who were often not paid as promised and endured unhealthy and unsafe living and working conditions. (Leonard Nadel/National Museum of American History/Reuters/Corbis)

relationship between the two nations (García 1980, 23).

The arrangement that emerged came to be known as the bracero (or farmworker) program. While the Mexican government believed that it was likely to be temporary, the program actually lasted 22 years from 1942 until 1964. During that time, more than 4.5 million temporary workers (braceros) entered the United States to work primarily in agricultural jobs. Generally, they contracted to work for one year and pledged to return upon completing the term of their contract. Under the original agreement, the U.S. government in return promised that braceros would receive transportation to and from the United States and the "prevailing wage" in the occupation in which they were engaged, and be free from discrimination during their time in the United States (García 1980, 24). Many of those promises would be very difficult for the government to fulfill.

Demand for bracero labor was not constant during the program's lifetime. Certain periods showed much greater demand. Between 1956 and 1959, for example, more than 400,000 braceros came to the United States annually. Corruption was common at most steps of the process. Many potential braceros paid bribes to Mexican officials to ensure they would be considered for the program (Garcia 2001, 176; García 1980, 37). Once they arrived in the United States, they discovered that they were not earning as much as their "permanent" peers, many of whom were Mexican immigrants or Mexican Americans.

Problems with Bracero Labor

The presence of temporary bracero workers led to some problems with their peers. Some workers complained that braceros worked too hard or failed to pick agricultural produce correctly. Braceros countered that in some instances they actually helped to raise wages; a strike by braceros in the first year of the program raised wages for the following season. Fights were not uncommon, either.

The conflict between Mexican Americans and braceros had complicated roots in economic and cultural divides. Braceros were less likely to complain about poor conditions or substandard wages because they were earning so much more than they would have in Mexico. Spanish-language ability was apparently another divisive issue; some Mexican Americans could no longer speak it fluently, if at all, and that could cause tension with the braceros. The perhaps inevitable romantic and sexual relationships that developed also added to tension; many Mexican American women who got involved with braceros faced ostracism from their communities (Garcia 2001, 180).

According to historian Matt Garcia, much of this tension came to a head in California's Pomona Valley in 1952 when four young Mexican American men killed bracero Ricardo Mancilla Gómez. Mexican officials immediately removed the remaining bracero workers from the region while the local community debated the import of this killing as well as the source of other acts of violence that had periodically affected the relationship between the two groups. Farmers eventually lobbied successfully for the braceros' return. Community leaders, in turn, worried simultaneously about the seeming delinquency of their young men while decrying the negative impact on wages they claimed was caused by imported workers (Garcia 2001, 181–183). Despite some efforts to reduce tensions, violent incidents continued throughout the decade.

Supporting Braceros

The bracero program had many supporters on both sides of the border. Employers liked it for obvious reasons; they got a relatively stable, relatively quiescent, low-paid workforce. Braceros themselves earned on average (despite high rents and other issues of corruption) much more than they would have in Mexico. The Mexican government recognized that money sent home by braceros, or remittances, were an incredibly important source of income for Mexicans and for the Mexican economy. A disproportionate percentage of braceros also came from a limited number of impoverished regions in Mexico, which helped to address potential unrest at home as well.

The U.S. government publicized what it felt to be the positive aspects of the program to Americans around the country. Employers went one step further. In 1959, the California Council of Growers commissioned a film called *Why Braceros?* to explain further the merits of bracero labor (Gonzalez 2006, 103). The film touted the efficiency of the system and stressed that braceros were willing to take on the most undesirable tasks that "Americans" were unwilling to do. It minimized the numbers of braceros in terms of the total farmworker population and denied arguments that bracero labor undermined wages and displaced "Americans." The film can be watched today online through the Prelinger Archives (2007).

Undocumented Workers and Braceros

The demand for bracero labor also had the impact of increasing the flow of undocumented workers across the border into Texas, California, and elsewhere. Some of these workers (often referred to pejoratively as "illegals") offered specific skills to employers and were in great demand. Some employers simply wanted to avoid the administrative hassles of arranging for bracero labor; this was especially true in the border states like Texas where many undocumented workers presented themselves to potential employers. Texas had also been denied bracero labor during the 1940s because the Mexican government, citing past discrimination, refused to permit it.

The relationship between the sanctioned bracero migration and that of undocumented workers illustrates one thing most of all: great demand existed for low-wage labor in the United States. The numbers of deportations were thought to represent at least in part the number of undocumented Mexican workers entering the country. Those numbers reached new heights in the 1950s, prompting one government commission, formed to investigate the issue, to conclude in 1951 that "in its newly achieved proportions, it is virtually an invasion" (President's Commission on Migratory Labor 1951, 69–88).

Debates over the bracero program inevitably involved the issue of undocumented labor. Critics of the bracero program wanted to tie compliance on undocumented workers to allotment of bracero labor. According to Public Law 78, which was a response by the federal government in 1951 to critics of the program and President Truman's Commission on Migratory Labor, employers would bear more responsibility for the costs of the bracero program, and those who also employed undocumented workers would lose their right to acquire bracero labor. Additionally, braceros would be restricted to employers who could establish that there was no other available labor in their area. Despite these efforts to control the influx of undocumented workers and reduce criticism of the bracero program, by the early 1960s, it became more and more difficult to silence the critics. Labor unions criticized the program for lowering wages and creating unfair labor competition. Others decried the abuses of braceros as evidence of the fundamental corruption of the program. President Kennedy reluctantly approved the extension of the program, but Lyndon Johnson allowed it to die in 1964 despite calls from the Mexican government to continue the program. It argued, not unreasonably, that the demand for labor motivated documented and undocumented migration across the border and that whether or not the bracero program continued, migration certainly would.

Deportations

When undocumented migrants entered the United States, they were subject to detention and the possibility of deportation. Historically, many more than those who are legally deported agree to "voluntary" deportation; the Department of Homeland Security suggests today that many of those who agree to be voluntarily deported are undocumented Mexicans. This was likely the case in the 1950s as well. During the decade, there was a significant spike in the numbers of those formally expelled and those deported voluntarily. At least in part, the low numbers of the early 1940s may have been a result of increased demand for wartime labor. By 1949, almost 24,000 people were expelled and 276,000 voluntarily deported. While the number of people expelled dropped in subsequent years, the voluntary deportations skyrocketed. The figures for 1950 were more than double those of the year before. Between 1950 and 1959, 4.4 million people "accepted" deportation.

Operation Wetback

The peak year for "voluntary" deportations was 1954, when more than one million people were deported voluntarily and the government formally expelled more than 30,000 (the highest number during the decade). This was at least in part a result of a government campaign to clamp down on the undocumented migration of "wetbacks." *Wetback* was the term derogatorily applied to a Mexican migrant who entered the country illegally. By 1954, Attorney General Herbert Brownell decided to act aggressively to curb the influx of undocumented migrants into the United States. His initial proposal to have the U.S. Army patrol part of the border met with opposition on both sides of the border. Brownell had sought a number of other solutions to the problem of undocumented migrants, few of them feasible.

By the end of the spring of 1954, immigration officials had marshaled several former generals to lead the offensive. In addition to urging better coordination among the different Border Patrol districts, they also formed a Mobile Task Force to react quickly to incursions. Operation Wetback itself was to commence in early June; it had the support of the State and Labor Departments as well as that of the Mexican government, which pledged to have trains waiting to take deportees away from the border.

The operation first focused on the border with California and Arizona; deportees would be carried mostly by bus to the border at Nogales, Arizona. The federal government asked for the support of local and state governments as well as local law enforcement. Within the first month, more than 50,000 undocumented immigrants had been rounded up and deported. Federal officials cited much higher numbers of people who chose to leave rather than face deportation; at least one scholar disputes those numbers as inflated (García 1980, 199–200).

The focus then shifted to Texas; there, the government faced more determined resistance from employers who preferred the lower rates of undocumented labor to the higher piece-wages demanded by local workers or braceros. Border

Patrol officials met with undisguised hostility from local employers and news-paper editorials. Employers desperate for help with harvests rushed to apply for braceros, some of whom were only recently deported. By September, the larger numbers of the initial roundups had dropped and immigration officials had switched to a new way of moving deportees as far away from the border as possible. They used two ships to ferry them far down the coast to the interior of Mexico. The voyages continued until 1956, when the drowning of seven un-documented migrants prompted a public outcry on both sides of the border (García 1980, 220–221).

The Increasingly Unnatural Environment and Environmental Activism

In some ways, the decade of the 1950s represents a period of transition in which many Americans began to realize that they could simply no longer build un-controllably without great consequence for the natural environment. While the following decade would show the first major burst of postwar environmental activism, many of the concerns that motivated those activists became evident in the 1950s. There were a host of concerns about the environment ranging from fears about population pressure, unrestrained suburban development, irriga-tion, and the damming of rivers to more difficult issues like the unwillingness of many Americans to think about conservation in a time (and land) of appar-ently plentiful and cheap energy.

The suburban landscape was one of the first sites of concern. While many would-be homeowners coveted suburban homes because of the apparent green-space and "natural" settings, most suburban developments were anything but natural and contributed to various environmental problems. From architectural style to the simple number of new homes being built, the suburbs put addi-tional pressure on many local ecosystems, some of which were ill-equipped to handle it.

Especially in the arid West, there were often more basic concerns about the environment and development; access to water was key to the sustainability of existing communities and even more important to the development of future ones. Coupled with concerns about access to water, however, was the problem of building where there was too much water at times. Building in floodplains risked devastating water damage and spurred demand for dams, which carried with them other environmental implications. During the decade, there were sev-eral efforts to alter or block dam development. Some of them were successful while others continued as a result of significant public pressure.

Finally, the post–World War II return to domestic consumption and economic prosperity, coupled with low prices for natural resources, affirmed the beliefs of many Americans that those resources were inexhaustible and could be used to fuel the increasing amenities (like air-conditioning) in American homes and offices.

Suburban Architecture and the Environment: Regionalism Gives Way to Universalism

Historically, architectural styles in the United States often reflected regional differences in climate. Houses in colder states were better insulated to keep out the chill of winter days. Similarly, houses in warmer climates might be surrounded by trees to provide welcome shade or have sleeping porches to allow residents to stay cool on summer nights. Multistory homes with basements provided better insulation from climatological extremes (Rome 2001, 62–63). Why, then, was there often so little variation in the style of new suburban homes being constructed around the country?

The most important answer to that question was cost. Home builders prospered most if they could build and sell houses as quickly as possible. As a result, using standardized plans for standardized lots facilitated quick and inexpensive construction. Single-level homes, lacking staircases and other more expensive features, allowed builders to provide the space desired by suburban families at a reasonable cost. The arrival of air-conditioning further undercut the argument for houses that conformed to the local environment (Rome 2001, 63–64).

There were efforts to encourage home builders to adapt suburban homes appropriately. In the late 1940s and 1950s, supporters of the "solar" house advocated the style as energy-efficient and powered by solar energy. Lacking government-research support, however, the concept never got off the ground in a significant way (Rome 2001, 49–58). With cheap energy generated by fossil fuels and, increasingly, the promise of nuclear power, few opted for the unproven styles.

Where Not to Build Becomes Why Not?

Another environmental concern that came to light in the 1950s was about filling or draining wetlands. Builders saw marshes or swamps near urban areas as opportunities; they could be filled in and even more houses could be built. Critics of the policy argued that wetlands were important not only for the flora and fauna of various ecosystems, but also because wetlands helped to maintain groundwater supplies and control flooding (Rome 2001, 154–157). Another issue was the growing number of people who sought to use wetlands for recreational purposes like hunting and fishing. Sportsmen and conservationists alike feared that wildlife was becoming increasingly scarce as wetlands disappeared.

By the early 1960s, many of the previous decade's arguments were being bolstered by increasing amounts of scientific evidence; wetlands were ecosystems to be treasured, not developed.

Hillsides and Erosion/Landslides

As builders sought more property for suburban development, they used techniques to build homes on lots located on hillsides. Hillsides presented unusual challenges; while the land itself tended to be cheaper, clearing lots for the homes was more challenging. In some cases, builders simply leveled the relevant lots, creating what historian Adam Rome calls "machine-made plateaus." Hillside homes exposed suburbanites to new risks; in addition to the obvious concerns about landslides, there were other issues as well. Soil erosion could carry soil into water supplies, increase the possibility of flooding, and "upset the ecology of streams and lakes" (Rome 2001, 167, 168).

Landslides, however, were the most immediate risk to people and property. Nowhere was that risk greater than California, where two-thirds of new homes in Los Angeles were built on hillsides in the 1950s. During the decade, numerous landslides caused millions of dollars in property damage. In one 1956 landslide, approximately 150 homes were damaged or destroyed; the landslide itself may have been the result of septic-tank systems saturating the soil (Rome 2001, 97–98, 169). Incidents like these spurred some to question the wisdom of hillside construction; by the 1960s, cities and towns were beginning to regulate hillside construction more stringently. Regulation, however, could not stop demand for homes in rapidly growing areas. Hillside homes had become a fact of life.

Suburban Toxicity: Septic Tanks

In the rush to create suburban neighborhoods, builders looked for the cheapest ways to get subdivisions up and running. Connecting every new suburban home to municipal sewer systems (where they existed) was expensive and more complicated than the alternative. That alternative was the septic tank, which provided simple and inexpensive waste processing in one's very own backyard. Septic tanks were ubiquitous; one government estimate from the middle of the 1950s suggested that approximately one-third of all new homes had septic tanks instead of municipal sewage (Rome 2001, 88).

Despite their apparent frugality, septic systems proved more complicated than many people hoped. Even more unfortunate, they failed at an alarming rate. As compared to sewer-line breaks under the street or further down the line, septic-tank failures were all too evident to suburban homeowners as waste could appear in the backyard. Even before 1950, the Federal Housing Authority estimated that one-third of all septic tanks failed in the first three years. Septic-tank failures were more than aesthetic problems; they could also lead to outbreaks of infectious disease and groundwater contamination (Rome 2001, 89).

Especially at the local level, public officials began to discuss regulation of septic systems. Builders opposed regulation because they feared it would restrict future development. Other than requiring all homes to be connected to sewer systems, there were few options. It would take another decade until regulation became commonplace and public officials made efforts to control groundwater contamination.

"My Cup Sudseth Over": Detergent in Water

While septic-tank breakdowns and contaminated well water were not new in the later years of the 1950s, historian Adam Rome notes that suburban homeowners had discovered that, in addition to the bad smells and taste that accompanied contaminated water, tap water now also seemed to contain suds when it came out of the faucet. Tests proved that this was actually synthetic detergent that had seeped through septic systems to wells and returned to the house in a very unfortunate cycle (Rome 2001, 105–106). By 1960, many scientists had identified the presence of synthetic detergents in drinking water as one of the most significant environmental problems in suburbia. Concern mounted as suds appeared in treatment plants, rivers, and lakes as well. The panaceas represented by suburban sewage systems, modern appliances, and chemical detergents suddenly seemed much more menacing than they had previously.

Air Unfit to Breathe

Los Angeles, California, had the distinction, according to one scholar, of creating the "world's first air pollution alert system" (Dewey 2000, 53). That the city needed such a system was a testament to its particular geographic location and the huge growth of both urban and suburban areas in Southern California. Air pollution itself was not particularly new to the region; it had been a periodic issue since the early 20th century when city residents had suffered from days in which the accumulated smoke created by city dwellers had failed to dissipate.

The problem in postwar Los Angeles, however, was smog (a fog created by smoke and other air pollutants), and the causes of smog had increased dramatically over the ensuing decades. In addition to pollution caused by industry and commerce, the growing network of freeways traveled by a vastly greater number of automobiles exacerbated the problem. By 1954, there were more than 2.3 million cars in Los Angeles; the city had the highest number of cars per capita (2.8 persons per vehicle) than any other major American city. Cars in the 1950s lacked catalytic converters, which reduce the pollutants going through vehicles' exhaust systems. As car numbers grew, so too did the gasoline used; it climbed

Smoke drifts across the Los Angeles area, 1954. Air pollution, increasingly identified with the dreaded smog, was one of the major environmental challenges facing Southern California as it became more and more developed. (Library of Congress)

to 4.8 million gallons per day in 1954. A disturbing percentage of that gasoline (approximately 10 percent) passed through engines unburned and went directly into the environment (Dewey 2000, 58–59).

Efforts to control air pollution more systematically began in the late 1940s. In 1947, Los Angeles County created a county Air Pollution Control District (APCD), which would institute many of the reforms mandated to reduce pollution over the next several decades. At least initially, the APCD focused on industrial pollution, restricting emissions from oil-storage facilities, steel mills, and others. By the late 1950s, it had also banned the burning of waste in backyard incinerators; this further cut down on some of the most visible contributors to smog (Dewey 2000, 43–46).

Despite the gains made by the APCD's efforts, smog was still all too common a phenomenon. Scientists conducted research to determine what else might be causing the problem. By the beginning of the decade, one California Institute of Technology scientist had simulated smog by using gasoline and its byproducts. That research pointed directly to the automobile as a principal cause of smog.

While some public and private organizations (including the private Southern California Air Pollution Foundation) pressed for greater regulation of automobile pollution, little happened before the end of the decade. Car manufacturers in particular resisted incorporating any pollution-control devices into their products; devices like catalytic converters added cost and were an admission of the complicity of automobiles in creating air pollution. By 1960, however, the state government forced the issue; passage of the California Motor Vehicle Pollution Control Act ensured that pollution control would feature prominently in the state's efforts and eventually require greater compliance from car makers (Dewey 2000, 57–64).

Too Much and Too Little Water: Damming

The issue of damming was hardly new in the postwar United States. A huge controversy had erupted in the first decades of the century with the authorization of the Hetch Hetchy Dam project in 1913; the dam's purpose was to stabilize and guarantee a water source for the San Francisco Bay Area more than 150 miles away. Even today, the Sierra Club continues to advocate for the restoration of the Hetch Hetchy Valley (which some liken to Yosemite).

Most Americans in the West saw dams as a necessary evil, however. They fulfilled a number of purposes that were increasingly important in the latter half of the 20th century. Depending on where one lived, dams could end or reduce the possibilities of flooding, provide hydroelectric power, and/or conserve water resources to provide a stable and continuous supply. In the arid West, where average rainfall was one-quarter or less than that of the eastern seaboard, most people agreed that dams were crucial guarantors of life and economic development.

People could not always agree, however, on many of the important questions surrounding the location of dams, who would build them, and what impact they might have on natural resources in those areas. Many agreed, for example, that the flooding of the Columbia River in Oregon in 1948 illustrated the need for flood-control projects. The U.S. Army Corps of Engineers released a report on flooding and a blueprint for development of the Columbia River system in 1950; it pushed for more dams on both the Columbia and its tributaries like the Snake River. This plan would eventually become enshrined in congressional legislation authorizing a new round of dams in the state (Robbins 2004, 70–74).

The Bureau of Reclamation and the Colorado River Storage Project

The federal agency with the responsibility for handling water projects in the American West was the Bureau of Reclamation. Created in 1902, the bureau was

Workers build a massive concrete wall across Glen Canyon in 1963. The Glen Canyon Dam, constructed of almost five million cubic yards of concrete, flooded Glen Canyon and created Lake Powell. (U.S. Bureau of Reclamation)

responsible for some of the largest water-reclamation projects (including the construction of the Hoover Dam) in the West. As part of a new effort to bundle numerous projects together into one grand plan (one writer termed it as being of "epic proportions"), the bureau released a draft plan for the Colorado River Storage Project (CRSP) in 1950 (Sturgeon 2002, 28–30).

Political conflicts and other delays resulted in slow initial progress for the CRSP. These complications increased with the election of President Eisenhower, who voiced concern about federal expenditures on water reclamation and sought to stop new construction on such projects. During his time in office, Eisenhower and his advisors pushed generally for private reclamation projects or public-private partnerships instead of wholly publicly funded ones. Despite that, the administration came to support the CRSP, and it began to move forward. Eisenhower's secretary of the Interior, Douglas McKay, was nicknamed "Giveaway" McKay because critics associated his tenure in office (and the Eisenhower administration more broadly) with being too close to businessmen and developers (Sturgeon 2002, 32).

Stopping the Echo Park Dam

No other part of the CRSP captured as much attention in the 1950s as the proposed Echo Park Dam. Plans called for the dam to be located inside the boundaries of the Dinosaur National Monument, a seldom visited but archeologically important site in Utah. Conservationists from a variety of different organizations mobilized to challenge the need for the dam and have it removed from the CRSP plan.

Led by the Sierra Club and the Wilderness Society, opposition to the dam grew in the early 1950s. As a dramatic public relations stunt, the conservation organizations ran river-rafting trips into the area in 1953 to dramatize its natural beauty and the desirability of keeping it from being flooded (Sturgeon 2002, 34–35). From 1950 onward, articles appeared in national publications questioning both the wisdom and utility of the dam (Schulte 2002, 58–59). The Department of the Interior received tens of thousands of pieces of mail on the subject, the vast majority of it opposing construction.

Removing the dam from the CRSP, however, required a complicated political solution in Washington. At congressional hearings in 1954, executive director of the Sierra Club David Brower testified that the engineering calculations and projections on which the justifications for the dam were based were simply wrong. While some immediately challenged Brower's ability to question those calculations, Brower's impassioned plea cemented public opposition to the Echo Park Dam. As debate continued into 1955, supporters of the CRSP (including Colorado's Rep. Wayne Aspinall) realized that if the plan were to go forward, it would have to do so without the dam. When the legislation finally passed the House in early 1956, it did so not only with the Echo Park Dam having been removed, but also with conservationists pushing that no reclamation projects would be built in national parks (Sturgeon 2002, 38–39, 49–51).

Building in Floodplains

The conversion of huge amounts of acreage into housing developments fundamentally altered America's landscape. The choice of where to build those subdivisions that were in such high demand, however, required a complex analysis of the costs of land and the costs to clear the land, not to mention the cost of building the homes themselves. Increasingly, developers chose to build in floodplains; as historian Adam Rome points out, floodplain property was inexpensive, flat, and usually easier to clear than some other property (Rome 2001, 174).

The principal problem of building in floodplains was, of course, the floods themselves. Several large floods in the late 1940s and through the 1950s illustrated the dangers inherent in living near rivers, creeks, or other bodies of water. The 1948 Columbia River flooding reinforced in the public mind the need for better flood-control measures. Midwestern floods in 1951 and floods in the Northeast resulted in numerous deaths and significant property damage (Rome 2001, 174). While the federal government pledged to incorporate flood control into its own conservation efforts, there were as yet no significant regulatory efforts underway to limit the ability of developers to expose homeowners to the risks of floods.

Throughout the decade, however, several scholars who studied flooding began to influence the debate; one of the most prominent was geographer Gilbert White. White's writings on flooding and flood control concluded that flood damage was largely a result of bad choices made by people and therefore almost wholly avoidable (Rome 2001, 176). By the early 1960s, White's ideas had begun to reach a mass audience. As the decade progressed, pressure for greater regulation of floodplain construction also increased.

Irrigation

In addition to periodically struggling with the phenomenon of too much water, it was much more common to suffer from a lack of water; this was especially true of western agriculture. Irrigation was vital for the sustainability of many farms in the arid region. Agricultural statistics show the major increase of farm acreage under irrigation in Arizona, California, and Texas, where the number of acres increased by 67 percent, 51 percent, and 250 percent, respectively, between 1940 and 1950. Nine years later, that acreage had increased once again. Between 1940 and 1959, irrigated acreage in Texas increased by an astonishing 532 percent; in California, there were almost 7.4 million acres of irrigated farmland in 1959. In addition to the large quantities of water consumed for golf courses, resort oases like Las Vegas, and other uses, the growth of the West and Southwest put an even greater strain on already limited water resources.

Monkeywrenchers and Violent Antidevelopment Protest

Not all Americans were content to sit back and allow development to continue in seemingly unregulated fashion. While much of the resistance to various forms of development (including water-reclamation projects) was in the form of peaceful protest, a new type of more violent activism arose by the end of the 1950s. While certainly lacking the drama of the fictional acts from Edward

Abbey's 1975 novel *The Monkeywrench Gang* (in which Glen Canyon Dam is the ultimate target of the antidevelopment protagonists), some Americans began to show their dissatisfaction with rampant development through destruction of property. By the late 1950s, they targeted billboards and other symbols of growth. Not yet the "eco-terrorists" decried by later supporters of development, the protesters of the late 1950s presaged the more violent and organized efforts of later decades.

Restaurant advertising air-conditioned interior, ca. 1950. Air-conditioning changed dramatically the spaces in which Americans lived and worked; it also consumed huge amounts of energy. (Library of Congress)

The All-Electric Landscape: Air-Conditioning

One of the technological developments that permitted builders to use standard

Table 5.3. Farmland Irrigation between 1940s and 1960s

Irrigation Statistics	1940	1950	1959	Change 1940–1950	Change 1940–1950 (%)	Change 1950–1959	Change 1950–1959 (%)	Change 1940–1959 (%)
Arizona farm acreage irrigated	575,464	963,560	1,152,000	388,096	67.44	188,440	19.56	100.19
California farm acreage irrigated	4,276,554	6,438,324	7,396,000	2,161,770	50.55	957,676	14.87	72.94
Texas farm acreage irrigated	894,638	3,131,534	5,656,000	2,236,896	250.03	2,524,466	80.61	532.21

Sources: U.S. Bureau of the Census. 1952. *U.S. Census of Agriculture: 1950.* Vol. III, *Irrigation of Agricultural Lands.* Washington, DC: Government Printing Office; U.S. Department of Agriculture. *Agricultural Statistics 1978.* Washington, DC: Government Printing Office.

architectural styles that varied little from region to region was air-conditioning. Push-button simplicity allowed climate control in even the most arid south-western suburbs. Air-conditioning also cooled offices, buildings, and other commercial ventures. Although air-conditioning was initially offered principally in more expensive homes, the home-building industry tried to capitalize on its appeal in suburban homes more broadly. Marketing campaigns promised numerous psychological, physiological, and financial benefits of an air-conditioned home. Those who purchased homes without air-conditioning might be left behind or suffer other negative consequences (Rome 2001, 64–70).

Utilities and the All-Electric Household

Especially as a result of the spread of air-conditioning, utility companies faced unusually high demand during warmer months; this presented the challenge of how to balance electric consumption year-round. Rather than encouraging conservation, the power utilities decided that the best course of action was to encourage homeowners to consume even more power in winter months. The most effective way to do this was through electric heating. Utility companies offered subsidies to builders to put electric heating in homes: the more electric appliances that builders incorporated into the homes, the larger the subsidy. This effectively passed along the higher costs of electric heating to consumers (electric heat was less efficient than either oil or natural gas). In 1956, General Electric began a promotional campaign called "Live Better Electrically" to tout the benefits of electric appliances and heat (Rome 2001, 72–77). Some power companies even lowered the cost of electricity for consumers who used the most.

THE CITY OF ANGELS EXPLODES: LOS ANGELES AND ORANGE COUNTY

The question of urban redevelopment (later called urban renewal) is a complicated issue tied into efforts by city governments to anchor residential and commercial populations in central cities and efforts to slow the "flight" of people and investment dollars into suburban areas. Los Angeles was no exception.

Different groups of people had different concerns about urban "blight" and the presence of "slums" in their cities. Some property owners who lived in neighborhoods near blighted areas feared decreasing property values. Property owners who either owned property or lived in "slum" neighborhoods needed the housing and/or welcomed the rents collected from less-affluent residents. They were understandably leery of redevelopment efforts. City officials often wanted to push the urban poor to the periphery and create commercial and cultural developments that would bring in larger numbers of tourists and the increasingly suburbanized middle class.

Perhaps even more important than agreement that there was a problem was the lack of consensus about the solution to it. Some felt any effort by local governments to engage in redevelopment smacked of communism and an encroaching state. Private property interests opposed almost any public effort to build affordable housing. Homeowners in areas near proposed projects feared their own property values would decline. Builders and contractors feared the loss of business in the face of monolithic city contracts. Those who faced displacement from slum clearance often preferred to be left alone, despite the at-times-squalid nature of their environments. Public housing supporters saw the process as an opportunity to significantly improve living conditions for those who would likely never realize the suburban American dream. Among supporters were city planners, labor unions (at least initially), and some religious and political organizations that represented less-affluent constituencies. In the case of Los Angeles, these debates would play out in numerous neighborhoods; while some of the details would differ, many of the key issues remained the same. At stake was who would design (and build) the modern metropolis. Equally at stake was who would be able to afford to live there once it had been built.

Eminent Domain in Bunker Hill

One of the first neighborhoods targeted by those who supported redevelopment in central Los Angeles was Bunker Hill. A century-old residential neighborhood, Bunker Hill had become an obstacle in the eyes of those who sought to simultaneously address issues of "blight," extend the business and commercial areas of downtown Los Angeles, and bring in some higher-profile centers of high culture. Redevelopment supporters hoped to anchor important corporations downtown and bring tourists in ever greater numbers into a cleaner, more modern landscape.

After the postwar failure of what urban historian and social critic Mike Davis calls "piece-meal private-sector redevelopment" in Bunker Hill, the neighborhood's critics sought to use the city government's new redevelopment efforts instead (Davis 2002, 148). As with Chavez Ravine, the site for another controversial development project, initial plans called for a project that included eleven apartment buildings (Avila 2004, 58–59). After changes in the city government, however, those plans for such an extensive program of public housing fell away, and there was a renewed emphasis on different kinds of construction; if housing was included, it tended to be housing accessible only to those with higher incomes than many of those displaced by eminent domain.

Despite protests by local residents who vigorously fought redevelopment of their neighborhood, the old Bunker Hill was doomed. Eminent domain and "blighted" status allowed the Community Redevelopment Agency to acquire much of the property in the neighborhood throughout the decade. Demolition began in 1960. One scholar calls this the "suburbanization" of downtown Los Angeles (Avila 2004, 62). Mike Davis sees the incident as indicative of how a city agency originally intended to promote public housing had become instead "the collective instrument of all the developers" (Davis 2002, 149).

Building High Culture on Bunker Hill

Sharp divisions between high and low culture in Los Angeles gained new momentum in the 1950s when wealthy socialite Dorothy Chandler began pushing for an elite music center in the struggling Bunker Hill neighborhood. Chandler's music center was a key cultural component of the private developers' alternative offered to contrast earlier redevelopment plans that included thousands of units of public housing. The Bunker Hill neighborhood became the battleground over these competing visions of downtown Los Angeles. Chandler offered a vision of a new music center in what had been Bunker Hill. Breaking through some traditional social barriers, she raised funds from Jewish contributors as well as the more usual WASP-y suspects (Avila 2004, 60–61). After the clearing of the land was completed in 1960, efforts went forward to begin construction of two new music venues; when the Dorothy Chandler Pavilion opened in 1964 (along with the Mark Taper Forum), it represented a glittering effort to prove the cultural credentials of Los Angeles. Those who remembered the displacement of a diverse community of lower-income Angelenos with few other residential options, however, were less delighted by the prospect of cultural enlightenment.

The 2003 completion of Frank Gehry's Walt Disney Concert Hall as the most recent of the buildings that comprise the Los Angeles Music Center represents yet another effort to legitimize the city as a nexus of high culture. The four-decade history of the Music Center illustrates that, during periods of urban renewal, cities sought to redefine what cultural activities were offered and who was welcome (and able) to participate in them. The Los Angeles Music Center and Lincoln Center in New York are two such examples.

Proposition B

Throughout 1951, opinions on the subject of public housing shifted dramatically on the Los Angeles City Council. Initially supportive of the projects, the majority had turned against the City Housing Authority (CHA) contract by the end of the year. Because the federal government had provided much of the funding to start acquiring and clearing property for redevelopment, however, the city could not simply walk away from the contract without repaying as much as $12 million in federal funds. Undeterred, the city council voted 8–7 in late December to revoke the contract (Parson 2005, 108–109).

A power struggle ensued between the mayor, the Los Angeles City Council, and the (CHA). While Mayor Fletcher Bowron claimed not to favor public housing personally, he argued that he felt there was no viable alternative to the program. The CHA began legal action to force the city to comply with the terms of the contract. For its part, the council decided to take the issue to the public and called for a referendum asking whether or not the voters wanted to reinstate the public housing contract. Thus, the question of Proposition B would be addressed in municipal elections in June 1952.

Ironically enough, the vote on Proposition B would have no legal standing. Even before the elections, court decisions determined that the city council had no standing to revoke the contract (Parson 2005, 110–111). That didn't prevent people from rallying to encourage voters to choose one position or another, however. A group called Citizens for Slum Clearance encouraged a "yes" vote supporting reinstatement of the public housing contract while the Chamber of Commerce spearheaded the "no" campaign. In the end, the "nos" outnumbered their opposition by more than 120,000 votes, suggesting at least that public housing had become hugely controversial among many citizens of Los Angeles.

Public Housing Eyes Chavez Ravine

When the Health Department declared the neighborhood in Los Angeles known as Chavez Ravine as the "worst slum area in the city," it was perhaps inevitable that it would become a target for the advocates of urban renewal (Parson 2005, 165). Unlike some other cases, however, what eventually happened in Chavez Ravine showed the very different motives that advocates of redevelopment shared and highlighted the limited influence of those who sought to replace low-income housing with affordable public housing. By the end of its redevelopment, Chavez Ravine had not become a residential haven for poorer Angelenos; instead, it became a symbol (however popular) of municipal largesse toward private developers.

The original plan imagined modern housing that would accommodate not just the original inhabitants of the area, but also many thousands of others who had been rendered homeless by other redevelopment efforts. By late 1950, the City Housing Authority had begun to purchase property that would go toward the creation of a large project that would eventually house 17,000 people (Parson 2005, 168–169). As with many other renewal efforts, the plan ran into opposition from existing home and property owners in the area, as well as those who opposed public housing as an unacceptable alternative to private development.

Red-Baiting Urban Renewal

Opponents of urban renewal used all of the tactics at their disposal to argue that public housing was undesirable for political as well as economic reasons. As critics often equated public housing with creeping socialism, the political loyalties of its advocates were subject to scrutiny. As the debate over Chavez Ravine raged, the political affiliations of Frank Wilkinson, a City Housing Authority employee and expert witness in the wrangling over the fate of the proposed Elysian Park Heights housing project, became central. When asked about this issue, Wilkinson refused to respond and was quickly suspended from his job. Several other fellow CHA workers met with the same fate shortly thereafter.

The allegations resulted in hearings by the California Un-American Activities Committee, which took place in the fall of 1952. Several past and present CHA employees testified; those who refused to answer questions were summarily dismissed from their jobs. The hearings concluded with a warning from the committee that public housing was much more likely to encourage Communist sympathies than other environments; this was a result of the "socially maladjusted" nature of many residents and the "high incidence of racial minority groups," which "made the field even more fertile" (Parson 2005, 125). Such pronouncements certainly lent credibility to private developers and more prosperous property owners who feared the impact of public housing on their own plans for the city.

The Aréchiga Family Resists Renewal

One of the last remaining holdouts resisting eminent domain in Chavez Ravine was the Aréchiga family. Having first moved into the area three decades before, the family occupied several houses (and owned several others) in the neighborhood. When the City Housing Authority condemned their homes in 1951, it offered them $11,500, far less than the $17,000 value established by an appraiser (Parson 2005, 171). After Mayor Norris Poulson canceled the Elysian Park Heights project in 1953, the Aréchigas appealed the condemnation. Since there was no longer a project planned for the site, they contended, there was no longer a reason for them to move.

The case made its way through a series of courts; the final decision in favor of the city came in 1958 and the city sought to remove the Aréchigas in May 1959. Police removed them from their homes and bulldozers promptly knocked the homes down. National television coverage illustrated the struggle over urban renewal, eminent domain, and what had by then become the issue of public subsidies for private development (in this case, Dodger Stadium). The deal with the Dodgers and the change in city government had shifted the terms of the debate. Whereas some of those who had opposed the public housing projects proposed in the late 1940s and early 1950s had decried the forcible removal of private property owners as reminiscent of either Soviet or Nazi authoritarian tactics, their tone changed once Norris Poulson became mayor in 1953. Using similar tactics to remove recalcitrant holdouts like the Aréchigas raised the ire of those who opposed the Dodgers' new stadium; using the same rhetoric of the police state, they were no less passionate about the eviction of the family. In the words of one scholar, incidents like this and others indicated the victory of "corporate modernism" over "community modernism" (Parson 2005, 185–186).

A New Kind of "Bum" in Chavez Ravine

When Rep. Norris Poulson returned to Los Angeles to run for mayor in the 1953 election, public housing was one of the central issues in the race. Then-Mayor Bowron had supported the proposed developments and thus became a target for conservative forces (rallied by the conservative *Los Angeles Times*). Poulson prevailed and immediately sought to halt or reduce the existing projects. As a result, the city ended its contract with the City Housing Authority and canceled the Elysian Park Heights development in Chavez Ravine as well as several others. This effectively halved the proposed number of units from the original plans.

The city did, however, promise to devote the property it had already acquired for redevelopment for public use. This pledge came into question in 1957 when city and county officials traveled to Florida to offer Chavez Ravine as the potential site for a major-league baseball stadium for the Brooklyn Dodgers, whose owner, Walter O'Malley, had been thinking about departing an aging Ebbets Field and an increasingly crowded New York City media market for several years.

In the course of its negotiations, the city offered the Dodgers (whose players had earned the nickname of "Bums" in the 1930s) over 300 acres of land as well as several million dollars for clearing it. In exchange, O'Malley promised little but a community youth center that was apparently never built. This was allegedly to pay lip service to the requirement that the property be used for "public purposes" (Avila 2004, 161–162). Even that no longer became necessary when Mayor Poulson and a politically sanitized housing authority simply changed the language of the agreement to remove that requirement from it, thus clearing the way for the "Bums" to leave Brooklyn for sunnier climes. Construction on Dodger Stadium began in 1959 and they played their first game there in April 1962.

Opposition to the deal struck with O'Malley centered around the perception that the city had given away too much in luring the team, not that the land originally intended for low-income public housing had become instead a privately owned shrine of commercialized recreation. It is also important to note that many of the poorer male Angelenos who might have benefited from better housing alternatives were still enthusiastic about the arrival of a baseball franchise.

Hispanic Civil Rights:
The Community Service Organization

One of the most prominent examples of community activism in Los Angeles came in 1948 when future councilman Edward Roybal and other Hispanic leaders formed the Community Service Organization (CSO). The CSO's stated mission was to be a "self-help, civic action agency." By 1953, the group claimed 3,500 members. While it was arguably a multiethnic organization, 85 percent of CSO members were Mexican or Mexican American. Margaret Rose characterizes the vast majority as low income and young "white collar, factory and field workers" (Rose 1994, 179, 180).

Women were an essential constituency in the CSO. Women like Hope Mendoza (later Hope Mendoza Schechter) were among its founders, and female members provided some of the domestic skills relied upon by activist organizations of the time. They also contributed much-needed financial support and pushed for improved community services in neighborhoods. Populated by a combination of women who brought "women's" issues into the group and men who returned from service in World War II angered by ongoing discrimination, the CSO welcomed members of both sexes. There were some limits on women's participation, however. Leadership remained almost wholly male. By the mid-1950s, the CSO had become a national organization. It would later become a launching pad for the organizing career of César Chávez, who became the organization's national head in 1960.

The issues that motivated the CSO were common to many other lower-income people of color nationwide. It protested police brutality, conducted voter registration drives, encouraged the city to improve services in lower-income neighborhoods, and formed a close alliance with organized labor in Los Angeles and elsewhere. It also challenged the more negative aspects of immigration reform embodied in the 1952 Immigration and Naturalization Act. The CSO had many successes and several notable failures, including the loss of the Chavez Ravine to the private development plan of the City of Los Angeles and the Brooklyn (soon to be Los Angeles) Dodgers. The organization did, however, provide what Margaret Rose calls a "bridge" between an older type of community mutual-aid organization and the social activists of the 1960s (Rose 1994, 194).

Sexual Politics: L.A. Communists
and the Mattachine Society

Given Cold War condemnations of some political and sexual activities as transgressive, gay and lesbian Communists were at a distinct disadvantage. Harry Hay was a founder of the Mattachine Society, which sought to provide support to gay men nationwide and to weaken the stigmas attached to homosexuality. He was also a Communist. As he sought to build a constituency for his fledgling organization, he turned to other local gay political radicals for support. Three of the five founding members of Mattachine were active in Communist Party politics. According to one analyst of the group, it was their beliefs (as Communists) in the possibility and desirability of social change that brought them to their efforts at making homosexuality more palatable to the general public (Hurewitz 2007, 241–243).

Daniel Hurewitz goes farther to argue that it was not just the radical political beliefs of individuals that determined the founding of organizations like the Mattachine Society. He claims that it was also the liberalizing influence of "bohemian" urban neighborhoods like Edendale in Los Angeles. In those neighborhoods, artists and intellectuals fostered a more welcoming atmosphere for diversity, including sexual diversity. Appropriating the rights consciousness of other groups (Mattachine founders identified themselves as a minority akin to racial and ethnic minorities), members started small groups in Los Angeles to discuss matters of mutual interest. Within several years, there were several thousand members in California alone (Hurewitz 2007, 249–251),

Freeways Lead to Autopia: Orange County and Its Real and Imagined Suburban Landscapes

Even though the American West was the beneficiary of some of the postwar population shifts, its own cities were undergoing a process in which either new migrants or existing residents chose to move to suburban communities in ever growing numbers. Perhaps no better example of this can be seen than Orange County, California. South of Los Angeles, Orange County experienced a population increase by almost half a million people between 1950 and 1960; this represented an incredible 225 percent increase over its 1950 population of 216,000 people. By 1967, Orange County was the second-largest county in the state.

Looking at what sociologists call the push and pull factors influencing migration illustrates why Orange County could, and did, grow so rapidly during the 1950s. First and foremost, more affluent (and usually white) residents of the Los Angeles area were seeking the same suburban dream that so many of their peers sought throughout the country. Orange County boasted a much lower population density and a number of willing developers who sought to capitalize on newfound demand. Second, the arrival of so many new migrants seeking to make their lives in Los Angeles strained the existing housing resources far beyond capacity. With the metropolitan area itself increasing in size by almost 2.5 million people (more than a 62 percent increase) during the decade, it was impossible for the city to do anything but grow outwards. Finally, Orange County was symbolic of the most recent developments that typified massive government investment in the West from World War II onward. The expansion of the military-industrial complex in the county meant that thousands of jobs were newly available there.

Suburban development was anything but axiomatic, however, around areas that were less developed than some of their eastern counterparts. In the case of Southern California, what enabled the extension of suburban development was the creation of massive freeways. They allowed suburban residents to get to jobs and cultural amenities in the city while escaping back to the landscaped suburban ranches that increasingly typified American suburbs in the 1950s.

The Military-Industrial Complex and the Growth of Orange County

During World War II, those who sought to transform the predominantly agricultural county looked for ways to bring military bases there. By the end of the war, the Army, Navy, and Marine Corps all had bases in the county. Not only did these bases bring in welcome revenue for merchants, but they also brought in thousands of new residents.

This trend continued in the 1950s. Wartime spending gave way to Cold War spending, which not only kept the military in the county, but also brought in defense contractors and other defense-related businesses. One estimate suggests that the total value of defense spending (and military payrolls) brought more than $50 billion into California during the decade. Southern California was the disproportionate beneficiary of that spending (McGirr 2001, 26).

By the end of the decade, tens of thousands of jobs were added to defense-related payrolls as defense contractors moved in. Manufacturing was the largest sector in the state by 1960, showing how far Orange County had come from its agricultural roots. The new jobs and new migrants created rapid growth in the real estate, service, and retail sectors as well (McGirr 2001, 27–28).

How "White" Is Your Valley? Orange County and Diversity

As Orange County grew, it remained overwhelmingly white. According to the 1960 Census, there were only 3,171 residents classified as "Negro." Another larger group appeared as "Other," 6,400 in total. ("Other" was a catch-all category used by the census when racial categories like "Asian" and "Indian" did not appear separately.) This did not account for those of Mexican ancestry; the census recognized a Mexican "race" in 1930 but had removed the category after protests among Hispanics. Thus, Mexican Americans began to be considered "white" unless they identified themselves as having Indian or other "racial" origin. Many Mexican Americans had in fact assimilated more than others from different racial backgrounds. Taken in that light, racial minorities comprised less than 1.4 percent of the more than 700,000 county residents. Even counting those of Mexican ancestry as part of Orange County's racial minority, the county was still more than 90 percent white.

Disneyland Connects Past and Future

Orange County's homogeneity found its way onto America's center stage after creation of the nation's first theme park. Disneyland was built in Anaheim on a site chosen because of its proximity to the extension of the Golden State Parkway, built as part of the 1950s freeway boom. In the park, Disney tried to create an idealized vision of America, recapturing history with frontier adventures and reaching into the future with visions of a technologically driven culture; however, his workforce reflected the real world of Orange County and other prosperous suburban areas where there was little room for minorities. The park did not hire its first African American "people contact" employee until 1968 (Avila 2004, 121, 135).

Master Planning and Private Cities: The Case of Irvine

Because so much suburban development in Orange County occurred in areas that were privately held, there were relatively few zoning restrictions or limits on haphazard residential development. The single-largest exception to this was the Irvine Company, which owned a massive piece of agricultural land in the county. Incorporated in the late 19th century, the company began a transformation during the late 1940s and 1950s from being a farming enterprise to being primarily in real estate development. Initially, however, the company only leased property near Orange County's coast. It provided a variety of amenities for leisure (paid for by assessments from homeowners) and implemented some restrictions on architectural styles. Because its intent was to cater to more affluent suburbanites, the initial development was even more exclusive than some others in the county (Schiesl 1991, 57).

By the late 1950s, there was even greater demand for property near and on Irvine property. The land was coveted by educational institutions as well as housing developers. The University of California (UC) system chose Irvine land for the site of a new campus. After the company resisted donating land for the campus, pressure from an Irvine family member (who supported the donation) prevailed, and the company and UC officials sought to develop a comprehensive plan for development of the area.

The architect chosen by the UC regents to find a new campus was William Pereira. Once Irvine became the frontrunner, company officials asked him to participate in a master plan for the broader community. Pereira prepared two reports; the 1959 report dealt with the campus while the one in 1960 presented a plan for the development of 10,000 acres in the area. The broader plan seemed like it would help to guide development in an increasingly chaotic suburban landscape. Its principles would eventually be adopted by the county government, which had many of the same problems. Unfortunately for the more inclusive vision that had driven Pereira and earlier planners, Irvine Company officials removed many of the requirements for green space, low-income housing, and greater social heterogeneity. As it evolved into the 1970s, Irvine ended up being an affluent suburban enclave, not balanced economically or culturally (Schiesl 1991, 64–67).

The Seeds of Modern Conservatism

Given the ethnic and racial homogeneity, high rates of home ownership, and higher than average incomes, it is perhaps not surprising that Orange County would develop into one of the most prominent sites of conservative political activism. According to historian Lisa McGirr, the origins of the county's new residents helped to define its subsequent political activism. More than one-third of the incoming migrants came from the Midwest, and they "brought the political baggage of their hometowns" with them (McGirr 2001, 46). They were avowedly anticommunist, avowedly religious, and increasingly conservative. In the 1960s, these residents would champion Barry Goldwater and then Ronald Reagan for office.

Sin City Lights Up: Las Vegas

Two events in the 1930s helped to pave the way for future prosperity for Las Vegas, Nevada. The construction of Hoover Dam (also called Boulder Dam for a time) only 30 miles from Las Vegas brought greater potential for industrial development. In 1931, the state legalized gambling. Thus, by the 1940s and 1950s, Las Vegas was a city in transition. Many people, including large numbers of African Americans, came to work at the Basic Magnesium factory during the war. The city and its surroundings changed further with the influx of federal defense monies; another wartime investment built the precursor to a major Air Force base; and nuclear testing started in the area in 1951.

The other major impetus behind the transformation of Las Vegas came from its increasing popularity as a destination for leisure and recreation. It became a major tourist destination with an average of eight million visitors a year by the middle of the decade. A new generation of casinos that appeared during the 1950s led the attractions. While still not the high-rise towers associated with Las Vegas today, they symbolized a massive investment in gambling; this generated jobs and brought further migrants into the area. The source of that financing, however, complicated enormously the political and legal issues involved. Many of the premier Las Vegas destinations were initially controlled by organized crime figures, and the city government struggled to root out organized crime without killing the city's golden goose.

As Las Vegas grew, the city government struggled to handle (as did many other cities facing similarly rapid growth) its new residents, visitors, and the demands placed on an infrastructure that was ill-equipped to handle them. One issue arising in the 1950s was the prospect of consolidating city services and incorporating newly valuable property into the city polity. As in other cities, the government also chose to delay crucial services to its less-affluent residents, many of whom were African Americans living in the segregated Westside neighborhood.

In addition to the residential segregation, African American Las Vegans also faced Jim Crow conditions in the casinos. Limited to service-sector jobs that offered low wages and long hours, African Americans struggled to realize a modicum of the wealth represented by the casinos and their promise of instant prosperity. Even high-profile African American entertainers struggled against segregationist thinking. While permitted to perform in the casinos, they could neither stay nor eat in them. Only after a public campaign, and the opening of a multiracial casino, did casino owners relent and begin to allow African American patrons into their establishments.

Wartime Origins of Population Influx: Basic Magnesium

Basic Magnesium was a massive enterprise formed with government and private funding to process magnesium for war production; at its height, it could produce 112 million tons of magnesium per year, far more than the total magnesium production of Germany in 1940 (Moehring 2000, 35). At one point, 13,000 workers were involved in the construction of the plant. Production began in 1942.

The impact of Basic Magnesium on the local economy and community continued to be significant in the 1950s. Since there were still relatively few people living in Las Vegas in 1940 (the census recorded just over 24,000 residents), the opening of the plant served as a magnet to migrants seeking well-paying defense jobs. Many of those job seekers were African Americans arriving daily from the South. Once the initial exodus began, many more followed to connect with family and friends already working in the region. Because the city of Las Vegas lacked the capacity to handle the large number of new migrants, the town of Henderson was created as a "temporary" stopgap.

As the number of African American employees rose, so too did the perceived need for racially segregated accommodation. In 1943, construction began on

Carver Park, a housing project with apartments, dormitories, and recreational facilities; according to Eugene Moehring, this made the fledgling town a "racially divided community" (Moehring 2000, 37). Schools were segregated, as were plant facilities, and would continue to be so in the 1950s. As greater numbers of migrants overcame the company's initial efforts to build housing for workers, more and more Basic employees found housing in Las Vegas and North Las Vegas.

Military Bases

Basic Magnesium was not the only beneficiary of wartime spending in the area. Early in the war, the government sought to secure property to build an airstrip for the Army Air Corps, the predecessor of the U.S. Air Force. The Army used the airport and the surrounding acreage for aerial gunnery training. Tens of thousands of trainees cycled through the program, with a new group arriving every six weeks. By the end of the war, more than 13,000 people were employed on the base (Moehring 2000, 32–33). Soldiers proved an important source of revenue for the casino industry as it blossomed in the fifties. In 1949, the base became Nellis Air Force Base, a major training center for pilots during the Korean War and a significant center for Air Force fighter operations into the contemporary period.

Atomic Research

The final linchpin of federal investment in defense spending in the Las Vegas region had somewhat more sinister overtones. In the late 1940s, the federal government was looking for a nuclear weapons testing site in the continental United States. By 1950, the government had chosen what would become the Nevada Test Site as its first choice. Within a year, nuclear testing had begun. Between 1951 and the moratorium on nuclear weapons testing in 1992, more than 1,000 detonations occurred at the site. It was adjacent to Nellis Air Force Base and only 60 miles or so from Las Vegas. In 1958 alone, with the looming implementation of a testing moratorium that lasted for several years, there were dozens of detonations at the Nevada Test Site. Even after the agreement on the 1963 Test Ban Treaty, which banned above-ground nuclear testing, underground testing continued at the site. Before the public became aware of the potential hazards of radioactive fallout and radiation poisoning, many in the area may have been exposed to a variety of health and environmental hazards; Annelise Orleck relates how residents of the city's Westside neighborhood would get up in the morning to see the mushroom clouds on testing days and were unaware of the possibility of radioactive dust and contaminated groundwater (Orleck 2005, 46).

The first and only test of the M65 atomic cannon, nicknamed "Atomic Annie," at Frenchman's Flat, Nevada, May 25, 1953. Atomic testing near Las Vegas provided employment for thousands in the region, but also exposed many to radiation. (Library of Congress)

The Growth of Sin in Sin City

Soldiers and defense workers flocked to Las Vegas, both from the immediate region and from the burgeoning urban areas of Southern California. Casino owners sought to expand and capitalize on that market. During the 1940s, developers began to acquire properties on what would become the Strip, and the predecessors of the monuments to excess that are contemporary casinos began to take shape.

Many of the older casinos were relatively utilitarian affairs, with Western themes and little pretense. As a new generation of hotel-casinos was constructed throughout the 1950s, however, this dynamic changed with casino owners seeking to attract a more-monied clientele. Offering more luxurious appointments and all of the amenities of a resort, these properties symbolized a major evolution in the approach to gambling (and leisure) in the city.

The first luxurious hotel arrived in 1947 when the Flamingo formally opened. More than 100 hotel rooms, a golf course, and many other options complemented the central focus on the casino and showroom. The opening of the Desert Inn in 1950 was another sign of how luxury and gourmet food had become watchwords for Las Vegas resorts. The Sahara and the Sands followed in 1952. Three years later, the Riviera improved upon its peers that sported only one or two stories by offering the first high-rise casino and hotel in the city. The Dunes opened in the same year. Another high-rise hotel, the Fremont, opened downtown in 1956. Other 1950s era resorts included the Tropicana and the Stardust (Moehring 2000, 47–48, 83).

The scramble for development of newer and fancier resorts was not without its pitfalls. The opening of so many resorts in such a short period meant that some failed or began cycles in which they were sold multiple times over the subsequent decades in efforts to make them more profitable. When resorts closed or scaled back operations, they sometimes stranded workers who had counted upon the rapid growth to furnish them with jobs and homes.

Organized Crime and Efforts to Stem Casino Corruption

Elements of organized crime arrived in Las Vegas as its gambling venues became more prominent during the 1940s. Tennessee senator Estes Kefauver led committee hearings about the presence and influence of organized crime in America in the early 1950s; the issue was taken up in 1957 by the Senate Permanent Subcommittee on Investigations, led by Sen. John McClellan. As the federal spotlight focused on the role of organized crime in the televised hearings, mobsters sought more discreet and more distant investments. Las Vegas, which historically had relatively little gaming regulation, became a popular destination. The state government claimed it was making strides in increasing regulation; local officials were more dubious. Historian Eugene Moehring describes one incident in which one county commissioner said in 1952 that the "state tax commission 'has let every syndicate in the country into Las Vegas'" (Moehring 2000, 54). In 1955, the state responded by creating the Gaming Control Board; its responsibilities were the investigation and enforcement of gaming licenses. The state further beefed up its regulatory efforts in 1959 with a state gaming control commission. While not as flamboyant as some earlier mobsters, like Bugsy Siegel who was killed in Los Angeles in 1947, organized crime figures would remain prominent in the management of numerous casinos throughout the decade.

Annexation and the Quest for Gaming Revenue

One of the dilemmas facing rapidly growing communities was how to keep providing necessary municipal services and how expansion of those services would be funded. Las Vegas was no exception. As it became increasingly clear that the so-called Strip, a section of Las Vegas Boulevard, would be a center of casino and hotel development, city officials scrambled to cash in on the Strip's new-found success. The problem was that the Strip was not technically part of the city of Las Vegas. Several times in the late 1940s and early 1950s, city officials sought to annex the Strip and its environs. Facing opposition from both suburban residents and the hotel and casino owners who preferred not to pay the tax levies that were sure to follow, the county sanctioned the creation of two unincorporated communities (Paradise, Nevada, and Winchester, Nevada) to block Las Vegas's annexation attempts.

Because the Strip remained outside city limits, and because state gaming revenues were distributed equally among all of Nevada's counties, the city of Las Vegas struggled to upgrade an aging sewer system and repair deteriorating roads while receiving little in return from its prosperous casino neighbors. Facing budget deficits, a political backlash developed against the leaders who seemed unable to handle the fiscal crisis (Moehring 2000, 70–72).

African Americans in Las Vegas

A group of people who were keenly aware of the dearth of municipal services in Las Vegas were the largely African American residents of the Westside neighborhood. At the beginning of the 1950s, neighborhood roads remained unpaved and, as historian Annelise Orleck reports, many houses did not have flush toilets and other basic amenities well into the 1960s (Orleck 2005, 38). They also lacked the air-conditioning that was becoming increasingly ubiquitous in casinos, hotels, and suburban homes. African American residents of the Westside provided valuable support for the 1951 mayoral run by C. D. Baker, who promised to pave some of the major streets on the Westside. Baker eventually delivered in 1955; the funding he used for paving, electric lighting, and a sewer system came from federal funds associated with highway construction. That construction eventually resulted in the destruction of hundreds of Westside homes (Orleck 2005, 48).

African American activists sought social change throughout the decade. At various points, they pushed unsuccessfully for state civil rights legislation and an end to the segregation of public accommodations throughout the city. In 1957, a group led by two prominent African American medical professionals formed to mobilize support for political candidates. In several key elections, the Nevada Voters League brought a thousand votes or more to their desired candidates. Eugene Moehring argues that despite these efforts, little progress against Jim Crow in Sin City had occurred. Inspired at least in part by national civil rights activism, African American community members finally convinced most owners of casinos and other public accommodations to integrate in 1960 (Moehring 2000, 180–186).

Segregation and Westside Culture

Because of local custom that barred African American patrons from casinos and hotels, African American military personnel working at Nellis Air Force Base and the Nevada Test Site were no more welcome in the casinos than were the residents of the Westside. There were periodic clashes on the Westside between police and African Americans. While military officials sought to quietly encourage greater tolerance for their servicemen, stubborn segregationism remained the norm.

In order to meet demand for multiracial alternatives, entrepreneurs used Westside venues to cater to a predominantly African American clientele. Clubs, bars, rooming houses, and hotels opened to serve them. The USO opened a Westside location for African American servicemen. The neighborhood thus developed a lively cultural scene; white and African American entertainers mingled at after-hours clubs, and residents found good jobs in these establishments that would have been denied them in the casinos on the Strip (Orleck 2005, 60–61).

Segregation of Entertainers

While some African American entertainers, like Lena Horne and Sammy Davis Jr., were in great demand as performers in the most prominent Las Vegas casinos, they discovered that they were unwelcome as patrons. After their shows or concerts, they headed to the Westside for rooming houses or hotel rooms.

Dorothy Dandridge dances at a nightclub in Las Vegas, 1955. (Library of Congress)

Over time, they became less and less patient with the Jim Crow conditions in the casinos and pushed for reform. In 1955, the Sands finally opened the doors of its hotel rooms to African Americans who were performing there (but not African American patrons more broadly). Few other resorts followed suit, however, and it would be another five years before there was broader integration in Las Vegas. Even after African American performers were deemed acceptable as guests, there were still incidents that showed the limits of racial tolerance even in an integrationist moment. Annelise Orleck relates an incident in the Sands' swimming pool. Several members of the Rat Pack, most pertinently Sammy Davis Jr., decided to play poker in the swimming pool at the Sands. After they had finished, the management drained and refilled the pool to mollify horrified white patrons (Orleck 2005, 62).

A Multiracial Casino: The Moulin Rouge

The opening in 1955 of the Moulin Rouge hotel and casino marked the first major effort to provide a racially integrated social venue for all Las Vegans. It also finally provided a more glamorous alternative for African American entertainers who had been forced to find ad hoc housing while performing in the city. The resort closed after only seven months because of financial shortfalls. It eventually reopened under new management in 1957. Ironically, the Moulin Rouge became the site of racial controversy at the end of the decade when it became public knowledge that the resort charged African American patrons more for drinks than white patrons. While it was apparently not uncommon in the city at the time, African American Las Vegans used the discriminatory practice as a basis for protest, which Eugene Moehring cites as valuable experience for later

The Moulin Rouge casino, the first racially integrated casino in Las Vegas, 1955. (Bettmann/Corbis)

activism. Throughout the early 1960s, the city revoked the hotel's liquor license as punishment (Moehring 2000, 182–184).

Low Wages and Long Hours in Casino Jobs

Work at the casinos became increasingly common for African Americans in Las Vegas during the 1950s. Yet very few of them were visible presences in the carefully controlled environs. Segregated occupationally, African American women could work as maids or in casino kitchens. African American men could be porters or janitors. None of them could aspire to be the better-paid (and better-tipped) dealers, waitresses, or clerks.

African American women who worked as maids in the casinos remembered ruefully how difficult the work was. While they were represented by trade unions, the unions had relatively little clout, especially when many Las Vegas casinos were under the control of organized crime. The speed at which Las Vegas was growing, however, did provide some protections for African American women workers. As with other workers in tight employment markets, workers who "voted with their feet" and left their jobs could often find other ones in short order. While conditions might not be any better, the ability to leave one job for another was an important psychological hedge against the discriminatory work environment. It is also important to note that while African American casino employees were not well paid compared to their white peers, they were still often earning significantly more than they had in previous jobs in the South (Orleck 2005, 49–60).

Urban Redevelopment and the Dropping of the "Concrete Curtain"

By the late 1940s, it was clear that most African American residents of Las Vegas lived in substandard housing. A 1949 survey determined that 80 percent of Westside homes failed minimum federal-housing standards. With help from NAACP members, Las Vegas secured a federally funded public housing development. After protests from white residents in an adjacent neighborhood, planners promised to place a buffer zone between the new development and them. Marble Manor opened in 1952 and offered 100 units. By the end of the decade, housing advocates secured another public housing development. The Madison Houses opened in 1959 and "filled immediately" (Orleck 2005, 48–49).

As it had in California and elsewhere, the darker side of urban renewal often disproportionately affected lower-income neighborhoods with higher proportions of minority residents. One of the main symbols of this darker side was the bulldozer; on the Westside, the culprit was the arrival in Las Vegas of Interstate

15, a beneficiary of the Federal Interstate Highway initiative. As engineers debated the routing of the interstate through Las Vegas, four options emerged. The option eventually chosen went through the Westside and required the demolition of several hundred homes (Moehring 2000, 102–103). The construction of the freeway "effectively cut off the city's black residents from commercial districts and white residential communities." Historian Annelise Orleck goes on to argue that, as was seen in Los Angeles and elsewhere, highway construction formalized racial divides, and many of the cities were "more segregated than ever" (Orleck 2005, 48–49).

BIOGRAPHIES

Patrick "Pat" McCarran, 1876–1954

Attorney, U.S. Senator

Pat McCarran played an important role in implementing national immigration reform, codifying anticommunist legislation, and encouraging the development of his home state of Nevada. Born in Reno, McCarran became a lawyer and served in a variety of public capacities at the state level, including as Chief Justice of the Nevada Supreme Court during World War I. After several unsuccessful efforts to secure a seat in the U.S. Senate, McCarran was elected in 1932.

While in the Senate, McCarran was a sponsor of the Internal Security Act, or McCarran Act, which was a key anticommunist effort in the early 1950s. Passed in 1950 (after two years of political wrangling), the bill required that members of the Communist Party and other organizations deemed "subversive" by the federal government register with the government. While the Supreme Court would find some parts of the law an unconstitutional infringement on Fifth Amendment rights, it took 15 years to vindicate the Communist Party's refusal to register.

Senator McCarran was also a cosponsor of the Immigration and Nationality Act of 1952 (the McCarran-Walter Act), which demolished some racial and gender preferences in immigration, continued restrictive quotas on certain countries, and provided the government with new powers to deny entry to political subversives. The city of Las Vegas memorialized McCarran by putting his name on the municipal airport

William Pereira, 1909–1985

Architect

William Pereira was the architect chosen by the University of California (and later the Irvine Company) to find a new campus in Orange County. He became

Edward Roybal, Hispanic city council member, congressman, and political activist. (Library of Congress)

the principal consultant on the master plan for both the campus and the community of Irvine more broadly. Later, he was the designer of the Transamerica Building in San Francisco.

Edward Roybal, 1916–2005

City Council Member, Congressman, Political Activist

Born in New Mexico, Edward Roybal arrived in Los Angeles in 1922. After stints with the New Deal's Civilian Conservation Corps and various public health organizations, Roybal lost his first attempt to win election to the Los Angeles City Council in 1947. One year later, he helped to found the Community Service Organization, an activist Hispanic civil rights organization that provided Roybal with a base of political support for his 1949 campaign. Roybal was elected to the Los Angeles City Council in 1949. As political loyalties shifted on issues like public housing, Roybal remained a steadfast supporter of publicly funded responses to the problems of insufficient and poor quality housing for the working class and the poor. He subsequently served in the House of Representatives from 1963 to 1993.

Hope Mendoza Schechter, 1921–?

Community Activist

Born in Arizona, Hope Mendoza Schechter arrived in East Los Angeles while still an infant. After work in a defense plant during the war, Mendoza Schechter went on to become an organizer for the International Ladies Garment Workers Union afterwards. She was a charter member of the Community Services Organization (CSO) and helped to cement a strong relationship between the mostly Mexican American activists and the labor movement. She served as chair of the CSO's labor relations committee and encouraged the organization to keep current on fair employment practices (Rose 1994, 183–188).

William Whyte, 1917–1999

Open Space Advocate, Author, "Urbanologist"

By the end of the 1950s, William Whyte had advocated several ways in which communities could increase their access to open space, an antidote to more densely packed suburban subdivisions. His 1959 book *Conservation Easements* advocated more open spaces in urban planning; he is credited with having an impact on calls for legislation in several states. He would expand upon these ideas during the 1960s as the idea of building "clusters" of houses situated around open spaces gained ground.

Whyte had been a social critic for some time; he first became widely known for his 1956 book *The Organization Man,* which criticized corporate culture for stifling creativity and the entrepreneurial spirit. Corporate environments had become overly bureaucratized, Whyte claimed, and this homogeneity was reflected in similarly undifferentiated suburbs. After serving as an officer in the Marines during World War II, Whyte became an assistant editor at *Fortune* magazine. After leaving *Fortune* to become a full-time observer of the American condition, Whyte conducted detailed studies of urban behavior; he did so first hand by watching people strolling the sidewalks of New York and elsewhere. He filmed street scenes in an effort to understand dynamics of pedestrian traffic.

He published several other works during his life dealing with many of the same issues. He later served as a consultant on urban development and zoning issues and taught at Hunter College, City University of New York. Adam Rome claims that Whyte's ideas about possible solutions to urban and suburban problems found popular acceptance because they were, in Whyte's own words, conservative ones (Rome 2001, 130).

REFERENCES AND FURTHER READINGS

Abbott, Carl. 1999. "Regional City and Network City: Portland and Seattle in the Twentieth Century." In *The American West: The Reader,* ed. Walter Nugent and Martin Ridge, 295–323. Bloomington: Indiana University Press.

Avila, Eric. 2004. *Popular Culture in the Age of White Flight: Fear and Fantasy in Suburban Los Angeles.* Berkeley: University of California Press.

Cassuto, David N. 2001. *Dripping Dry: Literature, Politics, and Water in the Desert Southwest.* Ann Arbor: University of Michigan Press.

Creagan, James F. 1965. "Public Law 78: A Tangle of Domestic and International Relations." *Journal of Inter-American Studies* 7 (4): 541–556.

Davis, Mike. 2002. *Dead Cities and Other Tales.* New York: New Press.

Dewey, Scott Hamilton. 2000. *Don't Breathe the Air: Air Pollution and U.S. Environmental Politics, 1945–1970.* College Station: Texas A&M University Press.

España-Maram, Linda. 2006. *Creating Masculinity in Los Angeles's Little Manila: Working-Class Filipinos and Popular Culture, 1920s–1950s*. New York: Columbia University Press.

Faderman, Lillian, and Stuart Timmons. 2006. *Gay L.A.: A History of Sexual Outlaws, Power Politics, and Lipstick Lesbians*. New York: Basic Books.

García, Juan Ramon. 1980. *Operation Wetback: The Mass Deportation of Mexican Undocumented Workers in 1954*. Westport, CT: Greenwood Press.

Garcia, Matt. 2001. *A World of Its Own: Race, Labor, and Citrus in the Making of Greater Los Angeles, 1900–1970*. Chapel Hill: University of North Carolina Press.

Geron, Kim. 2005. *Latino Political Power*. Boulder, CO: Lynne Rienner Publishers.

Gonzalez, Gilbert G. 2006. *Guest Workers or Colonized Labor? Mexican Labor Migration to the United States*. Boulder, CO: Paradigm Publishers.

Hawley, Ellis. 1979. "The Politics of the Mexican Labor Issue, 1950–1965." In *Mexican Workers in the United States: Historical and Political Perspectives,* ed. George C. Kiser and Martha Woody Kiser, 97–120. Albuquerque: University of New Mexico Press. Reprinted from *Agricultural History* 40 (1966): 157–176.

Hays, Samuel P. 2000. *A History of Environmental Politics since 1945*. Pittsburgh: University of Pittsburgh Press.

Hurewitz, Daniel. 2007. *Bohemian Los Angeles and the Making of Modern Politics*. Berkeley: University of California Press.

Kaufman, Michael T. 1999. "William Whyte, 'Organization Man' Author and Urbanologist, Is Dead at 81." *New York Times,* January 13, 1999. Accessed online at www.nytimes.com.

Kline, Benjamin. 2007. *First Along the River: A Brief History of the Environmental Movement*. 3rd ed. New York: Rowman and Littlefield.

López, Ian F. Haney. 2003. *Racism on Trial: The Chicano Fight for Justice*. Cambridge, MA: The Belknap Press.

McGirr, Lisa. 2001. *Suburban Warriors: The Origins of the New American Right*. Princeton, NJ: Princeton University Press.

McWilliams, Carey. 1951. "America's Disadvantaged Minorities: Mexican-Americans." *Journal of Negro Education* 20 (3): 301–309.

Moehring, Eugene P. 2000. *Resort City in the Sunbelt: Las Vegas, 1930–2000*. 2nd ed. Reno: University of Nevada Press.

Ngai, Mae M. 2004. *Impossible Subjects: Illegal Aliens and the Making of Modern America*. Princeton, NJ: Princeton University Press.

Nugent, Walter. 1999. "Where Is the American West? Report on a Survey." In *The American West: The Reader,* ed. Walter Nugent and Martin Ridge, 11–23. Bloomington: Indiana University Press.

Orleck, Annelise. 2005. *Storming Caesar's Palace: How Black Mothers Fought Their Own War on Poverty*. Boston: Beacon Press.

Parson, Don. 2005. *Making a Better World: Public Housing, The Red Scare, and the Direction of Modern Los Angeles*. Minneapolis: University of Minnesota Press.

Pastor, Robert A. 1984. "U.S. Immigration Policy and Latin America: In Search of the 'Special Relationship.'" *Latin American Research Review* 19 (3): 35–56.

President's Commission on Migratory Labor. 1951. *Migratory Labor in American Agriculture*. Washington, DC: Government Printing Office. Excerpted in George C. Kiser and Martha Woody Kiser, eds. 1979. *Mexican Workers in the United States: Historical and Political Perspectives*, 131–153. Albuquerque: University of New Mexico Press.

Robbins, William G. 2004. *Landscapes of Conflict: The Oregon Story, 1940–2000*. Seattle: University of Washington Press.

Rome, Adam. 2001. *The Bulldozer in the Countryside: Suburban Sprawl and the Rise of American Environmentalism*. New York: Cambridge University Press.

Rose, Margaret. 1994. "Gender and Civic Activism in Mexican American Barrios in California: The Community Service Organization, 1947–1962." In *Not June Cleaver: Women and Gender in Postwar America, 1945–1960*, ed. Joanne Meyerowitz, 177–200. Philadelphia: Temple University Press.

Sandos, James A., and Harry E. Cross. 1983. "National Development and International Labour Migration: Mexico 1940–1965." *Journal of Contemporary History* 18 (1): 43–60.

Schiesl, Martin J. 1991. "Designing the Model Community: The Irvine Company and Suburban Development, 1950–1988." In *Postsuburban California: The Transformation of Orange County since World War II*, ed. Rob King, Spencer Olin, and Mark Poster, 55–91. Berkeley: University of California Press.

Schulte, Steven C. 2002. *Wayne Aspinall and the Shaping of the American West*. Boulder: University Press of Colorado.

Self, Robert O. 2003. *American Babylon: Race and the Struggle for Postwar Oakland*. Princeton, NJ: Princeton University Press.

Shabecoff, Philip. 2003. *A Fierce Green Fire: The American Environmental Movement*. Rev. ed. Washington, DC: Island Press.

Sturgeon, Stephen C. 2002. *The Politics of Western Water: The Congressional Career of Wayne Aspinall*. Tucson: University of Arizona Press.

U.S. Department of Homeland Security. U.S. Citizenship and Immigration Services. *Legislation from 1941–1960*. N.d. Accessed online at http://www.uscis.gov/files/nativedocuments/Legislation%20from%201941–1960.pdf.

White, Richard. 1986. "Race Relations in the American West." *American Quarterly* 38 (3): 396–416.

Cold War and Peace

OVERVIEW

The Cold War hung like a specter over American life in the 1950s. In the American mind, fears of the Soviet Union and the prospect of nuclear war merged in nightmarish views of the nation's future. The Cold War mixed the horrors of shrouded science-fiction monsters with the realities of bright-eyed American children. Early in the decade, the Cold War gave birth to a limited "hot" war in Korea, but nuclear anxiety played a bigger role in setting the tone of the times. While many Americans became Cold Warriors, peace organizations struggled to break through the din of Cold War rhetoric at a time when religious leaders sometimes endorsed military might over peace on Earth.

The stage had been set for the Korean War shortly after World War II when Korea, which had been under Japanese domination since 1910, was divided. The area north of the 38th parallel fell under Soviet influence, and South Korea was established with closer ties to the West. After North Korean troops flooded into the south in 1950, President Harry Truman requested that the United Nations establish an international effort to regain South Korea's sovereignty. Although other nations took part, Americans made up the biggest part of the international force. China responded to the influx of troops from other nations by sending Chinese troops into Korea to bolster North Korea's military efforts. When the war began, 75 percent of Americans backed Truman's policy, and White House mail was 10-to-1 in favor of intervention (Tucker 2000, 40); however, about half of the American population eventually opposed U.S. policy in Korea. In this war, Truman had a simple goal: to regain South Korea's sovereignty without widening the war. He wanted to avoid involvement of Soviet forces in the war, and he hoped to reach a resolution without direct conflict between the United States and China. Some Americans thought the United States should take more aggressive action, going head-to-head with China, but Truman worried that this conflict might blossom into a nuclear World War III. The United Nations commander, Douglas MacArthur, disagreed with Truman—and their conflict would affect American public opinion.

The Korean War touched American life in differing ways. It destabilized some families because National Guardsmen and reservists were called to arms unexpectedly. At the same time, draft boards, which sought to augment the United States' fighting force, reported noticing a difference between the young men going into enlistment offices in 1950 and those who had lined up to join the military after the 1941 attack on Pearl Harbor. In New York City, the chairman of a local draft board reported that "the spirit—the sense of participating in something important, of doing a necessary job—that characterized World War II selectees is missing from the men being called up today. . . . There isn't the same cooperation. All we can do is explain to them that they have an obligation to their country that they must perform" (Rose 1999, 262–263). The war also accelerated integration of the armed services—a change that altered the military experience of most Americans.

While Truman struggled to limit the breadth and the deadliness of the Korean War, the Cold War between the United States and the Soviet Union generated extreme and widespread trepidation about communism as a godless and monolithic enemy intent on world conquest. These fears, which sparked a bunker mentality among many Americans, were pervasive. Even children were not spared the terrors of this ideological showdown: A bubble-gum manufacturer in Philadelphia began replacing baseball cards with cards from the anticommunist Children's Crusade in 1951. The existence of nuclear weaponry in the arsenals of both nations changed fears of defeat into nightmares of annihilation. Civil defense drills in preparation for nuclear war became a part of American culture in the 1950s. In retrospect, these rehearsals for mass destruction seem almost silly. School children were taught to duck under their desks and cover their heads in the event of nuclear attack. This action might protect them from falling debris caused by the blast or from eye damage as a result of the nuclear flash; however, it offered no real protection against a direct hit or against radioactive fallout.

In the 1950s, no international crises brought the world to the brink of nuclear war. But two close calls—the Berlin crisis in 1961 and the Cuban missile crisis a year later—had roots in the Cold War culture of the 1950s, which characterized peaceful coexistence with the Soviet Union as an impossibility. For many Americans, dark anticipation was amplified by the knowledge that the United

States had been the first nation to use nuclear weapons in war. As a Presbyterian minister in Syracuse told his congregation in 1958, "A sense of impending doom and helplessness hangs over us, and we know, in our heart of hearts, that we would not be in a position to pass judgment on their deed" (George 2003, 21).

Some Americans rejected Cold War rationales and continued to push for peace. However, many Americans began to equate calls for peace with appeasement and with sympathy for communism. As a result, the peace movement had difficulty making its voice heard in the decade's early years. Despite the unpopularity of the Korean War, conservative forces managed to muzzle peace organizations during that conflict. However, as McCarthyism faded and as the dangers of nuclear testing became clear, the peace movement found new life and embraced the issue of banning nuclear testing. Pacifists' use of civil disobedience affected the development of the civil rights movement and their perseverance provided a model for peace demonstrators in the coming years.

Churches sometimes are seen as proponents of peace, but as Americans began joining churches in record numbers, the idea of promoting world peace was not high on the agenda of many churches. The Soviet leadership's professed atheism led many to cast the Cold War as a holy war that Americans must win through military might if necessary. In a struggle against powerful and threatening nonbelievers, many church leaders and members believed that a strong commitment to U.S. military strength was consistent with their religious beliefs. Civic religion became more apparent, and many Americans believed that in the Cold War, God was on their side.

TIMELINE

1950   In the wake of the Soviet Union's successful development of the atomic bomb, President Harry Truman orders American scientists in January to regain supremacy by producing a hydrogen bomb.

North Korean troops invade South Korea in June, and in response, President Harry Truman orders U.S. naval and air operations against the invaders.

The U.S. government begins calling up reserves; Truman commits ground troops to Korea, where they serve as part of an international force.

The first ground troops leave the United States for Korea in July, and Truman names a World War II hero, Gen. Douglas MacArthur, to lead the United Nations Command in South Korea.

Chinese troops support North Korean forces, beginning in October.

African American leader and peace activist W. E. B. Du Bois faces federal charges that he is an unregistered foreign agent; he is acquitted.

The Billy Graham Evangelical Association is incorporated.

Religious denominations unite in the National Council of Churches.

1951   In a February statement, MacArthur criticizes the military policies of the United Nations and the United States in Korea; United Nations troops push the Chinese army back.

MacArthur demands Communist surrender in March.

MacArthur condemns Truman's policy in letter to Rep. Joe Martin of Massachusetts and openly favors invasion of China.

Truman relieves MacArthur of command in April because of his failure to support U.S. policy.

MacArthur addresses a joint session of Congress in May.

Intermittent Korean War armistice talks begin in July.

Catholic bishop Fulton J. Sheen launches his television series, *Life Is Worth Living.*

1952   Korean armistice talks stall over the issue of voluntary repatriation of prisoners of war.

The federal government allows an April atomic test in Nevada to be broadcast live on television.

Retired general and Republican presidential nominee Dwight D. Eisenhower declares in October that he will "go to Korea" if he is elected president.

The Atomic Energy Commission reports the United States' first successful detonation of an H-bomb in early November at Eniwetok Atoll in the Pacific Ocean.

United States voters elect Eisenhower as the 34th president in November.

Eisenhower goes to Korea in December.

Protestant leader and broadcaster Norman Vincent Peale's best-seller, *The Power of Positive Thinking,* is published.

Billy Graham launches weekly television program; he also produces a newspaper column that is syndicated in 125 newspapers.

1953   The Soviet Union's dictator, Josef Stalin, dies in March.

The Korean armistice, intended only to achieve a temporary ceasefire, is signed in July, effectively marking the war's end. Efforts to reach agreement on a fuller treaty fail.

In August, the Soviet Union announces that it has developed a hydrogen bomb.

President Eisenhower tries to put a happy face on nuclear science in December by promoting the idea of "Atoms for Peace"—the use of atomic power for productive, rather than destructive, uses.

1954   Eisenhower's secretary of state, John Foster Dulles, reveals new Cold War strategy that downplays the need for conventional military forces and relies on the threat of "massive retaliation" to deter Soviet expansionism.

Navy commissions USS *Nautilus,* the first nuclear submarine.

Congress acts in June to add the words "under God" to the Pledge of Allegiance.

In the annual Operation Alert civil defense drill, nuclear attacks are simulated across the United States; Eisenhower leaves the White House for a tent city outside the nation's capital.

1955   In this year's mock nuclear attack, Eisenhower hides in a bunker and goes through the motions of declaring martial law. Twenty-seven pacifists stage a protest in Manhattan's City Hall Park; all receive suspended sentences.

Pacifists issue a July appeal written by Albert Einstein and Bertrand Russell calling for an end to Cold War threats in light of nuclear war's potentially devastating effects.

Dial-a-Prayer telephone service begins in Evansville, Indiana.

The Soviet Union and Great Britain test their first hydrogen bombs.

1956   The United States drops a hydrogen bomb from an airplane in May test.

Democratic presidential nominee Adlai Stevenson endorses an end to atmospheric nuclear tests.

Eisenhower wins re-election by a landslide.

Congress makes "In God We Trust" the nation's official motto.

1957   Peace activists form the Committee for Non-Violent Action.

As pacifists' attention increasingly turns toward nuclear testing, Linus Pauling, Norman Cousins, and Homer Jack lead a mainstream organization, the Committee for a Sane Nuclear Policy, known as SANE.

The Atomic Energy Commission begins underground nuclear tests at Nevada test site in September.

"In God We Trust" appears on American paper money for the first time.

1958   Eisenhower initiates unilateral suspension of atmospheric nuclear tests.

The United States tests intercontinental ballistic missile in November; Atlas rocket hurtles more than 5,000 miles and scores a bull's-eye.

1959   Soviet premier Nikita Khrushchev tells the United States and its allies, "We will bury you." He also tours the United States as Cold War tensions appear to melt a bit.

The USS *George Washington,* the nation's first missile-firing submarine, is launched in June.

With growing fears of nuclear war, there is increasing consumer interest in building fallout shelters.

Protesters at the Mead Intercontinental Ballistic Missile base in Omaha draw public attention with their calls for a ban of nuclear weapons.

The Student Peace Union is formed and begins establishing chapters on various college campuses.

THE KOREAN WAR
AS SEEN FROM THE UNITED STATES

Because many U.S. citizens viewed communism as a monolithic threat to democracy around the world, most initially supported President Harry Truman's decision to intervene after Communist North Korea's forces invaded South Korea in June 1950. As the nation prepared for yet another war, it quickly became clear that the United States lacked adequate manpower and equipment to respond effectively. And even with the help of a United Nations task force, the United States had to take the lead in this fight. Across the nation, military reserve units were called up to fight in Korea. This created upheaval as many families were uprooted to follow husbands to military bases, where they prepared for deployment to Korea.

Some civilians wondered aloud why the U.S. military did not bring the war to a quick end by using the most powerful weapon in its arsenal—the atomic bomb. An August 1950 poll showed that 28 percent of Americans favored that option (Whitfield 1996, 5), and some members of Congress, such as Maine's Sen. Margaret Chase Smith, joined the call for a nuclear strike. The Truman administration rejected such pleas because of fear that the Soviet Union, which also had developed the atomic bomb, might join the fray.

Just as World War II arms production had transformed the American economy, the Korean War affected the economic climate at home. After a massive force of more than a million Chinese soldiers joined North Koreans on the battlefield in October, Truman declared a national emergency to bolster rapid military expansion. By the following year, America's defense budget was three times as large as it had been in 1949. In addition, the Office of Defense Mobilization, the Office of Price Stabilization, the Defense Production Administration, and the Wage Stabilization Board began controlling most wages and prices in the United States.

Although Truman's strategy avoided wartime rationing and runaway inflation, wage and price controls were unpopular. Economic growth was strong and jobs were plentiful, but the war derailed Truman's efforts to win passage of social legislation that might have helped Americans struggling to overcome poverty. Communist forces' ability to capture the South Korean capital, Seoul, at the beginning of the war and again after Chinese reinforcements joined the North Koreans' cause, led the American media to draw a grim picture for their readers. The *New York Times* described "hordes of Chinese Reds." *Time* reported that "140,000 U.S. troops . . . face possible annihilation" and said the men on the streets of the United States shared one sentiment: "It looks bad" (Mills and Mills 2000, 207). United Nations troops eventually managed to push the North Korean and Chinese forces back into North Korea, and by May 1951, a stalemate had been reached. Peace talks began in July 1951, but they dragged on for about two years before an armistice was declared. When the war was over, neither side could claim significant gains.

Remembering "The War"

To understand the Korean War's impact on American life, it is important to realize the continuing hold of World War II on the nation's imagination. More than any other foreign war, the United States' face-off against the Axis Powers seemed almost like a holy war for American forces. Because the United States itself had been the victim of a surprise attack and because the nation's enemies were known to have committed brutal acts of aggression, Americans rallied behind U.S. forces. In the simplest terms, World War II seemed to be black and white, a simple confrontation between good and evil. And the victory won by the United States and its allies also seemed just. Postwar Gallup polls showed that most Americans believed that entering that war had been the correct decision.

The halo effect of that war still touched everyday American life in many ways during the 1950s, a phenomenon that author Tom Englehardt has called "victory culture" (Englehardt 1995). On Sunday afternoons during the 1952–1953 television season, Americans gathered around their TV sets to watch the popular *Victory at Sea,* a documentary series about the U.S. Navy's role in World War II. It had been preceded by similar series, including *Crusade in Europe* and *Crusade in the Pacific.* The war, which had become a popular subject for films almost as soon as the fighting began, also continued to draw Americans to movie theaters. Between 1949 and 1953, some of the World War II films that attracted public attention were *Stalag 17, From Here to Eternity, Twelve O'Clock High, The Sands of Iwo Jima, Flying Leathernecks,* and *The Desert Fox.*

Because of its many manifestations in popular culture, World War II even changed the way American children played. This was especially true for boys who enjoyed playing war. Now, the enemies in childhood romps often were Nazis or Japanese. Production of toy soldiers wearing World War II–era uniforms and carrying equipment from that era also intensified identification of that conflict as "The War."

The presence of so many veterans among American civilians also affected the way Americans lived. Making use of the GI Bill, veterans promoted expanded demands for higher education and caused changes in the workplace. GI loans also made the expansion of American suburbs possible. Moreover, the same companies that produced World War II military materiel now provided appliances that changed American households.

The most popular potential presidential candidate for either party in 1952 was Dwight D. Eisenhower, supreme commander of the Allied Expeditionary Force. And many of the nation's leaders in the military arena remained men who had led forces to victory in World War II. Among them were Secretary of Defense and retired general George C. Marshall, General of the Army Omar Bradley, and Gen. Douglas MacArthur, who led United Nations forces in the Korean War.

Against this backdrop, the warfare in Korea seemed insignificant and confusing. Even Cold Warriors found that the American struggle in Korea lacked the high drama of World War II. The United States had not been directly attacked, and the Korean War offered a seesawing pattern of triumphs and defeats followed by a stalemate that lasted almost two years. Quite simply, the Korean War could not compete with the memory of World War II. In fact, historians later labeled the conflict as the "forgotten war" in American history.

Mobilization

When the Korean War began in June 1950, the United States had an inadequate number of troops available to fight—and that shortage guaranteed that the lives of many civilians would be disrupted by government efforts to fill the gap. Initially, three army divisions stationed in Japan were deployed in South Korea. Each division was shorthanded, with only two battalions per regiment rather than three. The men in these divisions also were not combat-ready because they had an insufficient number of tanks and other military hardware. In addition, some of their weapons were outmoded and could not stand up to the new Soviet-produced tanks used by the Chinese and North Koreans.

Congress approved the Selective Service Extension Act on June 30, 1950, giving the president power to call up National Guard and reserve units for up to 20 months. This legislation threw many men's lives into chaos because they did not know whether they would have to don uniforms and go to war. With Truman's approval, the Army called up 324,761 National Guardsmen, 184,015 active reservists, 324,602 inactive volunteer reservists, and 91,800 inactive reservists to complement a force of 591,487 regular troops. Inactive reservists did not receive pay for being on the reserve rolls, and they did not receive training, although most were World War II veterans. By mid-August, almost 1,500 National Guard units were part of the nation's active military forces. More than 244,000 Army reservists served during the war. Because the Marine Corps was similarly strapped for men, all Marine reserve units had been activated by October 1951. Navy reservists also were called up, including 22 reserve fighter squadrons, and naval forces restored mothballed ships into service. The Air Force called up about 100,000 individual reservists to serve as well as 10 Air Force reserve wings. Although its pilots lacked adequate training, the Air National Guard also contributed to the war effort (Tucker 2000, 456, 710).

At the same time, the draft added uncertainty to the lives of civilian men. In July 1950, the Selective Service issued a call for 50,000 draftees for September. Fifty thousand more were called in October, 80,000 in November, and 40,000 in December. In early 1951, 80,000 per month were drafted. Then, a slowdown was ordered as the Army surpassed its approved manpower levels. In fiscal year 1951, 587,000 men were drafted, and 630,000 volunteers were identified as draft-motivated—men who joined the Navy, Marines, or Air Force to avoid being drafted by the Army (Tucker 2000, 193).

Deployment of young men often meant that their families were uprooted as they followed the men to whatever training base would prepare them for service in Korea. In other cases, families merely stayed behind as men headed off to war. Many single men married quickly after learning that they were being called into the military, and they left behind young brides who had enjoyed only days or weeks of married life.

Capt. Johnnie Gosnell's family of Borger, Texas, waves good-bye as the Air Force pilot leaves for service in the Korean War, 1950. (National Archives)

Korean War Lingo

Brainwashing   The process of using physical or psychological coercion to win the loyalty of prisoners of war. There was much debate about collaboration by prisoners of war during the conflict, and many credited Communist brainwashing with weakening the loyalty of U.S. soldiers.

Bug out   Hastily retreat or fall back. The heavy flow of Chinese troops into North Korea in 1950 forced United Nations troops to bug out and return to South Korea, below the 38th parallel. "Bug-out fever" was the tendency to run from enemy forces.

M.A.S.H.   Mobile Army Surgical Hospital. Mobile hospitals had been used during World War I and during World War II in the Pacific. Five of these units had been established in the late 1940s, but none was in the Pacific. As a result, three units were activated in South Korea in 1950 and another in 1951. These units followed combat units up and down the Korean peninsula.

Table 6.1. Korean War Casualties

Americans serving in the Korean War	572,000
Pentagon estimate of battle-related deaths	36,914[a]
Pentagon count of Americans missing in action	8,177
American prisoners of war	4,714[b]
South Korean estimates of military deaths	184,573
South Korean estimates of civilian deaths	24,000
South Korean count of missing civilians	300,000
North Korea's estimated North Korean military deaths	294,931
Chinese estimates of Chinese deaths	152,400

Source of data, excluding prisoner-of-war count: Spencer C. Tucker, ed. 2000. *Encyclopedia of the Korean War: A Political, Social, and Military History,* 98–101. Santa Barbara: ABC-CLIO.

[a]American casualty numbers often list 54,246 American deaths, but that number reflects non-combat deaths during the period of the Korean War. This figure comes from the Washington Headquarters Services, Directorate of Information Operations and Report.

[b]The number of POWs attributed to the Korean War differs, according to the source. This is the total cited by the National Archives.

MacArthur's Rebellion

For Americans, the war's most controversial event was President Harry Truman's decision to oust Gen. Douglas MacArthur, who had commanded United Nations and U.S. forces in Korea. This bold move dominated headlines for weeks and created armchair debates in living rooms across the United States. To many Americans, MacArthur was a hero and Truman a politician afraid to pursue a wider war. Truman and his allies saw MacArthur as an insubordinate officer failing to follow the agenda set by the president of the United States as commander-in-chief of the military. In the winter of 1951, MacArthur had begun advocating a more aggressive approach to the war. Instead of merely chasing Communist soldiers back into North Korea, he wanted to attack Najin, a North Korean port near the Korean-Soviet border. While Truman saw the war as an effort to contain communism, MacArthur believed that the United States should attack communism head-on without fear of the consequences. Although he knew that Truman hoped to reach a negotiated settlement, MacArthur took his stand publicly, arguing against limitations on military action and demanding a Communist surrender. At first, Truman mildly rebuffed the general, reminding him that he was violating a directive that military leaders would not make public statements on diplomatic issues. However, Truman lost patience when MacArthur let the world know that he wanted to attack China and wrote to Joe Martin, a Republican member of the House of Representatives, that there was "no substitute for victory" (Park 1983, 254). Faced with such blatant insubordination, Truman felt compelled to act. Adding fuel to the fire were MacArthur interviews attacking Truman's policy.

After conferring with top officials, including the Joint Chiefs of Staff, Truman recalled MacArthur on April 10. MacArthur learned about his ouster from the news media. The American public responded to the news with great emotion. The White House was bombarded by mail, most of it supporting MacArthur. A California town hanged Truman in effigy, and some cities demonstrated their anger with the president by hosting receptions for MacArthur when he returned to the United States. Congress asked the general to address a joint session on April 19, and in that address, MacArthur ended his military career with the famous line: "old soldiers never die; they just fade away."

On the Home Front

The war's biggest impact on everyday life was economic. The stock market experienced its biggest drop in almost four years on the day after North Korea launched its invasion. On that day, the market also recorded its heaviest trading since May 1940. When Truman announced U.S. intervention, heavy trading again made the market plummet, but it soon stabilized.

As the war began, Americans who feared rationing started stockpiling items likely to become scarce. Included on this list were nylon stockings, tires, automobiles, bedding, soap, sugar, toilet paper, washing machines, refrigerators, and cigarettes. The Federal Reserve Board reported that installment purchases of durable goods in July 1950 alone had pushed consumer credit up $660 million. This was a significant jump in comparison with a May increase of $457 million and a June jump of $550 million (Mills and Mills 2000, 188). All of this spending led to inflation. The Truman administration succeeded in avoiding huge jumps in across-the-board inflation, but wage and price controls had mixed results.

At the same time, production of war materiel created a boom in manufacturing and employment. There was great demand for skilled workers. *Time* magazine reported in the war's first month that companies were beginning to count off the number of reservists and potential draftees on their payrolls so that they could gauge the need for future hiring. To keep its employees, automaker Chrysler Corporation offered significant pay increases in August 1950, and other companies followed suit. Cost-of-living raises built into union contracts made it simpler for millions more to live comfortably despite inflation. (See chapter titled "American Workers in the 1950s" for more information on work during the 1950s.) While some plants were devoted to war production, *Newsweek* reported in early 1951 that production of consumer goods would be adequate to forgo rationing, although there were reports of a lag in production of some goods during the war years. Unemployment fell to less than 2 percent by the spring of 1951.

Although most Americans supported the Korean War at its outset, Chinese intervention led to declining support. Surveys taken during the war showed that half of all Americans thought the Korean face-off was just the beginning of

World War III. Many others became tired of the long stalemate and wondered why the United States did not act more aggressively to end the conflict. An Edward A. Suchman survey of male college students in 1953 found that just one-fifth thought that the reasons for waging war in Korea were "tremendously important," and only 12 percent were "strongly in favor" of the United States' policy (Suchman, Goldsen, and Williams 1953, 173).

Because the cost of the war led to greater conflict between Truman and Congress, his proposed domestic agenda, known as the Fair Deal, became paralyzed. As a result, it seemed that all he could offer was stalemate in Korea and at home. By March 1952, half of Americans polled opposed the war (Mueller 1971, 360). In that same month, Truman announced that he would not seek reelection. Americans chose Dwight D. Eisenhower to replace him, and Eisenhower finalized the armistice six months after taking office.

Armed Forces Integration

The U.S. Air Force and Navy were in the process of implementing racial desegregation policies by the time conflict arose in Korea. These efforts were made in response to President Truman's 1948 order that all of the armed services must integrate. Truman's mandate, which applied to all units wherever they were deployed, promised an end to all–African American units, a change that would have a significant effect on the military experience of most people in the armed forces. African American units in previous wars had been typically assigned menial jobs behind the battle lines because of racist assumptions about cowardice and inferiority. In truth, the military usually provided African American soldiers with poor training and substandard weaponry, which placed them at a disadvantage when they were thrown into battle. As the Navy and the Air Force proceeded with integration, the Army frustrated the Fahy Committee, a panel appointed by Truman to approve desegregation plans. After months of delay, the Army finally adopted a plan in January 1950 to gradually end segregation. Although more than half of African American Air Force personnel were in integrated units just six months after implementation of the Air Force plan, Army leaders seemed intent on making the process move slowly.

The war in Korea made segregation unworkable. The Fahy Committee had convinced the Army to drop its racial quotas for enlistment in April 1950. When the war began and new troops flooded into training posts, it became clear that maintaining segregation was no longer possible because the number of African American troops was unpredictable without quotas. Ironically, the first suggestion for integrating training units came from a base in the South. The post commander in Fort Jackson, South Carolina, argued that integration was essential to the Army's success. Shortly afterward, basic training at all Army bases was integrated. Similar factors led to integration of units in Korea after commanders in the field specifically requested desegregation. Following a year of warfare with some integrated and some segregated units, the Army announced in July 1951 that it planned total integration of forces in Japan, Korea, and Okinawa within six months. The plan was the result of a study called Project Clear, which was conducted by social scientists for the Army and which recommended integration. Nevertheless, Army units in Europe remained segregated. In April 1952, the Army began the process of addressing that problem. By October 31, 1954, six years after Truman's initial order, the Army had eliminated all segregated units.

Prisoners of War

Prisoners of war (POWs) became an especially volatile issue in the Korean War because some analysts feared that American shortcomings at home had produced weak military men prone to collaboration with the enemy. Many Americans were appalled to learn about soldiers who cooperated with their captors rather than launching prison rebellions or masterminding clever escapes. They also were shocked by reports of healthy prisoners who merely gave up and died. And while Americans found it totally logical that 42,000 Communist POWs chose to stay in South Korea after the war's end, they were shocked to learn that 21 Americans decided to remain with their Communist captors.

Most civilians drew their understanding of POW camps from books and films in which defiant prisoners outsmarted their captors and escaped to safety. And with rabid anticommunism thriving in many corners of the United States, some believed that anyone who read Communist propaganda was demonstrating a moral failing—even if he was isolated in a camp with no other reading material available. Yet many Americans failed to realize the bleak conditions facing prisoners of war.

When the war started, poorly organized North Korean military men kept captured Americans in primitive living conditions and with little food. After the Chinese entered the war, there was a period of joint administration of the Communist POW operation. During this period, many POWs were forced to take part in long marches through frigid areas of North Korea, and many died as a result of exposure, malnutrition, dysentery, and pneumonia. Corporal punishment and solitary confinement were common. It has been estimated that 75 percent of all men captured between June 1950 and September 1951 died in captivity (McDermott 2000, 3). For the war as a whole, that rate was cut in half. In July 1951, the Communists began implementing a new approach to prisoner control. Americans and other United Nations soldiers faced interrogations aimed at gaining intelligence information and acquiring personal data about soldiers to make indoctrination easier. Although camp libraries usually held only Communist books, the real goal was not to convert prisoners to communism. Instead, their captors hoped to destroy their spirit and make them easier to dominate. In ad-

Former American and Australian prisoners of war warm themselves around a stove at a medical clearing station in February 1951. The men, who had been held by Chinese Communists fighting in the Korean War, were freed by their captors. The behavior of American POWs during the war became a topic of controversy in the 1950s. (National Archives)

dition to interrogation, indoctrination included reading, lectures, and discussions. Captured soldiers also were forced to perform hard labor.

Americans began hearing the term *brainwashing* to characterize the indoctrination carried out by Communist prisons. Some people blamed socialist subversion, American materialism, and permissive homes, schools, and churches for producing a generation of weaklings. The Army looked harshly on POWs facing charges of misconduct. Of the 11 percent of Army POWs accused of acting improperly, 58 percent were cleared quickly—and the Army was the only branch of the armed services to try former POWs, convicting 11 of 14 suspects. The Marine Corps quickly cleared 94 percent of those accused of misconduct and ultimately tried none of the suspected collaborators (Wubben 1970, 15).

Graves Registration

In previous foreign wars, Americans often waited months or years to receive the bodies of their lost loved ones—if they received them at all. The Korean War was the first war in which America's dead were not buried on foreign soil immediately after losing their lives. In previous wars, many soldiers had been buried abroad and later were transported to the United States. Those who died

Historians' Debate:
Did POWs Give in Too Easily?

During the 1950s, the two leading sources of information about the failures of American prisoners of war were freelance writer Eugene Kinkead, who authored *In Every War but One* in 1959, and Lt. Col. William E. Mayer, a psychiatrist who interviewed returning POWs and who spread his message of dismay through public speaking engagements and articles. Both reported that American prisoners lacked moral strength and a full commitment to the nation's traditional values. According to Kinkead and Mayer, soldiers displayed a lack of discipline, failed to help one another, and surrendered to their unfamiliar surroundings. These "experts" argued that the POWs of the Korean War were the first Americans to behave this way in captivity.

At the time, the assertions of Kinkead and Mayer were often accepted without further examination by a population that feared subversive threats to the American character. Even Eisenhower believed this analysis. Historians Robert Leckie and T. R. Fehrenbach were among those who adopted Kinkead's analysis almost without question. However, 21 scholars with intimate knowledge of the Korean POW experience signed a document in 1962 attempting to dispel the popular view, and a year later, sociologist Albert Biderman's *March to Calumny* refuted the contention that Korean War POWs were especially likely to collaborate with the enemy. Since then, other scholars, such as Russell Weigley and H. H. Wubben, have pointed out that the behavior of POWs has been an issue in every U.S. war since the American Revolution. In the face of the toughest ideological indoctrination ever confronted by U.S. soldiers, the conduct of Korean War prisoners probably was neither better nor worse than the behavior of POWs in other wars. In an article in the *American Quarterly,* Wubben argued that the American public simply was more gullible than ever before in the 1950s and more willing to accept enemy propaganda. This thesis turned Kinkead's analysis on its head; again, the problem was at home—not in Korea. In Wubben's interpretation, the civilian population's attitudes, rather than the prewar experiences of soldiers, were at fault.

in Korea were sent rapidly to a quartermaster graves registration unit. From there, the bodies of the dead were flown to Japan and then on to the United States. Often, the bodies of men killed in Korea arrived at their homes for burial within 30 days of their deaths.

Korean War Brides

With so many American servicemen in South Korea, it was inevitable that some U.S. soldiers would marry Korean women, some of whom worked within U.S.

military bases as office or store employees. Jobs on the bases introduced Korean women to American men and to some of the luxuries taken for granted in the United States, including flush toilets, pencil sharpeners, and typewriters. The image of America added impetus to involvement with American servicemen. The first bride apparently reached the United States in 1950. Frequently, these young women faced difficulty entering the United States because immigration legislation dating from the 1920s made it all but impossible for Asians to immigrate; however, intermittent exceptions were made. When they arrived in the United States, women were often disappointed to see that their husbands came from rural areas as primitive as the villages they knew in South Korea. Also, because there was no large Korean American community in the United States during the 1950s, these war brides faced strong pressure to Americanize themselves.

The Korean War and Popular Culture

The Korean War quickly made its mark on popular culture in the United States. Among the films that portrayed the Korean War experience during the 1950s were *The Steel Helmet* and *Fixed Bayonets* in 1951, *Retreat, Hell!* in 1952, *The Bridges at Toko-Ri* in 1954, and *Pork Chop Hill* in 1959. A separate genre of Korean War film was the prisoner-of-war saga. Among these were *The Bamboo Prison* and *Prisoner of War* in 1954, *The Rack* in 1956, and *Time Limit* in 1957. Perhaps the most famous popular-culture manifestation of the war in this era was *The Manchurian Candidate,* a novel written by Robert Condon in 1959 and turned into a film in 1962. It told the story of a brainwashed prisoner of war transformed into a political assassin. The Korean War did not find a home on American television until 1972, when a TV version of the 1970 film *M*A*S*H* debuted. The popular series, which mixed comedy with tragedy, was on the air for 11 years, lasting far longer than the war it portrayed.

Distant War Touches American Life

North Korea's surprise invasion of its southern neighbor had significant effects on American life. As outlined in his 1949 State of the Union address, President Harry Truman's Fair Deal aimed to help America's disadvantaged citizens with programs to guarantee equal rights, to provide public housing, and to provide health care; however, after the Korean War began, the administration found itself consumed by efforts to control inflation, shortages, and economic growth. While the economy boomed and Truman managed to avoid drastic actions such as rationing, his Fair Deal programs largely fell victim to a tug of war between the White House and the Capitol. As a result, the nation as a whole prospered, but the poor found little new assistance.

When Truman left office, the Korean War already had reached a stalemate, and his successor, Eisenhower, ended the conflict with an armistice that maintained the 38th parallel as the border between the two Koreas. This fell short of South Korean leader Syngman Rhee's desire for reunification of the two Koreas; nevertheless, Eisenhower saw it as the most prudent solution. He warned China against any further activity in Korea and began withdrawing troops from the peninsula in 1954.

As servicemen returned to the United States, they were released to civilian life at a slower pace than those who had served in World War II. Nonetheless, during his White House years, Eisenhower reduced the size of the armed services from 3.5 million in 1953 to 2.47 million, and he cut the Army from 1.5 million to 860,000 men over the same period. Military service, therefore, affected the lives of fewer Americans. After being caught undermanned at the start of this war, the federal government maintained the draft through the decade, so young men still faced the prospect of unwanted military service. However, deferments were available for specific occupations, for education, and for those with dependents.

Because Korea remained divided at the end of the war, containment of Communists in North Korea represented a continuing goal throughout the Cold War. After the fall of the Soviet Union, American politicians and policy makers moved North Korea into a new category, labeling it as a "rogue nation" that endangered other parts of the world. As a result of Cold War and post–Cold War priorities, the United States has continued to deploy thousands of troops in South Korea for more than half a century since the end of the Korean War. In 2006, 20,000 Americans were assigned to South Korea.

THE COLD WAR

Although no shooting war touched American soil in the 1950s, much of daily life was framed by the Cold War with the Soviet Union and the threat of nuclear war. Together, these two forces, separate and yet intertwined, dwelled in the American mind. Since the American bombings of Hiroshima and Nagasaki during World War II, nuclear war had been a nightmare looming over American life. The Cold War sometimes erupted into actual military confrontations; however, much of that long conflict, too, existed outside the physical world and in the psyches of ideological combatants on both sides. These were years of high anxiety about national and personal survival.

Events in the 1950s brought changes in Americans' view of both the Cold War and the threat of nuclear war. One significant development was a change in the leadership of the Soviet Union. Many Americans, both liberal and conservative, equated the repressive Josef Stalin with Adolf Hitler. Though their politics were quite different, both men were ruthless dictators, considered capable of almost any kind of evil. Like Hitler, Stalin had persecuted Jews and political opponents in inhumane concentration camps; the two leaders also embraced military aggression as a means of achieving their goals. Stalin's harsh rule ended when he died in 1953, but Americans did not immediately recognize that the threat of a hot war had lessened with his departure. Three years after Stalin's death, his successor, Nikita Khrushchev, stunningly denounced Stalin and his harsh policies. As a result, hope for a lasting peace with the Soviet Union, unimaginable a few years earlier, began to become an acceptable concept in the minds of some Americans. Conflict with the Soviet Union no longer seemed quite so inevitable.

The election of new leadership in the United States also had an impact. Although he was a veteran military leader, Dwight D. Eisenhower chose to reduce the armed forces during his presidency. After taking office in 1953, Eisenhower began developing a new approach toward the Cold War. At the heart of his policy was the belief that the United States could avoid war simply by maintaining a superior nuclear arsenal. Eisenhower believed that attacks on the United States could be prevented by simply promising massive retaliation using the largest nuclear-weapons cache in the world. This policy reduced the number of people serving in the military and made it possible to lower expenditures on conventional weapons. However, Eisenhower's strategy also positioned nuclear weapons front and center in the next anticipated war, raising the stakes significantly in a dangerous game of brinkmanship. As a result, the government began placing greater emphasis on the need to maintain nuclear strength and on the idea of saving lives through civil defense.

Typical Americans faced almost daily reminders of the possibility that nuclear war might come. The government conducted nuclear tests, sometimes broadcast live on television. Also, television and radio stations regularly tested the emergency broadcasting signal that would alert citizens if the threat of nuclear attack was imminent. At the same time, the government conducted civil defense drills on a massive scale, housewives were urged to prepare their homes to serve as shelters from radioactive fallout, and even small schoolchildren participated in civil defense drills. Popular culture also began to address nuclear war more directly as the mushroom cloud assumed a more prominent position in America's imagined future.

School children duck and cover their heads in a 1951 civil defense drill. (Bettmann/Corbis)

More Powerful Bombs, Less Chance of Survival

The 1950s represented a period of massive change in the technology that would power a nuclear war, and as a result, the concept of civil defense also underwent a rapid evolution. As the 1950s began, the United States knew that the Soviet Union had just begun to build its nuclear arsenal and so the nuclear threat was seen as affecting only a few major targets. People who lived away from large cities and military bases faced little threat of nuclear devastation and a minimal possibility of deaths caused by radioactive fallout. Consequently, civil defense drills were not universal.

The atomic bombs that hit Hiroshima and Nagasaki in 1945 seemed incredibly strong; however, development of the hydrogen bomb by the United States in 1952 and the Soviet Union in 1953 expanded the area of immediate destruction. The United States' first hydrogen bomb was hundreds of times more powerful than the bomb dropped on Hiroshima. Recognition that a hydrogen bomb blast could wipe out everything within a 14-mile radius made taking shelter meaningless for those living in a target area. Moreover, radiation sickness became a larger threat with hydrogen bombs. As a result, the government briefly shifted gears toward the idea of evacuating prime targets. Because airplanes were the only available delivery system for nuclear weapons at that time, some civil defense planners believed that air defense monitors would provide adequate warning to make broad-scale evacuation a workable idea. Even in a surprise attack, evacuating the area around a rural military base might be doable with the help of buses; however, there were obvious problems with evacuating a densely populated area. One target, Manhattan, is an island with limited escape routes. Inevitably, bridges and tunnels would become jammed with panicky drivers, public transit systems leading out of the city would be overtaxed, and chaos would follow. Many people who escaped the target might still be in the path of radioactive fallout. As a result, evacuation might save city dwellers from dying in the blast, but they still might die from radiation sickness.

Late in the decade, the development of missiles powerful enough to carry nuclear weapons from the Soviet Union to the United States again changed the parameters of nuclear war and governmental concepts of civil defense. With missiles, people living in target areas could receive as little as 15 minutes warning. This limited the possibilities of surviving a nuclear assault at the same time that it made a surprise attack more attractive to the aggressor. Evacuation no longer was feasible. Consequently, there seemed to be no real options for people living in target areas. Shelters in the basements of office buildings, schools, and homes could provide a minimal opportunity for survival to those living outside target areas, but because more powerful weapons aimed at more targets would create more pervasive fallout, the threat of radiation sickness ballooned.

Nuclear Tests

Testing of nuclear weapons was intended to help the governments of the United States and the Soviet Union produce better weapons, but these tests carried an implicit warning for average Americans about the true dangers of nuclear war. Although some tests were televised live, much of the truth about their results remained secret. And the small group of Americans who argued for a preemptive nuclear strike against the Soviet Union really had only a vague idea of how nuclear war could transform American life.

The United States conducted the first test of a hydrogen bomb, known as Operation Ivy, in the Marshall Islands on November 1, 1952. The blast created a fireball 3.5 miles wide and unexpectedly high levels of radioactive fallout. In announcing this new achievement, the government emphasized the pyrotechnic effects of America's newest weapon and downplayed the issue of fallout, which would have revealed greater danger to average Americans in a nuclear war. Officials saw no reason to worry civilians.

In March 1954, fishermen on a Japanese boat 85 miles away from the Bikini Atoll testing site developed radiation sickness as a result of a hydrogen bomb blast. Following this incident, the news media alerted Americans to the expanding danger of fallout, but the government again glossed over the details. What the government had learned in 16 months of testing hydrogen bombs was that use of a thermonuclear weapon created a huge amount of radioactive debris—so huge that fallout could take more lives than the explosion itself.

Acceptance of this new scientific evidence contributed to increased civil defense dependence on fallout shelters and changed the whole concept of nuclear war. Because fallout from multiple attacks on the United States would all flow eastward with prevailing weather systems, the entire East Coast probably would be shrouded in radioactivity, and people who lived far from target areas could fall victim to radiation sickness. Although the government promoted home fallout shelters in basements, there was little chance of survival for people near target areas unless they happened to be ensconced in a deep underground bunker, such as the ones that awaited Eisenhower and other government leaders. As of 1958, Eisenhower and other government leaders had a bunker awaiting them in Virginia called Mount Weather. Another bunker, intended to house the Congress, was under construction under the elite Greenbrier resort in West Virginia in the 1950s, but was not completed until the following decade.

For American civilians, the danger did not lie strictly in possible attacks from the Soviet Union. Atmospheric testing itself endangered Americans' health. Both the United States and the Soviet Union tested atomic and hydrogen bombs in the atmosphere in the postwar years. While testing usually occurred in isolated areas, it demonstrated that nuclear weapons employed in one of the earth's hemispheres could threaten the health of human beings in another. Hydrogen bomb blasts put the radioisotope strontium 90 in the air, where it drifted along with global weather patterns. Over time, it was absorbed by plants that were eaten by cows, and eventually, it entered the human body through cows' milk. Scientists of this era estimated that it would remain in the human body for 40 years, but they lacked adequate information to predict its short- and long-term effects.

Operation Alert

In the belief that a series of national drills would ease civilian panic if a real nuclear attack occurred, the Eisenhower administration began annual exercises under the name Operation Alert. These events tested government as well as civilian preparedness. Some cities were designated as the unfortunate victims of nuclear bombs and had to respond accordingly; others were spared and faced problems such as handling refugee populations from stricken urban areas and providing health care to victims of radiation sickness. Each year, the government planners changed the war scenario and the lessons to be learned.

In 1955, about 5 percent of the civilian population was "killed" in a nuclear attack that hit 53 cities; however, in 3 of the 53 stricken cities, civil defense officials decided that all bombers had been shot down, sparing their beloved homes. Along with 15,000 government employees, Eisenhower took refuge in a secret location and attempted to prove that the government could be run from a bunker (George 2003, 29). One Cabinet member reached the bunker too late after stopping on the way to get lunch. This strange mixture of a real-life threat and a fictitious national storyline reflected the ambiguous nature of civil defense in American life.

In one exercise, an entire hospital in Canton, Ohio, was evacuated, and all patients were moved to a field hospital. In another, instructions in self-control were given. Red Cross workers, civic leaders, auxiliary police officers, Boy Scouts, Girl Scouts, and B'nai B'rith volunteers all participated in these massive dramas intended to train Americans in "habits of thinking needed to cope with emergency conditions" (Oakes 1994, 95). It was a gigantic war game for civilians; participants knew they could return to the safety of their homes at the end of the day.

Nuclear False Alarms

1955   After an unidentified squadron of bombers was spotted off the California coast, air-raid sirens sounded in Oakland. Most residents took no action because they assumed it was a drill.

1957   Malfunctioning sirens blared in the early morning in Schenectady, New York, and only one family in the whole city responded to the alarm. That family evacuated instead of waiting for radio confirmation to act.

1959   Celebratory Chicagoans set off air-raid sirens to mark a White Sox victory that clinched the American League pennant. Many Chicagoans used telephones to confirm that the threat was real, and in the process, they jammed lines that would have been needed in a real emergency.

Civil Defense at Home

Because the government could not afford to build enough deep bunkers to protect the lives of all Americans in a nuclear war, discussion of civil defense in the 1950s often focused on the American home. *How to Survive an Atomic Bomb,* published by the government in 1950, warned readers that after a nuclear attack, survivors could expect that "things are probably going to look different when you go outside" (George 2003, 30–31). What survivors might see would be frightening, but the government wanted to stress the possibility of survival.

With more than one-third of the American population living outside target areas in towns of fewer than 50,000 residents, a large portion of the nation's population faced the greatest threat from radioactive fallout rather than blast effects. By the late 1950s, the Office of Civil and Defense Mobilization had begun churning out booklets that urged families to prepare basement areas as home fallout shelters, allowing 10 square feet per person, and they urged housewives to stock these areas with the necessities for survival. "Civil Defense training is

A Michigan housewife stands beside a 14-day emergency food supply she bought following general instructions from the Office of Civil Defense. These 113 food items, which would feed two people during two weeks of isolation following a nuclear attack, cost less than $28 and weighed 118 pounds. (National Archives)

Recommended Fallout Shelter Supplies

Canned foods	Portable radios
Bottled water	Soap
Powdered milk	Buckets
Crackers	Pet food
First-aid supplies	Books
Flashlights	Geiger counter
Candles	

almost akin to religious training," said Jean Wood Fuller, director of women's activities for the Federal Civil Defense Administration. "We must teach our children protection. . . . A mother must calm the fears of her child. Make a game out of it: Playing Civil Defense" (May 1988, 103–104).

The growing threat of fallout made the safety of basement fallout shelters debatable, and for those without basements, these plans were useless. At that time, basements were common in the North, but most southern homes had no basements to serve as refuges from nuclear war. And many Americans simply found planning for civil defense to be morbid, so by 1959, effective shelter spaces had been prepared for only about 1 percent of the nation's population.

Schools' Preparations for War

Although talk of imminent warfare might be considered a frightening subject for small children, youngsters in the 1950s routinely practiced for war. Drills became commonplace in major cities during the 1950–1951 school year. Children in New York, Chicago, Los Angeles, Detroit, Milwaukee, Fort Worth, and San Francisco participated in these exercises. When they heard air-raid sirens, children crouched under their desks with their hands covering their heads. These exercises represented meager attempts to protect children from the blast effects of an atomic bomb. By the mid-1950s, as Americans faced the threat of a hydrogen bomb attack, schools across the country began drills in which the children were hustled into dark hallways or basements that conceivably could serve as shelter areas. The potential use of missiles to deliver nuclear weapons late in the decade led to drills in which children were released from school in the hope that they could reach their homes within the 15-minute warning time before a missile could strike. Those who could not reach home in the designated time period faced the prospect of dying alone by the side of the road rather than in the arms of their mothers.

Visions of Nuclear War in Pop Culture

Nuclear war became a factor in the American imagination as soon as news of the Hiroshima attack spread through the nation, and during the 1950s, the dangers of the nuclear age had become a new theme in popular culture as nuclear weapons cast gloom across American life. A 1956 survey of college students showed that more than 70 percent believed that a third world war was likely. Just a little more than 60 percent of those students believed that they would survive such a war, and only a small percentage felt certain that they would survive (George 2003, 40).

British author Nevil Shute's 1957 novel *On the Beach* was popular in the United States, and it inspired a 1959 film starring Gregory Peck and Fred Astaire. Shute's concept was simple: a nuclear war in the northern hemisphere generated so much radioactivity that the entire world's population was at risk. The book focused on Australia, where many of the last survivors had gathered, including the crew of the only surviving U.S. submarine. By this time, radioactivity had killed all humans except those closest to the South Pole. In Australia, as it became clear that nuclear death was at hand, many chose suicide, either by driving at high speeds on a racetrack or by downing government-issued pills. The 1959 novel *A Canticle for Liebowitz,* written by American author Walter M. Miller Jr., took a different perspective. It examined the wasteland left behind by a long-past nuclear conflict and traced humanity's technological rebirth, which would lead inevitably to massive destruction once again. And *Level Seven* by Mordecai Roshwald chronicled a nuclear war fought by humans buried deep in the earth, where they were supposedly safe. The final irony hit home when the last man to die was the man who had callously pushed the button launching the war that destroyed humankind.

Fictional nuclear war found a place in episodes of Rod Serling's science-fiction television series, *The Twilight Zone,* in the late 1950s and early 1960s. In one such scenario, a bored banker hid inside a vault during his lunch break so that he could read in a quiet place. Because his wife discouraged his reading at home, he cherished this time. When he emerged one day, he found a world entirely destroyed. For a while, the dazed man wandered through the ruins of civilization aimlessly and then he found the remains of a public library. Hundreds of books waited there for him to read. Forgetting about the devastation around him, he found joy as he mapped out his future in the pages of so many books. Then, a small accident—the destruction of his eyeglasses in a world without optometrists—destroyed his dream and left him all alone without even a book for company.

These horrific explorations of nuclear war gave Americans dark expectations of one possible future. Even children's comic books warned about the evils of communism and the potential of war. Some analysts also have connected Cold War anxieties to the prevalence of dark science-fiction monster movies during the 1950s. Faced with grim expectations, many Americans openly discussed their own preference for dying in a nuclear conflagration rather than having to live in its aftermath.

Cold War Loses Much of Its Bite

At the end of the 1950s, the Cold War seemed less dangerous than it had been in 1950; however, the potential for nuclear destruction had grown during the decade. Though the threat of war weighed heavily on Americans, the nation experienced no near-misses where the United States and the Soviet Union appeared on the brink of war; those lay a few years in the future. Nevertheless, the United States of this era was swathed in a fear of communism that generated the politics of paranoia. At the same time, civil defense drills and alerts brought the prospect of nuclear war into American homes and schools.

Americans felt powerless when faced with the idea of a Cold War–spawned nuclear war. Not only were the weapons incredibly destructive, but voters also would have little voice in this kind of confrontation. Most wars had been declared by a vote of the nation's elected officials in Congress; even in the case of the Korean War, which was not officially declared, Congress could have crippled President Truman's initiative if that had seemed wise. However, nuclear war might require quick action in a matter of minutes. This narrowed the decision-making group to the president of the United States and a small group of unelected leaders, such as key Cabinet members and top-ranking military officers.

Although the Eisenhower administration made some efforts to lure the public into participating in civil defense drills, some administration officials and many American civilians believed that civil defense precautions were unlikely to save many lives in a massive nuclear war. Eisenhower himself thought that it was essential to give Americans hope of survival so that they would not surrender to their fear of nuclear war and accept Communist advances in other parts of the globe. Some Americans did stock corners in their basements with survival supplies and a few built fallout shelters. However, for most, not thinking about nuclear war seemed to be the most effective defense.

After the Korean War ended, the Cold War became largely a war of words. Americans were frightened by Nikita Khrushchev's threat to bury Western nations and by his shoe-banging United Nations theatrics, but he did not significantly expand the Soviet sphere of influence. The most shocking addition to the Communist sector came late in the 1950s when Cuba, just 90 miles off the American coast, decided to establish close ties with the Soviet Union. After Fidel Castro's revolutionary government chose to tie its fortunes to the Soviet Union, many Americans felt that communism had invaded the Western Hemisphere, and they feared its future spread in Latin America. The concept of being surrounded by monolithic communism was very real in the American consciousness. As a result, voters supported Eisenhower's cautious efforts to deter Soviet aggression in little-known nations like Vietnam. The ominously quiet Cold War was more expensive than many shooting wars because of the high cost of being militarily ready for nuclear war, and the Cold War generated more widespread fear of imminent destruction among civilians than any war in American history because it was the first conflict to threaten the lives of American civilians in all regions of the country.

THE PEACE MOVEMENT

In the early 1950s, the peace movement was a weak force in American culture. Current and former Communists often joined pacifist organizations and that provided an excuse for attacks on peace activists by right-wing emulators of Sen. Joseph McCarthy. Moreover, because many Americans believed that war represented the only answer to conflict between the United States and the Soviet Union, talk of peace seemed un-American to many. In the words of Supreme Court justice William O. Douglas, the pacifists' cause suffered because of "the prevalence of the belief that full-scale war is inevitable. Many men of good will have lost hope for any solution short of war." And as Albert Einstein told peace activist A. J. Muste, "the men who possess the real power in this country have no intention of ending the Cold War" (Wittner 1984, 212).

With the Cold War came anticommunism, and with anticommunist passions rising, congressional committees started to include pacifists among their targets for investigation. Even the hint of Communists or Socialists on a peace group's membership list could create serious problems. As debilitated peace groups purged their organizations of possible Communists, the most overt antiwar actions were individual young men's decisions not to register for the draft. Oddly, the muffling of the peace movement coincided with an unpopular war. Although as many as 50 percent of Americans opposed the Korean War at various times, peace organizations profited little from these sentiments. Divisions on the Left and fear of being

Pickets protest the development of nuclear weapons in a March 1950 demonstration. (Library of Congress)

labeled as Communists led pacifist groups to remain relatively quiet during the war. Many Americans who opposed the Korean War did not deplore the conflict's violence; instead, they opposed the Truman administration's efforts to limit the fighting.

Pacifists had many different reasons for opposing the war. Some were members of the "historic peace churches"—the Quakers, the Mennonites, and the Brethren—that opposed all military action and placed a special emphasis in the 1950s on nuclear weapons and the arms race. Others supported the idea of a single world government, a concept that first gained popular attention in the late 1930s and now raised fears of Communist rule. Some scientists focused their energies on educating the public about the dangers of nuclear war. And other peace backers belonged to the Third Camp movement, which endorsed a worldwide antimilitarist movement aimed at ending colonialism and building a new pacifist base in former colonies. Some of those supporting peace and rejecting nuclear war were not pacifists at all: they were mainstream Americans disturbed about the devastating effects of nuclear weapons.

As anticommunism waned late in the 1950s, peace activists regrouped. They found new strength by fighting for a ban on atmospheric nuclear tests and by supporting nuclear disarmament. Because contamination from nuclear tests affected typical American adults and children through the milk they drank, this issue fit into the devotion to family that was an important part of American life during this period. Drawing support from mainstream Americans, the peace movement found new life in this issue.

Peace Activists

Pacifism lost strength early in the 1950s largely because many Americans' attitudes toward the Soviet Union made it impossible for them to conceptualize existing peacefully in a world with the Communist giant. If Americans could not trust anything Soviet leaders said, then clearly no negotiated peace settlement was possible. Americans remembered all too well that British prime minister Neville Chamberlain thought he had guaranteed peace with Adolf Hitler in the 1938 Munich Pact, and they feared that any treaty with the Soviet Union would be equally misguided.

In 1948, Henry A. Wallace's Progressive presidential campaign challenged curbs on the rights of those suspected of Communist ties. Wallace opposed the hard line taken against the Soviet Union, but most Americans disagreed with his stand. After his defeat, the mere whisper of Communist ties could lead to ouster from a peace group. Pacifist organizations, whose leaders often shared widespread concerns about Communist infiltration, sometimes expelled members who were accused of representing "subversive" elements or of actively supporting communism. At other times, group leaders defended their members and paid a heavy cost. Greater government scrutiny hurt efforts to recruit new members, and in many cases, the targeted group was forced to adopt a formal resolution denying membership to supporters of communism. Lawyers for the accused often argued that individuals should be judged for their actions, not for their beliefs or their political associations; however, some peace groups shunned people who had ever taken any action to support communism in the United States or around the world.

Organizations like the Fellowship of Reconciliation, the Women's International League for Peace and Freedom, and the War Resisters League faced a flurry of accusations about Communist influences, and fear of being labeled as a Communist became so great among Americans that the War Resisters League found that New Yorkers were too frightened to accept mimeographed circulars being passed out by league members on Times Square. Even the Committee for a Sane Nuclear Policy, founded in 1957 after the worst of McCarthyism had been discarded, faced the same kind of charges and demands. When accusations were directed at a member of SANE's New York committee and when that member refused to state whether or not he had been a Communist, he was suspended. A new membership policy and an effort to oust chapters with questionable members soon took hold.

Clearly, being a pacifist carried risks. Activists handing out literature sometimes faced violent attacks on the street or lost their jobs because of their unwillingness to sign loyalty oaths. A city librarian in Bartlesville, Oklahoma, was ousted after 35 years in her job largely because she placed the *Nation,* the *New Republic,* and *Soviet Russia Today* on library shelves. Even the American Friends Service Committee, the Quaker peace organization, refused membership to Priscilla Hiss in 1954 because her husband, Alger, had been convicted of perjury three years earlier after being accused of being a Soviet spy. Some pacifists, such as members of the Committee for Non-Violent Action, used passive resistance as a tool in achieving their goals, which meant that those demonstrators faced the possibility of imprisonment to draw public attention to the era's dangers.

Einstein-Russell Appeal

Since the attacks on Hiroshima and Nagasaki, some scientists had urged the U.S. government to forgo future use of nuclear weapons. The Einstein-Russell Appeal, issued in July 1955, represented the first major statement by respected scientists and philosophers calling for an end to the development of nuclear weaponry. This document, written by physicist Albert Einstein and philosopher and mathematician Bertrand Russell, was signed by 11 men revered for their scholarship. Respected intellectuals from the United States, Great Britain, Poland, Germany, France, and Japan united to address "all the powerful governments in the world in the earnest hope that they might agree to allow their citizens to survive." This represented an important moment in opposition to the Cold War because the men who signed this appeal could not be dismissed as Communist subversives or hare-brained crackpots. Einstein, who died before the document was released, argued that "political passions, once they have been fanned into flames, exact their victims" (Pauling 1986, 79–80). A week after this appeal was released, 52 Nobel laureates, including 15 Americans, urged that violent force should no longer be a "final resort to policy."

Liberation

Liberation, a magazine founded in 1956 by radical pacifists, offered a new voice for those who opposed the government's foreign policy. It quickly won acceptance from those who favored direct, nonviolent action to bring change and from the anti-establishment Beat movement. The magazine condemned the silencing of radical voices in the American discourse of the 1950s. It shunned both liberalism, which was characterized as shallow and hypocritical, and Marxism, which "underestimated the seriousness of the growth of the State and its emergence as an instrument of war and oppression." The editors also voiced dissatisfaction with centralization, technology, and industrialization, all of which affected both American and Soviet society. A 1959 poll of *Liberation*'s readership found that most were middle-class intellectuals. When asked to choose an ideology they embraced, only 2 percent chose capitalism; 1 percent chose communism. Most members favored "cooperative communities." In addition to their pacifist tendencies, the magazine's readers denounced loyalty oaths and corporal punishment for children, and they defended homosexuality and extramarital affairs (Wittner 1984, 238).

The *Phoenix*

Opponents of nuclear testing sought to disrupt testing efforts in 1958 by sailing into an area of the Pacific Ocean where U.S. tests were conducted. After several efforts to invade the test zone, the peace activists' boat, the *Golden Rule,* had been boarded and the Quaker crew arrested. Coincidentally, an American anthropologist and his family happened to sail into Honolulu at the time of this confrontation, and on July 1, 1958, the Earle Reynolds family took on the *Golden Rule*'s mission in their boat, the *Phoenix*. Reynolds radioed the Coast Guard that his boat had entered the forbidden zone, and the boat and its crew were apprehended. The Reynolds family's efforts triggered protests at Atomic Energy Commission offices, and while he awaited trial, Reynolds visited 58 American cities on a speaking tour. Reynolds eventually was convicted and served a short prison sentence, but his family's efforts brought new support to the antinuclear movement.

Omaha Action

Members of the Committee for Non-Violent Action chose the Mead Interconti-nental Ballistic Missile Base in Omaha, Nebraska, as the site for a protest against nuclear weaponry. Sign-carrying protesters conducted a week-long demonstra-tion, but officials managed to keep the protest out of the news at first by limit-ing the group's access to locations where they could meet with the media. To attract more attention, the 75-year-old A. J. Muste and two other protesters climbed over the chainlink fence surrounding the base. All three were arrested and given suspended sentences. Fence climbing immediately became a daily event in the protest, and as a result, some people were arrested repeatedly, thus violating the conditions of their parole. Some faced sentences of six months in prison for trespassing on government property. The protest attracted spotty cov-erage from the media, but because it drew some attention, Muste considered it a triumph for nonviolent action.

Student Peace Union

In 1959, the Student Peace Union (SPU), the first campus-based national peace organization, was founded by young activists who believed that SANE's ap-proach to ending nuclear testing was too conservative. SANE, which was led by adult intellectuals, seemed out of sync with the temper of young people. Look-ing back, SPU appears to be a link between the political quietude of college campuses in the 1950s and the raucous student demonstrations in the latter half of the 1960s. By encouraging student activism, it also opened the door to white students' involvement in the civil rights movement. The organization's original goal was to promote nuclear disarmament and an end to nuclear testing. Even-tually finding a home on about 100 college campuses, SPU was critical of both American and Soviet policy. The group organized several protest marches on Washington and participated in the civil rights movement's 1963 March on Wash-ington before dissolving a year later.

Anti-Nuke Campaign

The campaign against nuclear tests and potential use of nuclear weaponry be-came the ultimate focus of peace organizations during the 1950s. Joining in these efforts were all of the major peace groups of the era, including what were known as the "historic peace churches." Anti-nuke activists attempted to gen-erate public opposition to ongoing tests of nuclear weapons in the earth's at-mosphere and to the continuing arms race between the United States and the Soviet Union. They also set out to discredit the very idea of nuclear war as an irrational manifestation of Cold War foreign policy.

To attract public notice, peace activists handed out information pamphlets, picketed sites associated with nuclear weapons, demonstrated against civil defense drills for nuclear war, invaded nuclear test areas, and placed advertisements in national publications that condemned nuclear arms. During this period, pacifists realized they could not win the battle to affect nuclear policy without the support of some nonpacifists. As a result, they asked Lawrence Scott of the American Friends Service Committee in Chicago to form two groups, each of which would campaign primarily for a nuclear test ban. They were the National Committee for a Sane Nuclear Policy, known as SANE, and the Committee for Non-Violent Action.

SANE was formed under the leadership of Linus Pauling, Norman Cousins, Clarence Pickett, and Homer Jack in 1957. This organization, which was intended to fit into the mainstream and to work through education and lobbying, grabbed national attention on November 15, 1957, when it placed a full-page ad in the *New York Times*. The ad argued that the "national interest" should not be the guiding force in human development. Instead, it contended that "the sovereignty of the human community comes before all others. . . . In the community, man has natural rights. He has the right to live and to grow, to breathe unpoisoned air, to work on uncontaminated soil." Within six weeks, the ad, which represented a plea for the end of the arms race, generated $12,000 in donations and 2,500 letters. Over the following months, SANE chapters popped up all over the country, growing to a total of 130 by the summer of 1958 (Wittner 1984, 243–244).

The second group, initiated in 1957 as Non-Violent Action against Nuclear Weapons, was a hard-core pacifist organization composed of activists willing to use civil disobedience in their struggle against war. The Committee for Non-Violent Action was reorganized and renamed a year later as the radical wing of the pacifist movement. The sailing of the *Phoenix* and the Omaha Action are just two examples of the committee's actions during the 1950s. On August 6, 1957, protesters from this group trespassed at the Atomic Energy Commission headquarters on the anniversary of the Hiroshima bombing, and 11 were arrested. Often, angry Americans urged anti-nuke activists to complain to the Soviet Union, and this group sent a delegation to the Soviet Union in 1958 to deliver its message that the arms race should be abandoned by both sides.

Concerned scholars contributed significantly to peace efforts. The Federation of American Scientists, founded in 1945 by atomic scientists who felt an ethical obligation to contribute to decisions relating to atomic weapons, frequently joined public discussion of these issues, but scientists also created new forums in the 1950s. During 1957 alone, scientists voiced their concerns in diverse manners. Physician Albert Schweitzer made a plea for an end to nuclear testing in a broadcast appeal to 50 nations. Philosopher and mathematician Bertrand Russell led the first international conference of scientists from both sides of the Cold War in Pugwash, Nova Scotia; at the meeting's conclusion, a statement against

Members of Non-Violent Action against Nuclear Weapons, later known as the Committee for Non-Violent Action, hold a prayer vigil before attempting to launch a demonstration inside the Nevada nuclear test site. (Library of Congress)

nuclear war was issued. And Linus Pauling issued a petition signed by more than 11,000 scientists that pleaded for an end to nuclear testing.

Another academic approach to ending the arms buildup was peace research, which attracted attention in the late 1950s. An eclectic group of social scientists at the University of Michigan founded the *Journal of Conflict Resolution* in 1957. One of the journal's founders, Kenneth Boulding, said that it could not be defined as being a pacifist publication; however, its goal was to advocate careful diplomacy leading toward a stable peace.

Ordeal of Robert Oppenheimer

Robert Oppenheimer, like many people in the United States, had doubts about the production of more and more powerful nuclear weapons. What set Oppenheimer apart from other Americans was his important position as a physicist and director of the Los Alamos laboratory, where the first atomic bombs were developed. Although Oppenheimer had a history of raising money for Spanish Republicans, participating in a teachers' union, and associating with some Communists, he was named to head the facility in 1943. Four years later, President Truman named him to the General Advisory Committee of the Atomic Energy Commission, and at that time, Oppenheimer joined the faculty of Princeton

Robert Oppenheimer, who headed the Los Alamos laboratory that developed the atomic bomb, opposed development of the hydrogen bomb in the 1950s. He subsequently was labeled as a security risk in 1953, ostensibly because of contacts with leftists that pre-dated his involvement in the Manhattan Project. Afterward, Oppenheimer continued to contribute to the study of quantum physics. (Library of Congress)

University as director of the Institute for Advanced Study.

Despite deep roots in the United States' atomic weapons program, Oppenheimer opposed development of the hydrogen bomb, and he often criticized the idea that the United States' ability to produce massive retaliation with powerful weapons would circumvent nuclear war. He promoted a mix of weapons and pushed for development of guided missiles and early warning systems. He also complained that the military showed inadequate concern for the potential effects of nuclear war on the civilian population. Because of his outspokenness, Oppenheimer had powerful enemies in the Atomic Energy Commission and the Department of Defense. By 1953, those adversaries had raised questions about Oppenheimer's past allegiances, and President Eisenhower reduced his access to classified material. After an investigation and interrogation, the Atomic Energy Commission's Personnel Security Board declared, based entirely on his activities before he headed the Manhattan Project, that Oppenheimer was a security risk.

Like many victims of McCarthyism, Oppenheimer faced career restrictions as a result of accusations based on very old information. He maintained his position at Princeton, but he was denied access to the latest research in his field of interest. In one significant way, Oppenheimer's experience differed from the ordeals of most blacklisted Americans: He was censured by the executive branch of government, with involvement of the president himself; others had been attacked by a handful of lawmakers.

Hiroshima Maidens

Ten years after the United States' attack on Hiroshima, 25 Japanese women arrived in New York for 138 separate plastic surgery procedures to repair the scars left on their faces by the atomic bomb that leveled the Japanese city. For almost two years, these young women, known as the "Hiroshima Maidens," lived in

Prominent Peace Organizations in the 1950s

American Friends Service Committee	The Quakers' activist arm
Mennonite Central Committee	The Mennonites' peace operation
Brethren Service Committee	The Brethren's pacifist organization
Fellowship of Reconciliation	Peace group founded in England in 1914, originally led by young Protestant clergymen
Women's International League for Peace and Freedom	U.S. section set up by Jane Addams in 1915 to oppose U.S. involvement in World War I
War Resisters League	Started in New York in 1923
Committee for Non-Violent Action	Organized in the United States in 1957
Committee for a Sane Nuclear Policy	Founded in New York in 1957
Student Peace Union	Initiated in the United States in 1959

the American homes of Quaker families while successive operations gave them new faces. Their treatment garnered national attention in the media. Three years earlier, in June 1952, nine women from Hiroshima received special treatment in Tokyo hospitals, and six months later, the Hiroshima City Hibakusha A-bomb Sufferers Treatment Council was founded, providing a mechanism to seek out treatment for those who needed it. *Hibakusha* is a widely used Japanese term to refer to victims of the Hiroshima and Nagasaki atomic bombings.

Peace Movement Shows Signs of Growth

The climate of the Cold War changed considerably in the late 1950s, although that change was not immediately apparent to all Cold Warriors. Despite his military background, President Eisenhower was anxious about giving too much power to what he called the "military-industrial complex" in his 1961 farewell speech. And despite his decision to crush a revolt in the Soviet satellite nation of Hungary in 1956, Khrushchev was not the murderous dictator that Stalin had been. The Russian leader intended to keep the Soviet bloc intact, but he did not crave a new world war.

With time, many people, including some who had been hesitant to support any cause tied to pacifism, realized that war with the Soviet Union might be avoidable. This applied especially to liberals who had embraced a tough Cold War stance because they feared the Soviet Union almost as much as they feared being labeled as leftists. Changes in leadership and in public opinion turned the international spotlight away from direct confrontation between the two superpowers and toward surrogate battles or proxy wars in Third World nations, where citizens supporting Western ideas battled leftists with Communist support. Within the United States, the idea of a nuclear test ban was drifting into the mainstream.

Though nuclear disarmament remained difficult because of distrust on both sides, the top priority of peace groups in the 1950s—an end to the testing of nuclear weapons in the atmosphere—was almost within reach as the decade ended. Pacifists had made a savvy decision when they recognized the need for nonpacifists in the anti-nuke movement. SANE brought the issue before a broader audience and established an example for another set of nonpacifists who soon would oppose nuclear testing and nuclear war. Women Strike for Peace, founded in 1961, put middle-class mothers on the streets protesting policies that threatened their children. Because of the women's fastidiously ladylike behavior, the group became a difficult target for right-wing militarists. Peace organizations laid the groundwork for approval of the Limited Test Ban Treaty of 1963, which came to pass after both President John F. Kennedy and Khrushchev accepted the prospect of peaceful coexistence and the rightness of ending atmospheric tests. The work of peace groups had made it easier for ordinary Americans to accept the possibility and the potential worth of a treaty with the Soviet Union.

RELIGIOUS AMERICA

Although religion is sometimes associated with the idea of peace, most churches in the United States did not embrace the pacifists' opposition to the United States' Cold War policies. In fact, many Americans saw prayer and other religious activity as a weapon to be used against "godless communism." According to the pacifist A. J. Muste, some ministers voiced apprehensions about discussing world peace in their sermons because they feared being identified as Communists. During these years, church membership rose, and the government's direct attachment to religion also expanded. Americanism and religion became tightly intertwined, with religion's greatest emphasis on individual salvation rather than world peace.

President Eisenhower helped in the effort to envelop American culture in a religious cocoon. There is irony in Eisenhower's role because he admitted that he had devoted little time to religion during his military career. However, as president, he made it clear from the start that religion would be an important factor in his administration and in his America. He read a prayer just before his inauguration ceremony and began each Cabinet meeting with a minute of silent prayer. By example, he hoped to show Americans that weekly church attendance should be a part of their routine. Democrats, too, gave religion a central spot in political thought. Adlai Stevenson, Eisenhower's Democratic opponent in 1952 and 1956, argued in their first contest that communism "seeks even to dethrone

God from his central place in the Universe. It attempts to uproot everywhere it goes the gentle and restraining influences of the religion of love and peace" (Whitfield 1996, 87).

The most visible warrior in the Christian battle against communism was a young North Carolina evangelist named Billy Graham. During the winter of 1950–1951, Graham sounded very much like Joseph McCarthy when he warned Christians against joining "over 1,100 social sounding organizations that are communist or communist operated in this country" (Whitfield 1996, 80–81). When he led the opening prayer in the U.S. Senate in February 1952, Graham spoke as a true anticommunist, referring to "barbarians beating at our gates from without and moral termites from within" (Wittner 1984, 214). And in September 1957, he attested to his belief that communism was "master-minded by Satan." With a weekly television series, a syndicated newspaper column, and evangelical events across the nation, Graham seemed ubiquitous. He promoted old-fashioned values and rejected such "sins" as card playing, smoking, drinking, swearing, dancing, failing to attend church, and reading steamy literature. He consistently endorsed the development and maintenance of strong American military forces, and he became a friend and associate to many Cold War presidents. Not everyone supported Graham, however. Theologian Reinhold Niebuhr called him "a personable, modest and appealing young man who has wedded considerable dramatic and demagogic gifts with a rather obscurantist version of the Christian faith" (Whitfield 1996, 79, 81).

In other parts of American life, the line dividing government from Christianity increasingly blurred during this era. Several states barred agnostics from adopting children, and some even barred agnostics and atheists from being notaries. In a Cold War with an enemy that embraced atheism, Americans clung to religious belief as if it were a lifeboat keeping the nation's hopes afloat.

Religion by the Numbers

Statistics confirm that religion held an important place in the American culture of the 1950s and that organized religion reached its zenith during the decade. This religiosity was not limited to one segment of the population. It was apparent in all classes and all races. Stronger affiliation to organized religion is not necessarily evidence that more people held religious beliefs; however, it does indicate that religion represented an increasingly important facet of Americans' public lives. No matter how deep their level of belief, Americans in the 1950s increasingly made church membership an important part of their identities, and like the suburban home and the stay-at-home mom, religion became an important part of middle-class identity. Church membership, which was a solid 43 percent in the century's early decades, began to climb in the 1940s, when it reached 49 percent. Membership pushed upward to 55 percent in 1950 and 69 percent

in 1960 before declining to 63 percent in 1970. The growth in church membership exceeded population growth in the 1950s. According to a 1954 survey, 90
percent of Americans believed in the divinity of Christ and more than 60 percent believed that the devil existed (Whitfield 1996, 83). A 1950 survey showed
that 99 percent of Americans over the age of 18 believed in a single god. Those
results indicated that women were slightly more faithful than men, and Catholics
were more likely than Protestants to say that they were "absolutely certain"
about God's existence (Hudnut-Beumler 1994, 41).

In all, 96.39 percent of Americans listed a religious affiliation in a 1957 Current Population Survey by the U.S. Census Bureau, and a Gallup poll taken in
1962 showed a total of 98 percent. Of those without a religious affiliation, 2.68
percent claimed no religion and approximately 1 percent simply took no position. This marked a significant change from 1947, when 6 percent of Americans
identified themselves as having no religion—a level that would not be reached
again until 1975. The nation remained predominantly Protestant, although the
number of American Catholics grew almost twice as fast as the number of Protestants during the 1950s. While 25.7 percent were Catholic and 3.2 percent were
Jewish in 1957, the survey showed that 66.2 percent were Protestant (Hudnut-
Beumler 1994, 33–34). At this time, politicians still wondered whether it would
be possible for a Roman Catholic to be elected president, given many Protestants'
aversion to Catholicism. The issue would be tested in John F. Kennedy's successful 1960 presidential campaign, which began unofficially in the late 1950s.

While church membership did not necessarily equate with church attendance,
many young baby boomers saw church as an important part of their lives. Prayer
was still common in public schools, and religious holidays, especially Christian
ones, received attention even in class-
rooms where more than one religion
was represented. As Americans rushed
to join churches, Congress moved to
formalize the nation's ties to God. Lawmakers added "one nation under God"
to the Pledge of Allegiance in 1954, and
"In God We Trust" became the nation's
official motto two years later.

Religion made its mark on popular
culture in the 1950s. Inspirational programming became standard fare on
American television and radio stations.
Even the telephone became a source of
religious comfort. Rock 'n' roll artists
recorded songs like "Big Fellow in the
Sky" and "The Teen Commandments."
And religious spectacles drew big crowds

Table 6.2. Total Church Membership

Year	Membership
1951	88,673,005
1952	92,277,129
1953	94,842,845
1954	97,482,611
1955	100,162,529
1956	103,224,954
1957	104,189,678
1958	109,557,741
1959	112,226,905[a]

Source: Based on G. F. Ketcham and
B. Y. Landis, eds. 1951–1960. *Yearbook of
American Churches.* Nashville: Abingdon.

[a] The U.S. Census Bureau estimated that
the nation's population in 1959 was
177,073,000.

to movie theaters. Among them were *Samson and Delilah* (1950), *David and Bathsheba* (1951), *Quo Vadis?* (1951), *The Robe* (1953), *Demetrius and the Gladiators* (1954), *The Ten Commandments* (1956), and *Ben-Hur* (1959).

New types of religious books also found an eager audience. Among them was the serious religious paperback. Doubleday led the way by introducing Image Books in 1954. This series was aimed at a Catholic audience, and within two years of its start-up, the series had sold 105,000 books, including its most popular entry, *A Popular History of the Catholic Church*. Meridian's Living Age series and Harper Brothers' Torchlight series soon reached out to Protestant readers. In 1957, the YMCA's Association Press launched Reflection Books. These series for the first time introduced many Americans to the work of philosophers and theologians. In both 1953 and 1954, the Bible held a place on the best-seller list.

This I Believe

Debuting in 1951, the CBS radio program *This I Believe* featured journalist Edward R. Murrow asking individual Americans of different faiths to explain their personal credos in five-minute essays read by the authors. Among the famous participants in the program were Helen Keller, Jackie Robinson, Eleanor Roosevelt, Albert Einstein, and Harry Truman. A hundred of the best essays were published as a 1952 book, *This I Believe: The Living Philosophies of One Hundred Thoughtful Men and Women in All Walks of Life*. The idea for the radio show sprang from a 1949 luncheon conversation among four men who feared that material values were superseding spiritual ideals. *This I Believe* took the spotlight away from public forms of religious worship and cast it upon the inner beliefs that guided individuals through daily life. Across the United States, the show aired 2,200 times each week. It was carried by 196 radio stations. About 39 million listeners made up its U.S. audience. It also was broadcast in six other languages on 150 foreign stations and Voice of America, a government effort to spread American ideals to other sections of the world. Because of the broadcast's popularity, the essays were spun off as a weekly feature in 85 American newspapers. The State Department made the show's essays available to newspapers in all 97 nations that enjoyed diplomatic relationships with the United States (Hudnut-Beumler 1994, 52–55).

The Power of Positive Thinking

Even before his greatest literary triumph in 1952, Norman Vincent Peale was widely recognized as a leading proponent of the idea that religion could generate psychological health. Well known in the United States for his inspirational programs on radio and television as well as his writing in *Guideposts* magazine,

Norman Vincent Peale, author of the best-selling book The Power of Positive Thinking, *was a leading proponent of the idea that religion could contribute to psychological health. (Library of Congress)*

Peale's reputation grew with the release of his best-selling book, *The Power of Positive Thinking,* which became the decade's most popular work of nonfiction. The book neatly served as a guidebook to attaining the middle-class American dream. In describing the good life that was available to Americans, it saluted affluence, joy, and health. Much of Peale's philosophy was conveyed through success stories often peopled by clever businessmen or prominent professionals. Peale's optimism about the state of the world at the middle of the 20th century was a welcome tonic for many Americans seeking an escape from the dreary Cold War. Peale produced another successful book, *Stay Alive All Your Life,* which appeared in 1957.

Life Is Worth Living

Television became a tool in spreading religion during the 1950s. Newly conse-crated Bishop Fulton Sheen debuted on television in 1952 in *Life Is Worth Living*. Sheen was not a newcomer to broadcasting. As a monsignor, he had presented

The Catholic Hour for 20 years on radio. His new TV show appeared on the Dumont Network during prime time. Appearing before a live studio audience of about 1,000 people, Sheen sought to lead his audience on the right path by using a combination of Bible stories, appeals for morality, and requests for charity. The series was extremely popular, even among non-Catholics. Appearing opposite Milton Berle's popular variety show, Sheen trounced the comedian. Because of the program's strong appeal, ABC picked it up from Dumont in 1954, and its message reached about 25 million Americans. The show, which aired for five TV seasons, ultimately was broadcast by 170 outlets in the United States and 17 in Canada. Sheen's 1953 book, *Life Is Worth Living,* climbed to the fifth spot on the best-seller list. An Iowa woman reportedly dressed up in her fancy clothes "just as if she were going to church" when she watched Sheen's show (Hudnut-Beumler 1994, 63), and a young actor named Rámon Gerardo Antonio Estévez adopted Sheen's name and became known as Martin Sheen, father of actors Emilio Estevez and Charlie Sheen.

Dial-a-Prayer

Magnetic audio recording tape made it possible for religious Americans of the 1950s to find inspiration while at work or at home. The Reverend Richard R. Schwambach started the nation's first Dial-a-Prayer line on Thanksgiving eve in Evansville, Indiana, in 1955. At first, the recorded prayers were such a hit that Indiana Bell Telephone Company reported 5,000 busy signals during two 24-hour periods. A similar service was initiated in New York in 1956 by John Sutherland Bonnell of the Fifth Avenue Presbyterian Church. The first advertisement sought callers with these words: "For a spiritual life in a busy day, Dial-a-Prayer. Circle 6–4200" (Hudnut-Beumler 1994, 17). Response to both phone lines led the phenomenon to spread rapidly across the nation.

Prayer

According to a 1950 survey, prayer held an important place in the daily life of American households. More than 40 percent of Americans prayed twice a day, and a 1959 poll showed that more than two-thirds of Americans said grace aloud before eating at home (Wuthnow 1998, 35). Many clergymen and writers of this era proclaimed the power of prayer and urged Americans to use that power to improve their lives. For example, the authors of *Your Way to Popularity and Personal Power*—James Bender and Lee Graham—described prayer as the answer to typical Americans' problems. "People who believe in God and ask him for help seem to have the greatest share of popularity and personal power. Why? Because their faith makes them the sort of individuals whom other folks instinctively like. Their inner strength attracts friendship and love like an irresistible magnet" (Hudnut-Beumler 1994, 44).

The *Reader's Digest* put its spotlight on celebrities' attitudes toward the power of prayer. An article in *McCall's* magazine asked a variety of religious experts about how Americans should pray, and, not surprisingly, the article did not find unanimity among the experts. Theologian Reinhold Niebuhr opposed asking for material success, while Norman Vincent Peale urged Americans to pray specifically for products that would make their lives better. In 1952, a *Newsweek* article told readers about athletes who had claimed victories immediately after asking God to help them win, and a book called *Pray Your Weight Away* found its way onto the best-sellers' list in 1957.

Theologians Look at America in the 1950s

This decade suffered no shortage of respected theologians. Here are a few of their comments on America in their era.

Protestant theologian Reinhold Niebuhr in 1952's *The Irony of History*:

If we should perish, the ruthlessness of the foe would be only the secondary cause of the disaster. The primary cause would be that the strength of a giant nation was directed by eyes too blind to see all the hazards of the struggle; and the blindness would be induced not by some accident of nature or history but by hatred and vainglory.

Catholic theologian Thomas Merton in notes taken in 1953 and 1954:

In our age everything has to be a "problem." Ours is a time of anxiety because we have willed it to be so. Our anxiety is not imposed on us by force from outside. We impose it on our world and upon one another from within ourselves. (Merton 1968, 82)

Protestant theologian Paul Tillich in 1959's *Theology of Culture*:

Organized Protestantism . . . is a social power of the highest degree. Through the democratic processes it influences political decisions, social ideals, ways of life, international actions. (181)

Jewish theologian Abraham Joshua Heschel in 1951's *Man Is Not Alone*:

We cannot endure the heartbreaking splendor of sunsets. Of what avail, then, are opinions, words, dogmas? In the confinement of our study rooms, our knowledge seems to us a pillar of light. But when we stand at the door which opens out to the infinite, we realize that all concepts are but glittering motes that populate a sunbeam. (Michaelson 2005)

Ministers as Counselors

At mid-century, Americans were very aware of Sigmund Freud's theories, and as *Life* magazine reported in 1957, the United States had "more psychologists and psychiatrists, engaged in more types of inquiry and activity, than all the rest of the world together." Despite the wealth of secular resources available to Americans who needed counseling, a National Institute of Mental Health survey showed that 42 percent of Americans who pursued emotional guidance first sought aid from members of the clergy (Hudnut-Beumler 1994, 9, 10). Carl Rogers, a theology student who switched directions and received a Ph.D. in psychology, provided the counseling model followed by most members of the clergy. Rather than pointing out the flaws of troubled individuals and directing them to improve themselves, Rogers's approach to counseling acknowledged that all humans attempted to reach their full potential. His counseling style led members of the clergy to elicit their subjects' innermost feelings and to help them understand themselves and the choices they faced.

Religion Offers Social Ties, Escape from Cold War

Many Americans of this era were true believers, but for some, religion became one more means of conforming to achieve social and economic success. In an atmosphere where "different" people were often viewed as subversive, embracing religion was one way of staking out a position in the middle of the crowd. In his book *Protestant-Catholic-Jew: An Essay in American Religious Sociology,* Will Herberg described the mood of the 1950s as "religiousness without religion." He concluded that rising church membership was "a way of sociability or belonging" rather than "a way of re-orienting life to God." He also decried religion's transformation into a big business.

During the 1950s, religion served as a palliative factor in an anxious world. With an increasingly mobile population, church membership offered an opportunity for establishing a sense of community even in a new city or neighborhood. It provided a new network of contacts that often filled gaps created by distance from family and old friends. Children as well as adults found a new peer group and new activities through involvement in church events.

Religion offered a possible escape from that threatening atmosphere of the Cold War. The power of anticommunism probably would have been significantly weakened without its religious component. It is difficult to imagine that the confrontation between superpowers would have been fired by so much passion if the opposing world power had been Anglican England or another nation that embraced Christianity. The atheism expounded by leaders of the Soviet Union helped to turn their nation into the quintessential enemy and enabled political leaders to use religion as a means of rallying the nation's population behind the American cause. A contest between religion and atheism struck a

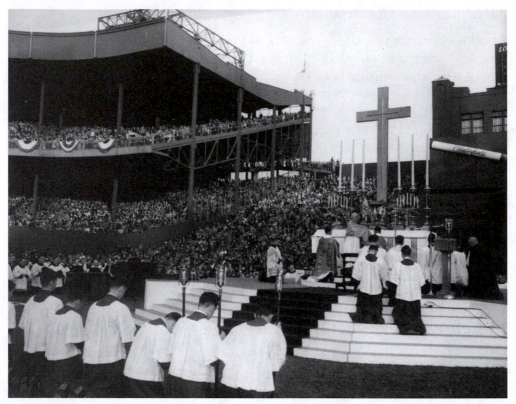

Cardinal Francis Spellman, archbishop of New York, presides over a Roman Catholic Mass during the Family Rosary Crusade Rally at New York City's Polo Grounds in 1952. (Library of Congress)

deeper emotional chord in Americans than a dry debate between capitalism and communism.

While the historic peace churches continued to exercise social activism, most churches in the 1950s either discouraged or ignored the possibility that religious Americans could apply their faith to helping the poor or cleansing the environment. Both Billy Graham and Norman Vincent Peale specifically rejected the idea of using religion as a tool to correct social problems. Graham's position is especially interesting because he so readily tied religion to a strong American military stance in the Cold War. Like many other parts of life in the 1950s, religion and its goal of personal salvation typically served as conservative forces intended to preserve order rather than to inspire change.

BIOGRAPHIES

Hanson W. Baldwin, 1903–1991

Journalist

As a reporter and military commentator for the *New York Times,* Hanson W. Baldwin was among the elite journalists who helped to shape public opinion during the Korean War. Although he generally backed the Truman administration, Baldwin sometimes criticized its military policies. A veteran war correspondent, Baldwin commented on the "unpopularity of the Syngman Rhee government" in South Korea as well as the "questionable political and military reliability" of the Republic of Korea's army and police. He strongly opposed the use of nuclear weapons in Korea at a time when some politicians advocated their use. Baldwin, who won a Pulitzer Prize for his work during World War II, also rejected the idea of widening the war by invading China, as Gen. Douglas MacArthur wanted to do. He supported Truman's decision to oust the popular MacArthur because he believed that the World War II hero had been guilty of insubordination.

Virginia Foster Durr, 1903–1999

Peace and Civil Rights Activist

Alabama-born Virginia Foster Durr spent much of her life working in the peace movement and the civil rights movement. She endorsed the American Peace Crusade, which opposed U.S. involvement in the Korean War. In the 1950s, her husband, Clifford, became one of the few white lawyers in Alabama who represented African Americans in civil rights cases. Like many outspoken liberals, she was the subject of anticommunist congressional hearings. Called to testify before the Senate Internal Security Committee in 1954 and to answer questions about Communists within the civil rights movement, she stated her name and declared that she was not a Communist, but she said nothing more. A year later, Durr personally paid the bail necessary to free civil rights pioneer Rosa Parks from jail in Montgomery, Alabama, after Parks refused to give up her seat on a city bus. Durr remained a strong supporter of both disarmament and equal rights through the rest of her life.

Bernard T. Feld, 1919–1993

Scientist

Bernard T. Feld helped to build the first atomic bomb, and in later years, he considered that to be the "original sin" of the nuclear age. After working in the Manhattan Project, which made the bombings of Hiroshima and Nagasaki possible, he became a leading opponent of the use of nuclear weapons. After earning his Ph.D. and becoming a faculty member at the Massachusetts Institute of Technology, he devoted much of his time to activism. He spearheaded lobbying efforts against military control of nuclear research. In 1957, he helped to found the Pugwash Conferences. These meetings provided a means for scientists to alert the public to the facts about nuclear war. To some degree, the Pugwash Conferences were an outgrowth of the Einstein-Russell Appeal for nuclear disarmament, written by Albert Einstein and Bertrand Russell in July 1955 and signed by a wide array of well-known scientists. In addition, Feld was an editor and board member of the *Bulletin of Atomic Scientists,* which has attempted to keep the public aware of the dangers of nuclear weaponry for more than 60 years.

Katherine Graham Howard, 1898–1986

Civil Defense Planner

As a woman with long-held ties to the Republican Party, Katherine Graham Howard worked to draw American wives and mothers into the Cold War civil defense program of Dwight D. Eisenhower's administration. Howard served as assistant administrator in the Federal Civil Defense Administration, and she made trips across the United States in an effort to elicit public support for civil defense preparations at a time when nuclear war seemed like a strong prospect. She launched a program called Rescue Street in 1953. It gave ordinary people a frighteningly realistic view of nuclear war's horrors. She also participated in the Eisenhower administration's yearly Operation Alert nuclear war drills. Howard became one of the nation's leading proponents of creating shelters within American homes, and she urged women to take the lead in defending their families. She recommended that women take American Red Cross classes and allocate basement space for a shelter. She also urged them to buy the supplies that would be needed if a family had to ride out a nuclear war at home, and she suggested that housewives become active in local civil defense efforts. She left the civil defense program in 1957 to become the U.S. deputy commissioner general for the Brussels Universal and International Exhibition of 1958. However, she served as a member of the National Civil Defense Advisory Council from 1959 to 1962.

Catherine Marshall, 1915–1983

Author

Catherine Marshall was a minister's daughter, and she married a man who would become a famous minister. Her husband, Peter Marshall, was an evangelistic young Scottish Presbyterian minister who had become chaplain of the U.S. Senate shortly before he died of a heart attack in 1949. Her book about his life, *A Man Called Peter,* arrived on the best-seller list in October 1951 and remained there for more than three years. Although the book traced everyday life without many grand dramatic moments, it was transformed into a popular and widely acclaimed movie starring Richard Todd in 1955. Four years later, she married Leonard LeSourd, executive editor of the religious periodical *Guideposts.* Marshall went on to write more than 20 inspirational fiction and nonfiction books with total sales exceeding 16 million copies. Her biggest seller, *Christy,* was a novel published in 1967 and later turned into a TV series.

Catherine Marshall wrote a popular book, A Man Called Peter, *about her late husband, Peter Marshall, who had been chaplain of the United States Senate. Her book, which was released in 1951, remained on the best-seller list for three years and was turned into a film in 1955. (Library of Congress)*

William E. Mayer, 1923–

Psychiatrist

In the aftermath of the Korean War, then–Lt. Col. William E. Mayer grabbed the national spotlight by condemning the behavior of American prisoners of war during the war. As a psychiatrist who graduated from Northwestern University and the University of Washington, Mayer served in the U.S. Navy from 1946 to 1952 and in the U.S. Army from 1952 to 1958 and from 1960 to 1965. He was one of the psychiatrists assigned to interview former POWs when they were released by their North Korean and Chinese captors. He believed that many American captives cooperated with the enemy because of weakness among the nation's youth. He especially condemned prisoners for not trying to escape from camps, although they were often isolated and frigid. In magazine articles and speeches, he contended that soldiers had been weakened by social welfare programs, reduced academic challenges, the availability of easy credit, reduced workweeks, and the failure of schools and the media to promote patriotism. In testimony before a Senate subcommittee, he urged educators to place greater emphasis on the teaching of American history. Mayer went on to head various mental health programs, and in 1981, he became administrator of the Alcohol, Drug Abuse, and Mental Health Administration under President Ronald Reagan. He also served as assistant secretary of health for the Department of Defense under Reagan.

Walter M. Miller Jr., 1923–1996

Science-Fiction Writer

One of the most successful novels about nuclear war was *A Canticle for Lie-bowitz,* written by American author Walter M. Miller Jr. A veteran of the Army Air Corps in World War II, Miller wrote many short stories, but his greatest success came with *A Canticle for Liebowitz,* published in 1959. The book won a Hugo award, also known as the Science Fiction Achievement Award. The events in his novel take place many years after a nuclear conflagration. He describes a civilized world that has been reduced to tatters. Against a barren landscape, illiterate and isolated individuals live in ignorance about what happened before nuclear weapons destroyed their world, but eventually, educational advancements lay the groundwork for scientific advancements and development of new weapons of mass destruction.

Red Cloud Mitchell, 1924–1950

War Hero

Red Cloud Mitchell, a Winnebago Indian from Wisconsin, posthumously won the Congressional Medal of Honor following his heroic actions on November 5, 1950, when he prevented Chinese forces from overrunning his company's command post near Chonhyon, Korea. When the Chinese made a surprise attack, he was on guard. He used his automatic rifle to shoot the Chinese at point-blank range and remained at his post even after being severely wounded.

Abraham Johannes (A. J.) Muste, 1885–1967

Pacifist

Abraham Johannes Muste, known in India as the "American Gandhi," was a leading advocate of nonviolent protest in the postwar years, and he became a model to civil rights activists such as Martin Luther King Jr. Muste served as executive secretary of the Fellowship of Reconciliation from 1940 until 1953, and he spent much of that time opposing U.S. involvement in both World War II and the Korean War. A strong opponent of nuclear weaponry, he established the War Resisters League in 1953, and five years later, as chairman of the Committee for Non-Violent Action, he attempted to dispatch a ship into a nuclear test zone in the Pacific Ocean. He received a nine-day jail sentence at the age of 75 for a protest at a Nebraska nuclear missile site. Born in the Netherlands, Muste had moved to the United States with his family in the late 19th century. As a young man, he was an ordained minister of the Dutch Reformed Church in America. During the 1920s and 1930s, he became a labor activist who advocated socialism.

Mildred Scott Olmsted, 1881–1990

Peace Activist

Born in Pennsylvania, Quaker Mildred Scott Olmsted was a political activist throughout much of her life. She attracted public notice as the national administrative secretary of the Women's International League for Peace and Freedom (WILPF) from 1946 until 1966. In that post, she helped the organization cope with growing fears about Communist infiltration of peace groups. In particular, she expressed concerns about the group's Miami chapter and urged the chapter's head to be wary of certain members in the 1950s. Hearings on Communist activity in the Florida city led to contempt charges against several members of the WILPF. Following Olmsted's lead, the Miami chapter's leadership chose not to take a stand in the case, although individual members were free to help the accused.

Val Peterson, 1903–1983

Politician

As the head of the Federal Civil Defense Administration (FCDA), Val Peterson changed the way Americans envisioned nuclear war—for a few years, at least. The former three-time Nebraska governor, who joined the Eisenhower administration in 1953, helped the Eisenhower administration reimagine nuclear war. Until that time, American civil defense drills had been based on the assumption that civilians would be best served by taking cover in their current locations. However, faced with the added destructive power of the hydrogen bomb and the massive fallout cloud it produced, Peterson steered Americans in target areas toward a new strategy—evacuation. At a time when bombs could be delivered only by planes, cities could expect some warning time in which evacuation could be carried out, he reasoned. The FCDA asked state and local governments to produce evacuation plans for target areas, which were primarily large cities and military bases. By the end of the 1950s, however, development of missile technology meant that nuclear bombs could be delivered with much less warning time.

Bayard Rustin, 1910–1987

Peace and Civil Rights Activist

Bayard Rustin played an important role in the peace and civil rights movements during the 1950s. He was a leading advocate of direct action in both movements. In 1950, he wrote to A. J. Muste, "I believe that people, including the churchmen and labor leaders of goodwill . . . are in so fearful and demoralized a position that they are prepared to give in on anything to stop the Russians

Bayard Rustin was a powerful organizer of pacifist and civil rights protests in the 1950s. (Library of Congress)

that the government calls for. The authorities know this. . . . We must find some way to let people know that now we are prepared to go to jail or even to give up all—to get shot down if necessary—but to cry out" (Lieberman 2000, 83). During the 1950s, he played a role in the 1955–1956 Montgomery bus boycott and joined with Martin Luther King Jr. in establishing the Southern Christian Leadership Conference (SCLC). He later was the chief organizer of the 1963 civil rights March on Washington. Rustin's commitment to peace and civil rights was the product of long-held beliefs. He had helped to found the Congress for Racial Equality (CORE) in 1942. And, when he was drafted during World War II in 1944, Rustin declined to serve because of his pacifist beliefs. As a result, he was arrested for violating the Selective Service Act. Later, he was convicted and imprisoned in Lewisburg, Pennsylvania.

REFERENCES AND FURTHER READINGS

Biderman, Albert D. 1963. *March to Calumny: The Story of American POWs in the Korean War.* New York: MacMillan.

Bogart, Leo, John Morsell, Robert Bower, Ira Cisin, Leila Sussmann, and Elmo C. Wilson. 1969. *Social Research and the Desegregation of the U.S. Army: Two Original 1951 Field Reports*. Chicago: Markham Publishing.

Breines, Wini. 1992. *Young, White, and Miserable: Growing Up Female in the Fifties*. Boston: Beacon Press.

Carlson, Lewis H. 2002. *Remembered Prisoners of a Forgotten War: An Oral History of Korean War POWs*. New York: St. Martin's Griffin.

Carter, Paul A. 1983. *Another Part of the Fifties*. New York: Columbia University Press.

Dalfiume, Richard M. 1969. *Desegregation of the U.S. Armed Forces: Fighting on Two Fronts, 1939–1953*. Columbia: University of Missouri Press.

"Dial-A-Prayer." 2006. Dial-a-Prayer International. http://www.dial-a-pray.com (accessed October 21, 2006).

Englehardt, Tom. 1995. *The End of Victory Culture: Cold War America and the Disillusioning of a Generation*. New York: Basic Books.

Fehrenbach, T. R. 1963. *This Kind of War: A Study in Unpreparedness*. New York: Macmillan.

George, Alice L. 2003. *Awaiting Armageddon: How Americans Faced the Cuban Missile Crisis*. Chapel Hill: University of North Carolina Press.

Geospatial and Statistical Data Center. University of Virginia Library. http://www2.lib.virginia.edu/geostat/index.html (accessed April 21, 2008).

Halberstam, David. 1993. *The Fifties*. New York: Fawcett Columbine.

Herberg, Will. 1955. *Protestant, Catholic, Jew: An Essay in American Religious Sociology*. Garden City, NY: Doubleday.

Hudnut-Beumler, James. 1994. *Looking for God in the Suburbs: The Religion of the American Dream and Its Critics, 1945–1965*. New Brunswick, NJ: Rutgers University Press.

Kaledin, Eugenia. 1984. *Mothers and More: American Women in the 1950s*. Boston: Twayne Publishers.

Karsten, Peter. 1966. "The American Democratic Citizen Soldier: Triumph or Disaster?" *Military Affairs* 30 (1): 34–40.

Kinkead, Eugene. 1959. *In Every War But One*. New York: Norton

Kleidman, Robert. 1993. *Organizing for Peace: Neutrality, the Test Ban, and the Freeze*. Syracuse, NY: Syracuse University Press.

Leckie, Robert. 1962. *Conflict: The History of the Korean War, 1950–53*. New York: Putnam.

Lieberman, Robbie. 2000. *The Strangest Dream: Communism, Anticommunism, and the U.S. Peace Movement*. Syracuse, NY: Syracuse University Press.

Mayer, William E. Interview. 24 Feb. 1956. "Why Did Many GI Captives Give In?" *U.S. News & World Report,* 56–72.

May, Elaine Tyler. 1988. *Homeward Bound: American Families in the Cold War Era.* New York: Basic Books.

McDermott, Kathleen. 2000. "Introduction." *Remembering the Forgotten War, Korea: 1950–53.* New York: History Book Club.

Merton, Thomas. 1968. *Thoughts in Solitude: Reflections on the Spiritual Life and the Love of Solitude.* New York: Image Books.

Michaelson, Jay. 2005. "Alone in Berlin." *Nextbook.* http://www.nextbook.org/cultural/feature.html?id=238 (accessed October 21, 2006).

Miller, Walter M. Jr. *A Canticle for Leibowitz.* Philadelphia: Lippincott.

Mills, Randy K., and Roxanne Mills. 2000. *Unexpected Journey: A Marine Corps Reserve Company.* Annapolis, MD: Naval Institute Press.

"Mitchell, Red Cloud." 2007. Medal of Honor Web site. http://www.medalof honor.com/MitchellRedCloud.htm (accessed October 24, 2006).

Mueller, John E. 1971. "Trends in Popular Support for the Wars in Korea and Vietnam." *American Political Science Review* 65 (2): 358–375.

Niebuhr, Reinhold. 1952. "The Significance of Irony." *The Irony of American History.* New York: Charles Scribner's Sons. http://www.religion-online.org/showchapter.asp?title=451&C=361 (accessed October 31, 2006).

O'Neill, William L. 1986. *American High: The Years of Confidence, 1945–1960.* New York: Free Press.

Oakes, Guy. 1994. *The Imaginary War: Civil Defense and American Cold War Culture.* New York: Oxford University Press.

Park, Hong-Kyu. 1983. "American Involvement in the Korean War." *The History Teacher* 16 (2): 249–263.

Pauling, Linus, ed. 1986. *World Encyclopedia of Peace.* New York: Pergamon Press.

Pells, Richard H. 1989. *The Liberal Mind in a Conservative Age: American Intellectuals in the 1940s and 1950s.* 2nd ed. Middletown, CT: Wesleyan University Press.

Prelinger Archives. 2006. Internet Archive. http://www.archive.org/details/prelinger (accessed November 20, 2006).

Rose, Kenneth D. 2001. *One Nation Underground: The Fallout Shelter in American Culture.* New York: New York University Press.

Rose, Lisle A. 1999. *The Cold War Comes to Main Street: America in 1950.* Lawrence: University Press of Kansas.

Roshwald, Mordecai. 1959. *Level 7.* New York: McGraw-Hill Book Co.

Rusk, Howard A. 1954. "Help for the Nurses of Korea." *American Journal of Nursing* 54 (4): 449–450.

Shute, Nevil. 1957. *On the Beach*. London: Heinemann.

Suchman, Edward A., Rose K. Goldsen, and Robin M. Williams Jr. 1953. "Attitudes Toward the Korean War." *Public Opinion Quarterly* 17 (2): 171–184.

Tillich, Paul. 1959. *Theology of Culture*. Edited by Robert C. Kimball. New York: Oxford University Press.

Tucker, Spencer C., ed. 2000. *Encyclopedia of the Korean War: A Political, Social, and Military History*. Santa Barbara, CA: ABC-CLIO.

U.S. Census Bureau. 1975. *Bicentennial Edition Historical Statistics of the United States Colonial Times to 1970, Part 1*. Washington, DC: Government Printing Office. Also available at http://www2.census.gov/prod2/statcomp/documents/CT1970p1–01.pdf (accessed October 10, 2007).

U.S. Census Bureau. 2004. "Census of Housing." http://www.census.gov/hhes/www/housing/census/historic/ownerchar.html (accessed September 5, 2006).

Weigley, Russell Frank. 1984. *History of the United States Army*. Bloomington: Indiana University Press.

Weiss, Jessica. 2000. *To Have and to Hold: Marriage, the Baby Boom, and Social Change*. Chicago: University of Chicago Press.

Whitfield, Stephen J. 1996. *The Culture of the Cold War*. 2nd ed. Baltimore: Johns Hopkins University Press.

Wiese, Andrew. 2005. *Places of Their Own: African American Suburbanization in the Twentieth Century*. Chicago: University of Chicago Press.

Wittner, Lawrence S. 1984. *Rebels Against War: The American Peace Movement, 1933–1983*. Philadelphia: Temple University Press.

Wubben, H. H. 1970. "American Prisoners of War in Korea: A Second Look at the 'Something New in History' Theme." *American Quarterly* 22 (1): 3–19.

Wuthnow, Robert. 1998. *After Heaven: Spirituality in America since the 1950s*. Berkeley: University of California Press.

Young, William H., and Nancy K. Young. 2004. *The 1950s*. American Popular Culture through History series. Westport, CT: Greenwood Press.

Yuh, Ji-Yeon. 2002. *Beyond the Shadow of Camptown: Korean Military Brides in America*. New York: New York University Press.

The Civil Rights Movement

OVERVIEW

As the 1950s dawned, African Americans had new hopes for change. World War II had transformed the world by fueling the decline of colonialism and opening the door to independence for the citizens of nonwhite nations in Africa and Asia. Moreover, at a time when recently defeated Nazi racism often was equated with pure evil, the United States' new position as a world leader and principal player in the Cold War had put the nation's ideals and its real-life practices under the international spotlight. Within the United States, the war had created a new wave of African American migration from the rural South to manufacturing jobs in urban factories, and as a result, the number of African Americans laboring in often-paternalistic southern farm operations plummeted in the 30 years after 1940. Finally, African American participation in a great war to defend the American way of life, whether it was on the battlefronts or in defense factories, had given many African Americans a sense of entitlement to their share of the American dream.

As African American hopes swelled, white opposition in the South hardened. In the states that once constituted the Confederate States of America, the racial divide remained a minefield. African Americans stepping across an often-indiscernible line could face a violent death at the hands of white supremacists. Racial hatred sometimes reached such heights that innocent African Americans

311

were chosen at random and lynched by angry white mobs. And whites had little reason to eschew violence against African Americans because even the unprovoked murder of an African American generally went unpunished in a region where all jurors were white. African American southerners could not depend on law enforcement officials to guarantee their safety, and they enjoyed virtually no civil rights. Laws and internal practices framed a world in which African Americans lacked human rights, including the right to vote. Working-class whites who had just begun to find their footing at the bottom of the middle class were the most vehement opponents of any change in African American status because of their own insecurity.

In the 1950s, when the civil rights movement began to score victories and gain supporters, new white-supremacist organizations also sprang up and found passionate backers. At least 568 such organizations were in operation by the end of 1955, and they reported a total membership of more than 200,000 (O'Neill 1986, 252). Racial issues generated much more passionate emotions in the South than they did in other parts of the nation. After May 1954, when the Supreme Court ruled in *Brown v. the Board of Education of Topeka, Kansas* that "separate but equal" schools were inherently unequal, a poll found that only 17 percent of nonsouthern whites had discussed the ruling by mid-1954, while 60 percent of southern whites had talked about it. In addition, one-third of southern whites saw segregation as a more important issue than atomic bombs, crime, or high taxes; only 6 percent of nonsouthern whites shared that point of view (Klarman 1994, 86).

For African Americans in the South and in some border states, daily life at home, at work, and even on the way to work was framed by a culture of segregation and distinct racial roles. African American women often found themselves restricted to careers as housekeepers or seamstresses, while most African American men had access to jobs in the lowest ranks of the blue-collar job market. Outside the South, African American life was somewhat better. African Americans could vote, and if they lived in an integrated neighborhood, their children attended integrated schools. However, many African Americans still had difficulty finding jobs that paid well and often lived in ghettoes. African Americans found a bit more flexibility in the job market, and they did not face indignities like segregated buses, restrooms, and water fountains. Urban crowding and inner-city crime added new threats to African American life, but lynching was not tolerated outside the South.

Despite the handicaps that they encountered, some African Americans thrived. Across the country, the growth of an African American middle class with some money and some power opened the way for great change. By 1960, more than one-fifth of African Americans held white-collar or skilled jobs (O'Neill 1986, 247). In the South, the existence of an isolated African American community had created demand for African American lawyers, teachers, dentists, ministers, and doctors; in areas outside the South, skilled African Americans had greater opportunities to get the education and training that would make it possible to move into the middle class. Martin Luther King Jr. and other civil rights leaders grew up in the middle class and profited from the learning that afforded them. In addition, the middle class contributed significantly to organizations such as the NAACP. These people enjoyed broader horizons and entertained brighter hopes than members of the working class. Although members of the African American middle class often encountered resistance when they tried to move into white neighborhoods outside the South, their ability to pay for such homes demonstrated significant progress, and in many cases, initial resistance from neighbors crumbled over time.

The NAACP, already more than 40 years old in 1950, fought for equal rights primarily in the political arena and the court system. Using African American voter clout, the NAACP had been able to win concessions like President Harry Truman's decision to integrate the armed forces in the late 1940s. With legal prowess, the organization set the goal of winning a ruling that would desegregate all of the nation's public schools. The Southern Christian Leadership Conference (SCLC), founded in the late 1950s, embraced a different approach to achieving equal rights. While it sometimes profited from court rulings, the SCLC's most powerful weapon was the use of nonviolent civil disobedience to achieve its goals. As leader of the SCLC, King banked on winning the support of many white Americans by allowing them to see peaceful, God-fearing African Americans, both young and old, standing up for the rights they had been promised. In fact, nationwide polling showed that most Americans supported school integration as well as a 1955 Interstate Commerce Commission order to end segregation in trains, buses, and stations. However, poll results from the South differed sharply, and civil rights leaders knew that they needed to break down the barriers erected by the region's Jim Crow culture. To do that, they had to make the rest of the nation care about what was happening in the South.

TIMELINE

1950	African American poet Gwendolyn Brooks wins the Pulitzer Prize for *Annie Allen*.
1951	The University of North Carolina joins the ranks of desegregated state universities in southern and border states.
	More than 3,000 whites riot in Cicero, Illinois, in a protest over an African American family's move into a previously all-white suburb.
	Despite African American protests, Virginia executes the Martinsville Seven for allegedly raping a white woman.

1953   White rioting breaks out in Chicago over integration of an apartment project.

1954   In a May decision, the U.S. Supreme Court rules in *Brown v. Board of Education* that segregated schools are not lawful.

                The first White Citizens Council meets in Mississippi in July.

1955   In a follow-up to its *Brown* ruling, the Supreme Court refrains from setting a school desegregation deadline.

                Emmitt Till, a 14-year-old Chicago youth visiting a friend's relatives in Mississippi, is slain after flirting with a white woman.

                Willie Mays dazzles baseball fans with 51 home runs and 24 stolen bases.

                The Interstate Commerce Commission bans segregation in interstate buses, trains, and stations.

                Montgomery seamstress Rosa Parks refuses to give up her seat on a city bus, triggering a year-long boycott by African American riders.

1956   Alabama attorney general John Patterson obtains a court order outlawing NAACP activities in the state.

                Autherine Lucy becomes the first African American enrolled at the University of Alabama but is suspended "for her own safety."

                Ruling on the Montgomery bus system's practices, the Supreme Court declares bus segregation illegal on November 13.

1957   Jimmy Wilson of Marion, Alabama, is sentenced to death for stealing less than two dollars from a white woman. After international publicity about the case, Wilson receives clemency.

                The nonviolent Southern Christian Leadership Conference is founded with Martin Luther King Jr. as its leader.

                A Prayer Pilgrimage leads 30,000 people to the Lincoln Memorial in Washington on the third anniversary of the *Brown* ruling.

                Arkansas governor Orval Faubus calls up the National Guard to block the integration of Central High School in Little Rock. Weeks later, federal troops enable nine African American students to start classes there.

The Cleveland Browns draft Jim Brown, the first dominant African American player in the National Football League.

Mobs protest the arrival of the Myers family, the first African Americans in Levittown, Pennsylvania.

1958   Althea Gibson, an African American athlete, wins the U.S. Lawn Tennis Association championship for the second consecutive year.

An African American woman stabs Martin Luther King Jr. in Harlem.

Members of the NAACP youth council begin sit-ins at segregated restaurants in Oklahoma City.

Little Rock's public high schools are closed for the 1958–1959 school year.

In *Cooper v. Aaron,* a case springing from requests for delayed integration in Little Rock, the Supreme Court reinforces the *Brown* ruling and issues an opinion supporting its role as the Constitution's ultimate interpreter.

1959   More than 10,000 students march on Washington, D.C., for the second consecutive year in the Youth March for Integrated Schools.

Faced with a court order to integrate its public schools, Prince Edward County in Virginia instead appropriates no money for schools.

Members of the Congress of Racial Equality (CORE) sit in at W. T. Grant's lunch counters in Miami and push to desegregate area beaches.

AFRICAN AMERICAN LIFE, PUSH FOR CHANGE

Newly urbanized African Americans helped the drive for civil rights gain momentum in the 1950s as the southern African American farm population continued its decline, diminishing the isolation of African American workers. At first, the chemicals and equipment that reduced the need for farmworkers had promised only economic ruin to African Americans; however, these technological changes eventually contributed to development of an African American population that enjoyed greater independence and less vulnerability to white intimidation. Escape from the plantation did not guarantee peace, however. Although

After the Interstate Commerce Commission banned segregation in interstate travel in 1955, an African American family stops to note a remaining segregation sign in the Santa Fe Depot in Oklahoma City, Oklahoma. (AP/Wide World Photos)

lynching was rare in the decade's first half, violence intensified in the South after the *Brown* decision.

In the region where slavery had made cotton king, African Americans still lived at the bottom of a caste system. Many limitations circumscribed their daily lives, and the specter of violence clouded their existence. As African Americans explored new opportunities outside the rural South, the shrinking African American farm population lived little better than their slave ancestors. If tenant farmers sent their children to school instead of putting them to work in the fields, they faced retaliation, including elimination of relatives' jobs, tenant farm evictions, and an end to the credit that enabled them to buy food. Life in southern urban areas offered wider opportunities; however, 17 states in the South or on its borders required segregation of public education in both urban and rural areas. Jim Crow laws segregated public transportation and restrooms in many places. Even water fountains sometimes were designated for use by a single race. For the most part, African Americans could not serve on juries, and several states erected legal obstacles, such as poll taxes and literacy tests, to block them from voting.

African Americans in the South developed an understanding of their subservient status at an early age. Psychologist Kenneth B. Clark studied the way that youngsters came to understand race at the middle of the 20th century, and his findings, which were released at a 1950 White House conference, showed that African American children as young as three understood race. Clark used dolls to determine youngsters' understanding of racial differences. He found that most three-year-olds knew the difference between a white doll and a "colored" doll. Even more striking, the majority showed a clear preference for the white doll (Williams 1988, 20).

Many expected racial relations in the United States to remain as they were. As late as 1957, only 43 percent of white southerners expected to live one day in an integrated society (Gallup 1958). Civil rights groups hoped to prove them wrong. The National Association for the Advancement of Colored People (NAACP) and the Urban League had represented African American rights for more than 40 years, while CORE had been founded in 1942 as an adjunct to the nonviolent

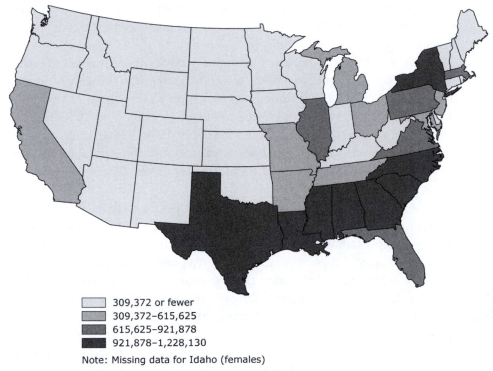

309,372 or fewer
309,372–615,625
615,625–921,878
921,878–1,228,130

Note: Missing data for Idaho (females)

Map 7.1 *Number of African Americans in each state.*

peace movement. During this decade, discontented African Americans backed these existing organizations and formed new ones. Like peace organizations, civil rights groups became common targets for conservatives seeking to label any advocacy of social change as Communist inspired. White southerners often labeled civil rights workers as "outside agitators," but by the end of the decade, it had become difficult to maintain the fiction that southern African Americans still accepted the status quo.

African American Life

Although African Americans faced the greatest challenges in the South, they were often marginalized wherever they lived within the United States. Outside the South, African Americans had many more legal rights than their southern counterparts. They could vote, serve on juries, and, in most states, attend integrated schools. However, African Americans often lived in poverty no matter where their homes were. Throughout the decade, the median income for white workers was twice as high as the median income for nonwhite workers. Integrated neighborhoods existed outside the South, but the population often was segregated by custom or by economics. Seattle's African American population of 26,901, for instance, resided in only 4 of the city's 110 census tracts, according to the 1960 census (Taylor 1995, 3).

The migration of African Americans from the rural South continued to redraw the nation's demographic picture. While about 80 percent of African Americans lived in the South in 1930, that figure had dropped to less than 70 percent in 1950. The central United States was home to about 15 percent in 1950, the East, 13 percent, and the West, less than 4 percent (Levy 1998, 42). In each southern state, the African American share of the overall population diminished during the 1950s, but it rose from 35 percent to 54 percent in the District of Columbia (Salzman, Smith, and West 1996, 2562).

The typical African American had a lower life expectancy than a white American. The average American born in 1950 could expect to live 68.2 years, while nonwhites' life expectancy was only 60.8 years of life. By 1960, 69.7 was the anticipated life span of a typical American. Nonwhites' anticipated lifespan still lagged behind, with a life expectancy of 63.6 years (Salzman, Smith, and West 1996, 2540). Infant mortality among African Americans also was significantly higher than the average for the overall population.

Across the nation, African Americans received less education than whites, and in the South, the education they received in segregated schools often was inferior. In 1950, almost one-third of African Americans had completed less than five years of elementary school, while only 11.1 percent of all Americans fell into that category. The median number of school years completed was 9.3 for the overall population and only 6.9 for African Americans. Figures for 1960 showed significant improvement among African Americans, but they still fell significantly behind the broader population. At a time when 7.7 percent of the population had completed four years or more of higher education, only 3.5 percent of African Americans could claim that achievement (Koslow 1999, 195). Late in the decade, nonwhite women tended to receive significantly more education than nonwhite men. In 1960, 53 percent of nonwhites who had completed four or more years of college were female. By 1963, among those who were aged 16 to 21 and out of school, the average nonwhite woman's education exceeded the average nonwhite man's by 1.1 years (Twombly 1971, 448–449). Education carried greater value for nonwhite women than white women because most of them expected to work throughout their lives rather than being full-time mothers.

Compared to their white counterparts, African Americans faced higher odds of going to prison and of facing execution. African Americans, who made up less than 12 percent of the nation's population in 1960, constituted 37 percent of the prison population (Twombly 1971, 457). African Americans also accounted for more than half of the 717 Americans put to death for their crimes, and they were far more likely to receive the death sentence for the crime of rape than their white peers (Koslow 1999, 195).

Table 7.1. Median School Years Completed by People 25 and Older

	All Men	Nonwhite Men	All Women	Nonwhite Women
1950	9.0	6.4	9.7	7.2
1952	9.7	6.8	10.4	7.4
1957	10.3	7.3	10.9	8.1
1959	10.7	7.6	11.2	8.4

Source: U.S. Census Bureau. 1975. "Years of School Completed, by Race and Sex: 1940 to 1970." *Bicentennial Edition: Historical Statistics of the United States Colonial Times to 1970, Part 1,* 380. Washington, DC: Government Printing Office. Also available at http://2www .census.gov/prod2/statcomp/documents/CT1970p1-01/pdf.

Organizing for Battle: The NAACP

The NAACP entered the 1950s with momentum provided by skyrocketing membership that had jumped from 50,000 to 450,000 between 1940 and 1946 alone (Klarman 1994, 89). Escape from the farm had made it easy for dissatisfied African Americans to communicate and share strategies, and the NAACP stood in the front lines of their battle. For the longtime civil rights advocacy group, the war against white supremacy proceeded on three fronts. As it had from its early years, the NAACP fought in the nation's courts to achieve recognition of African American rights. In addition, the organization sought to protect the victims of the oppressive white citizens groups, and it led sit-ins to expand African Americans' access to services.

The biggest goal of the NAACP's legal initiatives was a Supreme Court decision ordering the integration of public schools. The driving force behind this legal campaign was future Supreme Court Justice Thurgood Marshall. In 1950, the battle got under way with *Briggs v. Elliot,* a federal court case aimed at integrating South Carolina schools. This case eventually was joined with four others, leading to the groundbreaking *Brown* ruling in 1954.

The NAACP's battles against white supremacist groups often unfolded in small towns outside the sphere of the national media. Without even the limited safety provided by the national spotlight, African American activists faced great risks. African American southerners who signed petitions opposing state and local policies frequently were targeted. In Mississippi towns like Yazoo City and Clarksdale, the NAACP also attempted to assist African American farmers who suffered at the hands of white supremacist organizations or lost Farmers Home Administration credit. Its plan was to direct African American farmers' business to the African American–owned Tri-State Bank; however, most of the farmers were unable to satisfy the requirements set by Tri-State. As a result, this plan failed.

In 1956, the NAACP faced a direct challenge when Alabama's attorney general banned the organization's collection of membership dues, efforts to gain new

Perhaps as many as 30,000 people from 36 states attend a 1957 prayer pilgrimage in Washington, D.C., to mark the third anniversary of the Supreme Court's ruling in Brown v. Board of Education. *(Library of Congress)*

members, and all fund-raising projects. A state court also ordered the NAACP to pay a $100,000 contempt fine for refusing to turn over its membership list, but the Supreme Court blocked that action in a 1958 ruling. Also in that year, the organization received approval from President Dwight D. Eisenhower's administration to conduct a prayer pilgrimage to the Lincoln Memorial in Washington to mark the third anniversary of the *Brown* ruling. About 30,000 Americans participated.

CORE

Once an adjunct to the pacifist movement, the Congress of Racial Equality (CORE) suffered low membership and exhibited little power at the beginning of the 1950s. Until that time, the organization's priorities and its membership had largely existed outside the South. As the protest movement heated up in the South, CORE hired its first field worker in 1956 and made its first efforts to improve race relations in the South. At that time, CORE began using direct action to overcome barriers to African American success, and it eventually embraced a policy of generating African American jobs by selective buying crusades that punished employers who would not employ African Americans. CORE's activities in the South focused primarily on opening public accommodations to African Americans; elsewhere, unemployment was the organization's top concern. New aggressiveness on CORE's part brought significant growth in membership. Figures gathered in mid-1959 showed that in a single year the organization's national membership had doubled, as did the number of CORE affiliates across the nation.

Southern Christian Leadership Conference

The Southern Christian Leadership Conference (SCLC) was founded in February 1957. While the NAACP and CORE had individual members, the SCLC encouraged membership from existing groups with shared goals. Martin Luther King Jr., who stepped into the national spotlight in 1955 during his leadership of the Montgomery bus boycott, headed the organization. Although SCLC sometimes profited from court decisions, its primary tactic was the use of civil disobedience to bring policy changes. In SCLC, King was joined by other leaders of the Montgomery boycott as well as civil rights activists who launched similar campaigns in other cities. Although SCLC came into being late in the 1950s, it was one of the most influential and successful civil rights organizations in the coming decade. Other organizations emulated its form of protest. SCLC's tactics reflected lessons from struggles against colonialism and racism in other countries as well as the relatively weak peace movement of the 1950s. As the organization achieved success, SCLC strategies, in turn, provided operational models for the robust peace movement of the 1960s.

Gandhi and Civil Disobedience

Nonviolent civil disobedience became an important tool of the civil rights movement during the 1950s, and it would continue to play a vital part in the movement's campaigns in the following decade. The peaceful tactics used by Indian nationalist Mohandas "Mahatma" Gandhi to end British rule in his nation during the 1940s served as a model for Martin Luther King Jr. and others. Several civil rights leaders had roots in the pacifist movement. Bayard Rustin of the Congress of Racial Equality and James Lawson of the Fellowship of Reconciliation were two pacifists who had served time in prison rather than join the armed services, and both now were willing to take the same kind of risk in the effort to expand their civil rights.

King went to India in 1959 to meet with other Gandhians, and he proclaimed that the time had arrived for a daring campaign for equality in the South. Although civil disobedience had already scored victories in some places, he focused a great deal of attention on the need to educate demonstrators in the principles of Gandhian protest so that they would not allow frustration to boil over into violent acts. Nonviolence drew many African Americans into the movement, allowing SCLC to blossom as CORE experienced dramatic growth.

Leaders of the movement realized that African American protesters in the South would be more sympathetic figures to Americans across the nation if they were peaceful, respectful, and religious. The sight of nicely dressed people, both young and old, facing harsh treatment from white supremacists carried the potential to turn the tide in the civil rights crusade. Whether the protesters were boycotting segregated buses or "sitting in" at lunch counters, their behavior put the spotlight on their will to persevere and on the injustice of their treatment. Few Americans were totally free of racial prejudice, but the protesters' dignified attire and behavior made it easier for many whites to feel sympathy for their cause.

African Americans in Entertainment and Sports

At the same time that many African Americans battled for their rights, a privileged few won spots on center stage in American popular culture. African American writers, actors and actresses, singers, and athletes found new opportunities for stardom. These individuals served as role models for young African Americans and showed that talent could open doors once locked by prejudice. Songstress Mahalia Jackson gave a concert at Carnegie Hall in 1950; actress Dorothy Dandridge became the first African American nominated for Best Actress in the 1954 Academy Awards; Marian Anderson achieved another first by singing with the Metropolitan Opera in 1955; crooner Nat King Cole became the first African American to host his own TV show in 1956; and jazz singer Ella Fitzgerald won the annual Metronome poll for best musicians twice during the decade. Sidney Poitier, who was heading for superstardom as a film actor, also began to make his mark in the 1950s. At the same time, African Americans were making inroads in professional sports. Following in the footsteps of Jackie Robinson, Willie Mays earned fans' admiration as a baseball star, and in 1957, Jim Brown was drafted by the Cleveland Browns and soon became a dominant running back. The rise of these stars coincided with growing acceptance of music that sprang from African roots—jazz and rock 'n' roll.

As white teens danced to the music of Fats Domino, Chuck Berry, and others, some white supremacists saw dangers all around them. In one incident, an Alabama caravan of 75 cars managed to stop a drive-in theatre showing of *Island in the Sun*, which featured an integrated cast. On that night, white supremacists were able to shut down power to the theater and block the entrance. Over time, they learned that rock 'n' roll and the civil rights movement were unstoppable forces.

Changes in the Political Environment

The African American battle for equal rights would not be won in months or years, but it experienced a surge of activity during the 1950s. With a variety of organizations appealing to different constituencies, the movement gained strength in numbers and broadened the base of sympathetic whites who might contribute to the cause. At the same time, court rulings added legitimacy to African American ambitions.

Civil rights protests gained international attention because the United States was one of the two primary combatants in the Cold War. Civil rights was an ideal topic for Communists and others who wanted to intensify attention on American deeds versus American ideals in appealing to newly emerging Third World nations. Civil rights leaders acted with the knowledge that one tool in making the federal government take direct action was international opinion. Also, although most of the nation's whites had not yet endorsed swift and clear action to protect southern African Americans, the 1950s laid the groundwork for changes in public opinion in the years to come.

Many southern leaders throughout American history had been advocates of states' rights—and the politicians of the 1950s often adopted that refrain by opposing interference from the federal government or from Americans in other parts of the nation. However, broadening news coverage and the growing popularity of television made it impossible in the late 1950s to maintain the veil of secrecy that had shielded African American–white relations in the South from national view. Certainly, some Americans outside the South found reasons to defend white supremacists; the great emphasis placed on fears that African American men would rape or seduce white women reinforced many white Americans' misconception that African American men were inherently dangerous. However, over time, images of authority figures unfairly treating African Americans were beginning to touch the consciences of an increasing number of Americans.

As events unfolded in the South, religious groups began to feel a stronger pull to join the movement and stand against the mistreatment of African Americans. Some Southern Baptist periodicals urged members to show their Christianity by supporting African American rights. Four South Carolina ministers joined forces in 1956 to develop a book of essays on racial tolerance by ministers and laypeople in their state. When asked why religious Americans should support civil rights, the Reverend John B. Morris of Dillon, South Carolina, said, "In fact, we [all churches] have been so weak in this matter that history will read back and say that the armed forces, the effect of TV etc., and the power of the dollar did more to solve the problem than we have had the courage to do in the church" (Daniel 2000, 240).

At the same time that small steps forward raised hopes among African Americans, these advances siphoned support from some white supremacist groups. Many whites were drained of racist fervor when they saw that African American advances did not adversely affect their lives. The North Carolina Patriots, for example, experienced "apathy among the rank and file of the whites in the eastern and western . . . sections of the state," according to one leader. When some of the state's public schools began token integration in 1957 with little uproar, passions cooled even more. Many members lost interest in the group, which disbanded that year (Daniel 2000, 270).

THE RIGHT TO VOTE AND THE RIGHT TO LIVE

Two crucial issues for the civil rights movement in the 1950s were the right to vote and the right to live free from the threat of violence. Often, these two goals became intertwined as activists who promoted African American voting became victims of crimes committed by white supremacists. While public officials often bent voting laws to discriminate against African Americans, the results of voting lawsuits were mixed and largely ineffectual. At the same time, white violence against African Americans often went unpunished in the Deep South because African Americans were not allowed on juries and all-white juries tended to acquit white defendants in such cases. Many Americans believed that the existence of a population with no vote and without legal protection from violent attacks was incongruous with American ideals. This widened the chasm between the South and other regions where African Americans could vote, serve on juries, and live in relative safety. This differentiation between the South and the rest of the nation was especially noteworthy because it occurred during the years when the mass media was chipping away at the power of regional identity by providing the same products for people all over the nation. (The strange strength of southern identity is apparent in commentary from that era. Often, the nation was divided into two parts—the South and the North, with the "North" encompassing everything that was not in the Old South, including states like Nevada and California.)

Because the vast majority of African Americans still lived in the South, most were unable to vote in the 1950s. The number of African Americans on the voting rolls had been slowly rising through the 1940s and into the 1950s, until the mid-1950s when white backlash against African American rights gained new strength. A combination of poll taxes, subjective challenges, physical intimidation, and literacy tests stood as obstacles to African American voting. At times, local officials claimed that even African American college graduates had failed to pass literacy tests. Sometimes potential voters were asked whether they favored school integration or supported the NAACP before officials decided on their voting status. In response, civil rights groups pursued a variety of campaigns to increase the number of African Americans registered to vote. Sometimes, these efforts placed would-be voters in physical danger. In other cases, localized groups, such as the Montgomery Improvement Association, the Southern Leaders Conference, and the Palmetto Voters Association, tried to gather the political clout to block practices that limited African American voting and to expand opportunities to vote.

White violence against African Americans, like restrictions on voting rights, was not new in the 1950s. However, the South's violent tradition of lynching African Americans received unusual international attention when the leftist Civil Rights Congress accused the United States of genocide in documents delivered to the United Nations Committee on Human Rights in Geneva in 1951. The petition condemned the lynching of thousands of African Americans over the 85 years since the end of slavery. It also specifically cited 153 killings, 344 other violent crimes, and other human rights abuses inflicted on African Americans between 1945 and 1951. And violence against African Americans gained new fervor after 1954. Because victims often were civil rights advocates, the

Tennessee officials of the NAACP inspect a tent city in Fayette County. African Americans were driven from their homes and forced into this temporary sanctuary after they tried to vote in 1960. The drive to register African American voters accelerated in the late 1950s, but did not achieve total success until passage of the Voting Rights Act of 1965. (Library of Congress)

dead became martyrs to the larger cause. The fact that African Americans were willing to risk their lives to obtain the rights enjoyed by other Americans demonstrated a serious commitment to democracy that became increasingly difficult to ignore.

Conservative Federal Policy

African Americans in the 1950s looked toward the White House in hope of getting help to change their everyday lives. The president of the United States during most of the 1950s was Dwight D. Eisenhower, a grandfatherly figure and former military officer. After a career in the segregated army, Eisenhower, like many other white Americans, had little insight into African American problems because of his limited contact with African Americans. Eisenhower and many of his counterparts in the white middle class had never worked alongside an African American person whose power equaled his. While he could see from a distance that African Americans suffered from injustice, his public statements often conveyed what was then a common question: What's the hurry?

Eisenhower and many of his white constituents shared a common concern that rapid integration could be unhealthy for the nation as a whole. A 1958 Gallup poll demonstrated little impetus for rapid change. The survey showed the largest group of Americans—33 percent—believed that integration should be carried out in a few years or in 10 to 20 years. Thirty-one percent of Americans expressed total opposition to integration of southern schools in areas of the Deep South where African American children might outnumber whites, and only 29 percent believed that school integration should be carried out immediately (Gallup 1958).

Eisenhower, in fact, did not see a need for expansion of African American rights, much less a federal mandate forcing states to treat African Americans more fairly. He failed to support the Supreme Court's ruling that public schools should be integrated. Instead of urging progress toward integration, he often commented that "you cannot change people's hearts merely by law" (Sitkoff 1993, 30). When Autherine Lucy attempted to integrate the University of Alabama, he refused to support her admission in the face of racist violence. However, he later did send troops to Little Rock, Arkansas, when he saw no other way to integrate Central High School in the face of locally sanctioned violence and intimidation.

This president did not revolutionize the lives of African Americans, but he did demonstrate the growing impact of the civil rights movement by meeting at the White House with Martin Luther King Jr. as well as the AFL-CIO's A. Philip Randolph, the NAACP's Roy Wilkins, and the Urban League's Lester Granger in 1958. Unfortunately, Eisenhower was dismayed by the civil rights leaders' pleas for more action, and his four visitors, recognizing the historic nature of the meeting, especially for African Americans, did not express public disagreement with the president after the meeting. Eisenhower had become the first president to name an African American professional to his White House staff, but his closest aides sometimes berated E. Frederic Morrow for his frequent memos urging the administration to take a stronger stand against segregation. Eisenhower's frequent choice of inaction and his calls for patience reflected a state of mind shared by many of his constituents and demonstrated why African American frustrations grew, fueling the civil rights movement. The Eisenhower administration, however, was not unanimous in its chosen stand. Some administration officials saw southern segregation as a weapon to be used against the United States by its enemies in the Cold War.

Racial violence often received international coverage, and smaller incidents also had a potential effect on U.S. relations with developing nations. In reaching out to newly independent African nations, the Eisenhower administration suffered embarrassment in 1957. A Howard Johnson restaurant in Dover, Delaware, refused to allow Komla Agbeli Gbedemah, finance minister of Ghana, to eat inside the restaurant with white customers. Eisenhower's team quickly entered damage-control mode and invited Gbedemah to the White House for an official apology and a tour.

African American Voting Rights

Only a small percentage of African Americans living in the South during the 1950s were allowed to register to vote. The 1950 total of 1.2 million registered African American voters was twice as high as the number registered in 1947; however, only 24.9 percent of nonwhites in all southern states were eligible to vote in 1956. Heightened white anger following the *Brown* ruling had slowed registration growth in some states and led to a decline in others.

In the heart of the Deep South, only 5 percent of Mississippi's African Americans were registered to vote in 1956—3.04 percentage points less than in 1952. The state lost 7 percent of its African American population during the 1950s; however, the decline probably reflects increased oppression rather than new mobility. A similar pattern existed in South Carolina, where 33.33 percent of African Americans were registered voters in 1952, and only 27 percent could vote in 1956. And South Carolina's African American population actually grew during the decade. While two-thirds of African Americans remained unregistered in the five states traditionally identified as the Deep South, more than 40 percent were registered to vote in Florida and Tennessee in 1952. Those totals also dropped between the decade's two presidential election years. With 37 percent of voting-age African Americans registered, Texas led the South in 1956 (Salzman, Smith, and West 1996, 3017).

Opponents of the African American vote employed an array of tactics to limit African American participation in elections. The most common tool was the literacy test. Despite a growing trend toward abandoning literacy tests, by 1957, Alabama, North Carolina, Mississippi, and Virginia still required them. Often, white election officials had quite a bit of leeway in deciding whether an individual was qualified to register. Instead of examining potential registrants' understanding of the law, some literacy tests focused on inconsequential or ridiculous questions such as how many rooms were in the county courthouse or how many bubbles were in a bar of soap. Georgia, Louisiana, and South Carolina all called for a literacy test or some other criterion, which was often open to interpretation. Among the alternatives to the literacy tests were proof of property ownership, "understanding the duties of citizenship," and "good character and adherence to the principles of the state" (Irving 1957, 3950). In 1957, five states—Alabama, Arkansas, Mississippi, Texas, and Virginia—maintained poll taxes, and in that year, the Alabama legislature considered forcing African Americans to pay back poll taxes up to a total of $36—a lot of money for an African American in rural Alabama during the 1950s. White desperation about blocking

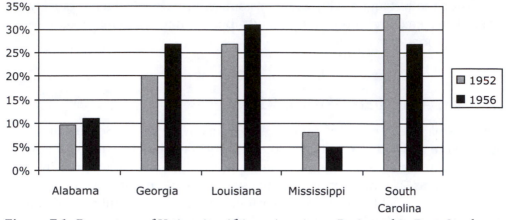

Figure 7.1 *Percentage of Voting-Age African Americans Registered in Deep South.*
Source: Salzman, Smith, and West 1996, 3017.

African American suffrage is apparent in the use of the poll tax, which also snatched voting rights from some poor whites.

By 1958, the NAACP had identified voter registration as its top priority. Activists Bayard Rustin and Stanley Levison, who was later investigated for ties to the Communist Party USA, produced a plan to give the Crusade for Citizenship a boost during that year, and SCLC followed through on their plan, leading simultaneous rallies in 21 cities on Abraham Lincoln's birthday. However, voter registration numbers did not show a significant improvement.

Civil Rights Legislation

No major civil rights legislation had been passed in the United States since the Reconstruction era that followed the Civil War, and despite Eisenhower's concern about endorsing rapid change, his administration attempted to broaden the citizenship rights of African Americans. Though this action occurred in Washington, it had the potential to touch African Americans throughout the South and to give them more power to affect the policies that shaped their lives. Immediately after his 1956 landslide re-election victory, Eisenhower proposed legislation to broaden voting rights of African Americans. Eisenhower's motives may not have been wholly unselfish. African American voters had been strong Democrats during the years of Franklin Roosevelt's presidency, and in 1952, 83 percent of African American voters cast their votes for the Democratic presidential candidate, Adlai Stevenson. However, four years later, when Eisenhower and Stevenson faced off again, Stevenson captured only 68 percent of the African American vote, thus leaving open the possibility that expanded African American voting would not merely be a boon to the Democratic Party (Koslow 1999, 74). Among those voting for Eisenhower in 1956 were Martin Luther King Jr. and his ally Ralph Abernathy, according to then–Vice President Richard Nixon. And after meeting with the two civil rights leaders, Nixon said that they believed most new African American voters would be Republicans (Branch 1988, 220).

The administration's bill faced a rocky road through Congress. When it finally passed, African American leaders and African Americans in general saw reason to celebrate in the first civil rights act in 82 years. And publicly, they did just that. However, Senate majority leader Lyndon Johnson made so many compromises to win Senate approval of the bill that its final form was virtually meaningless. The most crippling change guaranteed that officials accused of violating court orders on voting rights would receive jury trials. With states in the Deep South continuing to keep African Americans off juries, white election officials would feel little need to obey the legislation, civil rights leaders realized. Instead, they would simply act as they wished and count on an all-white jury to acquit them if they were charged with violating the law. As a result, historians have concluded that few if any African American Americans were able to achieve voter registration because of this bill.

Violence in the South

White violence against African Americans had been common for centuries, but there seemed to be an unofficial moratorium on lynching in the early 1950s. This development indicated a cooling of the vitriolic emotions that had caused so many deaths since the end of the Civil War. For African Americans in the South, the world was a bit safer; however, all of that changed after both the Supreme Court's *Brown* ruling in 1954 and the heightening of civil rights activity. Brutal race hatred and violence were reignited by the thought that the South might be forced to abandon the segregation that defined much of its culture. African Americans again commonly became victims of violent race crimes. Lynching returned, but guns took lives as well. In some cases, African Americans died for what they believed; in others, they died simply because of white people's fears and indignation.

During 1955 alone, several African Americans died or were wounded by white supremacists. Some of those who died were civil rights workers attempting to change their world, but the most notorious case involved a teenaged boy acting like a teenaged boy. Emmett Till was a Chicago youth who had traveled to Mississippi with his cousin, Curtis Jones, to stay with Jones's great-uncle. Details about Till's actions remain open to question. Jones later said that on August 24, 1955, he and Till were playing with some boys outside a small store owned by a white couple. At one point, Till reportedly pulled the photo of a white girl from

Mamie Bradley weeps as the body of her slain son, Emmett Till, arrives in the Chicago Rail Station. Till, who was only 14, had been killed by white vigilantes in Mississippi after flirting with a white woman. (Bettmann/Corbis)

his wallet and claimed that she was his girlfriend. Apparently, the other boys did not believe the 14-year-old Till's claim, and they dared him to approach the white woman running the store. Some say Till merely whistled at the woman; others claim that he bought candy from her and then grabbed her, suggesting that they get together. An older African American man playing checkers outside the store saw whatever happened between Till and the woman, and he advised Till and his cousin to leave because the woman might come outside with a gun.

The woman's husband was not in the store at the time. When he returned hours later, an African American witness told him what had occurred. The store-owner, Roy Bryant, and a gun-wielding comrade, J. W. "Big" Milam, went to the house of Moses Wright, the elderly sharecropper with whom the two boys were staying. The men threatened Wright, who allowed them to talk with Till. They forced Till into their pickup and drove off. The men stripped Till, pistol-whipped him, shot him, tied him to a 74-pound piece of a cotton gin that they had previously forced him to load onto the truck. Then, they threw him into the Talla-hatchie River.

Both killers later were arrested, tried, and ultimately exonerated by a white jury. The case attracted more national publicity than any previous case of white violence against an African American. Till's death may have received broader attention because his body was shipped to Chicago, where the brutality of his death became clear when his mother insisted on an open-casket funeral. Reporters from the *New York Times* and other media flooded into the town of Sumner, where the trial took place. The killers confessed their guilt to *Look* magazine writer William Bradford Hule, who produced a detailed account of the killing under this headline: "The Shocking Story of Approved Killing in Mississippi." Their greatest concern, they told Hule, was that someone would catch them with the stolen fan from the cotton gin. According to them, Till believed that they were bluffing when they threatened violence, and he refused to apologize for what he had done. "Well, what else could we do?" said Milam. "I'm no bully; I never hurt a nigger in my life. I like niggers—in their place—I know how to work 'em. But I just decided it was time a few people got put on notice" (Hule 1956).

In her 1968 autobiography, *Coming of Age in Mississippi,* Anne Moody wrote, "I was fifteen years old when I began to hate people. I hated the white men who murdered Emmett Till and I hated all the other whites who were responsible for the countless murders Mrs. Rice [my homeroom teacher] had told me about and those I vaguely remembered from childhood. But I also hated Negroes. I hated them for not standing up and doing something about the murders" (Carson et al. 1991, 41).

The Case of Harry T. Moore

NAACP activist Harry T. Moore struggled to protect African Americans in Florida from the mid-1930s until the early 1950s. In 1949, after a white mob beat three African American men accused of raping a white woman in Groveland, Florida, Moore charged Lake County sheriff Willis McCall with misconduct in the case of Charles Greenlee, Walter Irvin, and Sammy Shepherd. The three men were convicted in 1949; however, two years later, the U.S. Supreme Court overturned the convictions. In November 1951, when he was transporting Irvin and Shepherd to a pretrial hearing, McCall shot both men, killing Shepherd. He claimed that the two handcuffed suspects had attacked him in an attempt to escape from custody. Irvin, who was critically injured, claimed that McCall had pulled the two men out of the car and fired on them. The shootings attracted national publicity, and Moore took a strong stand, urging that McCall be indicted for murder. About six weeks later, Moore lay asleep in his bed beside his wife, Harriette, when a bomb exploded directly underneath the floor of their bedroom. The device had been wedged under floor joists beneath their bed. Moore died before reaching a hospital, and his wife succumbed nine days afterward.

In a period when white violence against blacks was somewhat rare, the double murder caused a national uproar. Both President Harry Truman and Florida governor Fuller Warren received a flood of protests in letters and telegrams. In 1952, the FBI initiated a probe into the murders and possible ties between the murderers and the central Florida branch of the Ku Klux Klan. Three members of the Klan were identified as suspects; one of the three took his own life just a day after being interrogated by the FBI. The investigation slowed Klan activity in the area, but no one was arrested for the Moore killings. Subsequently, four Klan members, all of whom were dead, were identified as having played a role in the crime. Despite two later investigations, no one has ever been tried for killing Harry and Harriette Moore.

White Violence against African Americans

Violence became more common, especially against civil rights activists, in the mid- to late 1950s. Till's cases attracted national publicity, perhaps because of his midwestern roots, while others were less prominent in the news. Following are some examples.

George Lee, vice president of the Regional Council of Negro Leadership and cofounder of the local NAACP chapter, was slain in May 1955 after threatening to file a lawsuit when the county sheriff denied his right to vote. Lee, who was a minister and a registered voter, was killed while driving alone on the dark streets of Belzoni, Mississippi. Apparently, someone shot at him from a vehicle that was following his car, and when another vehicle pulled alongside Lee's, someone shot out one of his tires. Lee then hit the brakes, and he was shot twice at point-blank range with a shotgun (Daniel 2000, 222).

Gus Courts, who led the Belzoni NAACP, also was shot in a separate 1955 incident for promoting African American voting. He survived his wounds (Daniel 2000, 224).

Lamar Smith of Brookhaven, Mississippi, was shot at close range and killed in August 1955 outside the Lincoln County courthouse in broad daylight. Smith, who was a farmer, had just cast his ballot in a primary election. He apparently was singled out because of his efforts to encourage other African Americans to vote (Lowery and Marszalek 1992, 483–484).

John Earl Reese, a 16-year-old, was shot while dancing in a Mayflower, Texas, café on an October evening in 1955. Gunmen fired through the establishment's windows, killing Reese and wounding two others. The attackers were trying to intimidate African Americans who had demanded improvement in African American students' schools (Southern Poverty Law Center 2005).

Willie Edwards Jr. was a truck driver forced at gunpoint to jump to his death from a bridge above the Alabama River. Edwards, who was mistakenly identified as a man who had been dating a white woman, was abducted on the road by four Klansmen in January 1957. His body was located three months later (Southern Poverty Law Center 2005).

Mack Parker, who was suspected of raping a white woman, was snatched out of a Poplarville, Mississippi, jail by an angry white mob. He was lynched, and his body was thrown into the Pearl River. The Federal Bureau of Investigation subsequently found evidence of police complicity in the crime, but a grand jury refused to allow FBI agents to testify. U.S. Atty. Gen. William P. Rogers called the Mississippi court proceedings "a travesty on justice, flagrant and calculated." Later attempts to bring federal charges against the killers were rebuffed by an all-white federal grand jury (Branch 1989, 257–258).

The Dangers of Protest

At the close of the 1950s, African Americans in the South understood that the threat of violence remained a prominent feature of their relationship with the white population. Most white southerners would never have resorted to violence against African Americans; however, a surprising number were quite willing to look the other way when these crimes were committed by others. Whether they refrained from demanding prosecution or actively served on a jury that absolved the guilty, many white southerners placed racial allegiances above all others. Some whites, like African Americans, succumbed to intimidation by hard-charging, brutal white supremacists. Those who disagreed with the lawbreakers did not always feel free to speak up and take a public stand. White southerners who openly condemned violence against African Americans could wake up in the night to find Ku Klux Klan crosses burning in their yards or bombs exploding on their porches. The issue of voting rights also was driven by strong emotions and by the kind of race hatred that made elected officials feel free to violate the law. When the Civil Rights Act of 1957 was approved, the emptiness of the triumph further clarified the realization that southern power in Congress made political victory difficult without changing the minds or touching the hearts of Americans outside the South.

On these issues and others, the civil rights movement functioned as both an expression of revolt and a public relations campaign aimed at evoking empathy among white Americans. Events in the South did not seem important to Americans in other parts of the country, and civil rights leaders placed great emphasis on why people should care. In the 1950s, African Americans put a great deal of time into showing their commitment to the struggle. From poor, raggedly dressed farmers to eloquent and educated orators, African Americans spent much of the decade drawing attention to the rights they had been denied. Throughout the South, activists would continue to push for voting rights for the coming eight years until the Voting Rights Act of 1965 removed southern barriers to African American voting. As King acknowledged more than once, no one could stop the lone gunman who might perch on a balcony to kill a civil rights advocate, but participants in the movement labored to make people care and to acknowledge how wrong racial violence was. For middle-class whites outside the South and for Dwight Eisenhower, right and wrong were a bit clearer on these issues. The issue of segregation was more difficult for them to judge.

BROWN RULING AND ITS AFTERMATH

Slowly and carefully, civil rights groups of this era assembled court challenges that had the potential to eliminate public school segregation. When those cases were combined to form *Brown v. the Board of Education of Topeka, Kansas,* the possibility of a momentous decision became clear. During the final months of Harry Truman's administration, the Justice Department filed an *amicus curiae* (friend of the court) document urging the high court to consider not just the case itself, but also the effect of racial discrimination on American standing in the world at large. With a full recognition of how big the issue of equal rights was in the United States, the Truman administration's Cold Warriors knew that international repercussions could make the U.S. Supreme Court's ruling even more important.

Indeed, the Court's 1954 opinion, which concluded that public schools should be integrated, was among the 20th century's most important rulings, and over the course of the next 20 years, it had a profound impact on the daily lives of many Americans. When enforced, the decision gave African Americans broader opportunities, starting in childhood. The possibility of receiving a better education and of interacting with whites from an early age represented a sea change in African American culture within the South. Since the *Plessy v. Ferguson* ruling of 1896 had given approval to the idea of "separate but equal" facilities for the races, African Americans had experienced a lot of separation with very little equality. In the *Brown* case, the Supreme Court ruled unanimously that "in the field of public education the doctrine of 'separate but equal' has no place. Separate educational facilities are inherently unequal" (Carson et al. 1991, 72–73).

In addition to setting into motion the journey toward school integration, the ruling helped to spur two important social developments: a reinvigoration of the civil rights movement and strong white backlash across the South. As white supremacists gathered forces to block African American progress and the end to a legally segregated society, they sought to intimidate both moderate whites and African Americans. Authors of books that were sympathetic to the civil rights movement found themselves suddenly silenced. The publisher of Lillian Smith's *Now Is the Time,* which supported integration, withdrew the book from the market, apparently to avoid retaliation against store owners who sold it. Two leading magazines—*Life* and *Time*—both refused to publish a written response by Smith to a states' rights article written by Mississippi novelist William Faulkner. When she appeared on the morning talk show *Today* after days of preparing a carefully worded five-minute introductory statement, she learned that it had

Nettie Hunt and her daughter Nickie sit on the steps of the United States Supreme Court in 1954. Hunt holds a newspaper announcing the court's decision in Brown v. Board of Education, *which found that segregated schools were unconstitutional. (Library of Congress)*

been cut, although the speaker endorsing segregation, Sen. James Eastland, was allowed to make his own opening statement. Wilma Dykeman and James Stokely, who explored southern race relations in their 1957 book *Neither Black nor White,* found that virtually all media were unwilling to give their work exposure. And as the power of the backlash became clear, George S. Mitchell of the Southern Regional Council noted that there was no parallel organizational boom of local white organizations that supported integration. Backlash to the ruling virtually eliminated white moderate views from southern politics.

Segregation as a Way of Life

At the time of the *Brown* ruling, segregation was required by law in Delaware, Maryland, West Virginia, Virginia, Kentucky, Missouri, Oklahoma, Arkansas, Tennessee, North Carolina, South Carolina, Georgia, Florida, Alabama, Mississippi, Louisiana, and Texas. Four more states—Wyoming, Kansas, Arizona, and New Mexico—offered segregation as an option for local school systems. And only 16 of the 48 states prohibited segregation in public schools.

An independent study repudiating segregation was released one day before the Supreme Court announced its unanimous decision. The study of southern schools conducted by the Ford Foundation concluded that southern school systems were not providing adequate educations for African American youngsters. However, the *Brown* ruling led segregationists to bombard elected leaders with angry missives and to begin more aggressive efforts to save segregated schools. Prosegregation pamphlets played on fears about white women succumbing to African American men. *The Kiss of Death,* a cautionary piece of literature, displayed on its cover an image of a white woman being kissed by an African American man. It warned readers that "The Russians regard every Negro in our midst as a weapon more deadly than the atomic bomb." Often segregationists defended their practices by claiming that African American students would pollute their children's lives. Reiterating an argument that dated back to the 19th century, one Tennessee woman asserted that African American children "come from homes where disease and vermin abound and baths are not taken too frequently" (Daniel 2000, 38–39). There was a powerful irony in white supremacists' stated revulsion to the very thought of allowing their children to interact with African Americans: For decades, prosperous white families had entrusted their children to the care of African American women, people to whom they denied an adequate education and whose children were seen as potential "pollution" of white youths.

While the South vibrated with newly amplified racial hatred, nationwide public opinion polls from 1954 until the end of the decade showed consistent support for school desegregation across the nation. The number of Americans backing the *Brown* ruling was 54 percent in 1954, rose to 64 percent in January 1957, and stood at 59 percent in July 1959 (Gallup 1959). It is important to note that many of those polled probably did not expect the ruling to affect their lives in any way. When a 1958 Gallup poll pushed that point and tried to test gut-level reactions to integration, the results showed that most nonsouthern white parents' support for integration was conditioned on very specific circumstances. While they voiced no objection to having their children attend integrated schools in which whites made up a majority or half of the student body, most expressed opposition to having their children assigned to schools in which whites represented a minority. In areas where the geography of de facto residential segregation guaranteed primarily white schools, nonsoutherners appeared to be more liberal than their counterparts in Dixie. However, there were limits to that liberalism.

Backlash

Much of the South defiantly opposed school integration plans throughout the 1950s. This revolt existed on a local level, but it also reached into the federal

government, as evidenced by the Southern Manifesto signed by nearly all
southern members of Congress in 1956.
Every U.S. senator from the South signed
the document except Estes Kefauver
and Albert Gore of Tennessee and Lyndon Johnson of Texas. This manifesto
called the *Brown* ruling "a clear abuse
of judicial power." Benjamin E. Mays,
who headed Morehouse College in Atlanta, warned that white leaders' reaction to the Supreme Court decision was
"an invitation to lawlessness all over
the place" (Daniel 2000, 206). Increasing
white supremacist activities throughout
the South during this era proved Mays's
point. Backlash included racial violence
but was not limited to it. Federal agricultural officials sometimes vented post-
Brown angst by mistreating African
American farmers and farmworkers.

*A woman and her child march in
front of Arkansas's state capitol in a
protest against integration of Little
Rock's public schools. (Library of
Congress)*

White Citizens Councils began to
spread across the South in the summer
of 1954. Although these groups opposed
integration, they were not violent like the Ku Klux Klan. Instead, council members often included community leaders, and they identified with civic virtues like
patriotism and anticommunism. The councils, which bristled with the pride of
an evolving middle class, viewed the NAACP as a radical organization seeking
to disturb what they perceived to be the natural and desirable racial order. Not
all of these groups claimed the title of "Citizens Councils." In North Carolina, the
leading group was the Patriots, in Louisiana the Southern Gentlemen. Like the
civil rights movement, this counterforce could lay claim to eloquent speakers and
writers. One leader, Tom P. Grady of Brookhaven, Mississippi, dubbed the day
of the ruling "Black Monday" and explained his imagery this way: "Black de-
noting darkness and error. Black signifying the absence of light and wisdom.
Black embodying grief, destruction, and death" (Carson et al. 1991, 83).

Segregationism became a unifying theme in a broader effort to maintain the
status quo. For example, antiunion forces forged links with segregationists.
Cannon Mills in Kannapolis, North Carolina, attempted to block unionization
by reporting that the United Auto Workers' leader, Walter Reuther, had contributed $75,000 to the NAACP. In rural areas, Farm Bureau officials used their
positions to create white supremacist networks within their states. Some agricultural officials withheld Department of Agriculture subsidies from African

Table 7.2. Number of Nonwhite Farmers in the South

	1950	1954	1959
Full owner	141,482	129,854	89,749
Part owner	51,864	50,736	37,534
Manager	239	381	290
Tenant	355,505	282,505	188,048
Sharecroppers	198,057	160,246	73,387

Source: U.S. Census Bureau. 1975. "Farms, by Race and Tenure of Operator, and Acreage and Value, by Tenure of Operator: 1880–1969." *Bicentennial Edition: Historical Statistics of the United States Colonial Times to 1970, Part 1,* 465. Washington, DC: Government Printing Office. Also available at http://2www.census.gov/prod2/statcomp/documents/CT1970p1-01/pdf.

American farmers while generously granting aid to their white neighbors. Tactics to control the African American population varied. A minority of white southerners still used violence to intimidate African Americans. Others embraced more sophisticated means, such as imposition of economic sanctions against African Americans by limiting their job options. Efforts to minimize the prospects of African American farmers were successful. In Mississippi, where African Americans made up 45 percent of the population in 1950 (Salzman, Smith, and West 1996, 2562), the number of African American farmers plummeted from 159,000 in 1940 to 38,000 in 1964 (Daniel 2000, 227). Citizens Councils in Mississippi routinely told complaining African Americans that they should move if they felt they were being treated unjustly.

The backlash thrived although prominent religious organizations within the South supported the *Brown* ruling and advocated obedience to the Court decision. The Southern Baptist Convention, Methodists, Presbyterians, and other churches favored peaceful compliance, but many members refused to hear their message. Despite their region's unofficial identification as the Bible Belt, many southern whites ignored religious pleas for harmony and accommodation as they embraced deepening racist militancy.

The Implementation Decision

By refusing to set a specific desegregation deadline in a 1955 decision, the Supreme Court gave new hope to segregationists and disappointed those who had hoped for speedy integration. The May 31 ruling required school systems to move with "all deliberate speed" as it acknowledged that desegregation would require detailed changes at the local level. The justices gave lower courts, often controlled by conservative white judges, the authority to accept or reject integration plans in the states under their oversight. This approach to enforcement of the original ruling offered segregationists the hope of finding enough loopholes to block the ordered changes. Many African Americans who were in first grade in 1954 would reach high school before "deliberate speed" had integrated their schools—or they would attend segregated schools throughout their public school years.

University of Alabama Integration

Autherine Lucy was a college graduate who wanted to earn a master's degree in library science. To do that, she applied to the University of Alabama; with the NAACP's help, she was able to overcome the obstacles thrown in her path and planned to start school in February 1956. Her arrival prompted rioting by white supremacists, and the federal government refused to take any action to protect Lucy or to control the angry mob. Within days, the university suspended her, claiming that it was acting to protect her from potential violence. Eventually, she was expelled because her lawyers accused university officials of complicity with white supremacists. Although the *Brown* decision had not focused on universities, historians believe that anxiety about the ruling may have heightened the violence that accompanied Lucy's enrollment.

Little Rock's Central High School

Central High School in Little Rock, Arkansas, was scheduled to become an integrated school on September 4, 1957; however, that did not happen. Instead, Gov. Orval Faubus called out the Arkansas National Guard to surround the school and block the students' admittance. Weeks later, a federal judge ordered that the National Guard had to be withdrawn. On the next school day, September 23, Little Rock police officers ringed the school to preserve order. The African American students slipped in through a side door of the school; however, when a loud mob of 1,000 outside the school learned that the students were inside, the police became fearful of being overwhelmed. As a result, the Little Rock Nine were removed from the school before noon. The city's mayor, Woodrow Mann, and U.S. Rep. Brooks Hays asked the federal government for help. On September 24, President Eisenhower, who had tried unsuccessfully to win Faubus's cooperation, sent U.S. Army troops to Little Rock. The president, who previously had opposed federal intervention in such cases, also decided to nationalize the Arkansas National Guard. Three weeks later, on September 25, the students finally entered the school under the protection of the 101st Airborne Division.

TV footage of this extended drama brought the crisis into American homes. Eight of the nine African American students finished the school year, and the group's only senior graduated. In the summer of 1958, the school board continued to seek legal barriers to integration. A lower court ruling supported a

Elizabeth Eckford ignores the hostile screams of students at Little Rock's Central High School as she attempts to enter the school in the fall of 1957. She was among nine African American students who joined the formerly all-white student body weeks later after federal troops interceded to ensure the peaceful integration of the school. (Bettmann/Corbis)

postponement of integration in Little Rock, but that decision was overturned. In September, the U.S. Supreme Court ruled that the planned integration should continue. Faubus then called the state legislature into special session and won approval of a bill allowing him to close the city's public high schools and lease them to private schools. The public high schools were closed for an entire school year. In June, a federal court ruled that the legislation allowing school closures was unconstitutional, and the schools reopened in August 1959. By this time, moderates had gained clout on the city's school board. Two of the Little Rock

The Little Rock Nine

Minnijean Brown	In the winter of 1958, she was suspended for the rest of the school year following several confrontations, including one in which she threw a bowl of chili on someone who verbally abused her in the cafeteria. A primary target of abuse, she transferred to an out-of-state school. As an adult, she became a fierce opponent of the Vietnam War before moving to Canada.
Elizabeth Eckford	Because she did not know that the other African American students were meeting elsewhere, Elizabeth Eckford arrived at school alone on September 4, 1957. Immediately, she became the target of taunts from thousands of segregationists; eventually, she escaped on a city bus. Later in life, she served in the U.S. Army and worked as a journalist and social worker.
Ernest Green	He was the first African American to graduate from Central High School. He earned a degree from Michigan State University and served as Assistant Secretary of Housing and Urban Affairs under President Jimmy Carter.
Thelma Mothershed	Although she was weakened by a heart condition, she wanted to attend Central High School so that she could prepare to become a schoolteacher. She did become a teacher and moved to Illinois, where she did volunteer work to help abused women.
Melba Pattillo	Then 15, she was denied the chance to sing in a school talent contest. She wrote *Warriors Don't Cry: A Searing Memoir of the Battle to Integrate Little Rock's Central High*. The book was based on a diary she kept during the ordeal. She later became a journalist.
Gloria Ray	She made the decision to attend Central High and take a position on the front lines of the civil rights movement without consulting her parents. She graduated from Illinois Technical College and did postgraduate work in Sweden. Ray became an author of computer science literature and made her home in Europe.
Terrence Roberts	A superior student, he spent one year at Central High School before his family moved to Los Angeles. As an adult, he earned a Ph.D. and became a clinical psychologist.
Jefferson Thomas	Described by observers as "tentative," he drew more attacks from segregationists than some of his comrades. Thomas later became an accountant.
Carlotta Walls	Known as the "Ridge Runner" because of her athleticism, she graduated from Central High and from Michigan State University. Afterward, she pursued a career in real estate.

Historians' Debate: *Brown*'s Impact

Did the *Brown* ruling serve as the catalyst for the civil rights movement, or were the movement's roots planted much earlier, perhaps during World War II? That question has led to debate among historians about the ruling's importance. Many have argued that the Court decision, indeed, marks the opening of the civil rights crusade. Harvard Sitkoff's influential *The Struggle for Black Equality 1954–1992*, which was first published in 1981, exemplifies works that have viewed the Supreme Court ruling as the starting point in the history of one of the nation's most dramatic social struggles.

As new research has traced the seeds of African American rebellion to the World War II experience, others have argued that at the very least the Supreme Court decision raised civil rights' position on the nation's priority list. Taking an opposing view, Michael J. Klarman contended in 1994 that the ruling's impact had been overstated, and political scientist Gerald N. Rosenberg went even further, calling the decision "merely a ripple" in the civil rights campaign. David J. Garrow took issue with both accounts. Specifically, he said there is ample evidence that the leaders of the Montgomery boycott were inspired by the *Brown* ruling, although Klarman and Rosenberg deny any such connection. To support his contention, Garrow notes public statements by both Rosa Parks and Martin Luther King Jr. While Garrow accepts Klarman's argument that the modern civil rights movement began before 1954, he rejects Klarman's contention that "a transformation in American race relations was . . . a virtual inevitability." Klarman did credit the ruling with setting into motion a powerful white backlash because it reawakened southern historical memory of federal government interference during Reconstruction, because it was "an unambiguous, high salient pronouncement that southern race relations were destined to change," and because it brought the issue of racial change very close to home by applying it to grade school education (Klarman 1994, 118). Again, Garrow took a different position. Stressing historian Michal Belknap's conclusion that backlash against the ruling was not immediate in all southern states, he rejects historical accounts that fail "to appreciate the interactive manner in which *Brown* and the newly intensified African American activism" enhanced white supremacist passions (Garrow 1994, 160).

Nine returned to Central High to earn their diplomas, and police began handling unruly white demonstrations outside the school by arresting the protesters. The Little Rock school system was not entirely integrated until 1972.

Other violent episodes occurred at scattered locations in the South when African American youths attempted to become students in schools that previously had been all white. Also in 1957, when two sisters attempted to join the student body at Birmingham's Phillips High School, an agitated crowd surrounded their car upon arrival at the school. The mob beat their father, a Baptist minister, with chains, and someone stabbed their mother.

Following *Brown*

In the years immediately following the *Brown* decision, hundreds of school systems in border states were integrated without significant turmoil. The percent of African American students attending integrated schools in Kentucky jumped from zero in 1954 to 38.4 percent in 1957–1958. In Oklahoma, no African American students attended integrated schools in 1954, but 18.2 percent did so in 1957–1958. While these percentages were not high, any increase in integration seemed like a victory to the civil rights movement. Arkansas and Texas also integrated some school districts after the ruling; however, that action was confined primarily to districts with small African American populations. While these states took somewhat limited steps forward with little difficulty, political leaders in the South remained defiant and refused to act. In the Upper South, North Carolina and Tennessee had placed less than 3 percent of African American students in integrated schools by the decade's end. Even as late as 1962–1963, no African American children attended integrated schools in South Carolina, Mississippi, and Alabama (Klarman 1994, 84).

Florida integrated some of its schools without incident, but for African Americans in neighboring states, integration remained a decade or more in the future. Knowledge that segregation was maintained in spite of the Supreme Court ruling contributed to simmering African American militancy. An NAACP official in Monroe, North Carolina, Robert F. Williams said, "I felt that at last the government was willing to assert itself on behalf of first-class citizenship, even for Negroes" (Sitkoff 1993, 22). However, Williams eventually became appalled by the open defiance of the law he witnessed on a daily basis. Embracing militancy, Williams and a group of comrades showed a willingness to meet violence with violence, and that led to his dismissal by the NAACP.

When the Supreme Court issued its *Brown* decision, it raised African American expectations to unprecedented levels. While many southern whites saw each African American victory as a threat to their culture, the government's failure to carry out the *Brown* decision expeditiously, and politicians' openly expressed caution about moving quickly, made it impossible to satisfy African American hopes. Many African Americans were angered by the very thought that school systems would be allowed more than a decade of postponements before being required to follow the Supreme Court's ruling. At the same time, white supremacists still rankled at the idea that a federal entity—the Supreme Court—could overturn decades of common practice in the southern states and potentially topple the South's Jim Crow culture. Dissatisfaction on both sides promised a future of turmoil and frustration. Two groups of deeply polarized people shared a sense of loss that served as a prelude to the even more unsettled 1960s.

Boycotts, Civil Disobedience

The year-long bus boycott in Montgomery, Alabama, was the civil rights movement's largest demonstration of the power of civil disobedience in the 1950s. It all began when Rosa Parks, a 42-year-old seamstress tired after a long day's work, refused to relinquish her seat on a city bus late on December 1, 1955. Parks, who had previous ties to the civil rights movement, was one of four African Americans sitting in the four-seat front row of the section of the bus set aside for African Americans. A white man boarded the bus and found that all of the whites-only seats had been taken. The bus driver asked all four African Americans to leave their seats so that the white man could sit alone. Three did stand up to clear the row, but Parks declined. The bus driver threatened to have her arrested, but she still refused to capitulate. Two policemen arrived, and Parks told them she did not believe that she should be forced to stand. The officers subsequently arrested Parks, who was freed within hours by white civil rights advocates Virginia and Clifton Durr, who provided her bail.

Parks's act of defiance inspired a 381-day boycott that involved 80 to 90 percent of Montgomery's African American population. The sharp decline in ridership hurt the city's public transit system, and it served as evidence that African Americans were willing to sacrifice by walking or sharing rides to obtain their goals. "My soul has been tired for a long time," said one woman who had walked to work instead of taking the bus. "Now my feet are tired and my soul is resting." A mother of six explained her involvement by saying, "We know now that we're free citizens of the United States. Now we are aiming to become free citizens of Alabama. Our state motto, you know, is 'We Defend Our Rights.'" After the boycott, Parks expressed pleasure with the steadfastness of its participants and said that African Americans had "acquired enough freedom to be able to be vocal and to . . . act as human beings" (Kaledin 1984, 151). The boycott originally sought fairer treatment for African Americans, not desegregation; however, with the help of the courts, the protesters exceeded their original goal.

The Montgomery campaign placed a young and eloquent minister, Martin Luther King Jr., in the national spotlight and drew attention to King's chosen strategy of nonviolence. Although the local media attempted to ignore or discredit the movement and its leaders, the national media took note of Montgomery African Americans' long struggle. Like several other boycott leaders, King faced arrests and physical attacks as a result of his leadership position. Others who participated in the boycott confronted the possibility of being arrested, losing their jobs, or being the victims of violence. Nevertheless, they maintained

Montgomery, Alabama, policeman fingerprints seamstress Rosa Parks after she refused to relinquish her seat to a white man on a city bus. Her arrest created the spark that ignited the African American community's Montgomery bus boycott. (Library of Congress)

solidarity for the most part. A network of African American churches served as a source of information and solace for those involved in the boycott. Mass meetings convened in their sanctuaries, where discussions of strategies and the tenets of nonviolent resistance filled the air.

Montgomery Grassroots Action

In 1954, when Martin Luther King Jr. came to Montgomery as the pastor at Dexter Avenue Baptist Church, the city was home to 70,000 whites and 40,000 African Americans. In many ways, it was a divided city. Whites had a broad array of job opportunities. According to the 1950 census, however, 63 percent of the city's African American women worked as domestics, and 48 percent of Montgomery's African American men were employed as domestics or unskilled laborers. The median annual income of whites was $1,730; of African Americans,

$970. Ninety-one percent of Montgomery's white residents had flush toilets, but only 31 percent of African American homes had indoor plumbing (O'Neill 1986, 257).

The effort to improve conditions on the city's buses was not new when Rosa Parks made her stand. At the time of its last fare hike, the city bus system had been asked by the Women's Political Council, led by Jo Ann Robinson, to institute three changes: allow African Americans to sit from back to front and whites from front to back until all seats were taken; let African Americans enter at the front of the bus where they paid; and order buses to stop at each corner in African American neighborhoods, as they did in white neighborhoods. After the fare increase took effect, Robinson noted in a letter to the mayor that buses had begun stopping at more corners in African American enclaves; however, the other two requests had not been addressed. Robinson reminded Mayor W. A. Gayle that African Americans represented 75 percent of bus passengers and warned him that "more and more of our people are already arranging with neighbors and friends to ride to keep from being insulted and humiliated by bus drivers" (Carson et al. 1991, 45). In her May 21, 1954, letter, she warned Gayle that talk of a citywide boycott had begun, and she pointed out that other cities, such as Atlanta, Macon, Savannah, and Mobile, all had changed their bus policies to better accommodate African American passengers.

The Women's Political Council had ironed out the details of a planned bus boycott by 1955. What the council and its backers awaited was an arrest that would outrage African Americans and serve as a catalyst for widespread participation. One of the city's civil rights leaders, E. D. Nixon, admitted that they needed a particular kind of person to serve as a catalyst for action. The strong and dignified Rosa Parks filled the bill. After paying Parks's bond, Virginia Durr and her lawyer husband, Clifton, told Parks that her case could be used to improve conditions for African American bus riders. After discussing it with her husband, Parks agreed to be the focal point of the campaign. Her arrest on a Thursday served as the impetus for a one-day boycott on the following Monday, the same day on which Parks was convicted and fined in court. That demonstration, spearheaded by Robinson, was surprisingly successful. Empty bus after empty bus made its way through the streets of Montgomery. Local civil rights activists met that night to discuss what their next action should be. The group formed the Montgomery Improvement Association (MIA) and named King as its leader. A vote was taken on whether to launch a longer boycott, and the idea received unanimous approval.

The Boycott Begins

The bus boycott that started as a one-day event on December 5 immediately became a regular fixture of life in Montgomery. Three days later, the leaders of the MIA held their first negotiations with city and bus company officials, but the talks deadlocked over plans to provide better service for African American passengers while continuing segregation. In the boycott's first week, African American taxi drivers ferried riders around town at an "emergency fare" of 10 cents; however, officials threatened to arrest drivers who did not collect the established minimum fare of 45 cents. As a result, the boycotters launched a car-pooling plan on December 13. Eventually, the car-pooling system expanded to include more than 200 vehicles. Money from outside contributors provided 15 new station wagons for the cause.

Meanwhile, the city paid a price for angering most of its passengers. Each day, city buses collected 30,000 to 40,000 fewer African American fares than were typical. In addition, Christmas sales in downtown stores suffered because fewer African Americans were shopping there. City Bus Lines readily acknowledged that the boycott had been almost totally effective, but politicians continued to minimize the campaign's impact. The bus company demanded and received an emergency fare increase in early 1956. The bus company's action demonstrated that African Americans could use their economic power to have an impact on white enterprises—and that suggested a strategy for future protests.

On January 21, the city announced an agreement with the protesters; however, boycott organizers soon discovered that the deal had been struck by three city pastors without the support of the boycotting passengers. Reports of a deal were soon dispelled. After it became clear that negotiations were not working, Montgomery mayor W. A. Gayle called an end to the talks January 23. Car-pooling drivers became a target for police as the city won praise from white supremacists for its tough stance. Some employers offered to fire African American employees who participated in the boycott. Three days later, King, who was driving a vehicle from the car pool, was arrested for driving five miles per hour above the speed limit. When he arrived in his cell, other prisoners recognized him and asked for his help in obtaining their freedom. "Fellows, before I can assist in getting any of you out," he said, "I've got to get my own self out" (Branch 1988, 160–161).

During the boycott, several leaders' homes were bombed. On January 30, a bomb exploded at King's home while his wife and infant daughter were home alone. When word of the blast reached King, he was leading a mass meeting. He calmly told the group what had happened and then rushed home. A lawsuit, *Browder v. Gayle,* soon was filed by some of the protesters. In it, four female plaintiffs claimed city and state bus segregation was unconstitutional. Several days after the suit was filed, thousands of White Citizens Council members rallied in Montgomery in support of city officials. Soon afterward, a grand jury was assembled to decide whether the African American citizens' action violated the state's boycott conspiracy law.

Protesters Stand Firm

On February 20, at a mass meeting, the protesters rejected a proposal put forward by nervous white businessmen to end the boycott. The next day, the grand jury indicted about 90 leaders of the boycott for violating state law, and they were arrested. At trial, King received a sentence of a $500 fine or one year in jail. He appealed the verdict. In March, many Americans participated in a National Deliverance Day to show sympathy for the boycotters. Coincidentally, many city bus systems across the South ended municipal bus segregation in late April because of widespread misunderstanding about the U.S. dismissal of a segregation case. City Bus Lines attempted to integrate buses in Montgomery, but city leaders challenged that action in court.

The boycott continued, and on June 4, federal judges declared that city and state bus segregation was unconstitutional. The ruling did not spur an immediate change. Instead, segregation was preserved because different federal judges issued a temporary injunction until the ruling could be reviewed by the Supreme Court. In November, as King sat in a courtroom listening to city attorneys make a plea for an injunction banning car pools and levying a $15,000 fine on the MIA to compensate the city for lost revenues, word arrived that the Supreme Court had upheld the lower court's ruling. A month later, the high court rejected a further appeal by the Montgomery City Commission. On December 21, the boycotters again became bus passengers—this time on desegregated buses. The legal victory did not stop opponents of integration from expressing their anger, however; just two days before Christmas, a shotgun blast hit King's home, and other violent attacks included sniper fire on buses. On January 10, an unexploded bomb was found on King's front porch, but by then, integration of city buses was a reality and tensions soon declined.

King's Transformed Role

Martin Luther King Jr. was a young man when he accepted the mantle of leadership in Montgomery, and through the course of the crisis he emerged on the national scene as the foremost civil rights leader of the 1950s. At the boycott's beginning, he was a 26-year-old recent recipient of a Ph.D. degree who had served Dexter Avenue Baptist Church as its pastor for a little more than a year. He was largely unproven as a leader, but he quickly revealed through his oratory that he could inspire individuals to unite and take action. He also impressed his followers by demonstrating remarkable calm during the mass meeting when he learned that his home had been bombed. People who knew him have commented that despite his vitality, he had the thoughtful nature often associated with a much older man. Growing to adulthood among Atlanta's privileged African American families, King suffered few of the hardships that affected most African Americans in the South. With his father serving as minister of an elite church, he enjoyed a comparatively easy life. Well educated and well read, he stood in contradiction to many white southerners' stereotypes of African Americans, and that distinction probably bolstered his position in Montgomery and in the minds of potentially sympathetic whites elsewhere. As an arduous student of religion and philosophy, he could not be ridiculed for ignorance or sidetracked by racist rhetoric.

King's prominence in the Montgomery effort put him in a good position to establish strategy for the civil rights movement. The birth of the Southern Christian Leadership Conference (SCLC) shortly after the boycott's resolution gave him a national platform, which he could command regardless of white supremacist tactics. In 1957, King also hoped to turn an African American religious organization, the National Baptist Convention, into a huge civil rights machine; however, without support from the National Baptist Convention's leader, J. H. Jackson, efforts to use its five million members as a civil rights vehicle failed.

The Reverend Martin Luther King Jr., leader of Montgomery's bus boycott, speaks to a mass meeting in 1956. The year-long boycott ended in late 1956 after federal courts ruled that segregation of city and state buses was unconstitutional. (Library of Congress)

Biographer Taylor Branch wrote that King used evangelist Billy Graham's crusades as a model for another approach to civil rights issues. Under this plan, King would attack segregation in a single locale through nightly rallies. A modified version of this approach came to fruition in the Crusade for Citizenship rallies held in cities around the country in 1958. However, many of his successes came not from grand plans but from his strong responses to specific crises in African American communities.

When the national media increasingly portrayed King as *the* leader of the civil rights movement, he found himself in an awkward position in relation to other leaders who were older men. The NAACP's Roy Wilkins rose to leadership before King, but he often stood in the younger man's shadow. King tried to demonstrate the appropriate deference to his colleagues who led the NAACP, CORE, and the Urban League. Yet, he was not shy about using his newfound fame to further his cause. In 1957, just days before he was scheduled to speak at the Lincoln Memorial, where 30,000 civil rights activists would gather in a prayer pilgrimage, King wrote to Vice President Richard Nixon suggesting a meeting. Three days after King's speech, which won favorable analyses in the media, Nixon responded and set up a private meeting with King and his ally in the SCLC, Ralph Abernathy. The session with Nixon led to a bigger meeting in

The Words of Martin Luther King Jr.

"If we are wrong—Jesus of Nazareth was merely a utopian dreamer and never came down to earth! If we are wrong, justice is a lie!" December 5, 1955, at mass meeting at Holt Street Baptist Church in Montgomery (Branch 1988, 141).

"We must love our white brothers, no matter what they do to us. We must make them know that we love them. Jesus still cries out in words that echo across the centuries: 'Love your enemies; bless them that curse you.' This is what we must live by. We must meet hate with love. Remember, if I am stopped, this movement will not stop, because God is with the movement. Go home with this glowing faith and this radiant assurance." Informal January 30, 1956, speech to a crowd outside his home after it was bombed (Carson et al. 1991, 57).

"The story of Montgomery is the story of 50,000 Negroes who were willing to substitute tired feet for tired souls and walk the streets of Montgomery until the walls of segregation were finally battered by the forces of justice." Recollections in his 1958 book *Stride Toward Freedom* (Williams 1988, 89).

"O God, our gracious heavenly father. We thank thee for the fact that you have defined men and women in all nations, in all cultures. We call you this name. Some call thee Allah, some call you Elohim. Some call you Jehovah, some call you Brahma. Some call you the Unmoved Mover." March 18, 1959, prayer offered on his return to the United States after his trip to India (Branch 1988, 255).

"There is more power in socially organized masses on the march than there is in guns in the hands of a few desperate men. Our enemies would prefer to deal with a small armed group rather than with a huge, unarmed but resolute mass of people. However, it is necessary that the mass-action method be persistent and unyielding." 1959 article in *Liberation* magazine (Carson et al. 1991, 113).

which President Eisenhower met with King and other civil rights leaders. In 1959, King left Montgomery and moved to Atlanta, where he led the SCLC and acted as co-pastor of his father's Ebenezer Baptist Church.

During the 1950s, King also raised his profile abroad through a trip to India, where he met with other disciples of Gandhi, and his visit to the newly independent African nation of Ghana. No longer just a young pastor at work in his church, King became an often-quoted voice heralding African American unity and strength. However, unlike Black Power advocates in the coming decade, King managed to wrap his defiance in a cloak of goodwill and Christian love. While white supremacists hated him, he became a revered peace advocate and spokesman for African Americans who increasingly inspired white liberals.

King's high profile brought a lot of media attention. In February 1957, *Time* featured him in a cover story that stressed his interest in Gandhi. Later, the *New York Times Magazine* prominently provided a history of the Montgomery boycott. Then he was invited to appear on NBC's *Meet the Press* and became only the second African American to do so. Though the civil rights movement was splintered into a number of organizations that embraced different strategies and goals, King became its recognized leader as the 1950s came to a close. For both friends and foes of the civil rights movement, he had become the face of African American America.

Montgomery Becomes a Model

The long Montgomery fight, which itself was modeled after a 1953 Baton Rouge boycott, helped to launch similar campaigns in both Tallahassee, Florida, and Birmingham, Alabama. African Americans began to make increasing use of another form of civil disobedience—the sit-in—after the successful Montgomery struggle. In most sit-ins of 1958 and 1959, African Americans filled the chairs at lunch counters and other spots that were segregated or refused to serve African Americans. NAACP youth councils in Oklahoma led such protests in Oklahoma City, Tulsa, and Stillwell, and in Wichita and Kansas City, Kansas. Other groups followed the same model in protests that occurred in Miami and Durham, North Carolina. These protests unfolded according to a familiar pattern. For instance, in Wichita, African American teenagers held a sit-in at a drugstore lunch counter, and for more than a month, store personnel ignored them. However, the owner eventually acknowledged that he had lost customers because of the demonstrations and ordered his employees to serve the African American demonstrators. Nashville activists also opened a two-year sit-in campaign in 1959 with department stores as their initial targets. Another kind of successful protest was the consumer boycott. In Marion, South Carolina, a boycott led to integration of an ice-cream stand.

The use of sit-ins to win concessions became a common tactic in 1960. The civil disobedience practiced in Montgomery and the lessons learned there established patterns that would be followed in the 1960s in places like Birmingham and Selma. Mobilization of almost the entire African American population within a single city brought new hopes for dramatic efforts by average African American citizens who had never considered themselves to be activists or risk takers. In addition, willingness to be jailed in the process of civil disobedience gave the civil rights movement a new weapon. Jails had a finite amount of space, and if a large portion of the population was arrested, the keepers of the jails would face new costs and inconveniences. In a way, the protesters' eagerness to be arrested reduced the appeal of making arrests. Violence was a continuing threat against those pushing for an expansion of civil rights, especially those who led the fight; however, peaceful civil disobedience made it easier for observers to see protesters as victims rather than troublemakers.

The Montgomery boycott helped to raise awareness of civil rights issues outside the South and led Americans to place a higher priority on civil rights as one of the nation's leading problems. After the boycott ended triumphantly, there was a sharp increase in the percentage of respondents in public opinion surveys who believed that civil rights was the most urgent problem facing the United States. The combination of the boycott and the Emmitt Till case had helped to move the issue to the top of the nation's agenda, and both had drawn representatives of the national media into the South, where they would cover ongoing protests over the coming years. The presence of television cameras forced some violent white supremacists to act in the shadows rather than boldly mistreating African Americans in public. And those who continued brutality despite the watchful eyes of television viewers often met with the disapproval of many white Americans.

Working alongside Martin Luther King Jr., Ralph Abernathy, who was both a Baptist minister and a civil rights activist, helped to form the Southern Christian Leadership Council in 1957. After King's assassination in 1968, Abernathy became the organization's leader. (Library of Congress)

BIOGRAPHIES

Ralph Abernathy, 1926–1990

Longtime Ally of Martin Luther King Jr.

A Baptist minister with a master's degree in sociology, Ralph Abernathy was pastor of the First Baptist Church in Montgomery, Alabama, in the 1950s. Alongside Martin Luther King Jr., he led the successful African American boycott of city buses. African American residents of Montgomery walked or carpooled to reach their jobs during the boycott, which lasted more than a year. It ended with a 1956 Supreme Court ruling that segregation of buses was illegal. Abernathy and King, along with Fred Shuttlesworth and Bayard Rustin, continued their civil rights efforts with the formation of the Southern Christian Leadership Conference in 1957. The organization was dedicated to the use of nonviolence to win civil rights. Initially, King was its president, and Abernathy was secretary-treasurer. Later, Abernathy became vice president, and when King was assassinated in 1968, Abernathy took over the presidency. He remained the SCLC's leader until 1977.

Daisy Bates, 1914–1999

Arkansas NAACP Leader

Born in a small Arkansas town, Daisy Lee Gatson married L. C. Bates in 1942, and both became important players in their state's civil rights battle. The couple first made their voice heard in the early 1940s by publishing the *Arkansas State Press* in 1941, but Daisy truly stepped into the national spotlight in 1957 through her work as an adviser to nine teenagers who integrated Central High School in Little Rock in 1957. She had been leader of the state conference of NAACP chapters since 1952, and when the Supreme Court ruled in 1954 that segregated public schools did not offer equal education for African Americans, she joined others in the NAACP in planning an Arkansas confrontation on the issue. When the 1957 school year began, she later recalled, "hysteria in all of its madness enveloped the city. Racial feelings were at a fever pitch" ("Daisy Bates" 2006). She was arrested on orders of the Little Rock City Council. She faced a fine for violating a city ordinance by failing to reveal information about her group's members. The case was appealed, and the U.S. Supreme Court eventually reversed the verdict. With Bates's guidance, the Little Rock Nine were able to enroll at Central High. Bates's prominent part in the showdown led advertisers to boycott the Bateses' newspaper, and it went out of business in 1959. She published a book, *The Long Shadow of Little Rock,* in 1962 and moved to Washington D.C., where she was active in antipoverty programs. She moved back to Arkansas in 1968. Four years after her husband's 1980 death, she renewed publication of the *Arkansas State Press.*

Dorothy Dandridge, 1922–1965

Actress and Singer

After gaining acclaim as one of the Dandridge Sisters on the nightclub circuit and appearing in parts in the movies during the 1940s, Dorothy Dandridge became a true star in the 1950s. At first, she got leading roles in low-budget films, such as *The Harlem Globetrotters,* but she later won more important parts. She costarred in MGM's *Bright Road* with Harry Belafonte in 1953. She claimed the part of Carmen Jones in an all–African American, Americanized version of Bizet's opera *Carmen.* The production featured lyrics by Oscar Hammerstein, and its release in 1954 put Dandridge on the cover of *Life* magazine at a time when many African American women were limited to domestic jobs. Her performance in *Carmen Jones* earned an Academy Award nomination. Dandridge also played a supporting role in *The King and I* and was featured in 1957's *Island in the Sun* as well as 1959's *The Decks Ran Red*. She costarred with Sidney Poitier in George Gershwin's *Porgy and Bess,* also in 1959. Subsequently, an unsuccessful marriage led to mismanagement of her finances, and she declared bankruptcy in 1963. When film roles began to disappear, she returned to performing on the nightclub scene, but she did not repeat her former success. In 1965, she died in an apparent suicide.

Orval Faubus, 1910–1994

Politician and Segregationist

Arkansas's Orval Faubus ran for governor of his state in 1954 as a liberal Democrat. He vowed to increase state spending on roads and on education, and although some considered him a left-wing radical, he won the governorship. In the early months of his term, Faubus took progressive steps, such as ending segregation on state buses and other forms of public transportation. However, he faced tough opposition from Jim Johnson, who led the conservative wing of the state Democratic Party. To secure his place in office, Faubus decided to stake out ground on the conservative's turf by opposing the Supreme Court's 1954 *Brown* ruling that mandated integration of public schools. Three years later, Faubus called up the Arkansas National Guard to block integration of Central High School in Little Rock. He later lost this battle when President Eisenhower sent federal troops to Arkansas to make it safe for nine African American students to take their places among students at the school. Faubus served a total of six consecutive terms over 12 years. His political career ended in the 1960s.

Frank Porter Graham, 1886–1972

Educator and Public Official

Frank Porter Graham headed the University of North Carolina for 19 years, ending in 1949, and immediately upon leaving the university, he served as an appointed U.S. senator. He lost an election attempt to keep his Senate seat because of his liberal views on civil rights, including support for African American voting rights and opposition to poll taxes. Graham also opposed the most deadly example of white violence against African Americans—lynching—and endorsed state and federal legislation to stop it. As an educator, Graham supported desegregation of higher education. Graham had favored gradualism in integration, but after the *Brown* decision, he wrongly expected white acquiescence to a more integrated society. His defeat in 1950 demonstrated strong white supremacist feelings, and that loss has been used to suggest that reinforcement of white supremacist thinking began before the *Brown* decision was handed down.

Autherine Lucy, 1929–

Civil Rights Activist and Teacher

Autherine Lucy made news in 1956 by attempting to study library science as the first African American graduate student at the University of Alabama. Lucy had graduated from the African American Miles College in Fairfield, Alabama, before applying to the state university. She had realized that she would not be welcomed, so she began her quest in 1953 by seeking aid from the NAACP. A legal battle to win her admission began in July 1953, and about two years later, the group's efforts reached fruition when a restraining order blocked the university from barring Lucy's admission because of her race. Just two days after the initial ruling, the court expanded its decision to apply to all African Americans. Lucy enrolled February 3, 1956, and confronted screaming and egg-tossing mobs.

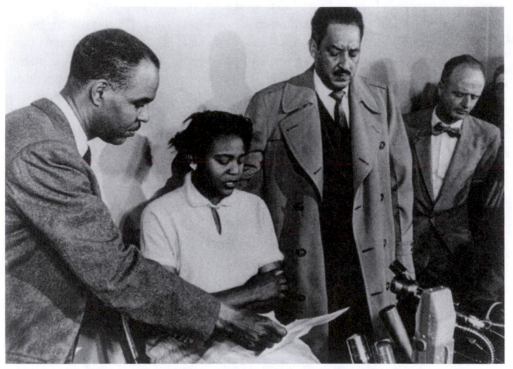

National Association for the Advancement of Colored People (NAACP) leader Roy Wilkins and future Supreme Court justice Thurgood Marshall, who was then special counsel for the NAACP's Legal Defense and Education Fund, appear at a 1956 press conference with Autherine Lucy. Lucy attempted to integrate the University of Alabama in 1956 by pursuing graduate studies in library science; however, university officials quickly suspended her, claiming that they were trying to protect her from potential violence. The NAACP argued that university officials were knowingly showing their approval of segregation. (Library of Congress)

She needed a police escort just to get to class. After being suspended and then expelled by university officials, she ended her battle. Like many activists of this era, Lucy was accused of having Communist ties, and she testified before the Alabama House of Representatives with Thurgood Marshall at her side. She married and became a teacher in Texas. When speaking at the University of Alabama in 1988, she was asked whether she had ever attempted to regain her status as a student there, and she said that she had not. Faculty members convinced the university to overturn her expulsion, and she began work on her master's degree in education a year later. She received her degree in 1992.

Robert B. Patterson, ?–

Founder of White Citizens Council

Plantation manager Robert B. Patterson, who founded Mississippi's original White Citizens Council in Indianola in 1954, spoke for many white southerners when he voiced fears about desegregation of schools. After the *Brown* ruling, he declared, "If red-blooded southern Americans submit to this unconstitutional 'judge made law' and surrender our Caucasian heritage of sixty centuries, the malignant power of communism, atheism, and mongrelization will surely follow" (Daniel 2000, 196). His organization boycotted African American merchants who supported integration or African American voting rights, established white-only private schools, and disseminated prosegregation literature throughout the South. Patterson, well known in his home state as a former captain of the Mississippi State University football team, continued to be a powerful voice for ultraconservatism in Mississippi more than half a century after he played a key role in launching the White Citizens Council. He helped to form the Council of Conservative Citizens in 1985 and remained an important contributor to its publication, the *Citizens Informer,* into the 21st century.

William Patterson, 1891–1980

Leader of the Civil Rights Congress

William Patterson, who was the grandson of a slave, headed the Civil Rights Congress. In Virginia, Patterson led the campaign in support of the Martinsville Seven, African American men convicted by an all-white jury of raping a white woman. Before the men were executed in February 1951, Patterson's efforts drew a crowd of about 500 people who marched from Richmond to Martinsville in a "pilgrimage." Later that year, Patterson was in the news again when he presented a petition to the United Nations Committee on Human Rights in Geneva. The petition claimed that the United States was responsible for the genocide of African Americans, and it charged that more than 10,000 African Americans had been lynched since the end of the Civil War. When Patterson attempted to return to the United States, he was asked to surrender his passport in Paris. He refused to relinquish it; however, officials seized his passport when he returned to the United States. Both Patterson and the Civil Rights Congress, which was a front for the Communist Party, were longtime targets of conservatives. The organization, formed in 1946, ceased to exist 10 years later. Patterson remained active and took part in the defense of Angela Davis and the Black Panthers in the 1960s.

Jo Ann Robinson, 1912–1992

Professor and Activist

Alabama State College professor Jo Ann Robinson led the Women's Political Council, an African American group modeled after the League of Women Voters in the early 1950s. In 1955, her group pushed white merchants in Montgomery to desegregate water fountains and to begin referring to African American women with the titles of Miss or Mrs. In addition, when Rosa Parks was arrested for refusing to give up her seat on a city bus, Robinson led a one-day African American boycott on December 5. The one-day protest was effective, with less than 10 percent of African American passengers riding. After that, she joined and worked behind the scenes in the Montgomery Improvement Association, which organized a sustained boycott that lasted for more than a year. Looking back, she said, "I think people were fed up, they had reached the point that they knew there was no return. That they had to do it or die. And that's what kept it going. It was the sheer spirit for freedom, for the feeling of being a man or a woman" (Sitkoff 1981, 37). Robinson, who was a member of Martin Luther King Jr.'s Dexter Avenue Baptist Church, later left Alabama and authored a 1987 book about her involvement in the boycott.

Modjeska Simkins, 1899–1992

Civil Rights Advocate

Modjeska Simkins became active in the South Carolina conference of the NAACP from its beginnings in the 1930s and continued her work through the turmoil of the 1950s. Simkins helped in the development of a school desegregation case, *Briggs v. Elliot,* which was later combined with *Brown v. Board of Education.* She helped to convince 20 poor African American residents of Clarendon County to become plaintiffs in the case, and afterward, she led efforts to help the plaintiffs following retribution by whites, who refused to allow them to obtain mortgages on their homes, to get installment loans, and to rent housing. She helped to generate publicity that brought in donations from across the country, and she traveled to Harlem to speak before a Young Women's Civic League about the plaintiffs' needs.

Robert F. Williams, 1925–1996

Militant African American Activist

A one-time NAACP official in North Carolina, Robert F. Williams became a leading advocate of African American militancy in the 1950s. He urged African Americans to arm themselves in self-defense as he watched the white community ignore the U.S. Supreme Court's *Brown v. Board of Education*. The NAACP ousted him because he advocated violence. He argued that nonviolence only worked in a civilized society, and he believed that the American South was not civilized. "Only highly civilized and moral individuals respect the rights of others. The southern brute respects only force," he wrote in *Liberation* (Williams 1988, 110). He produced *The Crusader,* a monthly newsletter, and headed the Revolutionary Action Movement. In 1961, he emigrated from the United States to Cuba to avoid prosecution on a false charge that he had abducted a white couple. He came back to the United States eight years later, but the charges were not dismissed until 1976.

References and Further Readings

Branch, Taylor. 1988. *Parting the Waters: America in the King Years 1954–63.* New York: Simon and Schuster.

Breines, Wini. 1992. *Young, White, and Miserable: Growing Up Female in the Fifties.* Boston: Beacon Press.

Carson, Clayborne, David J. Garrow, Gerald Gill, Vincent Harding, and Darlene Clark Hine, eds. 1991. *Eyes on the Prize Civil Rights Reader.* New York: Viking Penguin.

Carter, Paul A. 1983. *Another Part of the Fifties.* New York: Columbia University Press.

"Civil Rights Memorial." 2005. Tolerance.org. http://www.tolerance.org/memorial/memorial.swf (accessed November 16, 2006).

Crawford, Vicki L., Jacqueline Anne Rouse, and Barbara Woods, eds. 1993. *Women in the Civil Rights Movement: Trailblazers and Torchbearers, 1941–1965.* Bloomington: Indiana University Press.

"Daisy Bates." 2006. Thomson Gale. http://www.gale.com/free_resources/bhm/bio/bates d.htm (accessed October 24, 2007).

Dallek, Robert. 1991. *Lyndon Johnson and His Times, 1908–1960.* New York: Oxford University Press.

Daniel, Pete. 2000. *Lost Revolutions: The South in the 1950s.* Chapel Hill: University of North Carolina Press.

Dudziak, Mary L. 2000. *Cold War Civil Rights: Race and the Image of American Democracy*. Princeton, NJ: Princeton University Press.

Englehardt, Tom. 1995. *The End of Victory Culture: Cold War America and the Disillusioning of a Generation*. New York: Basic Books.

"From Segregation to Breakfast." 1957. *Time*. www.time.com/time/magazine/article/0,9171,937922,00.html (accessed October 22, 2007).

Gallup, George. 1958. *Gallup Poll*. http://brain.gallup.com (accessed April 22, 2008).

Garrow, David J. 1994. "Hopelessly Hollow History: Revisionist Devaluing of *Brown v. Board of Education*." *Virginia Law Review* 80 (1): 151–160.

Geospatial and Statistical Data Center. University of Virginia Library. http://www2.lib.virginia.edu/geostat/index.html (accessed April 21, 2008).

Halberstam, David. 1993. *The Fifties*. New York: Fawcett Columbine.

Hule, William Bradford. 1956. "Killers' Confession: The Shocking Story of Approved Killing in Mississippi." The Murder of Emmett Till. http://www.pbs.org/wgbh/amex/till/sfeature/sf_look_confession.html (accessed October 22, 2007).

Irving, Florence B. 1957. "The Future of the Negro Voter in the South." *Journal of Negro Education* 26 (3): 390–399.

Kaledin, Eugenia. 1984. *Mothers and More: American Women in the 1950s*. Boston: Twayne Publishers.

Klarman, Michael J. 1994. "How *Brown* Changed Race Relations." *Journal of American History* 81 (1): 81–118.

Koslow, Philip, chief ed. 1999. *The New York Public Library African American Desk Reference*. New York: Stonesong Press.

"The Legacy of Harry T. and Harriette Moore." http://www.naacp.org/about/history/moores_story/ (accessed April 22, 2008).

Levy, Peter B. 1998. *The Civil Rights Movement*. Westport, CT: Greenwood Press.

Lowery, Charles D. and John F. Marszalek. 1992. *Encyclopedia of African-American Civil Rights*. Westport, CT: Greenwood Press.

May, Elaine Tyler. 1988. *Homeward Bound: American Families in the Cold War Era*. New York: Basic Books.

Meier, August. 1963. "Negro Protest Movements and Organizations." *Journal of Negro Education* 32 (4): 437.

Myers, Daisy. 2005. *Sticks 'n Stones: The Myers Family in Levittown*. York, PA: York Heritage Trust.

O'Neill, William L. 1986. *American High: The Years of Confidence, 1945–1960*. New York: Free Press.

Pells, Richard H. 1989. *The Liberal Mind in a Conservative Age: American Intellectuals in the 1940s and 1950s.* 2nd ed. Middletown, CT: Wesleyan University Press.

Polenberg, Richard. 1980. *One Nation Divisible: Class, Race and Ethnicity in the United States since 1938.* New York: Penguin Books.

Rose, Lisle A. 1999. *The Cold War Comes to Main Street: America in 1950.* Lawrence: University Press of Kansas.

Rosenberg, Gerald N. 1994. "Brown Is Dead! Long Live Brown! The Endless Attempt to Canonize a Case." *Virginia Law Review* 80 (1): 161–171.

Salzman, David, Lionel Smith, and Cornel West, eds. 1996. *Encyclopedia of African-American Culture and History.* New York: Macmillan Library Reference.

Sitkoff, Harvard. 1981. *The Struggle for Black Equality 1954–1992.* New York: Hill and Wang.

Southern Poverty Law Center. 2005. *Forty-one Lives for Freedom.* Veterans of the Civil Rights Movement. http://www.crmvet.org/mem/41lives.htm (accessed November 16, 2006).

Taylor, Quintard. 1995. "The Civil Rights Movement in the American West: Black Protest in Seattle, 1960–1970." *Journal of Negro History* 80 (1): 1–14.

"They Changed the World." 2005. The Story of the Montgomery Bus Boycott. montgomeryadvertiser.com. http://www.montgomeryboycott.com/timeline.htm (accessed November 21, 2006).

Twombly, Robert C. 1971. *Blacks in White America.* New York: McKay.

Tyson, Timothy B. 1988. "'Black Power' and the Roots of the Freedom Struggle." *Journal of American History* 85 (2): 540–570.

U.S. Census Bureau. 1961. *Statistical Abstract of the United States 1961.* Washington, DC: Government Printing Office. Also available at http://www2.census.gov/prod2/statcomp/documents/1961–01.pdf (accessed November 12, 2006).

U.S. Census Bureau. 1975. *Bicentennial Edition Historical Statistics of the United States Colonial Times to 1970, Part 1.* Washington, DC: Government Printing Office. Also available at http://www2.census.gov/prod2/statcomp/index.htm (accessed October 23, 2007).

Whitfield, Stephen J. 1996. *The Culture of the Cold War.* 2nd ed. Baltimore: Johns Hopkins University Press.

Wiese, Andrew. 2005. *Places of Their Own: African American Suburbanization in the Twentieth Century.* Chicago: University of Chicago Press.

Williams, Juan. 1988. *Eyes on the Prize: America's Civil Rights Years, 1954–1965.* New York: Penguin.

Young, William H., and Nancy K. Young. 2004. *The 1950s.* American Popular Culture through History series. Westport, CT: Greenwood Press.

People and Events in the 20th Century

THE 1900s

THE 1910s

THE 1920s

THE 1930s

THE 1940s

THE 1950s

THE 1960s

THE 1970S

The 1980s

THE 1990s

1950s Index

About the Authors

John C. Stoner is assistant professor of history at Binghamton University, SUNY. He received a PhD from Columbia University and is currently finishing a manuscript on the activities of the AFL-CIO in Africa during the Cold War.

After 20 years as an editor at newspapers, including the *Detroit Free Press* and the *Philadelphia Daily News,* **Alice L. George** earned her PhD in history from Temple University in 2001. She is the author of *Awaiting Armageddon: How Americans Faced the Cuban Missile Crisis, Old City Philadelphia: Cradle of American Democracy,* and *Philadelphia: A Pictorial Celebration.* She works as an independent historian in Philadelphia.